DUE PROCESS IN SPECIAL EDUCATION

James A. Shrybman, J.D.

George Matsoukas

AN ASPEN PUBLICATION®
Aspen Systems Corporation
Rockville, Maryland
London
1982

Library of Congress Cataloging in Publication Data

Shrybman, James A.
Due process in special education.

Includes index.
1. Handicapped children—Education—Law and legislation—United States. I. Matsoukas, George. II. Title.
KF4210.S48   344.73'0791   82-3903
ISBN: 0-89443-686-4   347.304791   AACR2

Publisher: John Marozsan
Editorial Director: R. Curtis Whitesel
Managing Editor: Margot Raphael
Editorial Services: Dorothy Okoroji
Printing and Manufacturing: Debbie Swarr

AUTHORSHIP
James Shrybman researched and wrote *Due Process in Special Education*.
George Matsoukas was responsible for initiating this project with the
publisher and for editing a portion of the manuscript.
Mr. Shrybman and Mr. Matsoukas were partners in the consulting firm
of Education Due Process Services during which time they conceptualized
Due Process in Special Education.

Copyright © 1982 by Aspen Systems Corporation

Library of Congress Catalog Card Number: 82-3903
ISBN: 0-89443-686-4

Printed in the United States of America

1 2 3 4 5

To my parents, Werner and Edith Halpern.
Their acceptance and nurturing of a special needs child
helped turn a confused vildechaye into a mensch.
Ah groysn dank!

Table of Contents

Acknowledgments xiii

Citations of P.L. 94-142 Regulations Used in This Book xv

    PART I—LEGAL SOURCES 1

Chapter 1—Due Process 3

Chapter 2—Public Law 94-142 9

       Origins of P.L. 94-142 9
       Unique Characteristics of P.L. 94-142 12
       Congressional Perception of an Unmet Need 12
       The General Purposes of P.L. 94-142 13
       Key Provisions of P.L. 94-142 14
       Definitions of Three Critical Terms 19
       Implementing Concerns in a Cutback Era 24

Chapter 3—Section 504 29

       The Section 504 Regulation 29
       Criteria for Section 504 Protection 30
       Free Appropriate Public Education 31
       Procedural Safeguards 34

Chapter 4—States, Localities, and Courts 39

       The Role of States and Localities 39
       Annual State Program Plans 41

The Role of the Courts............................. 46

**Chapter 5—The Interrelationship of Federal, State, and Local
        Laws** 49

P.L. 94-142 and Its Regulations 49
P.L. 94-142 and Section 504 50
P.L. 94-142 and P.L. 89-313 51
U.S.-Funded Education and Medicaid 51
P.L. 94-142 and Employment 53
P.L. 94-142 and State Law.......................... 53

PART II—THE SPECIAL EDUCATION PROCESS 61

Chapter 6—Identification 65

The Role of Identification 65
Types of Identification Activities 68

Chapter 7—Evaluation 73

Evaluation's Role in Decision Making 73
The Importance of Evaluation....................... 74
The Legal Requirement 74
Preevaluation Procedures 75
The Evaluation Team Participants 80
Protection in Evaluation Procedures................. 80
The Components of an Evaluation 83
The Right to an Independent Evaluation 85
Reporting the Results of Evaluations 86

Chapter 8—Programming and the Written IEP 89

The Role of Programming 89
Programming and the IEP 90
The Legal Requirement of an IEP 91
An IEP Defined.................................... 91
The Purposes and Functions of the IEP 92
Out-of-State Placement............................ 95
When the IEP Must Be in Effect 95
The Law and IEP Meetings 96
Participants in the IEP Meetings..................... 98
When the Parties Disagree 103
Use of a Tape Recorder at IEP Meetings 104

Parent Signatures on the IEP 105
Parent Monitoring of the Child's Progress............ 105
Content and Format of the IEP 106
The Inclusion of Physical Education.................. 112
The Inclusion of Vocational Education 112
The Inclusion of All Services Needed 113
Accountability for the IEP 113
The IEP for Handicapped Gifted Children 114

Chapter 9—Placement **117**

Placement's Role in Special Education 117
Participants in the Placement Decision 119
'Temporary' or 'Interim' Placements 119
Three Legal Requirements for Placements 120
Placement Based on the IEP 120
The Least Restrictive Environment Rules 122
A Continuum of Alternative Placements 125
Least Restrictive Nonacademic Settings 129
Review and Reevaluation 130
Concerns about Misuse............................ 131
Guidelines on Proposed Placement 132
Placement Must Be at No Cost to Parents 132
Funding Handicapped Education Programs 142
Public Supervision of Placements Required............ 144

Chapter 10—Special Requirements for Specific Handicaps **149**

Hearing Impaired 149
Mentally Retarded................................. 153
Multihandicapped and Deaf-Blind 158
Orthopedically and Other Health Impaired 160
Seriously Emotionally Disturbed 162
Specific Learning Disability 166
Speech Impaired 173
Visually Handicapped 177

**Chapter 11—How to Determine Whether an IEP Placement Is
Appropriate** **181**

Step 1: Identification. 183
Step 2: Evaluation 184
Step 3: Translation of Data into Specific Educational
Needs 186
Step 4: Program Development....................... 189

Step 5: Placement 192
Conclusion 194
Guidelines for Special Education Program 195

PART III—ROLES, RIGHTS, AND RESPONSIBILITIES 203

Chapter 12—Students and Parents 205

Role of the Student................................. 205
Rights of the Student 205
Responsibilities of the Student...................... 208
Who Is Considered a Parent? 208
Role of the Parents 208
Rights of the Parents 209
Responsibilities of the Parents...................... 218

Chapter 13—Schools and Professionals 229

The Role of School Personnel....................... 229
Rights of School Personnel 230
Responsibilities of School Personnel.................. 232

Chapter 14—The Hearing Officer 245

The Role of the Hearing Officer 245
Selection of Individuals to Serve 246
Impartiality and Who May Serve 247
The Importance of Training......................... 248
Training Workshop Outline 249
Monitoring Hearing Officers 253
Liability of Hearing Officers 254
Rights of the Hearing Officer 255
Responsibilities of the Hearing Officer 256

Chapter 15—The Surrogate Parent 259

The Role of the Surrogate Parent.................... 259
The Need for Surrogate Parents 260
The Duty of the Public Agency...................... 263
Criteria for Selection of Surrogates.................. 265
Rights of Surrogate Parents......................... 267
Responsibilities of Surrogate Parents 268
Legal Problems in Providing Surrogates 269

PART IV—PROCEDURES OF THE DUE PROCESS HEARING **277**

Chapter 16—Notice Requirements and Timeliness of Proceedings **279**

The Purpose of the Notice Requirement 279
P.L. 94-142 and the Notice Requirement 279
Content of the Notice 280
The Form of the Notice 285
The Meaning of 'Notice' and 'Consent'. 287
Consent in Addition to Notice. 287
The Elements for a Valid Consent 289
When Parents Refuse Consent. 293

Chapter 17—Invoking the Hearing **295**

Right to Impartial Due Process Hearing 295
The Agency Responsible for the Hearing. 296
Initiating a Due Process Hearing 297
Informing Parents Where to Obtain Help 298
Administrative Reviews and Mediation 298

Chapter 18—Prehearing Activities **301**

Responsibility for Prehearing Coordination. 301
Receipt of the Request for a Hearing 302
Arranging Hearing Dates and Logistics 303
Providing a Verbatim Record 303
Determining the Need for an Interpreter 304
The Independent Educational Evaluation. 304
Placement during the Proceedings 305
Current Placement Representation 310
Providing Hearing Information to Parents 311
Open or Closed Meeting, Child's Presence. 311
Obtaining a Witness List and Written Evidence 312
Compelling the Attendance of Witnesses 314
Final Notice to the Parties 315

Chapter 19—Conducting the Hearing **317**

Hearing Room Seating Arrangement 317
Recording Equipment 319
Starting the Hearing 320
Administration of the Oath 324
Order of Presentation 324

The Presentation of Witnesses 328
Introducing Documents into Evidence 330
Continuance or Postponement of a Hearing 330
Ruling on Objections during the Hearing 333
Closing the Hearing 337

Chapter 20—After the Hearing: Alternatives and Procedures **339**

The Right to Appeal.............................. 339
'Appeal' Defined 340
What Is an 'Error'?............................... 341
Initiating an Appeal 342
Filing Appeal with Administrative Agency 342
Procedures for an Administrative Appeal 343
Right to Sue in State or Federal Court.............. 347
Decision Options of the Appellate Official 348
The Enforcement of Decisions 351
Timelines in Due Process Proceedings............... 354
Other Timelines to Be Established 355

**PART V—EFFECTIVE PRESENTATION AT THE
HEARING** **359**

Chapter 21—Evidence and Burden of Proof **361**

Evidence Defined 361
The Use of Evidence in a Hearing................... 361
Different Forms of Evidence 362
Admissible and Nonadmissible Evidence............. 362
Other Factors in Admitting Evidence 364
Assessing Weight and Credibility 364
The Burden of Proof 365

Chapter 22—Presenting Evidence **371**

Planning for the Hearing 371
Preparing Witnesses for the Hearing................. 372
The Opening Statement at the Hearing............... 376
Presenting the Evidence 377
Direct Examination 378
Cross-Examination 380

Admission of Evidence 384
Objections 385
The Way to State an Objection 385
The Use of Objections 386
Opinions and Expert Witnesses 387
The Closing Statement 389

Chapter 23—The Witness: A Guide 391

Preparing to Testify 391
Being Nervous and Not Showing It 392
Answering Questions 393
Surviving Cross-Examination 396
Presenting Your Information Effectively 400

PART VI—THE DECISION 403

Chapter 24—Arriving at a Decision 405

Step 1. The Perspective of an Observer 406
Step 2. The Weight and Credibility of Evidence 408
Step 3. Is the Child Handicapped? 408
Step 4. The Need for Special Education 409
Step 5. Aptness of Program and Placement 410
Step 6. Selecting a Decision Option 410
The Two Restrictive Requirements 411
Choosing among Options 411

Chapter 25—Writing a Decision 415

The Cover Page 416
Jurisdiction and Procedural Posture 418
The Issues 418
Applicable Law and Regulations 419
The Evidence Considered 420
Summary of the Evidence 420
Evaluation of the Evidence 421
Findings of Fact 421
Conclusions of Law 422
The Final Order and Appeal Information 423
Case Study of Peggy 423

PART VII—SPECIFIC CONCERNS 447

Chapter 26—Private Schools 449

　　Placements by Public Agencies 449
　　Placements by Parents 451
　　Personnel, Equipment, and Funding................. 453
　　The EDGAR Regulations 454
　　Difficulties in Implementation of the Private School
　　　　Provisions of P.L. 94-142/EDGAR 456
　　Case Example 457

Chapter 27—Confidentiality of Information 463

Chapter 28—Minimum Competency Testing 471

　　Minimum Competency Testing Programs 471
　　The IEP as a Management Tool 472
　　Diplomas 473

Chapter 29—Disciplinary Action 475

Glossary 479

Index 489

Acknowledgments

Several critical persons suffered through my last-minute deadlines, late payments, and general erratic behavior. In the end we all were a part of the production of this book. My special thanks to:

Curt Whitesel, who initiated this project so very long ago and who kept the candle flickering through its darkest periods.

Gloria A. Young, who produced manuscript copy from mounds of drafts to be finished yesterday.

Harvey Schweitzer, my unique part-time partner, who was behind the scenes assisting me with the legal research.

Alice Brandeis Popkin, who oversaw my legal training in the field of children's law.

Jean Bower, who has given me, and continues to give me, such valuable professional support in working on the legal problems of children.

Cory, whose constant interruptions enabled me to take little breaks every now and then.

Rochelle Testa, who worked with me, stood by me, and screamed at me throughout this ordeal—and has become my wife in spite of it.

and

The Dining Room Table on Castlebar Road. It was here that I received my education in the family business of children by partaking of the wisdom, experiences, and insights of those who came to share many meals and discuss every facet of child development.

CITATIONS OF P.L. 94-142 REGULATIONS
USED IN THIS BOOK

As a result of the creation of the Department of Education, the regulations implementing Part B of the Education of the Handicapped Act (20 U.S.C. 1411-1420), as amended by P.L. 94-142, were transferred to title 34 (Education) of the CFR (45 FR 77368, November 21, 1980), and redesignated as 34 CFR, Part 300.

However, individual section numbers have not changed. For example, the sections on IEPs, previously 45 CFR 121a.340-121a.349, have been redesignated as 34 CFR 300.340-300.349.

The citations in this book use the original reference numbers for the P.L. 94-142 regulations they were issued on August 23, 1977, and codified in the Code of Federal Regulations (CFR) at 45 CFR, Part 121a.

Part I

Legal Sources

The decades of the fifties, sixties, and the seventies undoubtedly will be remembered as the era in which the rights of individuals were reaffirmed and clearly established in law. That era yielded abundant local, state, and federal legislation, as well as court decisions, in support of the various civil rights movements. The subjects of the many legislative actions and legal decisions have been such groups as ethnic or linguistic minorities and women.

Advocates for the rights of the handicapped and children also won a number of such legal victories during that era. The legal rights of the handicapped were firmly established. Children became recognized as independent human beings with inherent rights of their own. But in many respects, these still are paper victories. The decade of the eighties appeared to be ushering in a new era of hard realities. It remained to be seen whether the sweeping legislative mandates and court orders of the previous decades actually would be implemented to the extent of their promise.

What is clear is that the decisions providing for a free appropriate public education for handicapped children are not necessarily self-executing. Advocates, parents, school system personnel, administrators, hearing officers, lawyers, and other persons interested in the promise must continue to be active and vigilant if they intend to ensure that the legal mandates are carried out.

However, persons who intend to advocate a position based on the law first must know concrete information about what that law provides. Part I provides the essential legal background of special education law. It discusses the concept of due process in special education, Public Law 94-142, Section 504, court decisions, local and state law, and their interrelationship. The part provides the basic legal foundation necessary upon which readers can build their positions effectively.

1

Due Process

The basic concept of due process in special education is derived from the 14th Amendment of the United States Constitution, of which the first paragraph states:

1. All persons born or naturalized in the United States, and subject to the jurisdiction thereof, are citizens of the United States and of the State wherein they reside. No State shall make or enforce any law which shall abridge the privileges or immunities of citizens of the United States; *nor shall any State deprive any person of life, liberty, or property, without due process of law; nor deny to any person within its jurisdiction the equal protection of the laws.* (emphasis added)

The general purpose of this amendment is to protect individuals from the state and its various public institutions. Whenever a state takes an action that adversely affects a citizen or group of persons, the protections of the 14th Amendment come into play.

There are two sections of that second sentence that are especially important in special education decision making. The first provides that a state may not "deny to any person within its jurisdiction the equal protection of the laws." The second provides that a state may not "deprive any person of life, liberty, or property, without due process of law." A public school system is one type of agency that is included in the term "state." Therefore, state and local public school systems may not deny to any children within their jurisdictions the equal protection of the laws, nor can they deprive them of life, liberty, or property without due process of law.

For many years, handicapped children were not provided with appropriate educational programs—nor, indeed, any educational programs at all. School authorities kept handicapped children out by using strategies

3

such as postponement, suspension, exclusion, and straightforward denial of entry. This was true even though most states' constitutions required them to provide a public education to all of their children.

Strangely enough, this exclusion of handicapped children generally was accomplished by reliance on the state compulsory school attendance laws. These laws typically required that all children between certain ages attend school unless some handicapping condition made this inadvisable. The determination of whether a handicapping condition made attendance inadvisable usually was left to the discretion of school authorities.

This exclusionary practice was challenged as being unconstitutional as a violation of the 14th Amendment. The basic argument was that the school system was discriminating against a class of children by not affording equal protection of the laws to the handicapped. In other words, every child within the jurisdiction of a public school system is, by virtue of the laws establishing that system, entitled to an equal educational opportunity. The Constitution does not state that children have a constitutional right to receive an education. What it says is that where a state has undertaken to provide education, it must provide it to all—equally—including handicapped children.

Cases in which the right of handicapped children to a public education was at issue were natural outgrowths of a line beginning with *Brown v. Board of Education*, 347 U.S. 483, which was decided by the Supreme Court in 1954. That historic case established the constitutional principle of equal educational opportunity:

> Today education is perhaps the most important function of state and local governments. Compulsory school attendance laws and the great expenditures for education both demonstrate our recognition of the importance of education to our democratic society. It is required in the armed forces. It is the very foundation of good citizenship. Today it is a principal instrument in awakening the child to cultural values, in preparing him for later professional training, and in helping him to adjust normally to his environment. In these days, it is doubtful any child may reasonably be expected to succeed in life if he is denied the opportunity of an education. Such an opportunity where the State has undertaken to provide it, is a right which must be made available to all on equal terms.

While the Court was focusing there on racial inequalities, subsequent litigation broadened this principle to apply to handicapped children. The first landmark case was *Pennsylvania Association for Retarded Children (PARC) v. Commonwealth of Pennsylvania*, 343 F. Supp. 279 (E.D. Pa.

1972). In this case a federal district court approved a consent agreement and order that enjoined the state from denying or postponing a mentally retarded child's access to a free program of education and training. The court order specifically provided that the state must:

1. provide all retarded persons between the ages of 6 and 21 years with access to a free public program of education and training appropriate to their learning capabilities
2. provide a free program of education and training appropriate to the learning capacities of every mentally retarded child less than 6 years of age whenever it offered a preschool program for the nonhandicapped of the same age

A second landmark case was *Mills v. Board of Education of the District of Columbia*, 348 F. Supp. 866 (D.D.C. 1972). This case expanded *PARC* to all handicapped children and was not limited to mentally retarded or other particular disabled populations. In *Mills*, the judge held that the denial of a publicly supported education to handicapped children violated the District of Columbia Code, the United States Constitution, and the District School Board's own policies and regulations. The court ordered that no children eligible for publicly supported education in the District of Columbia be excluded from a regular public school assignment unless they were provided with alternative educational services suited to their needs.

After the *PARC* and *Mills* cases, 28 states in 1972 passed legislation creating or extending educational programs for handicapped children. Tennessee, Massachusetts, and Wisconsin enacted comprehensive laws that required that all handicapped children receive an appropriate education at state expense. By the end of 1972, 43 states had legislation requiring some services for handicapped children. Congress later passed landmark legislation reinforcing and extending the constitutional rights of handicapped persons—Section 504 of Public Law 93-112 (1977), the Rehabilitation Act of 1973, and Public Law 94-142, the Education for All Handicapped Children Act of 1975.

The second part of the 14th Amendment that is important to special education decision making is that a state may not "deprive any person of life, liberty, or property, without due process of law." This commonly is referred to as the due process clause. This protection comes into play whenever a state agency takes an action that infringes on an individual's life, liberty, or property.

The due process clause is relevant here because the Supreme Court has stated that public education is a "property" interest within the meaning of that term as expressed in the 14th Amendment. It is a "property" interest because states have passed laws providing for free public education for children within their borders. Once a state has extended the right of education to all children, it cannot take away or substantially change that right without affording them "due process of law;" if it provides free education to any of its children, then they all—including the handicapped—have an entitlement to that education. The entitlement is very valuable, which is why it has been denominated a "property" interest.

The clause also forbids deprivations of liberty without due process of law. The term "liberty" in this context is not limited to incarceration in a prison. The Supreme Court has said that:

> Where a person's good name, reputation, honor, or integrity is at stake because of what the government is doing to him, the minimal requirements of the clause must be satisfied. (*Goss v. Lopez*, 419 U.S. 565 (1975))

In the context of special education, this means that before a school system can label or classify a child as "mentally retarded" or having any other handicapping condition, there must be some due process proceeding for the student (individually or through parents or guardian) to object to the label and the stigmatization that may result. Even if such a label may make the child eligible for certain benefits, the school system may not apply it over the individual's objections without due process of law. In the absence of procedural safeguards, inadequate identification and evaluation procedures can lead to mislabeling of children. These pupils then are likely to be removed from the regular classroom, placed in special classes for the handicapped, and accordingly suffer from the stigmatization that results.

In summary, the general protections of the due process clause can be triggered by:

1. a significant school-imposed change in the educational status of the student; children have a "property" interest in their education
2. the imposition of a label that carries a stigma for students who are placed in special programs; impact on a person's reputation is an aspect of personal "liberty" under the due process clause

Once it is clear that the state is about to take an action affecting an individual's interest in life, liberty, or property, the person has a right to due process of law. The next question becomes: What kind of due process is required? Should there be a full-blown hearing? Is the individual entitled to a court-appointed attorney? The Supreme Court has made it clear that the nature of due process depends on the situation. However, it has two basic elements that must be provided:

1. the right to be given adequate notice about what action is proposed, when, where, why, how it will occur
2. the right to an opportunity to be heard on the issue

In the context of special education decision making, P.L. 94-142 clearly sets forth the major requirements of due process. These include the right of the parents of a handicapped child to be given adequate notice a reasonable time before the state proposes, or refuses, to initiate or change the pupil's identification, evaluation, programming, or educational placement. The parents also have an opportunity to be heard on any issue regarding a free appropriate public education for their child. The public school system also has this right to be heard. Both parties are entitled to invoke the due process safeguards that afford each a panoply of rights.

The vehicle for resolving special education disputes is the due process hearing. This is an information-gathering forum conducted under the authority of state law or regulation by a qualified hearing officer. The evidence is presented by the parties involved so that the hearing officer can determine whether:

1. the student is a handicapped child as defined in state education law and regulation
2. the student requires any special education and related services because the handicapping condition adversely affects the pupil's educational performance
3. the individualized education program (IEP) recommended by the school system is appropriate to meet the special needs of the handicapped child
4. the educational placement recommended by the school system has the apparent ability to deliver the necessary services as specified in the child's IEP, and whether that placement is the least restrictive environment in which the pupil could successfully receive the special services

Generally, due process is a well-established principle in most areas outside of education. The principle comes into play during any substantial decision making between the state and an individual. It safeguards the rights of all those involved. Due process is based upon the philosophy that all parties involved in a decision that affects an individual's life, liberty, or property are entitled to (a) speak on their own behalf and (b) request a face-to-face meeting where they can have the fairest possible opportunity to dispute others' points of view.

Special education due process hearings apply this principle in the school system. Such a hearing is a mechanism for gathering information and resolving conflicts about that information. The primary duty of the hearing officer is to determine whether the school system's proposed educational program is appropriate to meet the child's learning needs and capabilities. The hearing officer gathers information from both the school system and the parents, weighs the material, and issues a decision in the best interests of the child within the limits of the law.

The law realizes that responsible persons can disagree over the use and interpretation of tests and data, definitions of handicapping conditions, due process rights, and the concept of appropriate education for a handicapped student. Experience shows that the basic causes of disputes over the education program are the result of

- the parents' demand for the best possible educational program to meet their child's needs and the legal requirement that the school provide an adequate and appropriate program to meet those needs
- the lack of communication between school personnel and parents during the identification, evaluation, and placement process, resulting in frustration and despair for both sides
- the struggle over who is to pay for which services needed by handicapped students

The special education decision-making process has become complex both educationally and legally. This book focuses on the legal requirements and procedures in that decision-making process of identification, evaluation, programming, and placement. These legal requirements and procedures, in the context of special education decision making, are defined collectively as "Due Process in Special Education."

Chapter 2

Public Law 94-142

[Public Law 94-142, the Education for All Handicapped Children Act, was signed into law by President Ford on November 29, 1975. It is the culmination of a movement to provide equal educational opportunity for all handicapped children. It incorporates many of the requirements that courts and state legislatures already had established to ensure that handicapped children within their jurisdictions received free appropriate public education. Its roots lie in federal legislation dating back to the 1950s. Although relatively new, P.L. 94-142 already has become recognized as landmark legislation whose impact on public school systems is likely to equal that of the Elementary and Secondary Education Act of 1965 and the Supreme Court decision in *Brown v. Board of Education* in 1954.]

ORIGINS OF P.L. 94-142

Many of the major provisions of P.L. 94-142 were in fact required in earlier federal laws, so it is the descendent of a long line of legislation aimed at the education of handicapped children.

The major federal law to which P.L. 94-142 is related is the Elementary and Secondary Education Act of 1965, P.L. 89-10. This provided federal funding for programs to help educationally deprived children. In the same year, P.L. 89-313 amended Title I of the Elementary and Secondary Education Act to assist in funding agencies to provide special education to handicapped children who were not covered initially under P.L. 89-10. These monies were aimed principally at handicapped children in institutions and other similar state-operated or state-supported residential settings.

In 1966, the Elementary and Secondary Education Act was amended again with the addition of a new Title VI, Education of Handicapped Children, P.L. 89-750. This authorized federal funds to assist states in initiating, expanding, and improving programs and projects for the education of the handicapped. Each state seeking a grant was required to submit a plan that provided for programs and projects for handicapped youth, including preschoolers. It also provided that federal funds be used to supplement—not supplant—state, local, and private funds.

The programs and projects were to be of sufficient size, scope, and quality as to give reasonable promise of substantial progress toward meeting the needs of handicapped children. They could include the acquisition of equipment and, when necessary, the construction of school facilities. The plans also must provide satisfactory assurances that they would include the handicapped enrolled in private elementary and secondary schools.

P.L. 89-750 also established a National Advisory Council on Handicapped Children consisting of representatives of government, research, and the teaching and training professions. A Bureau for Education of the Handicapped also was mandated, located in the then U.S. Office of Education, with responsibility for administering programs and projects related to the education of the handicapped, including training teachers for that population and research in special education.

In 1967, the Elementary and Secondary Education Act of 1965 was amended again by expanding Title VI. The amendments, P.L. 90-247, the Education of the Handicapped Act, authorized federal funds for establishing or operating regional resource centers for improving the education of the handicapped.

The amendments authorized federal funds to establish model centers and services for deaf-blind children. The new act authorized funds for grants or contracts to improve recruiting of educational personnel and to promote dissemination of information concerning educational opportunities for the handicapped. It provided for the expansion of instructional media programs to include all handicapped children, in addition to a loan service of captioned films for the deaf. The law authorized assistance for handicapped children in schools operated by the U.S. Department of Defense and on Indian reservations serviced by schools operated by the U.S. Department of the Interior.

In 1969, Congress again amended the Elementary and Secondary Education Act of 1965 with the passage of P.L. 91-230. The new Title VI of this act, which consolidated a number of previous provisions on handicapped children, again was titled the Education of the Handicapped Act. It divided into seven basic sections—Parts A through G—all of the categories of programs and services for the education of handicapped children who receive federal assistance.

The new Part B is the most important in terms of the history. It authorizes grants for the initiation, expansion, and improvement of state and local educational programs for handicapped children. Part B determines the kind and amount of federal funding that will be provided to public agencies for special education.

In 1974, Congress substantially enlarged the federal role in the education of handicapped children with the omnibus Educational Amendments of 1974, P.L. 93-380. This law amended and expanded the Education of the Handicapped Act (P.L. 90-247 and P.L. 91-230 discussed earlier). The most significant features of P.L. 93-380 were its modifications of Part B to increase sixfold the funds available to public agencies for the education of handicapped children.

P.L. 93-380 also provided that state plans must include greater rights for handicapped children and their parents. It required the states to provide assurances:

1. that all handicapped children residing in the state, regardless of the nature or severity of their dysfunction, would be given special educational services and that the state would work toward full educational opportunities for them
2. that confidentiality of data and information on these handicapped young persons would be protected
3. that full educational opportunities to all handicapped children would be established

It also specified that there be procedural safeguards in the special education decision-making process, including:

- prior notice to parents before a child's educational placement was changed

- opportunity for parents to obtain an impartial due process hearing

- opportunity for parents to examine all records involving the child's placement

- procedures to protect the child's rights when the pupil lacks parents or guardians

- procedures to ensure that, whenever possible, handicapped children were educated along with the nonhandicapped

- procedures to ensure that testing and evaluation materials were not racially or culturally discriminatory

In 1975, Congress passed P.L. 94-142, a comprehensive revision of Part B of the Education of the Handicapped Act. As noted, the original Part

B was in the Education of the Handicapped Act, P.L. 90-247, revised later by P.L. 91-230 and P.L. 93-380, as discussed.

The 1975 revision of Part B strengthened and built on the foundations that preceded it. The new section increased federal financing of elementary and secondary educational programs for all handicapped children. The other sections of the act remained substantially unchanged and continue in operation. However, the magnitude of the 1975 revision of Part B was so comprehensive that it has come to be designated the Bill of Rights for the education of handicapped children under its new title—The Education for All Handicapped Children Act of 1975.

UNIQUE CHARACTERISTICS OF P.L. 94-142

Public Law 94-142 is unique in several aspects. It addresses actual instruction at the classroom level more explicitly than does any other federal statute. It is the mandate for the development of an individualized education program (IEP) for each handicapped child. The aspect most open to controversy and challenge is its spelling out nine components of that program.

It is, moreover, the first federal law to require preservice education, i.e., in a teacher training institution, for both regular and special educators concerning handicapped children. It is noteworthy that the act is codified as both education and as civil rights legislation.

CONGRESSIONAL PERCEPTION OF AN UNMET NEED

In studying the needs of education for handicapped children, Congress found that:

1. there were more than eight million handicapped children in the United States
2. their special educational needs were not being met fully
3. more than half of these children did not receive appropriate educational services that would enable them to have full equality of opportunity
4. one million of them were excluded entirely from the public school system and would not go through the educational process with their peers
5. their handicaps prevented many of those participating in regular school programs from having a successful educational experience because their dysfunctions were undetected

6. the lack of adequate services in the public schools often forced families to find services outside the system, often at great distances from their residence and at their own expense
7. developments in teacher training and in diagnostic and instructional procedures and methods had advanced to the point that, given appropriate funding, state and local educational agencies could and would provide effective special education and related services to meet the needs of handicapped children
8. state and local educational agencies had a responsibility to provide education for all handicapped children but their financial resources were inadequate to do so
9. it was in the national interest that the federal government assist state and local efforts to provide programs to meet the educational needs of the handicapped in order to assure equal protection of the law

THE GENERAL PURPOSES OF P.L. 94-142

Congress stated that its general purpose in enacting P.L. 94-142 was:

1. To ensure that all handicapped children had available a free appropriate public education that emphasized special courses and related services designed to meet their unique needs. This frequently was not available previously but enactment of the law made it a fundamental right that now must be provided to all handicapped children. This education must be at no cost to the parents and must be designed to suit the child's individual needs.
2. To ensure that the rights of handicapped children and their parents or guardians were protected. These include the right to nondiscriminatory testing in evaluation, to an individualized education program (IEP), to confidential handling of personally identifiable data, to placement in the least restrictive environment, and to a special education due process hearing and decision by an impartial hearing officer. These rights were intended to assure fairness and appropriateness in making decisions about providing special education to the handicapped.
3. To assist states and localities in providing for the education of all handicapped children. The law provided federal funds to support the educational programs as well as state monitoring activities, personnel training, and other activities.
4. To assess and assure the effectiveness of efforts to educate handicapped children. The law required that state and local education

agencies establish clear management and auditing procedures to assure that the federal funds were being spent properly and the rights were being extended appropriately to the handicapped children. The act required each state to submit to the then U.S. Office of Education for approval, a detailed plan outlining how it would assure compliance with the law's mandates. Each state agency similarly was required to obtain from each local educational entity an application outlining how it would ensure compliance with the law and with the state plan. States must establish clear procedures for supporting, monitoring, and policing local educational agencies' compliance. The required structure is intended to hold the local systems accountable to their respective state agencies.

5. The parents of each handicapped child can hold the public agency responsible for their child's education accountable through the mechanism of the IEP. The IEP must include appropriate objective criteria, evaluation procedures, and schedules for determining, at least annually, whether instructional objectives are being achieved.

KEY PROVISIONS OF P.L. 94-142

The provisions of P.L. 94-142 are discussed in greater detail later. The following list of the key provisions is presented here as an introduction.

The Right to a Free Appropriate Public Education

The fundamental element of P.L. 94-142 is the right to a free appropriate public education for every handicapped child who needs special help. As noted, Congress stated that its purpose in passing the law was "to assure that all handicapped children have available to them . . . a free appropriate public education which emphasizes special education and related services designed to meet their unique needs. . . ."

The entire thrust of the law is based on the right of all children, with no exceptions, to an education. Its intent is to give all children, including the most severely handicapped, the learning opportunities they need to achieve their potential and become as self-sufficient as possible.

To qualify for federal assistance, each state was required to submit a plan to the then U.S. Office of Education showing how it proposed to carry out its commitment to the goal of free and appropriate education for all handicapped children. All of the law's other requirements stem from this fundamental goal.

Priority for Services

The paramount goal of the U.S. Congress in enacting P.L. 94-142 was to make a free appropriate public education available to every handicapped child in the nation. The act required that the highest priority for services must be given, first, to handicapped children who were not receiving an education, and, second, to the most severely handicapped who were receiving an inadequate education. The act required that an appropriate education be available to all handicapped children aged 3 to 18 by September 1, 1978, and all handicapped children aged 3 to 21 by September 1, 1980.

Unfortunately, this goal was not reached for all eligible handicapped children. According to a report by the Comptroller General of the U.S. General Accounting Office (GAO) issued in September 1981, most handicapped children not in school (the unserved) had been identified. However, there were a substantial number of handicapped children in regular classrooms (the underserved) not receiving special education. The GAO reported that these underserved were found in the populations of preschool, secondary, and postsecondary handicapped children. Also underserved were seriously emotionally disturbed and migrant children.

Identifying Those in Need of Special Education

The local educational agency is responsible for ensuring that all handicapped children within its jurisdiction are identified, located, and evaluated, including those in all public and private agencies and institutions in its area. Collection and use of data are subject to the confidentiality requirements.

Congress believed that early identification was crucial to preventing a child's handicap from becoming worse or leading to further learning problems. To meet this requirement educational agencies must undertake such activities as child-find programs, which use a variety of approaches to discover children with handicaps that may have gone undetected. These approaches might include such elements as advertising in various types of media, house-to-house canvassing, screenings of children at different grade levels, community workshops on handicaps, etc.

Safeguards for Parents in Decision Making

State and local education agencies must guarantee parents and children strong safeguards to protect their due process rights in all steps of the special education decision-making process. School authorities must provide the parents with a written notice before making changes in the identification, evaluation, program, or placement of their child. The notice must: (1) inform parents of available procedural safeguards; (2) describe and explain the action proposed or taken by the school; (3) state the options the school has considered and, if they are rejected, why; (4) describe each evaluation procedure, test record, or report the school uses to reach a decision; and (5) describe other factors included in making the decision. Finally, the notice must be written so that parents can understand it.

Parents have the right to challenge the school's decision on their child. They may initiate an impartial due process hearing to obtain what they may regard as the appropriate educational placement. They have a right to be represented at the hearing by counsel or by specialists in education for the handicapped.

Parents can present evidence; confront, cross-examine, and compel the attendance of witnesses; and prohibit the introduction of any evidence at the hearing that was not disclosed to them five days before the hearing. Moreover, they can obtain a written or electronic verbatim record of the hearing and can appeal the decision of the impartial hearing officer.

During the time the educational program is being challenged, the student has the right to remain in the present program.

Surrogate Parents

A child is assigned a surrogate parent when the parent or guardian is not known, the parents are unavailable, or the pupil is a ward of the state. The surrogate represents the child as a parent in all matters pertaining to the identification, evaluation, program, placement, and provision of a free appropriate public education.

Consent from the Parents

School authorities must obtain the written consent of parents before conducting initial evaluations and before placing a child in a special education program for the first time.

Multidisciplinary and Nondiscriminatory Evaluations

Before any action is taken on the initial placement of a handicapped child in a special education program, a full and individual evaluation of the pupil's needs must be conducted. The child must be assessed in all areas related to the suspected disability by a multidisciplinary team or group of persons, including at least one teacher or other specialist with knowledge in the area of the apparent dysfunction.

All methods used for testing and evaluation must be racially and culturally nondiscriminatory. They also must be in the child's primary language or mode of communication. No one test or procedure may be the sole means of making a decision about an educational program.

A Written IEP for Each Child

Individualized education programs (IEP) are to be prepared for each child. The parents, and the child where appropriate, are to participate. These programs must include short-term and long-term educational goals and specific services to be provided. The IEPs are to be reviewed at least annually and revised according to the child's changing needs.

Independent Educational Evaluations

Parents can obtain an independent educational evaluation of their child, at public expense in certain cases. On their request, the school authorities must furnish them with information about obtaining such assistance.

Programs in the Least Restrictive Environment

The law mandates that handicapped children be educated to the maximum extent possible with their nonhandicapped peers. Pupils must be placed in special or separate classes only when it is impossible to work out a satisfactory placement in a regular class with supplementary aids and services. State and local education agencies must ensure that a range of alternative placements is available to accommodate handicapped children in the least restrictive setting possible.

Confidentiality of Information

The state and local education agencies must ensure that they will protect the confidentiality of the information gathered and used with regard to handicapped children. The parents of such a pupil have a right to:

1. know what records involving the child are being collected, maintained, or used by the school district and where they are located
2. inspect and review all such records
3. make copies of the child's records at a reasonable cost

4. have someone at the school explain or interpret any item in the child's records
5. give consent before the records can be seen by someone not involved in the child's education
6. know who, other than the persons involved in the child's education, has seen the pupil's records and why
7. ask for a change in the records because they think a statement is wrong or misleading; parents have a right to a hearing upon request if the school refuses to change the statement; they also have the right to add to the records a statement commenting on the information, or stating reasons why they disagree with the hearing if the decision there upholds the accuracy of the information in the records.

Services in Private School Placements

When children are placed in private schools by state or local education systems in order to receive an appropriate education, this must be done at no cost to parents. Private school programs must meet standards set by the law and must safeguard the rights of parents and of the children who are placed there. Special needs children enrolled in private or parochial schools by their parents also have a right to receive some special education and related services from the public school system.

Schools' Adaptation to Needs of Handicapped Children

The law requires that training must be provided for teachers and other personnel who deal with handicapped children. Regular educators need to learn how to teach such pupils. More special education teachers must be trained and hired to meet the increased demand. Curriculums including academic and vocational courses must be adapted for children with special education needs. Handicapped children must be afforded greater access to programs and buildings in which nonhandicapped students receive education.

Advisory Boards

Each state must set up an advisory board, including handicapped individuals, teachers, and parents of dysfunctional children. This board is to advise the state on unmet needs, comment publicly on rules and regulations, and assist in evaluating programs.

Penalties for Failure to Comply

The law provides for jurisdictions to be penalized for noncompliance. Funds can be withheld if, after reasonable notice and an opportunity for a hearing, a state is found by the U.S. Department of Education to have failed to comply with the law. Federal payments that are passed through to local school systems also may be suspended for noncompliance.

DEFINITIONS OF 3 CRITICAL TERMS

1. 'Handicapped Children'

As used in the law, the term "handicapped children" refers to those children who are mentally retarded, hard of hearing, deaf, speech impaired, visually handicapped, seriously emotionally disturbed, orthopedically impaired, other health impaired, deaf-blind, multihandicapped, or have specific learning disabilities. It involves children who, because of those impairments, need special education and related services. (§ 121a.5(a))

The definition of handicapped children sets two criteria for determining whether a pupil is eligible for special education. First, the child must have been evaluated and found to have one or more of the handicaps listed in the definition. For example, one who simply presents a difficult behavior problem in the classroom may not qualify for a special education program unless found to be seriously emotionally disturbed or to have one of the other listed handicaps.

The second criterion is that the child must need special education and related services because of the handicap. A pupil may have one or more of the disabling conditions but not necessarily need special educational services. For example, a student who is orthopedically impaired may or may not require special education because of that disability. It is possible that the student can and should attend school without any program modification. It is important to emphasize that a child who does not require special education services is not considered handicapped for purposes of this law.

2. 'Special Education'

A child who is handicapped and needs help is eligible for "special education" and "related services." Special education is defined in P.L. 94-142 (§ 121a.14) as:

> *specially designed instruction*, at no cost to parents or guardians, *to meet the unique needs of a handicapped child*, including class-room instruction, instruction in physical education, home instruction, and instruction in hospitals and institutions. (emphasis added)

The critical italicized phrases clearly indicate that the law is designed to respond only to a child who has special needs in educational programming. The law does not respond simply because the child is handicapped. The instruction required to be provided is specially designed to meet the unique needs of a child that result from the handicap, and no further.

From this definition of special education (and the requirements concerning placement in the least restrictive environment) it is clear that the goals of general education predominate for all children. Only when a handicap impairs a child from functioning in a general school program does special education become appropriate. Even then, special education is appropriate only to the extent that it is necessary to bridge the gap between the child's ability to function in the general school program and the deficits in doing so because of the handicap. Indeed, for most handicapped children, special instruction will not be the totality of their education. They will participate in the general education program to the maximum extent possible.

The example of Jackie illustrates the term special education. Jackie is a 6-year-old girl who is mentally retarded. The law does not require special intervention because she is mentally retarded. It does not require that Jackie be placed in a classroom established for the mentally retarded.

It does not require that she receive math instruction for the mentally retarded, reading instruction for the mentally retarded, self-help training for the mentally retarded, socialization activities for the mentally retarded, physical education for the mentally retarded, art for the mentally retarded, lunch for the mentally retarded, recess for the mentally retarded, etc.

It does not require that Jackie receive a program for the mentally retarded at all. In fact, it would be absurd and unlawful to place her in a total education program for the mentally retarded simply because she is so impaired.

Rather, the law requires that the focus of special intervention is not on Jackie's handicap of mental retardation, but rather on her individual educational needs that result from her mental retardation. Every mentally retarded person is not affected in the same way or to the same extent. Jackie may require only itinerant or resource help with certain academic subjects while spending most of her day in the general education program with her nonhandicapped peers. On the other hand, she might require a 12-month residential education program with little or no integration with her nonhandicapped fellow pupils. Her handicap of mental retardation does not alone identify her unique educational needs.

The law requires that the special education provided for Jackie involve only instruction that is specially designed and directed to meet her unique needs, such as those that result from the adverse effect of her handicap on her ability to function in the general education program. The law does not require the school system to provide all kinds of programs to meet Jackie's unique needs that may result from her home environment, personal interests, etc.

3. 'Related Services'

As noted, a child who is handicapped and needs help as a result of the impairment is eligible for special education and "related services." Special education is defined above. The term "related services" as used in the law is defined (§ 121a.13) as:

> the term "related services" means transportation and such developmental, corrective, and other supportive services *as are required to assist a handicapped child to benefit from special education*, and includes speech pathology and audiology, psychological services, physical and occupational therapy, recreation, early identification and assessment of disabilities in children, counseling services, and medical services for diagnostic or evaluation purposes. The term also includes school health services, social work services in schools, and parent counseling and training. (emphasis added)

As discussed, a child is defined as handicapped, for purposes of this law, only if special education and related services are required. Special education is instruction designed specifically to meet unique needs. The definition of related services follows the logical progression by stating that they are the additional services necessary for the child to benefit from special education.

The definitions of handicapped and special education make it clear that, under the law, a child is not handicapped unless special education is needed. The definition of related services also depends on these factors since related services must be necessary for a child to benefit from special education. Therefore, if a child does not need special education, there can be no related services, and the pupil (because not "handicapped") is not covered under P.L. 94-142.

The terms included under related services are defined as follows:

(1) "Audiology" includes:

(i) Identification of children with hearing loss;

(ii) Determination of the range, nature, and degree of hearing loss, including referral for medical or other professional attention for the habilitation of hearing;

(iii) Provision of habilitative activities, such as language habilitation, auditory training speech reading (lip-reading), hearing evaluation, and speech conservation;

(iv) Creation and administration of programs for prevention of hearing loss;

(v) Counseling and guidance of pupils, parents, and teachers regarding hearing loss; and

(vi) Determination of the child's need for group and individual amplification, selecting and fitting an appropriate aid, and evaluating the effectiveness of amplification.

(2) "Counseling services" means services provided by qualified social workers, psychologists, guidance counselors, or other qualified personnel.

(3) "Early identification" means the implementation of a formal plan for identifying a disability as early as possible in a child's life.

(4) "Medical services" means services provided by a licensed physician to determine a child's medically related handicapping condition which results in the child's need for special education and related services.

(5) "Occupational therapy" includes:

(i) Improving, developing or restoring functions impaired or lost through illness, injury, or deprivation;

(ii) Improving ability to perform tasks for independent functioning when functions are impaired or lost; and

(iii) Preventing, through early intervention, initial or further impairment or loss of function.

(6) "Parent counseling and training" means assisting parents in understanding the special needs of their child and providing parents with information about child development.

(7) "Physical therapy" means services provided by a qualified physical therapist.

(8) "Psychological services" include:

(i) Administering psychological and educational tests, and other assessment procedures;

(ii) Interpreting assessment results;

(iii) Obtaining, integrating, and interpreting information about child behavior and conditions relating to learning;

(iv) Consulting with other staff members in planning school programs to meet the special needs of children as indicated by psychological tests, interviews, and behavioral evaluations; and

(v) Planning and managing a program of psychological services, including psychological counseling for children and parents.

(9) "Recreation" includes:

(i) Assessment of leisure function;

(ii) Therapeutic recreation services;

(iii) Recreation programs in schools and community agencies; and

(iv) Leisure education.

(10) "School health services" means services provided by a qualified school nurse or other qualified person.

(11) "Social work services in schools" include:

(i) Preparing a social or developmental history on a handicapped child;

(ii) Group and individual counseling with the child and family;

(iii) Working with those problems in a child's living situation (home, school, and community) that affect the child's adjustment in school; and

(iv) Mobilizing school and community resources to enable the child to receive maximum benefit from his or her educational program.

(12) "Speech pathology" includes:

(i) Identification of children with speech or language disorders;

(ii) Diagnosis and appraisal of specific speech or language disorders;

(iii) Referral for medical or other professional attention necessary for the habilitation of speech or language disorders;

(iv) Provisions of speech and language services for the habilitation or prevention of communicative disorders; and

(v) Counseling and guidance of parents, children, and teachers regarding speech and language disorders.

(13) "Transportation" includes:

(i) Travel to and from school and between schools,

(ii) Travel in and around school buildings, and

(iii) Specialized equipment (such as special or adapted buses, lifts, and ramps), if required to provide special transportation for a handicapped child. (§ 121a.13(b))

The list of related services is not exhaustive and many lists include other developmental, corrective, or supportive services (such as artistic and cultural programs, and art, music, and dance therapy) if they are required to assist a handicapped child to benefit from special education.

Certain kinds of services might be provided by persons from varying professional backgrounds and with a variety of functional titles, depending upon requirements in individual states. For example, counseling services might be provided by social workers, psychologists, or guidance counselors; psychological testing might be done by qualified psychological examiners, psychologists, or psychometrists, depending upon state standards.

However, with respect to related services, the Senate Report states:

> The Committee bill provides a definition of "related services," making clear that all such related services may not be required for each individual child and that such term includes early identification and assessment of handicapping conditions and the provision of services to minimize the effects of such conditions. (Senate Report No. 94-168, 1975, p. 12)

It also is important to note that each related service may include the administrative and supervisory activities necessary for program planning, management, and evaluation.

IMPLEMENTING CONCERNS IN A CUTBACK ERA

P.L. 94-142 established a payment formula based upon a gradually escalating percentage of the national average expenditure per public school child times the number of handicapped pupils receiving publicly financed special education and related services in each state. That percentage was scheduled to escalate on a yearly basis until 1982, when it was to become a permanent 40 percent for that year and all subsequent years. Yet, regardless of the dollars generated under this formula, they are potential dollars only. The entitlements become reality only if Congress actually appropriates the money.

Although most public officials and school administrators have an ethical commitment to the philosophy expressed in P.L. 94-142, i.e., the right of all handicapped children to education, there is some divergence of opinion. Certain assumptions that society has accepted are not really commensurate with special education as it is currently espoused.

For instance, the tenet that decisions be made in order to provide "the greatest good for the greatest number" certainly is at odds with this act.

A second tenet, that of efficiency and cost-effectiveness, is increasingly popular in this age of accountability and spending reductions. But P.L. 94-142 runs contrary to those concepts because it contains a legal mandate to provide education regardless of the cost involved, for these children, who at times must be taught by one or two adults per pupil.

It is reassuring to note that compliance with the guarantee of the availability of a free appropriate public education is in no way dependent on whether this law is funded fully. Regardless of the actual federal appropriations, if a state accepts the money under the law it must comply with the basic guarantee. If a state chooses not to participate under P.L. 94-142, essentially the same compliance still will be required under Section 504. In addition, most states have their own state laws, regulations, and court orders requiring the provision of a free, appropriate public education to all handicapped children within their state borders.

In addition to reductions in funding, this decade is likely to see major efforts to limit the federal role in education policy making, such as replacing most of the categorical grant programs with combined block grants—one block to the state education agencies (SEAs) and one to the local education agencies (LEAs).

In April 1981, The Council for Exceptional Children, a lead organization in the field of public policy and special education, published a document titled "Effects of Federal Block Grant and Budget Proposals on Special Education." The document summed up the concerns of the special education community over trends of the current decade to reduce funding and restructure the categorical programs into block grants:

Budget Reductions

- The [proposed budget cuts would] mean that many handicapped students will not receive adequate special education; some will be unable to find a program at all; others will be denied needed related services.

- In many states, funding cuts will result in staff reductions, increases in class size, fewer curricular materials, loss of paraprofessional assistance, and longer distances for pupils to be transported.

- There will be reduced opportunities for earning a degree in special education at a time when many districts are experiencing shortages of such personnel. Faculties in many teacher training institutions are on "soft" money and may be laid off.

- Early intervention programs will be hit hardest in some states where federal money is not used largely at the preschool level.

- Districts in 40 states are faced with tax caps, statutory spending limits, and tax reductions and will be unable to raise money to replace lost federal aid.

Under the block grant structure, federal funds could be spent on any one program or combination of programs that had been grouped together. In other words, money once targeted only for handicapped children could be used toward any other educational program grouped in the same "block."

The idea behind this concept is to shift control over educational policy from the federal government to state and local authorities. This objective would be accomplished by limiting the federal role to simply making resources available. The choices and decisions about those resources would be made by the individual SEAs and LEAs. The regulatory and paperwork burden on the education agencies would be lessened and thereby result in lower administrative costs.

Most advocates of the handicapped staunchly oppose the budget reductions and block grant restructuring. They feel that funding for P.L. 94-142 has not been adequate and any reduction would adversely affect the ability of SEAs and LEAs to deliver on the law's promise.

They further believe that the block grant structure would mean the total demise of P.L. 94-142 and the protections it guarantees. They feel that it is unlikely that its provisions would be carried into any block grant legislation.

The Council for Exceptional Children declared:

Block Grants

- With the repeal of P.L. 94-142, protections guaranteed under the act will not be specified in the block grant legislation. Issues such as right to education, procedural safeguards, least restrictive environment, related services, nondiscriminatory assessment, and others would be left to state policies or litigation. A decade of progress will be seriously threatened.

- There will be no earmarking of federal funds so special education will be forced to compete at the state and local level with many other interests for their share of the funds.

- States and school districts will no longer be required to use federal funds to supplement their local money. Federal money could be used to replace state and local resources, which would result in reduced resources for special education.

- There will be no provision or recognition of the importance of child-find or early screening, identification, and early childhood programming, even though the preschool incentive grant is folded into the LEA block grant.

- There will be no recognition of state education agencies, only the "state," which is not defined as state education agencies (SEAs). Funds could be used by a governor or state legislature for political purposes.

- There will be no [specific] recognition of institutions of higher education. Present programs in personnel development will be seriously threatened.

- The 25 percent SEA set aside under P.L. 94-142 will no longer exist.

- Allocations of portions of the funding will be based on state average per pupil expenditures rather than on the national average.

- The formula for allocations will not be uniform but will be determined by states. It will not be tied to a count of exceptional children or children served.

- Many services currently authorized for funding under P.L. 94-142 will no longer be specifically mentioned as eligible for funding, i.e., transportation, counseling, recreation, social work, early identification and assessment, and school health.

- There will be no assurance that funds generated under the two state block grants will be allocated to public education agencies.

- There will be no provision for a sole state agency responsibility for assurance of special education services for exceptional students.

However, even if the federal budget for education is cut and P.L. 94-142 eventually is repealed, a decade of court decisions in nearly every state granting handicapped children the right to a free appropriate public education still stand. Those decisions are based on the constitutional rights of handicapped children to such an education. Therefore, it is unlikely that any major effort to wholly replace P.L. 94-142 and Section 504 will be successful for a long time to come.

The right of handicapped children to an appropriate education in the least restrictive environment has been firmly established in society and is certain to endure in one form or another.

Chapter 3

Section 504

Section 504 is the basic civil rights provision for ending discrimination against America's handicapped citizens. The section was enacted through the Rehabilitation Act Amendments of 1973, P.L. 93-112. The act has been codified as 29 U.S.C. 794. The act prohibits discrimination against any qualified handicapped person in any program or activity receiving federal financial assistance:

> No otherwise qualified handicapped individual in the United States . . . shall, solely by reason of his handicap, be excluded from the participation in, be denied the benefits of, or be subjected to discrimination under any program or activity receiving federal financial assistance.

THE SECTION 504 REGULATIONS

The final regulations for Section 504 were published May 4, 1977. Written by the then U.S. Department of Health, Education, and Welfare (HEW), they explain how the federal government will interpret and enforce its responsibilities under the Rehabilitation Act to ensure that handicapped persons are protected from discrimination in federally funded programs.

The Section 504 regulations apply only to recipients of financial assistance from what are now the Department of Health and Human Services and the Department of Education. These two originally constituted HEW when the regulations were first published. Other federal agencies and departments issue regulations for programs and activities they fund.

Recipients of funding from federal health and education agencies and all programs or activities benefiting from such assistance are subject to the nondiscrimination provisions of the Section 504 regulations.

A recipient is any person, public or private agency, governmental unit, institution, or other entity that receives funds, the services of personnel, property (automobiles, buildings, furniture, equipment, etc.), or any other assistance directly or indirectly from federal agencies. Thus, local service providers, school districts, and consumer organizations representing the handicapped that receive federal funds from a state agency must comply with the regulations; so, too, must state agencies that receive funds directly from the federal government.

Examples of recipients include hospitals, public and private schools, universities and colleges, state agencies, county welfare and rehabilitation agencies, nursing homes, day care centers, and consumer and advocacy organizations.

CRITERIA FOR SECTION 504 PROTECTION

Section 504 protects "qualified handicapped persons." To be so safeguarded a person must (a) be handicapped, and (b) be qualified to be employed in, benefit from, or participate in a federally assisted program or activity.

Section 504 defines a handicapped person as anyone who:

1. has a physical or mental impairment that substantially limits one or more major life activities (such as manual skills, caring for self, walking, seeing, hearing, speaking, breathing, learning, and working); or
2. has a record of such an impairment (including persons who no longer have the handicapping condition, such as those with a past history of epilepsy, or who in fact never had the impairment but were classified erroneously as handicapped, such as individuals misclassified as mentally retarded); or
3. is regarded as having such an impairment (including a person without a substantially limiting physical or mental impairment who may be handicapped, such as a facially scarred yet otherwise nonhandicapped woman who is denied employment because an employer finds her appearance repulsive).

Examples of physical or mental impairments covered by the regulations include: cerebral palsy; cancer; diabetes; heart disease; muscular dystrophy; mental retardation; epilepsy; mental illness; autism; specific learning disabilities; orthopedic, visual, speech, or hearing impairments; and loss of extremities.

A handicapped student is protected from discrimination in public pre-school, elementary, secondary, and adult education programs if the individual

1. is of an age during which nonhandicapped students are provided such services, or
2. is of an age during which state law mandates delivery of such services to handicapped students (originally ages 5 to 21 but 3 to 21 effective September 1, 1980), or
3. is one to whom a state must provide a free appropriate public education under P.L. 94-142 (ages 3 to 21 effective September 1, 1980).

For example, if a school district provides early childhood educational services to 3-year-old and 4-year-old nonhandicapped children, it also must provide the same services to handicapped children of the same ages.

Handicapped children are protected from discrimination in private pre-school, elementary, secondary, and adult education programs if they meet the essential eligibility requirements for receiving such educational services. For example, a private school that admits only girls 5 to 12 years old may not exclude a hearing-impaired 9-year-old girl who can participate in the institution's regular education programs with only minor accommodations.

FREE APPROPRIATE PUBLIC EDUCATION

A recipient who operates public elementary and secondary education programs must provide a free appropriate public education to each qualified handicapped student in its district, regardless of the nature or severity of the pupil's impairment. If a recipient places a child in a program other than its own, it remains financially responsible for the pupil, whether or not the other program is operated by another recipient or educational agency. However, in no case may a school system refuse to educate a handicapped child living in the district because of another district's failure to pay.

Public schools must provide educational and related services to handicapped students without cost. For example, a school district may not charge for such services as special classroom adaptive equipment, phonic ears, study carrels, Braille materials, vocational and academic counseling services, medical diagnostic services, physical and occupational therapy, teacher aides, resource teachers, private educational services, or special transportation.

However, schools may collect the same fees as are imposed on the parents or guardians of nonhandicapped students. For example, a school district may not charge the parents of a cerebral palsied child for the cost of specially adapting a lunchroom table. However, it may charge the daily fee for lunch normally required of all parents.

If a school district does not itself provide its handicapped students with the requisite services, it must offer free alternate placement, including its paying tuition fees and the cost of any related services or aid the child requires. For example, if a district places a severely emotionally disturbed, learning disabled student in a private day school program, the parents do not have to pay for the tuition fee or the services of attending professionals such as a psychologist.

The school also must arrange for transportation to and from this special placement at no greater cost to the parents or guardian than the district charges for regular school bus service, regardless of the actual expense of conveying the child.

Identification, Evaluation, Programming, and Placement

Each year, public elementary and secondary schools must locate and identify handicapped children who live in their districts who are not receiving a public education. These schools must inform students and parents or guardians annually of the district's duty to provide a free appropriate public education to each handicapped child.

Public schools must meet the individual educational needs of handicapped students just as they must of the nonhandicapped. An appropriate education may consist of:

1. schooling in regular classes with the use of supplementary services, or
2. special education in regular or separate classrooms, at home, or in public or private institutions accompanied by such related aids as psychological, counseling, transportation, and medical diagnostic services.

For example, a school could not offer a handicapped child a program that averaged only four hours of instruction a day while giving nonhandicapped students six hours a day.

A handicapped child's appropriate education and placement are determined by special evaluation methods that include tests and procedures designed to minimize misclassifications and inappropriate assignments.

The identification, evaluation, programming, and educational placement of a handicapped child also are subject to due process procedures, which provide parents or guardians an opportunity to challenge the school's proposed actions.

Residential Placements

If a public or private residential placement is required for a handicapped student to receive a free appropriate public education, the residential program, including room and board and nonmedical care, must be provided at no cost to parents or guardians. However, if other factors, such as an impaired student's home life, brought about the residential placement, then the school is not required to provide room, board, and nonmedical care.

A public school's Section 504 duties continue even when it places a handicapped child in or refers the pupil to a program it does not operate. For example, if a school places a handicapped child in a state institution, the district must ensure that (1) the pupil receives a free appropriate public education, (2) the pupil is properly evaluated and reevaluated, and (3) the child and parents are provided opportunities to challenge the state school's actions.

Integration of Handicapped Students

Private and public schools must make every effort to educate handicapped students in the most normal setting appropriate to their needs. Schools may not operate separate facilities for impaired pupils unless they are absolutely essential for assuring that such students receive an appropriate education.

Schools must try continually to place handicapped students in the regular programs and activities, with as much contact as appropriate with the nonimpaired. For example, a hearing impaired junior high school student may participate appropriately in regular classroom instruction if provided with the support of a sign language interpreter.

A handicapped student may be removed from the regular educational setting only when the school can show that the pupil cannot be educated satisfactorily in its normal programs or activities with the use of supplementary aids and services. For example, an elementary school cannot automatically segregate an entering visually handicapped first grader into a special program without first determining that the child cannot be educated in a regular classroom using aids and other services.

Schools also must try to place handicapped students in programs located as close as possible to their homes. These pupils also have the right to participate with nonhandicapped students in nonacademic and extracurricular services and activities. Even if impaired students have to be educated solely with others who are handicapped, they may be integrated with the nonhandicapped for transportation, recess, physical education, music, art, assemblies, lunch, etc.

If separate facilities (or services or activities) are provided to handicapped students, they must be comparable in quality to others operated by the schools. For example, a high school may not relegate its handicapped students to basement or portable substandard classrooms or buildings or provide them with inferior materials and staff.

Public schools may not initially place handicapped students in regular or special education programs or significantly change their placement without first thoroughly and professionally evaluating their educational needs.

Schools may not rely solely on standardized IQ tests in determining handicapped students' educational placement. They must draw upon a variety of sources in evaluating and placing these pupils, including aptitude and achievement tests, teacher recommendations, physical condition, social or cultural background, and adaptive behavior. The information from these sources must be well documented. The placement decision must be made by a group of persons familiar with the student, based on their knowledge of the child, the evaluation data, and placement options. Placements must be reevaluated regularly.

PROCEDURAL SAFEGUARDS

Elementary and secondary public schools must establish a system of procedural safeguards that permit a handicapped student's parents or guardian to participate in or contest decisions regarding the child's identification, evaluation, programming, and placement. The procedural safeguards must include the following:

- notice
- opportunity for the parents or guardians to examine the child's records
- an impartial hearing with an opportunity for the parents or guardian to participate
- representation by counsel
- an appeal procedure.

Parents have a right to request an impartial hearing if the school proposes to:

- transfer a child from a regular classroom to a separate, segregated setting
- refuse to provide related services and aids such as speech therapy, vocational rehabilitation, or physical therapy
- classify a child as handicapped
- refuse to pay for private residential placement
- place a pupil in a private program that discriminates against the handicapped

If a public school does in fact offer a free appropriate public education to a handicapped child but the parents or guardian choose to place the pupil in a private school, then the public school does not have to pay for the private education. But if parents believe the school, in fact, cannot appropriately educate their child, they have the right to settle this disagreement or any other question about the educational program in an impartial hearing.

Compliance

As of June 3, 1977, no recipient could exclude any handicapped child from its public elementary or secondary education program and was required to provide each such qualified student with a free appropriate public education no later than September 1, 1978.

Discrimination Ban in Nonacademic Services

Handicapped students must have an equal opportunity to participate in their school's nonacademic and extracurricular services and activities. A school may not deny handicapped students such elements as:

- cafeteria services
- intramural athletics
- interscholastic athletics
- transportation
- health services
- school-sponsored clubs
- student employment

- social activities

- special interest groups or clubs

These services and activities must be provided in the most integrated setting appropriate to the handicapped student's own needs.

Disciplinary Expulsions

Public schools may not expel handicapped students because the nature or severity of their impairments pose problems. For example, a highly destructive, emotionally disturbed child may not be expelled because the school is unable to cope with the disruptive behavior; however, the school may change the pupil's placement in accordance with its normal procedures to protect the safety of the other students.

A school may not expel a handicapped child who is difficult to serve. If it is truly unable to educate a disruptive pupil appropriately and effectively, it must seek out and pay for an alternate educational placement.

Preschool and Adult Education

Qualified handicapped students may not be excluded from preschool education, child day care, or adult education programs solely because of the nature or severity of their impairment. For example, a 4-year-old asthmatic child may not be excluded from the school district's early childhood program for those 3 to 5 years old.

Private Schools

Private elementary or secondary schools do not have to accept handicapped students with special education requirements if they do not offer programs or services designed to meet those needs. For example, a private school that has no programs or services designed for the deaf is not required to admit hearing impaired students. But they may not exclude handicapped children who, with only minor adjustments, can participate in their regular programs and activities.

A private school is subject to the evaluation and due process requirements of the Section 504 regulations only if it operates special education programs. If it does not have any such programs, it may expel a handicapped child from its regular classes without providing the parents with an impartial hearing to challenge the expulsion.

Program Accessibility

No qualified handicapped person may be excluded from or be denied the benefits of a public preschool, elementary, secondary, or adult education program because the facilities are inaccessible to or unusable by the impaired. For example, an elementary school cannot refuse to educate orthopedically impaired students because classrooms are located on an upper floor of a building without an elevator.

Programs in existing facilities must be operated so that, when viewed as a whole, they are readily accessible and usable. Therefore, a school need not make each and every part of its existing facilities accessible if it can relocate or reschedule enough classes and activities so as to offer all required courses and a reasonable selection of electives and other activities in already accessible areas.

Programs in existing facilities had to be made accessible by December 2, 1977, and where structural changes were necessary, they had to be completed no later than June 2, 1980. A recipient's newly constructed facilities must be designed and built so that they are accessible to and usable by handicapped persons.

Chapter 4

States, Localities, and Courts

P.L. 94-142, Section 504, and the accompanying regulations provide the legal mandates and a framework for implementing the right to a free appropriate public education for every handicapped child. However, those laws also intentionally leave many of the details to be filled in by the states and by local authorities. Frequently, the courts are called upon to interpret and clarify the application of a law to a particular set of facts. This chapter discusses those roles of the states, localities, and courts as they fit into the context of special education law.

THE ROLE OF STATES AND LOCALITIES

Originally, public education was solely the responsibility and domain of the individual states and localities. Over time, the federal government slowly began to intervene. Initially it limited itself to education programs that were temporary, voluntary, or developed in response to a particular national problem.

The historical federal reluctance to intervene in education derives from the earliest days of the republic and the development of the Constitution. The Constitution itself clearly distinguishes between areas of authority that belong to the federal government and those reserved to the states. It provides federal authority over all subjects that concern the interests of the nation as a whole and reserves to the states all other matters relating to local affairs and the welfare of their own territory and people. It left education to the states.

However, the federal government became heavily involved in education in the 1950s and 1960s. The nation was concerned about the advancement of the Soviet Union and the launching of Sputnik. The government began to support technological research and many other education programs in response to the perceived threat to national security. It also provided carrots and sticks to the states to bring them into compliance with court decisions involving unequal educational opportunity and racial discrimination in the public schools.

The courts also issued numerous decisions in the late 1960s and early 1970s related to the handicapped that have had sweeping social consequences, especially in public education. Congress adopted P.L. 94-142 because it found this approach to be necessary to establish the guidelines and financial incentives for providing handicapped children with access to full educational opportunities.

The Primacy Factor

Congress and federal agencies repeatedly assert, however, that education in the United States is a state function. They often have reaffirmed the principle that the states and local communities have, and must retain, control over and primary responsibility for public education. Congress and these agencies generally hold that the role of the federal government is limited to providing financial aid and technical assistance to the states in meeting their education obligations.

The issue of primacy in education becomes academic when considering the series of interlocking responsibilities through which P.L. 94-142 is administered. The basic arrangement between the federal and state governments resembles a business contract.

The federal government agrees to provide financial and technical assistance to the states for the education of handicapped children. In return, the states agree to comply with federal regulations and standards for such schooling. A state theoretically could refuse to participate under the P.L. 94-142 "contract" but it still would be required to meet the generally identical requirements of Section 504, and there is no federal funding scheme behind that law for public education.

However, the act and its regulations recognize that the states differ in their laws, practices, and special circumstances. Although it is clear and strict on many points, P.L. 94-142 differs in numerous ways from state law and practice, as well as on the judgment of the state educational agency.

For example, notice to parents about a proposed action is one right that is central to the due process protections. The regulations require that written notice be given a reasonable time before the school takes or refuses to take some action in the special education decision-making process. The interpretation of what constitutes a "reasonable period of time" is left to the states. Another example is the responsibility under P.L. 94-142 for monitoring local implementation of the mandates. This responsibility is left to the individual states but with federal authority to suspend funding to a locality that fails to comply.

The 1980s appear to be ushering in an era in which the trend of the federal government returning to the states and localities more control over their special education policy will increase. The U.S. Department of Education has adopted the general objective of reducing the burdens and costs of existing and future P.L. 94-142 regulations. The department will continue to review the regulations in an on-going process to:

- Avoid unnecessary regulation
- Reduce compliance requirements
- Increase agency accountability for regulatory actions
- Ensure the societal benefits of the regulations outweigh the cost to society
- Eliminate burdensome, unnecessary, and unproductive paperwork
- Minimize the cost of rulemaking to the federal government
- Ensure that the department is collecting only the information it needs
- Specifically, reduce burdens for small entities.

Sources of Legal Support

Generally, the states and localities have numerous legal sources affecting special education services for handicapped children. These include state statutes, state regulations, court orders, state attorney general opinions, and other state policy documents.

In addition, the act gives the states and localities the responsibility of adopting operating procedures and interpretations of the federal regulations to promote the purpose of the law and to facilitate its application in local circumstances.

Regulations and procedures also are necessary to implement court orders and assure a uniform state response to federal requirements. Each state must assure that it has in place the legal authority to carry out each provision of the P.L. 94-142 regulations. If they lack legal authority to comply with a requirement, they are supposed to adopt legislation to enable them to comply or reconcile the discrepancy in some other way.

ANNUAL STATE PROGRAM PLANS

To receive funds under P.L. 94-142, the states must submit annual program plans to the U.S. Department of Education through their own agencies. A state plan must represent the basis for the operation and administration of the activities to be carried out under the act. Each state has the responsibility of ensuring that its plan is consistent with its own law and that it complies with the act. The state plan must contain statements that correspond to each of the federal requirements for the education of handicapped children. The state also must include a copy of each state statute, court order, regulation, state attorney general opinion, and other policy documents to support the statements it made in the plan.

The state program must contain certain assurances, specifics of certain procedures, and a detailed resource plan. Generally, it must include information that shows:

- the state has in effect a policy that ensures that all handicapped children have the right to a free appropriate public education within the age ranges and timelines under federal law

- the state has policies and procedures designed to ensure that a free appropriate public education is available for all handicapped children aged 3 through 21

- the state's policies and procedures ensure that it has a goal of providing full educational opportunities to all handicapped children from birth through age 21 and a detailed timetable for accomplishing it

- the number of handicapped children from birth through age 2 who are receiving special education and related services, such as a parent-infant program or physical therapy stimulation activities

- the number of handicapped children who: (a) are enrolled in public or private institutions who are receiving a free appropriate public education, (b) need but are not receiving a free appropriate public education, and (c) are enrolled in public and private institutions and are not receiving a free appropriate public education

- the estimated numbers of handicapped children expected to receive special education and related services during the next school year

- the basis used to determine the required data

- the kind and number of facilities, personnel, and services necessary throughout the state to meet the goal cited above

- efforts to ensure that federal requirements on procedural safeguards are met

- procedures that ensure that the federal requirements of a least restrictive environment are met

- the state's policies and procedures to ensure that: (a) all handicapped children, regardless of the severity of their impairment who are in need of special education and related services are identified, located, and evaluated; and (b) a practical method is developed and implemented to determine which pupils are receiving special education and related services and which are not

- each public agency in the state is maintaining records of the individualized education program for each handicapped child and reviews and revises the programs annually

- the state's policies and procedures to ensure the protection of the confidentiality of any personally identifiable information collected, used, or maintained

- procedures that ensure that federal requirements on evaluations are met

- the supervisory responsibility of the state educational agency for all programs

- state monitoring and evaluation activities to ensure that all agencies comply with the federal law

- procedures the state educational agency follows to inform each public entity of its responsibility for assuring effective implementation of procedural safeguards for the handicapped children it serves

- procedures provided for consultation with individuals involved in or concerned with the education of handicapped children, including impaired individuals and parents of such pupils

- programs and procedures established to ensure that funds received by the state or any of its agencies under any other federal program are used only in a manner consistent with the free appropriate public education goal; this includes funding under Section 121 of the Elementary and Secondary Education Act of 1965 (20 U.S.C. 241e-2), Section 305(b)(8) of that act (20 U.S.C. 844a(b) (8)) or Title IV-C of that act (20 U.S.C. 1831), and Section 110(a) of the Vocational Education Act of 1963, which includes specific authority for assistance for the education of handicapped children

- procedures for the implementation and use of a comprehensive system of personnel development as required by federal law

- the priorities established for providing a free appropriate public education to all handicapped children, first for those not receiving such an education and second for those within each disability with the most severe handicaps who are receiving an inadequate education

- policies and procedures that ensure that the federal requirements on handicapped children in private schools are met

- policies and procedures that ensure that the state will seek to recover any funds provided under P.L. 94-142 for services to a child who is determined to be classified erroneously as handicapped

- control of funds provided under the act, and title to property acquired with those funds, is in a public agency for the assigned uses and purposes and that such an agency administers the funds and property

- procedures for keeping records and affording access to them as the U.S. Department of Education may find necessary for verification of the reports and of proper disbursements of federal funds

- procedures to ensure that the state educational agency does not take any final action on an application from a local educational agency before giving it reasonable notice and an opportunity for a hearing

- an assurance satisfactory to the U.S. Department of Education that funds provided under P.L. 94-142 are not commingled with state monies

- procedures for evaluation at least annually of the effectiveness of programs in meeting the educational needs of handicapped children, including evaluation of individualized education programs

- how federal funds for state administration are to be used

- positive efforts to employ and advance in employment qualified handicapped individuals in programs assisted under P.L. 94-142

- procedures and format that local educational agencies in the state must use in preparing and submitting their applications.

Similarly, local educational agencies must prepare and submit an application to the state agency in order to receive federal payments under P.L. 94-142. A state educational agency may not allow a local agency's funding entitlement to pass through to the locality until it has approved the latter's application.

Local agency applications must contain certain assurances, a detailing of certain procedures, and a resource plan, all similar to what are required of the state in its annual program submitted to the federal government. More specifically, each local educational agency application must:

- include procedures to ensure that all handicapped children residing within its jurisdiction, in all public and private agencies and institutions, regardless of the severity of their impairment, who are in need of special education and related services are identified, located, and evaluated, including a practical method of determining which ones currently are receiving those benefits

- include policies and procedures to ensure that the federal criteria on confidentiality of personally identifiable information are met

- include a goal of providing full educational opportunity to all handicapped children, aged birth through 21, and a detailed timetable for accomplishing that objective

- provide a description of the kind and number of its facilities, personnel, and services necessary to meet the goal of full educational opportunity

- include procedures for the implementation and use of the comprehensive personnel development system established by the state educational agency

- assign service priorities that meet federal requirements

- include procedures to ensure that the local agency makes provision for participation of and consultation with parents or guardians

- include procedures to ensure that, to the maximum extent practicable, local agencies provide special services to enable handicapped children to participate in regular educational programs

- describe the types of alternative placements available, and the number of handicapped children in each disability category who are served in each type of placement

- provide assurances satisfactory to the state educational agency that control of funds under P.L. 94-142 and title to property acquired with those monies are vested in and administered by a public agency for the uses and purposes prescribed in the act

- provide assurances satisfactory to the state that the local agency uses P.L. 94-142 funds only for costs directly attributable to the education of handicapped children

- provide assurances satisfactory to the state that the local educational agency uses P.L. 94-142 funds to supplement and, to the extent practicable, increase the level of state and local expenditures for the education of handicapped children and in no case to supplant those state and local funds

- provide assurances satisfactory to the state that the local agency does not use P.L. 94-142 monies to provide services to handicapped children unless it uses state and local funds for services that, taken as a whole, are at least comparable to those it provides to other handicapped children

- provide that the local agency furnishes information (including data on specific performance criteria it developed concerning program objectives) as the state educational agency requires; this includes information on the educational achievement of handicapped children participating in the local programs

- provide that the local agency keeps records, and affords access to them, that the state needs to verify their correctness

- make the application and all documents related to it available to parents and the public; however, the local educational agency is not required to hold public hearings

- provide assurances satisfactory to the state that all local agency policies and programs are consistent with P.L. 94-142 and state law

- describe how the local educational agency will use the federal funds during the next school year

- provide assurances satisfactory to the state that the local educational agency's procedural safeguards meet the P.L. 94-142 requirements

- include an assurance that the program assisted under P.L. 94-142 will be operated in compliance with Title 45 of the Code of Federal Regulations, Part 84 (Nondiscrimination on the Basis of Handicap in Programs and Activities Receiving or Benefiting from Federal Financial Assistance, otherwise known as Section 504 Regulations); the local educational agency may incorporate this assurance by reference if it already has been filed with HEW or one of its successors, the Department of Health and Human Services or the Department of Education

- include additional procedures and information that the state educational agency may require in order to meet state annual program plan requirements

THE ROLE OF THE COURTS

The powers of the federal, state, and local governments are divided into three departments: legislative, executive, and judicial. No individual or group in any one of these departments is permitted to exercise powers properly belonging to either of the others unless expressly directed to by law. The courts are in the judicial domain. Their role is to interpret legal principles and apply them to the specific facts in a controversy.

However, even a lay person recognizes that the judiciary does not simply limit itself to interpreting the law; in actual fact, it makes law. Sometimes these lawmaking ventures are viewed positively as being creative applications of legal principles to difficult situations. Regardless of how such actions are viewed, however, it is clear that the judiciary often has encroached on the lawmaking function delegated to legislatures around the nation.

To protect the rights of individuals who have been victimized by discrimination, the judiciary has issued many decisions that have had sweeping social ramifications. Federal, state, and local legislatures and agencies have been obliged to adopt laws and regulations to implement these court directions. The history leading up to P.L. 94-142 is an example of this judicial lawmaking process.

The process of judicial intervention is continuous. Once major acts such as P.L. 94-142 are passed, the judiciary inevitably is called upon to construe or interpret its provisions. Court decisions predominate over interpretations by government agencies, parent groups, or the public. A decision of a higher court obviously is controlling over a lower court. For example, a decision by a state's highest court on the meaning of the term "appropriate" as used in P.L. 94-142 is controlling over a lower state tribunal or a county court. Such a decision also would be controlling over interpretations by the state department of education or a local director of special education.

A court does not initiate proceedings to interpret a law. It acts only in response to a suit brought by a party who can assert adverse effects of the law. A law may be challenged by such a party in two ways: (1) the validity of the statute itself, and (2) its application to the situation involved.

Such issues present questions of law that only courts have the authority to determine. When a court decides that a law is valid or invalid or applies or does not apply to a situation, its action is a judicial determination. It is that determination that is binding and final unless appealed.

The hearing officer in a special education due process proceeding has authority to carry out judicial functions of interpreting the law and applying it to the facts in a specific case. Such hearings are held under the aegis of state or local educational agencies.

This function normally would be reserved to the judicial department of government. But Congress expressly delegated it to state and local educational agencies in the interest of providing an effective dispute resolution mechanism to settle complaints about the special education of a handicapped child.

However, a decision of a hearing officer does not carry the same weight as a determination by a judge nor does it, by itself, carry the force of law. The ramifications of the decision are limited to the particular facts and parties involved in the specific case.

A hearing officer's decision may be appealed by one or both of the parties to an appropriate court of law. If the decision is upheld by the judge, then it becomes binding over all those in the court's jurisdiction. However, it is the court's imprimatur, its judicial determination, that makes the ruling binding.

In special education, federal, state, and local courts have clarified some of the provisions of P.L. 94-142 and of state laws enacted as a result of the federal law. Some courts have gone beyond the minimum requirements of the federal law and expanded the rights of handicapped children in their jurisdictions. Some have even taken over the administration of a school system to supervise the provision of special education services, either through detailed court decrees and constant monitoring or through the appointment of special masters.

Another court role in special education is the creation and award of remedies to individuals aggrieved by actions taken or not taken by a school system. The courts may punish individuals responsible, award damages, or direct that compensatory education be provided.

Courts have played, and will continue to play, a critical role in special education for the handicapped. It therefore is important for participants in the special education decision-making process to inform themselves about what courts in their jurisdiction have determined regarding schooling for handicapped children. State and local laws and regulations are important sources of protection but it is equally important to be aware of court decisions because they may interpret, expand, or supersede the law as it is found in statutes and regulations. Such decisions provide crucial guidance to parents, school systems, and hearing officers regarding their roles, rights, and responsibilities.

Chapter 5

The Interrelationship of Federal, State, and Local Laws

Previous chapters have discussed the types of laws that affect the special education decision-making process. It is only natural that some of these laws may conflict with one another. They also may present questions regarding their interrelationship. This chapter addresses some of these conflicts and questions of interrelationship.

P.L. 94-142 AND ITS REGULATIONS

The P.L. 94-142 regulations were designed to implement the parent law. The regulations were published in final form in the *Federal Register* (Vol. 42, No. 163, August 23, 1977). They implement the act by (1) amending existing regulations governing assistance to states for education of handicapped children, (2) adding a new part (Part 121m) on incentive grants programs for those ages 3 through 5, and (3) making conforming amendments to the general provisions for state-administered programs.

The regulations govern the provision of formula grant funds to state and local agencies for educating handicapped children. They are designed (1) to assure that all disabled children have available a free appropriate public education, (2) to assure that their rights and those of their parents are protected, (3) to assist states and localities in providing for their education, and (4) to assess and assure the effectiveness of such efforts. The regulations also include the final rules for counting and reporting handicapped children.

The U.S. Department of Education saw the development of regulations for implementing P.L. 94-142 as being an evolutionary process that would continue over several years. The actual impact and consequences of problems that state and local educational agencies might face in implementing these provisions were unclear. Therefore, the department felt that the most rational approach to follow was to write minimum regulations, then to amend and revise them over time as need and experience dictated.

Because the statute itself is comprehensive and specific on many points, the department elected to incorporate the law's basic wording and substance directly into the regulations and to expand on the statutory provisions only where additional interpretation seemed necessary.

Although some who commented on the proposed rules said they should be more extensive, many others felt that the federal government already had over-regulated the issue and should cut back.

P.L. 94-142 AND SECTION 504

Section 504 of the Rehabilitation Act of 1973 deals with nondiscrimination on the basis of handicap and basically requires that recipients of federal funds provide equal opportunities to disabled persons. For example, recipients must meet the needs of handicapped persons to the same extent they do those of the nonimpaired. These regulations dealing with preschool, elementary, and secondary education (Subpart D) share some basic requirements with P.L. 94-142. Both require:

- that handicapped children, regardless of the nature or severity of their impairment, be provided a free appropriate public education

- that handicapped students be educated with the nonimpaired to the maximum extent appropriate to their needs

- that educational agencies identify and locate all handicapped children not receiving public schooling

- that evaluation procedures be adopted to ensure appropriate classification and educational placement

- that procedural safeguards be established to allow parents and guardians to influence and contest decisions regarding their children's evaluation and placement

In several respects, however, the Section 504 regulations are broader in coverage than P.L. 94-142. For example, the definition of "handicapped person" and "qualified handicapped person" under Section 504 covers a broader population than "handicapped children" under the act. P.L. 94-142 defines a handicapped child as one who has one of the impairments listed in the act, because of which the pupil requires special education and related services. Under Section 504, a handicapped person is one who has a physical or mental impairment that substantially limits one or more major life activities, has a record of that type of dysfunction, or is regarded as having that disability.

Section 504 also deals with a number of subjects not covered in P.L. 94-142 such as barrier-free facilities and program accessibility; employment; postsecondary education; and health, welfare, and social services. On the other hand, P.L. 94-142 contains a substantial number of administrative requirements not in Section 504, such as annual program plans and local applications, and in many instances requires more detailed procedures (such as due process) and policies.

In several instances, Section 504 specifically references where a requirement may be met by complying with one under P.L. 94-142. For example, the Section 504 provision on appropriate education cites implementation of an individualized education program (IEP) as one means of meeting the requirement. Section 504 indicates that reevaluation and due process procedural safeguards consistent with P.L. 94-142 will meet the former's requirements.

It should be noted that the term "free appropriate public education" (FAPE) has different meanings under P.L. 94-142 and Section 504. For example, under the former, FAPE is a statutory term that requires special education and related services to be provided in accordance with an IEP. However, under Section 504, as noted, each funding recipient must provide regular or special education and related aids and services designed to meet individual needs of handicapped persons as adequately as those of the nonimpaired.

P.L. 94-142 AND P.L. 89-313

Children who were counted or eligible to be counted for purposes of generating an entitlement under P.L. 94-142 may not also be counted under the formula for P.L. 89-313, the program of supplemental educational services for the handicapped in state-operated or state-supported facilities (the 1965 amendments to Title I of P.L. 89-10, the Elementary and Secondary Education Act of 1965). However, federal funds under both P.L. 94-142 and P.L. 89-313 may be mingled programmatically where the target populations of these two laws coincide.

Whether or not children under P.L. 89-313 enjoy the fiscal benefits of P.L. 94-142, all of the rights and protections of the latter apply to them as well.

U.S.-FUNDED EDUCATION AND MEDICAID

P.L. 94-142 requires states to assure that a free appropriate public education is available to all handicapped children. Implementation of this requirement has resulted in many handicapped children receiving educational services, who previously were excluded from public schools. An example of such children are the mentally retarded who are served in intermediate care facilities. However, under Title XIX, Medicaid Intermediate Care Facilities for the Mentally Retarded (ICFs/MR), it is difficult to differentiate clearly between a habilitative and an educational service.

The actual service provided in ICFs/MR can be defined either as special education or a related service or as Medicaid habilitative service. At any rate, many of these children require round-the-clock care, services, and supervision. Experience indicates that a variety of human service agencies must be involved in formulating a comprehensive service program for such children.

In determining the most equitable and effective means of organizing, financing, and delivering comprehensive service programs for children in ICFs/MR, there are several important points.

First, all "related services" need not be paid out of education funds. P.L. 94-142 does not require that an education agency bear all of the cost. Each state may use whatever federal, state, local, and private sources of support are available.

Thus, if a state determines that certain specified services to a Medicaid-eligible child in an ICF/MR are reimbursable under Title XIX, their cost may be reimbursed under the federal-state Medicaid program even though they also are considered "related service" needs in the child's IEP. Therefore, a service may be included in an IEP and be provided and paid for by Medicaid.

However, although P.L. 94-142 does not make all "related services" generally available through the education agency, states may have statutes that do. If a state statute extends responsibility for payment of specific health services to the education agency, then the Medicaid agency cannot pay for them. Such services may be made available to Medicaid children only if no other source of funding is available.

Second, most states have statutes that require legally responsible relatives (generally limited to parents and legal guardians) to pay support charges for residents of public institutions for the mentally retarded. However, parents may not be charged for special education and related services under P.L. 94-142.

Third, children in intermediate care facilities for the mentally retarded are required to have both an IEP under P.L. 94-142 and an Individual Plan of Care (IPC) under Medicaid. Where both types of plans are required, it may be possible to draw up a consolidated program, provided that it contains all the required information and that all parties participate in its development.

P.L. 94-142 AND P.L. 94-482

P.L. 94-142 defines vocational education as involving organized programs directly related to the preparation of individuals for paid or unpaid employment or for additional preparation for a career requiring other than a baccalaureate or advanced degree. (§ 121a.14)

This definition is taken from the Vocational Education Act of 1963, as amended in 1976 by P.L. 94-482. Under that act, "vocational education" includes industrial arts and consumer and homemaking education programs.

As noted earlier, P.L. 94-142 requires that each public agency ensure that its handicapped children have available the same variety of educational programs and services as do the nonimpaired, including art, music, industrial arts, and consumer, homemaking, and vocational education.

This list of program options is not exhaustive and could include any class or activity in which nonhandicapped children participate. Moreover, vocational education programs must be specially designed if necessary to enable a handicapped student to benefit fully from them. The set-aside funds under the Vocational Education Act of 1963, as amended by P.L. 94-482, may be used for this purpose.

P.L. 94-142 AND EMPLOYMENT

Each state annual program plan and local agency application must include an assurance that the programs assisted under P.L. 94-142 are operated in compliance with 45 CFR 84 (Nondiscrimination on the Basis of Handicap in Programs and Activities Receiving or Benefiting from Federal Financial Assistance). The state educational agency may incorporate this assurance by reference if it already has been filed with the Department of Education.

P.L. 94-142 AND STATE LAW

P.L. 94-142 regulations apply to each state that receives federal funds under that act. The annual program plan is submitted by the state educational agency on behalf of the state as a whole. Therefore, this part applies to all political subdivisions of the state that are involved in the education of handicapped children.

These include: (1) the state educational agency, (2) local agencies and intermediate educational units, (3) other state agencies and schools (such as departments of mental health and welfare and state schools for the deaf or blind), and (4) state correctional facilities.

Each public agency in the state also is responsible for ensuring that the rights and protections under this part are given to children the entity refers to or places in private schools and facilities.

The regulations define "public agencies" as including all political subdivisions in the state that have direct or delegated responsibility for educating handicapped children, regardless of whether or not they receive P.L. 94-142 funds. In other words, the term "public agencies" is all-inclusive. This term refers to government agencies such as a Department of Education or a Department of Public Welfare, as well as state and local educational agencies.

Unfortunately, the P.L. 94-142 regulations mandate certain activities or programs that the states often find to be in conflict with their own laws or constitution or are not specifically covered by legal provisions at their level. For example, the federal requirements for serving handicapped children specify certain timelines for certain age categories. State law might permit education for only certain children within the federal mandates. However, the federal government has given the states some flexibility in this area.

Another example of conflict involves identifying and counting handicapped children. Federal law requires that such counting be done by categories and percentages but this runs counter to state practice in some jurisdictions. For instance, the state education agency in Massachusetts has a policy of noncategorical descriptions to define handicapped children by their special educational needs rather than by specific disabling condition.

Other conflicts between federal and state law arise from the fact that P.L. 94-142 requires the state education agency (SEA) to be responsible for the education of all handicapped children regardless of whether other entities actually provide the services. Under this provision, the SEA sets the standards for education and exercises general supervision.

The requirement of state education agency responsibility was included in the law to provide a point of final legal responsibility for the education of the child precisely because of fragmented service delivery, responsibilities, requirements, and commitment.

While this does not require all service provisions to be transferred to the state education agency, it does mandate that:

1. the SEA be responsible for assuring the availability of a free appropriate public education for all handicapped children within the state and for assuring that all of the provisions of P.L. 94-142 are carried out

2. all educational programs for handicapped children meet the standards of the SEA and be under the general supervision of persons in that agency responsible for the schooling of such pupils

The provision requiring SEA supervisory responsibility has resulted in two types of implementation problems. The first involves the relationship between the SEA and other state agencies. This has been most prevalent in the Western states and where there is a strong tradition for local governance and weak technical-assistance-oriented state agencies. In such areas, it has been difficult to work out monitoring and sanctioning procedures necessary to assure implementation of the law.

The second set of concerns centers on the relationship of the SEA to other state or local programs that are responsible for or provide educational services to handicapped children.

These programs include day training, institutional and other programs supported by departments of mental health or of mental retardation or by federal funding sources such as Title XIX or Title XX, Medicaid and EPSDT, the Crippled Children's program, vocational rehabilitation, S.S.I., Head Start, and vocational education.

The federal law adopted a convenient approach to resolving the issues presented by this second set of concerns. It established a clear accountability mechanism. The act and regulations provide that the SEA is the agency within each state that is legally responsible to the federal government for assuring that the right to education for every handicapped child is, in fact, implemented.

However, these issues are not as easily resolved by the states. At the state level, inter-agency responsibilities must be continually worked out. This process is on-going and involves political, informational, logistical, and practical problems. The following is a list of some of the factors which contribute to these problems at the state level:

1. the existence of legal obstacles (statutory or regulatory)
2. the advantages and disadvantages of particular kinds of inter-agency agreements
3. the appropriate roles of different agencies or programs, given their overall mandate
4. dollar responsibility for various aspects of program services
5. utilization of private and other federal financial resources
6. methods of monitoring and sanctioning service delivery failures

The following is one typical example of the problem arising from the federal requirement that the SEA have general supervision of special education programs administered by other state agencies:

Federal Law and Regulations

P.L. 94-142, Section 612(6): Specifies that educational programs for handicapped children administered by other state agencies will be under the general supervision of the state education agency.

Regulation § 121a.600: Stipulates that, in addition to the above, the educational standards established by the state agency must be met and that agreements be signed to show this section is being complied with by the SEA as well as other state agencies.

Regulation § 121a.14(a)(1): Defines special education as including "at no cost to the parent or guardian . . . instruction in hospitals and institutions."

State Law and Policy (State of Texas)

Texas Education Code Section 1.04(b): Excludes the Texas Department of Mental Health and Mental Retardation (TDMHMR) and the Texas Youth Council. In addition, the Moody State School is under the administration of the University of Texas system. State statutes authorize TDMHMR and the Moody State School to assess parents of students under age 21 fees for support and maintenance.

Discrepancies

Potential differences involve the following areas:

1. clarification of general supervision
2. assurances of compliance with all procedural safeguards
3. educational programs meeting standards established by state boards of education
4. support and maintenance be at no cost to the parent or guardian

The first provision above—that of P.L. 94-142—reflects the desire of Congress for a central point of responsibility and accountability in the education of handicapped children in each state. Congress believed that without this requirement, there would be an abdication of responsibility for these pupils' schooling. In many states, responsibility is divided, depending upon the age of the child, sources of funding, and type of services. While different agencies may, in fact, deliver services, P.L. 94-142 requires that the responsibility must remain in a central oversight agency so that failure to provide services or any violation of the students' rights can be laid squarely at the door of one agency.

In meeting these requirements, there are a number of acceptable options, including the following:

- Written agreements may be developed among state agencies concerning educational standards and monitoring. These agreements would be binding on the local or regional counterparts of each state agency.

- The governor's office may issue an administrative directive establishing state educational agency responsibility.

- State law, regulation, or policy may designate the state agency as responsible for establishing standards for all educational programs for the handicapped and may include responsibility for monitoring.

- State law may mandate that the state agency be responsible for all educational programs.

The Office of Special Education in the Department of Education (originally the Bureau for Education of the Handicapped in HEW) established working agreements with other federal programs, including EPSDT, SSI, Vocational Rehabilitation, Vocational Education, and Title XX. These agreements involve facilitation of cooperative programming and responsibilities for resource allocation and for communication with state agencies about these arrangements.

Another example of a conflict between P.L. 94-142 and state law is in serving nonpublic school students. In some cases, the federal requirement directly contradicts state laws and constitutions. An example is the Texas law on providing related services for handicapped pupils in private schools:

Federal Law and Regulations

P.L. 94-142, Section 613(a)(4)(B): directs that handicapped pupils placed in or referred to private schools have all the benefits, services, and protections authorized by the act.

Section 613(a)(6): provides assurances that the control of funds and title of property will be under the authority of a public agency.

P.L. 94-142 Regulations (§ 121a.403(a)): stipulate that where the parent chooses placement of a child in a private facility when an appropriate public school is available, the local or state agency is not required to pay any part of the pupil's education.

P.L. 94-142 Regulations (§ 121a.457(a)): stipulate that equipment may be placed on the premises of a private school for a limited time when used by an eligible handicapped child as long as the ownership and control remains with the public agency.

P.L. 94-142 Regulations (§ 121a.13): define related services in such a manner that the parent may place a pupil in a private school for basic education; however, if eligible, the child must receive related services, materials, equipment, and professional help for such needs as speech and hearing therapy. Parents of pupils in private schools also may request and expect to receive pupil appraisal and diagnostic services at public expense.

State Law and Policy

Chapters 15 and 16 of the Texas Education Code, "State Funds for the Support of Public Schools" and "Foundation School Program:" authorize the use of state education funds for pupils in public schools.

State Board of Education Policies: make no provision for pupils enrolled in private schools at the choice of the parent to receive services, materials, or equipment provided by taxes.

Discrepancies

Texas education statutes and corresponding State Board of Education policies prohibit the use of public funds for the benefit of pupils who are, at the choice of their parents, enrolled in private schools.

When federal and state law conflict, it usually is the state that must yield. Courts have established in a variety of contexts that properly promulgated federal agency regulations have the force and effect of law. This doctrine is so well established that agency regulations implementing federal statutes, such as P.L. 94-142, have been held by courts to preempt state law under the supremacy clause of the Constitution. Frequently, however, there are ways to reconcile state and federal legal conflicts that are less drastic than a win-lose confrontation in court.

The federal government could include in future regulations such phrases as "unless otherwise provided by a state" or "as determined by the state education agency," as it did in some of the P.L. 94-142 regulations. Federal officials also could be more sensitive to the particular needs, practices, and laws of a state when they are issuing official interpretations of their regulations.

The states could conduct an analysis of the perceived and reported legal conflicts between the federal requirements and their own laws. The states then could redraft or amend their laws and regulations to conform more smoothly with federal demands. If necessary, the states may even need to propose new legislation or revamp their structure for providing education to handicapped children in order to comply with P.L. 94-142.

Part II

The Special Education Process

Public Law 94-142 did not create new ideas in the schooling of handicapped children or require anything revolutionary in special education. For example, the concept of individualized programs or learning plans is not a recent innovation. Teachers have used versions of such an approach virtually since the beginning of pedagogy.

Many professionals raised the concern that, even if the P.L. 94-142 concepts are not new, the amount of paper work the act requires actually results in less time to provide services to the children. While this may have indeed been true in some situations, most state education laws already closely paralleled the act in terms of the substantive requirements. Therefore, in most respects, there should not have been a significant increase in the workload or paper requirement beyond that already imposed by state and local school systems.

The individualized education program (IEP) is essentially the only requirement of P.L. 94-142 that might have been considered a new substantive provision in some states. Yet in implementing this provision, a number of states and local school systems elected to include additional requirements of their own that exceed the federal requirements.

In requiring a written IEP for each handicapped child, P.L. 94-142 formalized a process that:

- is basic to good educational practice

- has traditionally been followed by good teachers under whatever name it might be called

- has been required by many state and local education agencies for a number of years

This also is true with most of the act's other requirements. There essentially is little difference in the legal and educational concepts involved in special education because the legal requirements have their roots in sound educational practice. For example, the use of nondiscriminatory testing is both a legal requirement and sound educational practice.

What is new is that the P.L. 94-142 legal requirements, based on sound educational practice, must be applied consistently from state to state and used with all handicapped children. The law requires that educational agencies identify, evaluate, program, and place every handicapped child who requires special schooling.

Some agencies may have had good evaluation procedures, others may have had an excellent continuum of alternative placements to accommodate differing needs of impaired children. Some may have followed sound educational practices in providing special instruction for all children with mild or moderate handicaps but felt less obligated to do so for those at the more severe or profound level.

P.L. 94-142 is designed to ensure that *all* education agencies adhere to *all* of the basic standards or requirements for identification, evaluation, programming, and placement for *all* disabled children, regardless of the type or severity of their handicapping condition. These requirements are not new. What is new is that they must be applied by all school systems and to all handicapped children.

This part discusses in Chapters 6 through 9 precisely what those legal standards or requirements are for identification, evaluation, programming, and placement of handicapped children in general. Chapter 10 analyzes legal considerations for such children in specific categories. It is critical that to understand special education concepts and how they interface with the legal concepts be understood so that participation in the decision-making process can be effective.

Finally, this part addresses in Chapter 11 the problem of how to determine whether a special education program is appropriate to meet the handicapped student's needs. The fundamental requirement of the law is that all handicapped children who need special schooling are to be provided with a free appropriate public education designed to meet their unique needs.

The term "appropriate" is, of course, highly subjective. It is precisely the point at which school personnel and parents often come into conflict. Each party has its own idea as to what the student needs in terms of an educational program. Each designates its proposed program as being the one that is appropriate. How can it be decided which program is truly appropriate for a particular child? What standards or elements should a program contain in order to make it appropriate? How can it be determined whether the assessment of a particular program is appropriate?

Chapter 11 presents a step-by-step procedure for determining the appropriateness of a special education program for a particular child. This process is designed for all of the participants in the special education due process situation. By following this procedure, participants can better determine whether their proposed program is appropriate, and also can present it more effectively at a special education due process hearing.

Chapter 6

Identification

If handicapped children are to have an opportunity to reach their potential, they first must be identified as possibly having special education needs. The term "identification" is not defined as such in the act. Rather, it uses the term to refer to activities that lead to the recognition that children have or may have a handicapping condition that interferes with their ability to learn.

THE ROLE OF IDENTIFICATION

Identification is the entry step in which the child first comes to the attention of professionals. They are responsible for ensuring that the child is channeled toward an appropriate evaluation, program, and placement. Identification itself does not include those three factors. It simply means that the child "identified" is suspected of having some special education needs.

The Legal Requirement of Identification

Public Law 94-142 requires that each state include in its annual program plan, submitted to the U.S. Department of Education certain assurances regarding the identification of children in its jurisdiction. Specifically, the regulations require that:

Each annual program plan must include in detail the policies and procedures which the State will undertake or has undertaken to insure that:

(1) all children who are handicapped, regardless of the severity of their handicap, and who are in need of special education

and related services are identified, located, and evaluated; and

(2) a practical method is developed and implemented to determine which children are currently receiving needed special education and related services and which children are not currently receiving needed special education and related services. (§ 121a.128(a))

The law contains essentially the same requirement for local educational agencies. It makes states and localities responsible for ensuring that all handicapped children are identified, located, and evaluated, including those in all public and private agencies and institutions in the state.

The Importance of Identification

The literature on special education emphasizes the early identification of handicapped children, especially those with severe problems. Identification is important because it is the step that begins the sequence in special education decision making.

Frequently, the nature and scope of an evaluation are determined largely by what kind of handicapping condition is suggested by the identification characteristics. Many school systems follow a prescribed set of evaluation procedures regardless of what the type of handicap appears to be. Many others tailor the evaluation to the presenting problem.

An evaluation is not appropriate unless it addresses every problem area, or potential problem area, presented by the referral characteristics. That is why a proper understanding of how the child first came to be identified as possibly in need is so important.

Unless an educator or practitioner has that understanding, the expert is likely to miss the target with evaluation assessments. The program and placement, which are outgrowths of the evaluation, would be likely to be deficient. Without an identification, the child would not be able to even start the special education decision-making process. Without an understanding of how the child came to be identified, subsequent steps in the sequence are likely to be defective.

The Purposes of Identification

As noted earlier, handicapped children first must be identified if they are to have an opportunity to reach their potential. Identification activities have two basic objectives:

1. Public Awareness: Many activities are designed primarily to make the public aware of the needs of handicapped children, of state and federal laws mandating the education for all such individuals, and of programs, services, and facilities provided for them.
2. Referrals: Other child-find activities are designed primarily to identify through referrals and screening procedures those who may have special education needs.

Confidentiality

The law requires that each state develop policies and procedures to ensure the protection of the confidentiality of any personally identifiable information collected, used, or maintained in connection with identification activities. The confidentiality regulations were published in the *Federal Register* in final form February 27, 1976 (41 FR 8603–8610), and met the requirements of P.L. 94-142. Those regulations are incorporated in § 121a.560–121a.576 of Subpart E (Procedural Regulations) of the P.L. 94-142 regulations.

Notice Requirements to Parents

The law requires that the school system or public agency conducting identification activities provide written notice to the parents of a child before initiating this procedure. (§ 121a.504(a)) The notice must include a complete description of the activity and a full explanation of the reasons why the agency proposes to undertake the procedure. (§ 121a.505(a)) The notice must be provided in a manner the parents can understand and they must be given an opportunity to present complaints about the proposed activity if they have any.

However, the school system or public agency need not obtain parental consent before conducting identification activities. Parental consent need be sought only before conducting a preplacement evaluation before assigning a handicapped child to a program providing special education and related services. Identification activities generally do not include assessments that could be characterized as a preplacement evaluation. (The term preplacement evaluation means procedures used selectively with an individual child and does not include basic tests administered to all pupils in a school, grade, or class.)

A preplacement evaluation includes procedures used to determine whether a child is handicapped and the nature and extent of the special education and related services needed. Identification activities are undertaken to determine whether a child should be referred for such a preplacement evaluation. Such activities cannot be construed in any way as an initial placement. Therefore, parental consent for identification activities is not required before conducting them.

TYPES OF IDENTIFICATION ACTIVITIES

School systems across the country have developed different approaches to identification using a variety or combination of activities. The following are examples of common identification activities:

Census and Community Survey Activities

Conducting a census as a means of identifying and counting a specific population has long been a common practice in many states. Educational agencies have used methods such as a census or school registration for predictive planning and budgeting. A census also can be used for locating handicapped children or a special education survey component could be added to a regular census.

A census is an effective identification activity. It can be adapted to collect information on any specific group of concern and allows for predictive planning by yielding data on the children in need of special education. The data can be obtained from a variety of sources such as teachers, doctors, parents, etc., and lend themselves well to computerization.

However, a census has certain inherent limitations. For example, the interpretation of the questions or answers is left up to the person completing the census form. The whole activity relies heavily on the cooperation of those responding and their ability to read, understand, and follow through with the census. A census form is difficult to design in such a way as to obtain all the desired information about a child's special needs.

There are other activities less formal than a census that also survey populations in the community. For example, a questionnaire could be developed for parents of preschool children. Parent volunteers could be sought from community organizations and trained for a house-to-house or telephone canvass of the targeted homes. Children could take questionnaires home from school. Questionnaires could be mailed to parents or printed in local newspapers, with parents requested to complete them and return them by mail. Volunteers could be stationed at some publicized central location on certain dates, with parents encouraged to come in and fill out a form.

Such community survey activities can cover large geographical areas and serve a secondary function of alerting the locality to the importance of early identification and intervention. Such a questionnaire also is likely to yield both planning and service information about a child that would have more depth and breadth than a census.

The questionnaire type of activity involves members of the community and gives planners an opportunity to experiment with a number of collection methods for future activities. However, it should be noted that such a survey is likely to require the cooperation of the local media to assure a high visibility public awareness campaign. It also will require careful development of the questionnaire and an efficient organization of volunteers.

Public Awareness

Public awareness is a broadly used term to describe any method of disseminating information on, among other things, special education rights and services. The law requires state and local agencies to conduct assertive child-find programs within their jurisdictions at least annually. The program may consist of one or more of the types of identification activities discussed earlier but, regardless of which are undertaken, there must be a public awareness campaign to gain the full benefit of the particular effort.

The awareness campaign really is the starting point for identification. People in the community must be alerted to their rights and need for participation before any activity can be successful. The campaign can help solicit public support in determining how many children have special needs and who they are.

The campaign can use a variety of information techniques and media. The message can be addressed to the various sensory channels and adapted to the educational level of the viewer/listener/reader. Information can be disseminated through newspapers, letters to parents and community organizations, advertisements on television and radio, brochures, posters, bumper stickers, pamphlets, civic meetings, and interviews.

Of course, public awareness activities are somewhat limited when used alone. They reach only the portion of the population that comes into contact with the campaign. Such campaigns often require large numbers of volunteers to disseminate materials effectively. They also must rely on the radio, television, and newspapers to contribute a substantial amount of time and space to the effort. Moreover, educators and community volunteers usually are not familiar with media advertising techniques and consequently do not take full advantage of the resources available.

However, the major problem with a public awareness activity by itself is that, in the end, successful identification depends upon parents' receiving the message and contacting the appropriate agency personnel for information and processing. The response rate for such an approach is simply too low to depend upon it alone. When used in conjunction with other identification activities, however, a public awareness campaign is a critical component of an overall child-find program.

Screening

Screening is an activity in which a test or tests are administered to a population group to identify the individuals most likely to manifest a handicap. It is a formal procedure for identifying persons with suspected conditions that might require special education services. Screening is not an educational evaluation, an assessment to label individuals, or a basis to prepare specific program objectives.

A school system should conduct screening procedures at least annually for all kindergarten children. The screening battery should test the areas of visual and auditory acuity, medical history, social-emotional development, speech articulation and language development, and cognitive and motor ability. If it is permitted under state statute, screening also should be administered to preschool children to determine their potential special education needs. After screening, they might be referred for a complete evaluation or for further assessment in a particular area, or simply passed because they evidenced no developmental delay.

Screening is an effective identification activity that can lead to more in-depth evaluation where appropriate. Parents are notified when their children are being screened and may be requested to fill out a questionnaire or respond to questions in an interview. This provides an opportunity for parents to become aware of, and involved with, the special education decision-making process at the earliest stage.

However, there are a number of considerations that can impair the efficacy of the screening program if they are not addressed properly. For example, the logistics of having the child and parents present must be arranged. There must be adequate and appropriate space to carry out the different types of screening, including individual and small group stations and interview areas.

A comprehensive screening program requires a substantial number of professional staff persons working with paraprofessionals and volunteers, who need to be trained. The staff also must interview parents and provide them with test results and information about special education services. Day care centers and nursery schools must be willing to cooperate with the screening program. A significant number of preschool children are likely to be missed if they do not attend such facilities that are part of the screening program.

Referrals

A referral is a written request for an evaluation by a person who suspects that a particular child might be in need of special education. A referral can come from a variety of sources, such as parents, teacher, family court, doctors, clergy, public health centers, nursery schools and day care centers, social service agency, etc. A frequent difficulty is the excessive delay between the referral and the evaluation. Therefore, school systems should have established referral procedures and routes in place to process referrals expeditiously.

In certain circumstances, children's cases automatically ought to be reviewed and considered for referral—for example, pupils in a regular education program who are doing so poorly at midyear that they are in danger of failing two or more core subjects, or who are not promoted at the end of the school year. Other examples might be children in the regular education program who have been suspended, absent with a medical excuse, or otherwise not in school for an excessive number of days. Students who demonstrate a significant negative change in alertness, learning, or general behavior shortly after returning from an illness also should be referred for further evaluation.

Referrals are an especially important means of identifying youngsters who need special education but were not so identified during the preschool and early grades of school. However, a weakness of the mechanism is that it depends so largely on the perceptions by the person making the referral.

The early referral of a mildly handicapped child may be a mixed blessing because of possible changes in significant adults' expectations for the pupil. If the person considering making a referral is in the school system, it generally is considered sound educational practice to first make and document all efforts to meet the child's needs in the context of services that are part of the regular school program before initiating formal action.

Generally, the referral is the most important component of an identification program. Parents and teachers are the most likely source of referrals. They know the child best and notice special problems sooner than others, especially if the problem is not obvious or severe. They are in a position to observe subtleties in the child's behavior or performance that others may not perceive. When a child has difficulty seeing television or keeping up with schoolwork, has frequent physical complaints, trouble speaking correctly, etc., parents and teachers usually are the first to pick up on such clues that special help may be needed. That is why a properly functioning referral system is so important.

The four types of identification activities described generally are used in some combination by state and local education agencies to meet their requirement under the law to identify children who show indications they might need special services. These activities may be conducted solely by state and local education agencies or in cooperation with other public or private entities.

Obviously, the more broad-based the partnership between the public agencies and community organizations, the more effective the child-find activities will be in generating information to help identify and locate all persons between the ages of 3 and 21 who may be in need of special educational services.

Chapter 7

Evaluation

The Public Law 94-142 regulations define "evaluation" as meaning procedures used

> to determine whether a child is handicapped and the nature and extent of the special education and related services that the child needs. The term means procedures used selectively with an individual child and does not include basic tests administered to or procedures used with all children in a school, grade, or class. (§ 121a.500c)

From this definition it can be seen that an evaluation under P.L. 94-142 has two clear purposes:

1. to determine whether or not the child is indeed handicapped and in need of special education services
2. to obtain the information necessary to design an individualized education program if the child is handicapped and in need of special schooling

EVALUATION'S ROLE IN DECISION MAKING

Evaluation follows identification in the sequential process of special education decision making. Evaluation, in the strict sense, does not encompass identification. The regulations state that evaluation does not include basic tests administered to, or procedures used with, all children in a school, grade, or class. Those generally are considered part of identification activities, such as screening. Such activities are designed to pinpoint children who may require special education.

At the evaluation stage, the question is whether or not a particular child is handicapped and in need of special education. If the answer is "yes," then the evaluation also should yield the information necessary to develop a program to meet those needs. If the answer is "no," then the child receives no special education. Pupils who do not have handicapping conditions that adversely affect their ability to learn are not entitled to such a program under the law.

Evaluation also is different from program development, which is the stage that comes after evaluation in the decision-making process. If it is determined from the evaluation that the child is handicapped and in need of special education, the information derived from the various assessments then will be used to develop an IEP for the pupil.

THE IMPORTANCE OF EVALUATION

As noted, there are two purposes for evaluation—one to certify that a child is handicapped and in need of special education, and the other to obtain information to design an IEP if necessary. The importance of evaluation is in gathering information to build the foundation for decisions later in the process. When the evaluation team believes this stage has been completed and is valid, a decision will be made as to whether or not the child is eligible for special education because of a handicap that interferes with the ability to learn.

If the pupil is determined to be eligible, then specific data relevant to the educational performance are extracted and organized as a basis for preparing an IEP that is developmentally rational. The heart of the IEP is the specific objectives that are to be used as guidelines in providing a quality education. These objectives are based directly on the data from the evaluation that identify the child's strengths and weaknesses and the constraints on the ability to perform in the classroom.

THE LEGAL REQUIREMENT

The importance of a sound evaluation is clear from the professional literature in the field of special education. It also is required by law. The law unequivocally states that:

Before any action is taken with respect to the initial placement of a handicapped child in a special education program, a full and individual evaluation of the child's educational needs must be conducted (§ 121a.531)

It also is a well-established principle in the field of special education that the evaluation of a child's strengths and weaknesses is a continuous process that should be repeated in full at periodic intervals. Assessment information forms the basis for all long-term and short-term goals and instructional objectives necessary to meet the child's special education needs. The law requires that a reevaluation be "conducted every three years or more frequently if conditions warrant or if the child's parent or teacher requests an evaluation." (§ 121a.534(b))

PREEVALUATION PROCEDURES

Before conducting an evaluation, the law requires the school system staff persons to first notify the parents in writing and explain:

1. what they propose to do, what tests they propose to administer (with descriptions), which experts will be involved, and what types of interviews will be necessary
2. why they think the evaluation is necessary and which tests, behavior, or records support their view
3. what options they have considered and why they selected or rejected them
4. what other reasons they may have for recommending the evaluation
5. what, in full detail, are the parents' rights and privileges in this situation

This notice should be written in language that is understandable to parents and, to the extent possible, to the child. The school team will need to ascertain whether the parents received the notice and if they can read and understand it. There may be a need for an interpreter or other person. (§ 121a.505(b)(2), (c)(1,2))

The law further requires that the school obtain parental consent before conducting a preplacement evaluation. (§ 121a.504(b)(i)) (This requirement is addressed fully in Chapter 16.) The law does not require consent for all evaluations—only for the initial or preplacement evaluation. However, prior notice is necessary before conducting a reevaluation.

If a parent refuses to give consent or otherwise fails to agree to the evaluation, the school may elect either to pursue or to drop the matter. If the team firmly believes that an evaluation is warranted and cannot obtain parental consent, P.L. 94-142 regulations provide the following procedures:

(1) Where State law requires parental consent before a handicapped child is evaluated . . . State procedures govern the public agency in overriding a parent's refusal to consent.

(2)(i) Where there is no State law requiring consent before a handicapped child is evaluated . . . the public agency may use the hearing procedures . . . to determine if the child may be evaluated . . . without parental consent.

(ii) If the hearing officer upholds the agency, the agency may evaluate the child without the parent's consent . . . (§ 121a.504(c))

The regulations simply mean that where state law requires parental consent before the evaluation and the parent refuses (or otherwise withholds) approval, state procedures, (such as obtaining a court order authorizing the agency to act) must be followed.

If, however, there is no state legal requirement for consent outside of these regulations, the public agency may use the due process procedures to obtain a decision to allow the evaluation without parental consent. The agency must notify the parents of its actions, and they have rights of appeal as well as at the hearing itself.

The procedures are designed not to interfere with existing state laws that may require consent. Where state law does not require consent, the parents are afforded a due process hearing. These rules are intended to provide protection to the parents, the child, and the agency.

In addition to the formal written notice and consent form, the requirements can best be accomplished with a preevaluation conference. This can give the school personnel and parents an opportunity to meet each other. Such a conference also can help the parents develop a better understanding of the evaluation and its purpose and provide them with better information to enable them to make sound decisions regarding their child. It also can give the school staff an opportunity to ascertain the parents' primary language or mode of communication. Finally, such a conference could be used to make arrangements with the parents for a home visit, medical assessment of the child, etc.

Notice and Consent as They Pertain to Evaluation Tests

As discussed, school personnel must consider the notice and consent requirements before conducting an evaluation of a student. A number of questions frequently arise in this regard. The basic concern is whether, in providing notice to the parents and in obtaining their consent, the public agency must list the specific tests it proposes to use or actually used in evaluating the child.

The following requirements in the regulations relate to this basic concern:

- **Prior Notice.** Written notice must be given to parents a reasonable time before the public agency proposes or refuses to initiate or change the identification, evaluation, or educational placement of the child or the provision of a free appropriate public education to the child. (§ 121a.504)

- **Content of Notice.** The notice must include . . . (3) A description of each evaluation procedure, test record, or report the agency uses as a basis for the proposal or refusal (§ 121a.505(a)(3))

- **Consent.** Parental consent must be obtained before (i) conducting a preplacement evaluation; and (ii) initial placement in a program providing special education and related services. (§ 121a.504(b)(1))

- **Definition of Consent.** The term "consent" means that (a) the parent has been fully informed of all information relevant to the activity for which consent is sought . . . and (b) the parent understands and agrees in writing to the carrying out of the activity . . . (§ 121a.500)

Again, it is important to note that written notice *and* consent are required for both (a) preplacement evaluation and (b) initial placement. However, only written notice is required for reevaluation, changes in placement, or any other action which the agency proposes or refuses to take with respect to the identification, evaluation, educational program, or placement of the child.

In accordance with the U.S. Department of Education interpretation, the following are six questions and answers which arise in connection with the above requirements and evaluation tests:

1. *In meeting the "prior notice" requirement for preplacement evaluation, must the public agency list the specific tests that it proposes to use in evaluating a child with a suspected disability?*

    No. It is not necessary for the notice to list the tests that will be used in the preplacement evaluation. This is because the "content of notice" requirement in § 121a.505(a)(3) is concerned with tests that have already been given to a child and not with those that might be used in the future.

§ 121a.505(a)(3) calls for a description of each evaluation procedure, test, record, or report an agency uses as a basis for proposing or refusing to initiate or change the identification, evaluation, program, or placement of a handicapped child. Thus, if an agency decides to propose that a preplacement evaluation be conducted for a given child, the written notice to the parents would include a description of any teacher records or reports and previously administered group or individual tests the agency used as a basis for its decision. It is not necessary for the notice to include a description of any tests that will be used in the preplacement evaluation of a child with a suspected disability.

2. *In meeting the "consent" requirement for preplacement evaluation, must the public agency inform the parents about the specific tests that it proposes to use in the evaluation?*

In general, the answer is yes. Under the consent requirement, a parent must be "fully informed of all information relevant to the activity for which consent is sought . . ." Thus, in obtaining consent for preplacement evaluation, if the agency plans to give a particular test to a child, then the parents must be fully informed about that test.

In cases where the actual tests to be given to a child are not known in advance of the testing situation, the agency must give parents a description of the general *kinds* of tests that will be used (e.g., "an individually administered test of general intelligence, such as the *Wechsler Intelligence Scale for Children* or the *Stanford-Binet Intelligence Scale.* These kinds of tests are designed to measure different types of abilities, such as being able to remember numbers and knowing the meanings of different words.")

In conducting educational evaluations, there are often several different tests which are designed to assess a particular skill(s) or a specific area(s) of educational need. These tests often are used interchangeably by qualified examiners on a case by case basis, as a matter of common practice. Because of the unique reactions of individual children in the educational testing situation, examiners often cannot select the specific tests they will use with a given child until they are actually in the testing situation.

The consent statement which the parent signs must describe the activity for which consent is sought (§ 121a.500). While signatures could be obtained through correspondence, the most effective way to ensure that the "informed consent" requirement is met is by meeting personally with the parents, as discussed. In such a meeting, school staff will be able to ensure (a) that the parents are fully informed of all information relevant to the activity for which consent is sought, and (b) that they understand and agree in writing to the carrying out of the activity.

3. *In meeting the "prior notice" requirement for initial placement, must the public agency list the actual tests that were used in the preplacement evaluation?*

    Yes. § 121a.505(a)(3) states, in effect, that the written notice must include a description of any tests which the agency used as a basis for proposing that a handicapped child be placed in a special education program. The description of the tests could be similar to that used in Answer No. 2, above, except that it would focus on the actual tests given. The notice would, of course, also have to include all other information required under § 121a.505.

4. *In meeting the "consent" requirement for initial placement, must the public agency inform the parents about the actual tests that were used in the preplacement evaluation?*

    In general, the answer is yes. In order to inform the parents of all information relevant to the activity for which consent is sought (i.e., initial placement in special education), the agency would have to (a) provide information about the actual tests used in the preplacement evaluation and describe the results of the evaluation (this could be covered in part through the written notice), and (b) describe the proposed special education placement.

    As with preplacement evaluation, the most effective way to implement the consent requirement is through a personal meeting with the parents. If the school staff does not meet with the parents, then the notice would have to be expanded, as necessary, in order to fully inform them "of all information relevant to the activity. . ."

5. *Is it permissible for prior notice and consent to be combined into one overall statement?*

    Yes. An agency could use a combined consent-notice statement, if the statement (1) meets the definition of consent in § 121a.500, and (2) contains all of the information required for prior notice in § 121a.505. However, whether the two requirements are combined into one statement or handled through separate statements, public agencies should find it more cost effective and efficient to implement both requirements (a) on a simultaneous basis, in concert with each other, rather than handling them as two totally separate processes, and (b) through meeting personally with the parents (whenever possible), rather than handling these procedures only through correspondence.

6. *In meeting the "prior notice" requirement for reevaluation, must specific tests be listed in the notice?*

The answer depends, in part, on why the reevaluation is being proposed. If the purpose is simply to meet the three-year reevaluation requirement in § 121a.534, then the agency would not be requested to list any tests in the notice. On the other hand, if the reevaluation is requested by a teacher or other member of the school staff, then the notice would include a description of any tests or records or reports that were used as a basis for requesting the reevaluation.

If the parents request the reevaluation, and the agency agrees to carry it out, then the notice to the parents would indicate this fact, and would not likely list any tests. However, if the agency refuses to conduct a reevaluation, then the notice must (1) indicate the reasons for the refusal and (2) include any tests or records or reports, which the agency uses as a basis for its refusal.

Regardless of the circumstances under which a reevaluation is proposed or refused, the "content of notice" requirement in § 121a.505(a)(3) is concerned only with tests that have already been given to a child, which the agency uses as a basis for its decision, and not with tests which might be given to a child in the future. (See answer to Question No. 1.)

THE EVALUATION TEAM PARTICIPANTS

The regulations are clear as to who should conduct the evaluation of the child:

a multidisciplinary team or group of persons, including at least one teacher or other specialist with knowledge in the area of suspected disability. (§ 121a.532(e))

The intent is that evaluation be conducted by multidisciplinary professional teams to ensure that the child's status and needs are considered from a variety of expert views. This principle is supported widely in the field of special education and has long been practiced by many school districts. The selection of the team members is particularly important because some will be involved later in helping develop the child's IEP.

PROTECTION IN EVALUATION PROCEDURES

The evaluation consists of specific in-depth assessments designed to assist in defining the child's status and needs. The information derived must be analyzed, validated, integrated, and aligned with parental priorities to prepare an IEP properly if it is determined that one is needed. Sound educational practice requires that evaluations be conducted in ways that will provide information upon which to base accurate decisions about a child's abilities.

However, many children traditionally have been evaluated at certain tasks in terms of the performance of their peers. Far too much of the testing has been largely subjective, culturally biased, highly narrative, and scale dominated. Educators and parents alike have complained about evaluation approaches as being disjointed, irrelevant, and ultimately inaccurate. A number of courts have ruled that certain ethnic minority children were labeled improperly as mentally retarded because of bad evaluation practices. In such litigation the courts have ruled consistently that certain individual intelligence tests discriminated unfairly against minority children, resulting in incorrect classification of many of them as handicapped learners.

According to a report by the Comptroller General of the U.S. General Accounting Office in September 1981, certain types of children were overrepresented in special education programs. For example, a disproportionate share of minority children participated in some special education programs. Forty-one percent of black students in special education programs in school year 1978 were in classes for the educable mentally retarded as compared with only 10 percent of Asian American students receiving special education and 17 percent of Hispanic students receiving services. Almost one half of the American Indian students in special education programs in the public schools were in learning disabled classes in 1978. Fifty percent of Asian Americans in special education were in speech impaired programs in 1978.

Also, the GAO report found that a disproportionate share of male children participated in some special education programs. Males were 3 times as likely as females to be found in programs for the seriously emotionally disturbed. Males were two and one half times as likely as females to be in learning disabled programs.

The over-representation of certain types of children in some special education programs emphasizes the need for reliable evaluation in the special education decision-making process. To ensure that an evaluation produces a full and fair picture of the pupil's strengths and weaknesses, the regulations provide protection by requiring that:

> Testing and evaluation materials and procedures used for the
> purposes of evaluation and placement of handicapped children

must be selected and administered so as not to be racially or culturally discriminatory. (§ 121a.530(b))

The regulations add more specific requirements:

State and local educational agencies shall insure, at a minimum, that:

(a) Tests and other evaluation materials:
✓ (1) Are provided and administered in the child's native language or other mode of communication, unless it is clearly not feasible to do so;
✓ (2) Have been validated for the specific purpose for which they are used; and
✓ (3) Are administered by trained personnel in conformance with the instructions provided by their producer;
✓ (b) Tests and other evaluation materials include those tailored to assess specific areas of educational need and not merely those which are designed to provide a single general intelligence quotient;
✓ (c) Tests are selected and administered so as best to ensure that when a test is administered to a child with impaired sensory, manual, or speaking skills, the test results accurately reflect the child's aptitude or achievement level or whatever other factors the test purports to measure, rather than reflecting the child's impaired sensory, manual, or speaking skills (except where those skills are the factors which the test purports to measure);
(d) No single procedure is used as the sole criterion for determining an appropriate educational program for a child; (§ 121a.532(a–d))

It is clear from these regulations that all types of discriminatory tests, or the discriminatory usage of tests, is prohibited. However, the law does not state what criteria are to be used to ascertain whether or not a particular test or testing procedure is discriminatory.

The regulations do suggest some approaches to minimize bias. The primary one is to ensure that evaluations are multifactored, multisourced, and carried out by qualified personnel. These protections are designed to prevent children from being misclassified or unnecessarily labeled as being handicapped because of inappropriate selection, administration, or interpretation of evaluation materials.

The major thrust is that there be a multiple approach to evaluation. The law does not specify particular materials, tests, or procedures that must be used except to the extent that they be properly validated for the specific purpose for which they are to be used. There is repeated emphasis on the importance of a variety of approaches in evaluating the child's level of functioning. The evaluation materials must be selected and administered so that their results accurately reflect what the particular test is supposed to measure. Sound educational practice requires that evaluators stay abreast of new research on instruments and approaches that have proved most effective with children from various cultural, racial, or handicapped groups.

THE COMPONENTS OF AN EVALUATION

As noted, the law does not detail any specific tests or materials to be used in evaluations but it does indicate what areas must be assessed as part of the procedure by requiring that:

> The child is assessed in all areas related to the suspected disability, including, where appropriate, health, vision, hearing, social and emotional status, general intelligence, academic performance, communicative status, and motor abilities. (§ 121a.532(f))

This information should be gathered from a variety of people and sources. It can be obtained from diagnostic, aptitude, achievement, or intelligence tests; extensive interviews with parents and teachers about the child's performance and development in and out of school; psychological testing of behavior and functioning; observation of the pupil in school and home settings; medical examinations; and other expert assessments.

Sound educational practice and law suggest that at a minimum there should be the following basic assessments in order to complete an appropriate multifaceted evaluation:

Social/Family Assessment

This should be conducted by a social worker or counselor who should attempt to make contact with the child's parents, guardians, or caretakers. The objective of the evaluation is to obtain historical and family background information. It also can obtain developmental history and information on adaptive behavior at home and in the neighborhood including identifying what the parents see as typical performance in the home environment. The parents also can provide information on their attitude toward their child as well as the pupil's relationships with peers and other family members. Detailed information regarding family constellation, cultural background, specific interpersonal family dynamics, and socioeconomic stresses should be included.

Health Assessment

This should be conducted by a physician and/or other pertinent medical professional. It should review present and past medical history, including prenatal, perinatal, and postnatal information. Details of all childhood illness should be obtained, including the age at the time of the ailment, symptoms, severity, course, medications, and care provider. The developmental history should include details of adaptive, personal-social, language, and motor development.

The evaluators should look for facilitators as well as constraints on the child's performance. These constraints can be very obvious when considering sensory handicaps but sometimes they are less obvious when examining metabolic, neurological, or even medication implications. Generally the major purpose of the medical examination is to determine and report on any physical factors that may influence the student's performance in the classroom or at home. It also should take into account various strengths that may facilitate the child's schooling and thus have an impact on the development of an educational program.

Educational Assessment

This should be conducted by a current or recent teacher of the child. It should include a summary of the educational history and observations regarding school behavior as well as academic progress, achievements, and demonstrated skills. School records, including samples of classwork and test results, should be included or incorporated by reference. The assessment should involve a complete analysis of academic abilities and levels and methods of skills acquisition.

It also should discuss previous educational strategies used to remediate the child's problems. The evaluator should describe the pupil's typical classroom and school performance with all the significant qualifying information that may explain specific actions. As in the social/family assessment, it is important to identify performance observed under general and special conditions in the school. The assessment also should contain information on the child's behavioral adjustment, attentional capacity, motor coordination, activity levels and patterns, and social relationships with others. There should be a language evaluation with detailed information on the child's speech and language behavior, articulation, voice quality, and expressive and receptive aspects of language.

Psychological Assessment

This obviously should be conducted by a psychologist. It should include behavioral observations in a variety of settings and measures of complex visual-motor-perceptual functioning as well as of personality characteristics and indexes of learning modalities or styles. Where possible, information derived from testing should be presented with much less emphasis on scores and more on individual strengths and weaknesses.

The assessment should provide an inventory of sensorimotor, language, perceptual, attentional, cognitive, affective, self-image, interpersonal, and behavioral factors with regard to the child's maturity, integrity, and interaction with the educational and home environments. This assessment should provide insight into the child's psychological makeup based on an appropriate examination and the pupil's developmental history. It should be drafted with descriptive and prescriptive recommendations for teaching.

THE RIGHT TO AN INDEPENDENT EVALUATION

The law provides that parents have the right to obtain an independent educational evaluation of their handicapped child. An "independent" evaluation means one conducted by a qualified examiner not employed by the public agency responsible for the child's education. (§ 121a.503(a), (i))

The agency is required to provide to parents, upon their request, information about where an independent educational evaluation may be obtained. Parents have the right to such an evaluation at public expense if they disagree with the one provided by the public agency. However, the agency may initiate a hearing to attempt to show that its conclusions are appropriate. If the final decision is that the assessment is appropriate, the parents still have the right to an independent evaluation, but not at public expense. Under the law, "public expense" means that the public agency either pays for the full cost of the evaluation or ensures that it is otherwise provided at no cost to the parents.

If parents obtain an independent evaluation at private expense, the results of the evaluation (1) must be considered by the public agency in any decision on providing a free appropriate public education and (2) may be presented as evidence at a hearing regarding that pupil.

If a hearing officer requests an independent evaluation, it must be at public expense.

Whenever an independent evaluation is at public expense, the criteria under which it is obtained, including the location of the analysis and the qualifications of the examiner, must be the same as those that the agency uses when it initiates an assessment.

REPORTING THE RESULTS OF EVALUATIONS

As noted earlier, the information received during the evaluation is used to develop the handicapped child's IEP. The various assessments are conducted to gather information about the pupil's performance in school. The end product must be readily translatable by educators into programming. It is critical that assessment findings be stated in educational terms so they can be used directly in the design of the IEP. Evaluators seeking to fulfill their role in the special education decision-making process should approach their task with an intention to determine:

- what the child can do

- what the child's current performance characteristics are

- what the specific constraints on the child's performance are

- what performance skills the child can be expected to attain over time, given an IEP that is developmentally rational

Many evaluators report their results in professional vocabularies that are not readily understandable by teachers, parents, or administrators. In terms of developing an educational program, it may not be particularly important for all of the team members to understand the full ramification of a student's childhood diabetes, for example. However, it is very important to know that the child will become tired more easily than others or may experience great physical discomfort if not medicated properly. This particular constraint can affect the implementation of the child's educational program. It is crucial to the development of a workable program that this information be stated in terms of functioning in school.

Evaluators should use tests with which they are comfortable and from which they can identify the student's highest observed performance. The test results then should be translated into specific performance statements. In anticipating the task of developing objectives for the child, evaluators must try to identify more complex functions and skills that the student can perform. Labels of handicapping conditions and descriptions about what children cannot do are of limited usefulness.

The emphasis of the evaluation process should be positive. Information about the student's current abilities is derived from data about the performance assessed by other evaluation team members and material on constraints on performance from medical professionals. If the results of the various assessments are reported in this positive manner and stated in terms of performance, educational objectives that are very specific and readily observable can be prepared in detail. Such objectives are likely to be understood easily by all persons involved and provide a basis for analyzing progress. Exhibit 7-1 is a checklist for evaluating the evaluation.

Exhibit 7-1 Checklist for Evaluating the Evaluation

	The Overall Evaluation Was consent for the assessments obtained from the child's parents?
	Were the tests and other evaluation materials provided and administered in the child's native language or other mode of communication, unless clearly not feasible to do so?
	Were the tests and other evaluation materials validated for the specific purpose for which they were used?
	Were the tests and other materials administered by trained personnel in conformance with the instructions provided by their producer?
	Did the tests and other evaluation materials include those tailored to assess specific areas of educational need and not merely those designed to provide a single general intelligence quotient?
	Were tests selected and administered so as best to ensure that when they were given to a child with impaired sensory, manual, or speaking skills, the results accurately reflect the pupil's aptitude or achievement level or whatever other factors they purport to measure, rather than demonstrating the child's impaired skills (except where they are the factors the test is intended to evaluate)?
	Was it certain that no single procedure was used as the sole criterion for determining an appropriate educational program for the child?
	Was the evaluation by a multidisciplinary team or group of persons, including at least one teacher or other specialist with knowledge in the area of the suspected disability?
	Was the child assessed in all areas related to the suspected disability, including, where appropriate, health, vision, hearing, social and emotional status, general intelligence, academic performance, communicative status, and motor abilities?

Exhibit 7-1 continued

	Were data obtained that included but were not limited to the following: • case history—educational, family, medical • educational achievement • language dominance of the home • current intellectual functioning level • school behaviors • information as required for specific handicapping conditions • measures of adaptive behavior • particular learning strengths and weaknesses
	Were the parents provided, on request, with information about where an independent educational evaluation could be obtained?
	Was an independent evaluation, if obtained by the parents, considered by the school system in any decision about providing a free appropriate public evaluation to the child?
	Each Assessment Report
	Was the report written in language understandable to the general public?
	Were the tools, tests, assessment instruments, and processes that were used identified in the report?
	Were the setting and any particular circumstances relevant to the assessment described?
	Was there a concise statement of the specific results or findings from each test?
	Was it clear which problem areas were identified from particular tests, which from behavioral observation, and which from reviews of other records?
	Were the assessment results stated in terms of performance so that the information would be useful in developing educational objectives?

Chapter 8

Programming and the Written IEP

Traditionally, the purpose of an educational evaluation was to determine whether a student was eligible for a particular placement, e.g., the educable mentally retarded class. This emphasis, as reflected in some of the terminology such as Admissions Committee, was to determine the presence of a specific handicap, with the automatic assumption that if such a handicap existed then placement in the special class for children so categorized was the appropriate action.

In contrast, current educational practice and P.L. 94-142 emphasize the concept that the major purpose of evaluation is to facilitate individualized programming to meet the handicapped child's unique needs. Certification and classification purposes of evaluation will continue to be necessary for administrative concerns but do not apply directly to programming.

"Programming" is the stage in the special education decision-making process in which the evaluation results are considered and specific objectives are developed, along with a recommended service delivery plan to meet those goals. The term programming is not defined as such in the law, but is derived from the process required to develop the individualized education program (IEP).

THE ROLE OF PROGRAMMING

Programming follows evaluation in the sequential process of special education decision making. It is closely related to evaluation because the quality of the programming depends largely upon the information about the child gathered through the assessment process. The first task of the persons developing an IEP is to prepare a statement of educational goals that is developmentally rational, sensitive to parental priorities, and related directly to the student's needs as derived from the evaluation data. The goals should represent increments toward prestated criteria.

Based on the goals, a series of short-term instructional objectives are then derived. This list of rank-ordered, performance-oriented objectives should represent a developmental approach to projections of anticipated achievement in terms of calendar time frames for one year. Then the type of service (e.g., physical therapy) necessary for the attainment of each objective can be recommended. Finally, the type of instruction (such as self-contained classroom, small group, etc.) most conducive to success can be decided.

Programming is different from placement, which is the stage that follows programming in the decision-making process. Programming is the heart of the special education the handicapped child receives. Placement is the manner or place or means by which the program is carried out—how and where it is implemented.

The law requires that an IEP must be in effect before special education and related services are provided to a child. Appropriate placement cannot be determined until after decisions have been made about what the child's needs are and what will be provided. Since these decisions are made at the IEP meeting, it is not permissible to place the child first and then develop the IEP.

PROGRAMMING AND THE IEP

The IEP clearly is at the heart of P.L. 94-142. It is both the process and the end product through which a program of free appropriate public education (FAPE) is assured to each handicapped child. The act defines a free appropriate public education as special education and related services that "are provided in conformity with an individualized education program which meets the requirements" on FAPE. (§ 121a.4(d)) In its requirement for an IEP, P.L. 94-142 can be credited with having codified what has long been recognized as superior teaching practice. The IEP for several reasons is of particular importance in the education of children with handicaps.

First, the IEP is individualized which means that it must be developed to meet the unique needs of one child rather than a class or group of pupils. It provides a natural point of departure from the conventional tendency to see the handicapped primarily in terms of their disabilities rather than as individuals, of viewing them as homogeneous and failing to recognize the wide variations that they, no less than nondisabled children, display.

Second, the IEP is education, which means that it is limited to special education and related services as those terms are defined in the law. It is not a plan to completely rehabilitate a child or deal with a pupil's family life situation.

Third, the IEP is a program which means that it is a written commitment of what actually will be provided. It is not a recommendation or a plan that offers guidelines from which a program is to be developed later.

The IEP is important for a number of other reasons. It provides accountability for achieving specific goals in specified time periods. It serves as a quality control mechanism, requiring the discipline of developing plans that are well reasoned and well considered. By calling for the involvement of parents, it fosters closer communication and greater trust between the school and the community. It replaces random instructional activities, based on standardized goals, with particularized steps calculated to achieve objectives important to the particular student. By virtue of the requirement that it be a written document that can be referred to readily, it promotes term-to-term continuity and consistency.

It can accommodate varying arrays of children (e.g., one-to-one tutoring, small groups, large groups, hospital or homebound instruction, and special resource activities). By using an interdisciplinary team approach, it can produce more balanced and comprehensive planning that results in an atmosphere far more supportive of the classroom teacher.

The concept of individualized programs or learning plans is not a recent innovation. Progressive teachers have used versions of such an approach virtually since the beginning of pedagogy. However, its formal application on a day-to-day basis has presented the vast majority of the nation's school staffs with a new experience. As shown by several references in P.L. 94-142, Congress clearly intended the IEP to be the key to attaining the act's goal of assuring free appropriate public education to every handicapped child.

THE LEGAL REQUIREMENT OF AN IEP

Under Part B of P.L. 94-142, the Department of Education makes federal funds available to states to help them in providing special education and related services to handicapped children. To receive assistance under this grant program, a state must demonstrate that it has met various provisions of the act, including the requirement that FAPE be available to all of its handicapped children.

AN IEP DEFINED

An individualized education program (IEP) is defined by the act (§ 4(19)), as:

a written statement for each handicapped child developed in any meeting by a representative of the local educational agency or an intermediate educational unit who shall be qualified to provide, or supervise the provision of, specially designed instruction to meet the unique needs of handicapped children, the teacher, the parents or guardian of such child, and, whenever appropriate, such child, which statement shall include (A) a statement of the present levels of educational performance of such child, (B) a statement of annual goals, including short-term instructional objectives, (C) a statement of the specific educational services to be provided to such child, and the extent to which such child will be able to participate in regular educational programs, (D) the projected date for initiation and anticipated duration of such services, and (E) appropriate objective criteria and evaluation procedures and schedules for determining, on at least an annual basis, whether instructional objectives are being achieved. (20 U.S.C. 1401(19)) (also, essentially the same, at § 121a.346)

THE PURPOSES AND FUNCTIONS OF THE IEP

The law divides the IEP requirement into two parts:
(1) the IEP meeting, at which parents and personnel jointly make decisions about a handicapped child's educational program, and (2) the IEP document itself, which is a written record of the decisions reached at the meeting. The IEP has a number of purposes and functions:

1. The IEP meeting serves as a communication vehicle between parents and school personnel and enables them, as equal participants, to decide jointly what the child's needs are, what services will be provided to meet them, and what the anticipated outcomes may be.
2. The IEP process provides an opportunity for resolving any differences between the parents and the agency concerning a handicapped child's special education needs through the IEP meeting and, if necessary, through the procedural protections available to the parents.
3. The IEP is a written commitment of resources necessary to enable a handicapped child to receive needed special education and related services.
4. The IEP is a management tool to ensure that each handicapped child is provided appropriate special education and related services.
5. The IEP is a compliance/monitoring document that may be used by authorized personnel from each governmental level to determine

whether a handicapped child actually is receiving the education agreed to by the parents and the school.

6. The IEP serves as an evaluation device for use in determining the extent of the child's progress toward meeting the projected outcomes. However, the law does not require that teachers or other school personnel be held accountable if a child does not achieve the goals and objectives in the IEP.

State Responsibility for the IEP

With regard to the responsibility for IEPs, the regulations state:

(a) *Public agencies.* The State educational agency shall insure that each public agency develops and implements an individualized education program for each of its handicapped children.
(b) *Private schools and facilities.* The State educational agency shall insure that an individualized education program is developed and implemented for each handicapped child who:
(1) Is placed in or referred to a private school and receives special education or related services from a public agency, or
(2) Is enrolled in a parochial or other private school and receives special education or related services from a public agency. (§ 121a.341)

This section applies to all the public agencies, including other state entities such as mental health and welfare departments, that provide special education either directly, by contract, or through other arrangements. Thus, if a state welfare agency contracts with a private school or facility to provide special education to a handicapped child, that agency would be responsible for ensuring that an IEP was developed for that pupil.

The Role of Agencies Other Than the LEA

As noted, the law provides that in each state the state education agency (SEA) ultimately is responsible for ensuring that each entity is in compliance with the IEP requirements and the other provisions of the act and regulations. However, the actual responsibility may vary from state to state, depending upon their law, policy, or practice.

The SEA must ensure that every handicapped child has a FAPE available, regardless of which agency, state or local, is responsible. While the SEA has flexibility in deciding the best means to meet this obligation (e.g., through interagency agreements), there can be no failure to provide FAPE because of jurisdictional disputes among agencies.

The requirements apply to all political subdivisions of the state that are involved in the education of handicapped children, including (1) the SEA, (2) local education agencies (LEAs), (3) other state agencies (departments of mental health and welfare, and state schools for the deaf or blind), and (4) state correctional facilities.

The following paragraphs outline (1) some of the SEA's responsibilities for developing policies or agreements under a variety of interagency situations, and (2) some of the LEA's responsibilities when it initiates the placement of a handicapped child in a school or program operated by another state agency.

SEA Policies or Interagency Agreements

The SEA, through its written policies or agreements, must ensure that IEPs are properly written and implemented for all handicapped children in the state. This applies to all interagency situations, including any of the following:

1. when an LEA initiates the placement of a child in a school or program operated by another state agency
2. when a state or local agency other than the SEA or LEA places a child in a residential facility or other program
3. when parents initiate placements in public institutions, and
4. when the courts make placements in correctional facilities.

This is not an exhaustive list. The SEA's policies must cover any other interagency situation that is applicable in the state, including placements that are made for both educational and noneducational facilities.

Frequently, more than one agency is involved in developing or implementing a handicapped child's IEP (e.g., when the LEA remains responsible for the child, even though another public agency provides the special education and related services, or when there are shared cost arrangements). It is important that SEA policies or agreements define the role of each agency involved in order to resolve any jurisdictional problems that could delay the educational process. For example, if a child is placed in a residential facility, any one or all of the following agencies might be involved in the development and/or implementation of the IEP: the LEA, the SEA, another state agency, an institution or school under that agency, and the LEA where the institution is located.

LEA-Initiated Placements

When an LEA is responsible for the education of a handicapped child, it also must develop the IEP even if the process results in placement in a state-operated school or program.

As noted earlier, the IEP must be developed before the child is placed. When placement in a state-operated school is necessary, the LEA must involve the affected state agency or agencies in the development of the program.

After the child enters the state school, meetings to review or revise the IEP could be conducted by either the LEA or the school, depending upon state law, policy, or practice. However, both agencies should be involved in any decisions about the IEP (either by attending planning meetings or through correspondence or telephone calls). There must be a clear decision, based on state law, as to whether responsibility for the child's education is transferred to the state school or remains with the LEA, since this decision determines which agency will review or revise the IEP.

OUT-OF-STATE PLACEMENT

When a child is placed out of state, the placing state is responsible for developing the IEP and ensuring that it is implemented. The determination of which agency in the placing state is responsible for the IEP would be based on state law, policy, or practice. However, as indicated above, the SEA in the placing state is responsible for ensuring that the child has available a free appropriate public education.

WHEN THE IEP MUST BE IN EFFECT

The regulations provide that:

(a) On October 1, 1977, and at the beginning of each school year thereafter, each public agency shall have in effect an individualized education program for every handicapped child who is receiving special education from that agency.

(b) An individualized education program must:

(1) Be in effect before special education and related services are provided to a child; and

(2) Be implemented as soon as possible following the meetings (to develop the IEP). (§ 121a.342)

It is expected that the child's program will be implemented immediately following the IEP meeting. Exceptions would be (1) when the meetings occur during the summer or a vacation period, or (2) where circumstances require a short delay (e.g., working out transportation arrangements). However, there can be no undue delay in providing education and services.

As used in the regulations, the term "be in effect" means that the IEP (1) has been developed properly (i.e., at a meeting involving all of the participants specified in the act such as the parent, teacher, agency representative, and, where appropriate, the child); (2) is regarded by both parents and agency as appropriate in terms of the pupil's needs, specified goals and objectives, and the services to be provided; and (3) will be implemented as written.

If a handicapped child has been receiving special education in one LEA and moves to another community, it would not be necessary for the new LEA to hold an IEP meeting if: (1) a copy of the child's current program is available, (2) the parents indicate that they are satisfied with it, and (3) the new LEA determines that it is appropriate and can be implemented as written.

If the LEA or the parents believe the current program is not appropriate, an IEP meeting would have to be conducted. This should take place soon after the child enrolls in the new LEA (normally, within one week).

If the LEA or the parents believe additional information is needed (such as school records from the former LEA) or that a new evaluation is necessary before a final placement decision can be made, it would be permissible to place the child temporarily in an interim program before the IEP is finalized.

THE LAW AND IEP MEETINGS

With regard to IEP meetings, the regulations state that:

> (a) *General.* Each public agency is responsible for initiating and conducting meetings for the purpose of developing, reviewing, and revising a handicapped child's individualized education program.
> (b) *Handicapped children currently served.* If the public agency has determined that a handicapped child will receive special education during school year 1977–1978, a meeting must be held early enough to insure that an individualized education program is developed by October 1, 1977.
> (c) *Other handicapped children.* For a handicapped child who is not included under paragraph (b) of this section, a meeting must

be held within thirty calendar days of a determination that the child needs special education and related services.

(d) *Review.* Each public agency shall initiate and conduct meetings to periodically review each child's individualized education program and if appropriate revise its provisions. A meeting must be held for this purpose at least once a year. (§ 121a.343)

Thus, when a child is first determined to be handicapped and in need of special education, there is a 30-day time frame in which to conduct an IEP meeting. This deadline ensures that there will not be a significant delay between the evaluation and when the child begins to receive special education. However, except for new handicapped children, the timing of meetings to develop, review, and revise IEPs is left to the discretion of each agency.

If the parents believe the child is not progressing satisfactorily or that there is a problem with the current IEP, they can request an IEP meeting. The public agency should grant any reasonable request for such a session.

A teacher who feels that the placement or IEP services are not appropriate to the child should follow agency procedures with respect to calling or meeting with the parents and/or requesting the agency to hold another session to review the program.

There is no prescribed length for IEP meetings. In general, they will be longer for initial placements and for children who require a variety of complex services and will be shorter for pupils who require only minimum services. In any event, agencies must allow sufficient time to ensure meaningful parent participation.

A local education agency need not hold a separate meeting, in addition to the IEP session, to determine a child's eligibility for special education. The law provides that the evaluation of each handicapped child must be "made by a multidisciplinary team or group of persons. . . ." The decisions regarding whether the team members actually meet together and whether such conferences are separate from the IEP session are left to the discretion of state or local agencies.

In practice, some agencies hold separate eligibility conferences with the multidisciplinary team before the IEP meeting. When these sessions are separate, placement decisions are made at the IEP meeting. However, placement options could be discussed at the eligibility meeting.

Other agencies combine the two steps into one. If a combined meeting is conducted, the parents must participate. If, at a separate eligibility meeting, a decision is made that a child is not eligible for special education, the parents should be notified.

With regard to IEP review meetings, the basic requirement still applies: the program must be in effect at the beginning of each school year. Meetings must be conducted at least once each year to review and, if necessary, revise each IEP. However, they may be held at any time—at the end of the school year, during the summer, before the new school term begins, or on the anniversary date of the last IEP meeting on the particular child.

PARTICIPANTS IN THE IEP MEETINGS

The regulations require that:

> (a) *General.* The public agency shall insure that each meeting includes the following participants:
> (1) A representative of the public agency, other than the child's teacher, who is qualified to provide, or supervise the provision of, special education.
> (2) The child's teacher.
> (3) One or both of the child's parents . . .
> (4) The child, where appropriate.
> (5) Other individuals at the discretion of the parent or agency.
> (b) *Evaluation personnel.* For a handicapped child who has been evaluated for the first time, the public agency shall insure:
> (1) That a member of the evaluation team participates in the meeting; or
> (2) That the representative of the public agency, the child's teacher, or some other person is present at the meeting, who is knowledgeable about the evaluation procedures used with the child and is familiar with the results of the evaluation. (§ 121a.344)

The Public Agency Representative

The public agency representative could be any member of the school staff, other than the child's teacher, who is qualified to provide or supervise special instruction for handicapped children. The agency representative could be a qualified special education administrator, supervisor, or teacher (including a speech-language pathologist), or a school principal or other administrator qualified to provide or supervise special education.

Each state or local agency may determine which specific staff member will serve as the agency representative. However, the individual should be able to ensure that whatever services are prescribed in the IEP actually will be provided and that the program will not be vetoed at a higher administrative level within the agency. Thus, the person selected should have the authority to commit agency resources (i.e., to make decisions about the specific special education and related services that the agency will provide).

For a handicapped student who requires only a limited amount of special education, the agency representative could be a special education practitioner or a speech-language pathologist—other than the child's teacher. For a child who requires extensive special education and services, the representative might need to be a key administrator in the agency. IEP meetings for continuing placements could be more routine than those for initial placements and thus might not require the participation of an administrator.

The question then is raised as to who is the "representative of the public agency" if a handicapped child is served by an entity other than the SEA or LEA. The answer depends on which state agency is responsible for any one or all of the following: (1) the child's education, (2) the placement, and (3) the provision (or payment for) special education and related services.

In general, the agency representative would be a member of the entity or institution responsible for the child's education. For example, if a state agency (1) places a child in an institution, (2) is responsible under state law for the education, and (3) has a qualified special education staff at the institution, then a member of the institution's staff would be the agency representative at the IEP meeting.

Sometimes there is no special education staff at the institution and the children are served by professional personnel from the LEA where the facility is located. In such a situation, a member of the LEA staff usually serves as the agency representative.

Teacher Participation

In deciding which teachers will participate in IEP meetings, the agency may wish to consider the following possibilities:

1. For a handicapped pupil receiving special education, the instructor could be the special education teacher. If the handicap is a speech impairment, the teacher could be the speech-language pathologist.
2. For a handicapped pupil being considered for placement in special education, the instructor could be the child's regular teacher or one qualified to provide the type of program in which the child may be placed, or both.

3. For a child who is not in school or who has more than one teacher, the agency may designate which one will participate.

In any event, there should be at least one member of the school staff at the meeting (the agency representative or the teacher) who is qualified in the child's area of suspected disability.

Sometimes more than one meeting is necessary in order to finalize an IEP. If, in this process, the special education teacher who will be working with the child is identified, it would be useful to have that person participate in the meeting with the parents and other members of the IEP team in finalizing the program. When this is not possible, the agency should ensure that the teacher is given a copy of the IEP as soon as possible after it is completed and before beginning to work with the child.

If a handicapped child is enrolled in both regular and special education classes, the practitioner at the IEP meeting should be the child's special education teacher. At the option of the agency or the parent, the pupil's regular teacher also might attend. If the regular teacher does not, the agency should either provide that instructor with a copy of the IEP or inform the person of its contents. Moreover, the agency should ensure that the special educator or the appropriate support person can consult with and be a resource to the regular teacher.

Some students have numerous teachers, such as in high school. In such a situation, only one teacher is required to attend the IEP meeting. However, at the option of the LEA, more of the pupil's teachers may be present. The following points should be considered in making this decision:

1. The number of participants at IEP meetings generally should be small. Small groups have several advantages over large ones: they (a) allow for more open, active parent involvement, (b) are less costly, (c) are easier to arrange and conduct, and (d) tend to be more productive.
2. Large meetings generally are inappropriate but, there may be specific circumstances in which the presence of additional staff would be beneficial. When the participation of the regular teachers is considered by the agency or the parent to be beneficial to the child's success in school (e.g., in terms of the regular education program), it would be appropriate for them to attend.
3. The regular teachers do not routinely attend IEP meetings but should either (a) be informed about the child's program by the special education teacher or agency representative, and/or (b) receive a copy of it.

If a child's primary handicap is a speech impairment, a speech-language pathologist would serve as the "teacher" for purposes of the IEP meeting.

The regular teacher also could attend, at the option of the school. No specific person represents the evaluation team but a speech-language pathologist normally would be the most appropriate. For many speech-impaired children, there may be no need to involve other evaluation personnel.

Those with a speech impairment as their primary handicap may not need a complete battery of assessments (psychological, physical, or adaptive behavior). However, a qualified speech-language pathologist would (1) evaluate such a child, using procedures appropriate for the diagnosis and appraisal of those disorders, and (2) make referrals, where necessary, for any additional assessments needed to assist placement decision.

Generally, a handicapped child should attend the IEP meeting whenever the parents decide this is appropriate. Whenever possible, the agency and parents should discuss this step before a decision is made in order to help them determine whether or not the child's attendance will be helpful in developing the IEP and/or directly beneficial to the pupil. The agency should inform the parents before each IEP meeting that they may invite their child to participate.

Parent Participation

The law requires that public education agencies provide extensive opportunities for parental involvement in the IEP process. The regulations declare:

> (a) Each public agency shall take steps to insure that one or both of the parents of the handicapped child are present at each meeting or are afforded the opportunity to participate, including:
> (1) Notifying parents of the meetings early enough to insure that they will have an opportunity to attend; and
> (2) Scheduling the meetings at a mutually agreed on time and place.
> (b) The notice under paragraph (a) (1) of this section must indicate the purpose, time, and location of the meeting, and who will be in attendance.
> (c) If neither parent can attend, the public agency shall use other methods to insure parent participation, including individual or conference telephone calls.
> (d) A meeting may be conducted without a parent in attendance if the public agency is unable to convince the parents that they should attend. In this case the public agency must have a record

of its attempts to arrange a mutually agreed on time and place such as:

(1) Detailed records of telephone calls made or attempted and the results of those calls.

(2) Copies of correspondence sent to the parents and any responses received, and

(3) Detailed records of visits made to the parents' home or place of employment and the result of those visits.

(e) The public agency shall take whatever action is necessary to insure that the parent understands the proceedings at a meeting, including arranging for an interpreter for parents who are deaf or whose native language is other than English.

(f) The public agency shall give the parent, on request, a copy of the individualized education program. (§ 121a.345)

The parents of a handicapped child are expected to be equal participants, along with school personnel, in developing, reviewing, and revising the IEP. Parents have the right to bring someone else to the meeting, e.g., a friend or neighbor, someone outside of the agency who is familiar with applicable laws and with the child's needs, or a specialist who conducted an independent evaluation of the pupil. The agency can ask whether they intend to do so. The law is silent concerning any modification of the rights of parents when the student reaches the age of majority.

In notifying parents of the meeting, the agency must indicate its purpose, time, and location, who will attend and where possible the name and position of each person who will be present. In addition, the agency should inform the parents of their right to bring other participants to the meeting.

An agency may not present a completed IEP to parents for approval before there has been a full discussion of the child's need for special education and related services and what services the agency will provide.

Agency staff members should come prepared with evaluation findings, statements of present levels of educational performance, and a recommendation regarding annual goals, short-term instructional objectives, and the kind of special education and related services to be provided. However, the agency must make it clear at the outset that the services proposed are only recommendations for review and discussion.

The agency must appoint a surrogate parent to represent the interests of a handicapped child when that pupil has no other parent to act. The surrogate has all of the rights and responsibilities of a parent and thus is entitled to participate in the IEP meeting, see the child's education records, and receive notice, grant consent, and invoke due process to resolve differences.

WHEN THE PARTIES DISAGREE

If, during the IEP meeting, the two parties are unable to reach agreement, the agency should remind the parents that they may seek to resolve their differences through a due process hearing. If a dispute persists, the agency and parents can agree on an interim course of action for serving the child (i.e., in terms of placement and/or services) until the disagreement is resolved. The manner in which this interim measure is developed and agreed to by both parties is left to the discretion of the agency. However, if the parties cannot agree even on an interim measure, the child's last agreed-upon IEP would remain in effect until the dispute is resolved. The following suggested approaches may be helpful when there are disagreements:

(a) There may be instances where the parents and agency are in agreement about the basic IEP services (e.g., the child's placement and/or the special education services), but disagree about the provision of a particular related service (e.g., whether the service is needed and/or the amount to be provided). In such cases, it is recommended (1) that the IEP be implemented in all areas in which there is agreement, (2) that the document indicate the points of disagreement, and (3) that procedures be initiated to resolve the disagreement.

(b) Sometimes the disagreement is with the placement or kind of special education to be provided (e.g., one party proposes a self-contained placement, and the other proposes resource room services). In such cases, the agency might, for example, carry out any one or all of the following steps: (1) remind the parents that they may resolve their differences through the due process procedures, (2) work with the parents to develop an interim course of action (in terms of placement and/or services) which both parties can agree to until resolution is reached; and (3) recommend the use of mediation, or some other informal procedure for resolving the differences without going to a due process hearing.

(c) If, because of the disagreement over the IEP, a hearing is initiated by either the parents or agency, the agency may not change the child's placement unless the parents and agency agree to otherwise. The following two examples are related to this requirement:

(1) A child in the regular fourth grade has been evaluated and found to be eligible for special education. The agency and parents agree that the child has a specific learning disability. However,

one party proposes placement in a self-contained program, and the other proposes placement in a resource room. Agreement cannot be reached, and a due process hearing is initiated. Unless the parents and agency agree otherwise, the child would remain in the regular fourth grade until the issue is resolved.

On the other hand, since the child's need for special education is not in question, both parties might agree—as an interim measure—(1) to temporarily place the child in either one of the programs proposed at the meeting (self-contained program or resource room), or (2) to serve the child through some other temporary arrangement.

(2) A handicapped child is currently receiving special education under an existing IEP. A due process hearing has been initiated regarding an alternative special education placement for the child. Unless the parents and agency agree otherwise, the child would remain in the current placement. In this situation, the child's IEP could be revised, as necessary, and implemented in all of the areas agreed to by the parents and agency, while the area of disagreement (i.e., the child's placement) is being settled through due process.

(U.S. Department of Education, Office of Special Education. Notice of Interpretation, published in the *Federal Register,* January 19, 1981.)

USE OF A TAPE RECORDER AT IEP MEETINGS

There are situations in which parents, school personnel, or both would like to use a tape recorder at IEP meetings. The use of tape recorders at IEP meetings is not addressed in P.L. 94-142 or its implementing regulations. Nor is there any formal policy statement from the U.S. Department of Education to either require or prohibit the use of tape recorders at such meetings.

However, it is recommended that a recorder should be allowed if either the parents or school officials request it. Probably the vast majority of IEP meetings will be conducted without either party being concerned with recording the proceedings. In those instances where a request is made to use a recorder in a meeting, however, there is little to be gained by denying the request.

If the parents are the ones making the request, it is unlikely that there would be any violation of the confidentiality requirements under either

P.L. 94-142 or the Family Educational Rights and Privacy Act (see Chapter 27). If made or used by school officials, the recording would be considered an "educational record" and therefore would be subject to the confidentiality requirements in both the statutes and their implementing regulations.

PARENT SIGNATURES ON THE IEP

' Parent signatures are not required by either the act or regulations. However, their inclusion is considered by parents, advocates, and public agency personnel to be useful. The following are some of the ways in which IEPs signed by parents and/or agency personnel might be used:

- A signed IEP is one way to document who attended the meeting. If signatures are not used, the agency must document attendance in some other way.

- An IEP signed by the parents is one way to indicate that they approved the program. If after signing the parents feel that a change is needed, they can request another meeting.

- An IEP signed by an agency representative provides the parents with a record of the services the entity has agreed to provide. Even if school personnel do not sign, the agency still must provide, or ensure the provision of, the services called for in the IEP.

The parents' signatures would satisfy the consent requirement concerning initial placement of the child only if the IEP includes a statement that meets the definition of "consent:"

> "Consent" means that: (a) The parent has been fully informed of all information relevant to the activity for which consent is sought . . .
> (b) The parent understands and agrees in writing to the carrying out of the activity for which his or her consent is sought, and the consent describes that activity and lists the records (if any) which will be released and to whom; and
> (c) The parent understands that the granting of consent is voluntary and may be revoked at any time. (§ 121a.500)

PARENT MONITORING OF THE CHILD'S PROGRESS

The law states that "the public agency shall give the parent, on request, a copy of the individualized education program." (§ 121a.345(f)) Parents should be informed of this provision at the IEP meetings and/or receive a copy of the program itself within a reasonable time afterward.

The IEP document includes agreed-upon items, such as goals and objectives, and the specific special education and related services to be provided.

The goals and objectives should be helpful to both parents and school personnel in checking on a child's progress. However, since the IEP is not intended to include the specifics about a child's total educational program that are found in daily, weekly, or monthly teacher instructional plans, parents often will need to obtain more specific, continuing information about progress through parent-teacher conferences, report cards, and other procedures the agency ordinarily uses.

The IEP is not required to include specific "checkpoint intervals" (i.e., specific dates to be met) for reviewing progress. However, in individual situations, specific dates could be designated if the parents and school believe that would be helpful.

There are specific provisions in the regulations on agency responsibilities in initiating IEP meetings, including the following: (1) public agencies must hold meetings periodically, but not less than annually, to review, and if appropriate, revise, each child's IEP; (2) there should be as many meetings a year as the pupil needs; and (3) agencies should grant any reasonable parental request for a meeting.

CONTENT AND FORMAT OF THE IEP

The regulations state that:

> The individualized education program for each child must include:
> (a) A statement of the child's present levels of educational performance;
> (b) A statement of annual goals, including short term instructional objectives;
> (c) A statement of the specific special educational and related services to be provided to the child, and the extent to which the child will be able to participate in regular educational programs;
> (d) The projected dates for initiation of services and the anticipated duration of the services; and
> (e) Appropriate objective criteria and evaluation procedures and schedules for determining, on at least an annual basis, whether the short term instructional objectives are being achieved. (§ 121a.346)

These IEP components are discussed individually next. In general, the format and length of an IEP are left to the discretion of state and local agencies. The document should be as long as necessary to describe a child's program adequately. However, it is not intended to be a detailed instructional plan. The federal IEP requirements usually can be met in one to three pages.

In instances where a handicapped child must have both an IEP and an individualized service plan under another federal program, it may be possible to develop a single, consolidated document provided that it contains all of the information required in an IEP and that all parties participate in its development.

Examples of individualized service plans that might be consolidated with the IEP are: the Individualized Care Plan (Title XIX of the Social Security Act—Medicaid), the Individualized Program Plan (Title XX of the Social Security Act—Social Services), the Individualized Service Plan (Title XVI of the Social Security Act—Supplemental Security Income), and the Individualized Written Rehabilitation Plan (Rehabilitation Act of 1973).

Present Levels of Performance

The statement of present levels of educational performance will be different for each handicapped child. Thus, determinations about the content of the statement are left to the discretion of participants in the IEP meetings. However, the following are some points that should be taken into account in writing this part of the IEP.

- The statement should accurately describe the effect of the handicap on the child's performance in any area of education that is affected, including (1) the academic (reading, mathematics, communication, etc.), and (2) the nonacademic (daily life activities, mobility, etc.). Labels such as "mentally retarded" or "deaf" may not be used to describe levels of performance.

- The statement should be written in objective measurable terms to the extent possible. Data from the evaluation are a good source of such information. Test scores that are pertinent to the child's diagnosis can be included, where appropriate. However, the scores should be (1) self-explanatory (i.e., they can be interpreted by all participants without the use of test manuals or other aids), or (2) an explanation should be included. Whatever test results are used should reflect the impact of the handicap on the child's performance. Raw scores usually would not be sufficient.

- There should be a direct relationship between the present levels of educational performance and the other components of the IEP. If the statement describes a problem with the reading level and points to a deficiency in a specific reading skill, this should be addressed under goals and objectives and under specific special education and related services to be provided.

Annual Goals and Short-Term Objectives

The statutory requirements for including annual goals and short-term objectives and for having at least an annual review of the IEP provide a mechanism for determining (1) whether the anticipated outcomes are being met (i.e., whether the child is progressing in the special education program), and (2) whether the placement and services are appropriate to the pupil's needs. In effect, these requirements provide a way for the teacher(s) and parents to track progress in special education.

The annual goals in the IEP are statements that describe what a handicapped child can reasonably be expected to accomplish in a 12-month period in the special education program. There should be a direct relationship between the annual goals and present performance levels.

Short-term instructional objectives (also called IEP objectives) are measurable, intermediate steps between present performance levels and the annual goals that have been established. The objectives are based on a logical breakdown of the major components of the annual goals and can serve as milestones for measuring progress.

In some respects, IEP objectives are similar to those used in daily classroom instructional plans. For example, both kinds of objectives are used (1) to describe what a given child is expected to accomplish in a particular area within some specified time period, and (2) to determine the extent to which the pupil is progressing toward those achievements.

In other respects, IEP objectives are different from those in regular instruction plans, primarily in the amount of detail they provide—general benchmarks for determining progress toward meeting the annual goals. These objectives should be projected over an extended period (e.g., an entire school quarter, semester, or year). On the other hand, the objectives in classroom instructional plans should be accomplished on a daily, weekly, or monthly basis. Class plans generally include details not required in an IEP, such as the specific methods, activities, and materials (e.g., flash cards) that will be used.

The heart of the IEP is the objectives that are to be used as a guideline in providing a quality education. Three basic criteria should be considered in developing these objectives:

1. They must be developmentally rational. If the student is using two-word sentences, the objective should be three-, four-, and five-word sentences. The long-term goal is that the student use compound and complex sentences but the most immediate objectives should indicate gradual increments toward that ultimate point.
2. They must be sensitive to parental priorities. If the student is demonstrating acting out behaviors such as hitting people or destroying property, objectives should be set to eliminate this conduct so that the pupil can function in an increased number of environments, if that is a parental priority.
3. They must relate to the student's progression to a less restrictive educational environment. If a student is in a substantially separate program, objectives should be established so that, when they are met, the pupil can be in a regular special education class at least part of the day.

However, it should be kept in mind that IEP goals and objectives are concerned primarily with meeting a handicapped child's need for special education and related services and are not required to cover other areas of the pupil's education. Stated another way, these goals should focus on offsetting or reducing problems resulting from the handicap that interfere with learning and educational performance in school.

For example, if a learning disabled child is functioning several grades below the pupil's indicated ability in reading and has a specific problem with word recognition, the IEP goals and objectives would be directed toward (1) closing the gap between the indicated ability and current level of functioning, and (2) helping increase the student's ability to use word attack skills effectively (or to find some other approach to increase independence in reading).

For a child with a mild speech impairment, the IEP objectives would focus on improving communication skills either by correcting the impairment or by minimizing its effect on the ability to communicate. On the other hand, the goals for a severely retarded child would be more comprehensive and cover more of the pupil's school program than if the handicap were only mild.

There should be a direct relationship between the IEP goals and objectives and those in the special education instructional plans because, through its goals and objectives, the IEP sets the general direction to be taken by those who will implement it.

IEP objectives must be written before placement. Once a handicapped child is placed in a special education program, the teacher can develop lesson plans or more detailed objectives based on the IEP; however, they are not required to be a part of the document itself. Since a change in short-term instructional objectives also constitutes a revision of the child's program, the agency must notify the parents of the proposed action and initiate an IEP meeting. However, if the parents are unable or unwilling to attend such a meeting, their participation in the IEP revision can be obtained through other means, again including individual or conference telephone calls.

Special Education and Related Services

This component of the IEP is designed to deliver the types of services necessary for the attainment of each short-term instructional objective. It should cover specific information on who will provide the services, what related ones will be included, and the extent to which the child will be able to participate in regular educational programs.

It must include all of the specific special education and related services needed by the child, as determined by the current evaluation. This means that they must be listed in the IEP even if they are not directly available from the local agency and must be provided by the agency through contract or other arrangements.

The public agency could provide IEP services directly, through its own staff resources; indirectly, by contracting with another public or private agency; or through other arrangements.

In providing the services, the agency may use whatever federal, state, local, and private sources of support are available. However, the services must be at no cost to the parents, and responsibility for ensuring that the services are provided remains with the public agency. The IEP also must include all services necessary to meet the child's identified special education and related needs. The agency must provide all services in the IEP if it is to be in compliance with the law.

The IEP is required to include only matters concerning the provision of special education and related services and the extent to which the child can participate in regular education programs. For some handicapped children, the IEP may address only a very limited part of their education (e.g., it would be limited to a speech impairment). For other children, such as the profoundly retarded, the program might cover their total education. An IEP for a child with no mental impairment might consist only of specially designed physical education. However, if there also is a mental impairment, the program might cover most of the child's education.

The amount, not just the types, of services must be stated in the IEP so that the level of the agency's commitment of resources will be clear to parents and other team members. The amount of time to be committed to each service must be appropriate to that specific effort and must be stated so that it is clear to all involved in both the development and implementation of the IEP.

The services listed in the program cannot be changed without holding another IEP meeting. However, as long as there is no change in the overall amount, some adjustments in scheduling services should be possible (based on the professional judgment of the provider) without another meeting.

If modifications (supplementary aids and services) to the regular education program are necessary to ensure the child's participation, those modifications must be described in the IEP (e.g., for a hearing impaired child, special seating arrangements or assignments in writing). This applies to any regular classes in which the student may participate, including physical education, art, music, and vocational education.

In addition, the law provides that this component include a statement of the extent to which the child will be able to participate in regular educational programs. One way of meeting this requirement is to indicate the percent of time the child will be spending in regular special education with nonhandicapped students. Another way is to list the specific regular classes the child will attend.

If a severely handicapped child, for example, is expected to be in a special classroom most of the time, it is recommended that, in meeting the requirement, the IEP include any noncurricular activities in which the pupil will be participating with nonhandicapped students (e.g., lunch, assembly periods, club activities, and other special events).

Projected Dates and Duration of Services

In general, services would be expected to run no longer than 12 months. There is a direct relationship between their anticipated duration and the other parts of the IEP (e.g., annual goals and short-term objectives), and each part of the plan should be addressed whenever there is a review of the child's program. If it is expected that the pupil will need a particular service for more than one year, the duration could be projected beyond that time in the IEP. However, the extent of each service must be reconsidered whenever the IEP is reviewed.

Criteria, Evaluation, and Schedule

The evaluation procedures and schedules need not be a separate item in the IEP but must be presented in a recognizable form and be clearly linked to the short-term objectives. In many instances, these components are incorporated directly into the objectives.

THE INCLUSION OF PHYSICAL EDUCATION

The regulations provide that:

> physical education services, specially designed if necessary, must be made available to every handicapped child receiving a free appropriate public education. (§ 121a.307(a))

Following are some of the different physical education (PE) program arrangements for handicapped students and whether, and to what extent, they must be described or referred to in an IEP:

- Regular PE with nonhandicapped students: If a handicapped pupil can participate fully in the regular PE program without any special modifications to compensate for a disability, it would not be necessary to describe or refer to PE in the IEP. On the other hand, if some modifications are necessary for the student to be able to participate, they must be described in the IEP.

- Specially designed PE: If a handicapped student needs a specially designed PE program, it must be addressed in all applicable areas of the IEP (e.g., present levels of educational performance, goals and objectives, and services to be provided). However, these statements need not be presented in any more detail than the other special education services in the IEP.

- PE in separate facilities: If a handicapped student is educated in a separate facility, the PE program must be described or referred to in the IEP. However, the kind and amount of information to be included in the IEP would depend on the child's physical/motor needs and the type of PE program that is to be provided. Thus, if a student is in a separate facility that has a standard PE program, such as a residential school for the deaf, and if it is determined—on the basis of the most recent evaluation—that the child can participate in that program without any modifications, then the IEP need only note such participation. On the other hand, if special modifications to the PE program are needed, they must be described in the IEP. Moreover, if the student needs an individually designed PE program, it must be addressed under all applicable parts of the IEP.

THE INCLUSION OF VOCATIONAL EDUCATION

If a student is able to participate in the regular vocational education program without any modifications to compensate for a disability, it is not necessary to include such instruction in the IEP. On the other hand, if modifications are necessary for the pupil to participate, those changes must be in the IEP. Moreover, if the student needs a specially designed vocational education program, it must be described in all applicable areas of the IEP (e.g., present levels of educational performance, goals and objectives, and specific services to be provided). However, these statements need not be any more detailed than the other special education services in the IEP.

Regulations under the Vocational Education Act provide that certain funds available for programs for handicapped persons must be used in a manner consistent with the state's plan under P.L. 94-142. They also require the five-year State Vocational Education Plan to describe how each handicapped child's program will be planned and coordinated in conformity with the IEP as stipulated by the Education of the Handicapped Act.

THE INCLUSION OF ALL SERVICES NEEDED

IEPs must include all services a handicapped child needs for an appropriate education in the least restrictive environment. The content of the IEPs may not be limited to the services currently available in the school district.

According to a report prepared by the Comptroller General of the U.S. General Accounting Office in February 1981, many LEAs limited the content of their IEPs to the special education and related services currently available in the district, even if the child needed other services. The report stated that school officials feared that if the specified needed services were not available, this could lead to legal charges that the LEA had violated the act's mandate.

ACCOUNTABILITY FOR THE IEP

With regard to the accountability of a teacher or education agency for the objectives in the IEP, the regulations provide that:

> Each public agency must provide special education and related services to a handicapped child in accordance with an individualized education program. However, Part B of the Act does not require that any agency, teacher, or other person be held accountable if a child does not achieve the growth projected in the annual goals and objective. (§ 121a.349)

This section makes it clear that the IEP is not a performance contract that imposes liability on a teacher or public agency if a handicapped child does not meet the IEP objectives. It is intended to relieve concerns that the IEP constitutes a guarantee by the agency and teacher that a pupil will progress at a specified rate. However, the section does not remove the need to make good faith efforts to help the child achieve the IEP objectives and goals in the IEP. It also does not limit the parents' right to complain and ask for revisions of the program or to invoke due process procedures if they feel these efforts are not being made.

While the IEP is seen as neither a legal document nor a legal contract, it does represent a commitment of resources necessary to enable a handicapped child to receive needed special education and related services. In fact, the delineation of services to be provided is one of the primary purposes of the document. In effect, the IEP is an agreement (with LEA and parental approval) for services to be provided. Stated another way, the services set out in the IEP must either be provided to the child, or the IEP must be amended.

THE IEP FOR HANDICAPPED GIFTED CHILDREN

The education of a handicapped gifted child under the law is treated the same way as any other disabled pupil. The following excerpt from a Maryland State Department of Education decision is an example of how a problem involving a handicapped gifted child might arise in the context of an IEP. The State Hearing Review Board's decision also provides a sound analysis of the legal issues involved.

Neither Public Law 94-142 nor the State Education Article mandates the provision of educational services to students who are gifted. Nor do these laws authorize educational agencies to resolve disputes relating to the provision of services to gifted students through a due process hearing. Public Law 94-142 and the State Education Article apply only to "handicapped children" who require "special education" because of their handicapping condition. These laws do not address children who are gifted and require different special education services from the majority of students. These laws only distinguish between "handicapped" and "nonhandicapped" students, and between "special education" and "general" or "regular" education. They do not segregate out gifted students from the general education population.

However, this case presents the question of a student who is both handicapped and gifted. The parents contend that their child meets the eligibility requirements for special education because the child is handicapped. But since the child is also gifted, the education to which he is entitled must be such that it takes into account his superior intellectual strengths. The parents argue that the individual education program for their child must include goals, objectives, services, etc., which address the whole child rather than just the child's needs resulting from his handicap.

In considering these contentions raised by the parents, the Hearing Review Board reviewed the legal definitions of "handicapped children" and "special education" under P.L. 94-142, as well as the requirements pertaining to placement in the least restrictive environment. . . .

From these definitions and the legal requirements regarding placement in the least restrictive environment, it is clear that the goals of general education predominate for all children. Only when a child's handicap impairs him or her from functioning in a general education program, does special education become appropriate. Even then, special education is only appropriate to the extent it is necessary to bridge the gap between the child's ability to function in the general education program, and the deficits in doing so because of the handicap. Indeed, for most handicapped children, special education is not the totality of their education. They participate in the general education program to the maximum extent possible.

In the case at hand, Michael is a child who is learning disabled. But the law does *not* require special intervention with Michael because he is learning disabled. It does *not* require that Michael receive math instruction for the learning disabled, reading instruction for the learning disabled, self-help training for the learning disabled, socialization activities for the learning disabled, physical education for the learning disabled, art for the learning disabled, lunch for the learning disabled, recess for the learning disabled, etc. His handicap of learning disabilities alone does not automatically entitle him to a full school day of special education programming.

Rather, the law requires that the focus of special intervention not be Michael's handicap of learning disabilities, but *his individual educational needs that result from his learning disabilities*. Learning disabilities do not affect every learning disabled child in the same way and to the same extent. It is conceivable that Michael may only require itinerant or resource help with certain academic subjects, while spending most of his day in the general education program with his nonhandicapped peers. Or, he might require a 12-month residential education program with little or no integration with his nonhandicapped peers. The law requires that the "special education" provided for Michael only involve that instruction which is specially designed to meet his unique needs. The unique needs referred to are those which result from the adverse effect his *handicap* has on his ability to function in the general education program. The law does not require specially designed instruction to meet Michael's unique needs which result from his superior intellectual abilities.

This interpretation, that the law requires special education to meet Michael's unique needs which result from his specific learning disabilities, is further supported by the requirements pertaining to the content of the IEP. The law requires that an IEP contain a statement of the child's present levels of educational performance. The law also requires a statement of the specific special education and related services to be provided to the child, and the extent to which the child will be able to participate in the regular educational programs. The law does not require that a detailed description of goals, objectives, and services for the regular education portion of the child's day be included in the IEP.

In this case, Michael's gifted educational needs are subsumed under the umbrella of regular education. The Hearing Review Board determines that a detailed description of goals, objectives, and services for the regular education portion of Michael's day need not be included in his IEP. The IEP for Michael must include a statement of the specific education and related services to be provided to him to meet his unique needs which result from his learning disabilities. The IEP must also include a statement of the extent to which Michael will be able to participate in classes or activities for gifted children. The IEP must address goals, objectives, and services regarding Michael's giftedness *only* if they are relevant within the context of the special education program being provided to Michael.

Chapter 9

Placement

Traditionally, if children were determined to have particular handicaps, they would be placed in the special class with other pupils who had the same categorical label. If no such class were available, or the child was too severely handicapped for the school to accommodate, the pupil frequently was excused from the compulsory attendance requirement. Placement decisions related directly to the classification of such children and the availability of existing programs for them.

That approach to placement decisions has been rejected by most progressive educators for years and now is a violation of P.L. 94-142. Under that law, all placement decisions on the education of handicapped children must be made within the context of each one's individualized education program (IEP). The law now requires that placement decisions be designed to fit the individual needs of the child as set forth in the IEP, not to fit the child into the available openings. The IEP concept requires that existing program placements be modified or new ones created, if necessary, to deliver the particular services specified in the program.

"Placement" is the model and facility in which the special education that the child needs, as already indicated on the IEP, will be delivered. The term placement is not defined as such in the law but rather derives from the procedures required to ensure that the IEP is carried out.

PLACEMENT'S ROLE IN SPECIAL EDUCATION

Placement is the last major stage in providing a handicapped student with a free appropriate public education. Before the placement may be determined, it is necessary to have properly identified the pupil's potential special needs, evaluated the strengths and weaknesses, and developed an IEP. The placement will determine how and where the IEP will be delivered.

Placement and the IEP: The Difference

Placement frequently is confused or lumped with the development of the student's IEP. The concepts are closely related but do involve two separate stages in the special education process.

As discussed in Chapter 8, the IEP essentially is a written agreement that must be provided for every handicapped child receiving special education. The IEP must:

- determine the extent of the child's ability to participate in regular educational programs
- determine the starting date of the pupil's program
- anticipate the duration of the services
- select appropriate objective criteria and evaluation procedures to determine whether instructional objectives are being achieved
- describe the child's present levels of educational performance
- state annual goals
- state short-term instructional objectives
- describe specific educational and related services to be provided

On the other hand, the placement is the means by which the individualized education program is carried out and determines the appropriate educational model and facility.

As noted, the IEP must be in effect before special education and related services are provided. Placement cannot be determined until after decisions have been made about what the pupil's needs are and what will be provided. Since these decisions are made at the IEP meeting, it is not permissible to first place the child and then develop the IEP.

The Importance of Placement

Perhaps the most critical decision in the special education decision-making process is the determination of the actual placement in which the student's IEP will be provided. The public schools and the parents may agree on the goals, services, etc., as specified in the IEP but disagree strongly on which particular placement would be appropriate to carry it out.

In most special education due process hearings, placement is the focal issue. Parents are especially concerned because they believe it is the placement that determines the quality of the education program their child will receive. School administrators are concerned because they believe it is the placement that will determine the actual expense they will incur in implementing the IEP.

PARTICIPANTS IN THE PLACEMENT DECISION

The regulations require that the public school system

> insure that the placement decision is made by a group of persons, including persons knowledgeable about the child, the meaning of the evaluation data, and the placement options . . . (§ 121a.533(3))

This requirement is similar to the one on multidisciplinary staffing teams discussed in Chapter 7, on evaluation. Here, the law is requiring public school systems to adopt procedures that will assure that placement decisions will be multifactored and multisourced in order to provide a comprehensive view of the child from the perspective of the school, home, and community.

The law does not appear to require any particular composition for the team charged with making the placement decision. It does not specify, for example, that a special educator or administrator is expected to base the placement decision on the recommendations of the multidisciplinary staffing team responsible for the evaluation and program development of the child.

'TEMPORARY' OR 'INTERIM' PLACEMENTS

As discussed earlier, placement cannot be determined until after the child has been evaluated and services decided upon. This does not preclude temporary assignment of a handicapped child in a program as part of the evaluation process, before the IEP is finalized, to aid in determining the most appropriate placement. It is essential that the temporary placement not become final before the IEP is approved. To ensure that this does not happen, the state might consider requiring LEAs to:

1. develop an interim IEP for the child that sets the specific conditions and timelines for the trial placement

2. ensure that the parents agree to the interim placement before it is carried out and that they are involved throughout the process of developing, reviewing, and revising the IEP
3. set a specific timeline (e.g., 30 days) for completing the evaluation and making judgments about the most appropriate placement
4. conduct an IEP meeting at the end of the trial period in order to finalize the program

THREE LEGAL REQUIREMENTS FOR PLACEMENTS

The regulations require that the public school system ensure that each handicapped student's educational placement decision:

1. is based on his or her individualized education program. (§ 121a.552(a)(2))
2. is made in conformity with the least restrictive environment rules. . . . (§ 121a.553(a)(4))
3. can provide the required special education and related services "at public expense, under public supervision and direction, and without charge." (§ 121a.4(a))

These three are the basis of all the other requirements discussed in this chapter. They appear to be very simple but that appearance is deceptive. It is their application in the special education process that gives rise to the most disputes among the schools, parents, public welfare agencies, etc.

The law still is relatively new and there are not yet sufficient cases from which to distill clear guidelines for clarifying the placement requirements. However, the safest approach is to follow sound special education practice. It is important to keep in mind, again, that the law is designed to follow sound special education practice, rather than the other way around.

PLACEMENT BASED ON THE IEP

As noted, the public schools are required to ensure that all handicapped student educational placement decisions are based on their IEPs. This again demonstrates that the special education process consists of a series of sequential components (see Chapter 11). The placement decision must relate back to the specifications of the IEP.

A placement must be designed so it can fulfill its purpose of carrying out the IEP. The law in essence requires that the public schools make certain that the shoe fits before asking the student to wear it.

The requirement that the placement decision be based upon the IEP also is grounded in the fundamental right of all handicapped children to a free appropriate public education. The term "appropriate" is defined for each child through the IEP (see Chapter 11).

The placement must be based on the IEP because the program is the major factor in determining whether or not the free public education is appropriate. If the placement is not designed to carry out the IEP effectively, then the child will not receive the appropriate education to which the pupil is entitled. The program as drafted may be excellent but its value will be diminished if the placement is not designed properly to deliver it to the child.

The requirement that the placement decision be based upon the IEP is a protection for both the school system and the parents. It protects the public schools by assuring that the decision is based on bona fide educational considerations. Frequently, parents will urge a placement different from that proposed by the school because of a variety of considerations not truly related to the child's education. For example, parents may argue for a residential placement because the child is a tremendous strain on them and the rest of the family.

The IEP, however, focuses strictly on the child and how the special needs impact on the pupil's education. The school system cannot be held responsible for providing additional services that might be needed to ameliorate a whole host of other problems that arise as a result of the child's being handicapped. Its role is limited to education.

The requirement also is a protection for the parents in that it ensures that the placement decision can implement the IEP. The actual benefit the child receives from the IEP is determined by how well the placement delivers on the promise. One placement may be better equipped than another to implement the program.

Many factors must be considered when making a placement decision— physical plant, training of personnel, student population, supplemental services, number of hours, etc. The placement also must be individualized and not simply based on a categorical label. For example, a school system may recommend placing an emotionally disturbed child with a visual dysfunction in a program for either the emotionally disturbed or the visually impaired because those are the ones it has available. However, this child's IEP probably includes goals and objectives relating to both of these special education needs. The requirement that the placement be based on the IEP protects the parents by assuring that it will be individually designed to implement the IEP and by not allowing the school to place the child simply on the basis of its administrative convenience.

THE LEAST RESTRICTIVE ENVIRONMENT RULES

As noted, the law requires that the school system assure that the placement decision conforms with the least restrictive environment rules. More specifically, the regulations require that the school ensure:

> (1) That to the maximum extent appropriate, handicapped children, including children in public or private institutions or other care facilities, are educated with children who are not handicapped, and
> (2) That special classes, separate schooling or other removal of handicapped children from the regular educational environment occurs only when the nature or severity of the handicap is such that education in regular classes with the use of supplementary aids and services cannot be achieved satisfactorily. (§ 121a.550(b))

Up to the placement stage, the special education decision-making process of identification, evaluation, and program development has focused attention strictly on the child's educational needs because they may require specially designed instruction.

Special education is defined in P.L. 94-142 as instruction designed specifically to meet the unique needs of a handicapped child. The pupil does not receive special education because of a handicap; the child is eligible for special education only if the handicap adversely affects educational performance.

However, the placement decision actually impacts upon the pupil's life in a much broader way than just on educational development. It affects the child as a whole person. Personality growth and development are influenced strongly by the range of everyday experiences and opportunities to which the child is exposed in the surrounding environment.

It follows that the best environment in which to provide an educational program is one that is the "most normal" or the "least restrictive" setting appropriate to the child's learning needs. This principle has long been recognized as sound educational practice because it provides for the child's psychosocial growth as well as academic achievement. This is essentially the reasoning behind the legal requirement that the child's educational placement be in the least restrictive environment.

It is important to emphasize that the principle of the least restrictive environment focuses primarily on with whom rather than where the child is to be educated. Usually, the restrictiveness of a particular placement is thought of in terms of the degree of isolation or security of the intended facility. Such a focus is perhaps appropriate in the field of criminal corrections but is not what the law requires in special education. The concept of restrictiveness in special education focuses on the appropriate extent or degree for educating a handicapped student with nonhandicapped peers.

Legal Origins of the Principle

As a legal concept, the principle of selecting the least restrictive alternative has undergone tremendous development in the last two decades. It has received legal recognition in a wide variety of social issues. The most frequently quoted and definitive rationale for the least restrictive alternative principle was provided by the U.S. Supreme Court in *Shelton* v. *Tucker*, 346 U.S. 479 (1960):

> In a series of decisions this Court has held that, even though the governmental purpose be legitimate and substantial, that purpose cannot be pursued by means that broadly stifle fundamental personal liberties when the end can be more narrowly achieved. The breadth of legislative abridgement must be viewed in the same light of less drastic means for achieving the same basic purpose.

In *Shelton*, the Court struck down an Arkansas affidavit statute requiring all public school teachers to disclose the organizations to which they belonged. Other courts and legislatures have incorporated the principle in laws affecting such matters as commitment of mentally disabled persons, child abuse and neglect, limitations on the media, and national security classification.

In education law, the principle of least restrictive alternative was noted first in the landmark case of *Brown* v. *Board of Education* (1954) in which the Court declared that the concept and practice of segregation was not permissible in public education.

In the years since, the principle of least restrictive alternative has been expanded and clarified. The principle was definitively articulated and applied to the education of handicapped children in the well-known cases of *Pennsylvania Association for Retarded Children v. Pennsylvania*, 343 F. Supp. 279 (E.D. Pa. 1972) and *Mills v. Board of Education of the District of Columbia, et al.*, 348 F. Supp. 866 (D.D.C. 1972).

The most significant legal recognition of the principle of least restrictive alternative in education has come from Congress in Public Law 94-142. Section 612(5)(B) of the act requires states to establish

> procedures to assure that to the maximum extent appropriate handicapped children, including children in public or private in-

stitutions or other care facilities, are educated with children who
are not handicapped, and that special classes, separate schooling,
or other removal of handicapped children from the regular educational environment occurs only when the nature or severity of
the handicap is such that education in regular classes with the use
of supplementary aids and services cannot be achieved satisfactorily. . . .

This policy of educating handicapped children in the least restrictive
environment is mandated in substantially identical terms in the U.S. Department of Health, Education, and Welfare regulations for implementation of Section 504 of the Vocational Rehabilitation Act of 1973. Those
regulations prohibit discrimination against handicapped persons ". . . under
any program or activity which receives or benefits from Federal financial
assistance." (§ 84.4(a))

Least Restrictive vs. 'Mainstreaming'

There probably is little real difference between the terms least restrictive
and mainstreaming. However, in recent years mainstreaming has become
a sort of code word with highly negative connotations. Many persons attach
a distorted meaning to the term. To them, mainstreaming refers to a whole-
sale return to regular classes of all handicapped children who are in special
classes. Nowhere do the laws mandate that all handicapped children should
be educated in regular classrooms. Consequently, those who refer properly
to P.L. 94-142 avoid the emotion-laden term of mainstreaming.
   Actually, the two concepts of mainstreaming and least restrictive environment are so close in meaning as to be indistinguishable. Any nuance
of difference disappears completely if practitioners accept the definition
of mainstreaming as approved by The Council for Exceptional Children's
Delegate Assembly in April 1976:

> Mainstreaming is a belief which involves an educational placement
> procedure and process for exceptional children, based on the
> conviction that each such child should be educated in the least
> restrictive environment in which his educational and related needs
> can be satisfactorily provided. This concept recognizes that ex-
> ceptional children have a wide range of special educational needs,
> varying greatly in intensity and duration; that there is a recognized
> continuum of educational settings which may, at a given time, be
> appropriate for an individual child's needs; that to the maximum
> extent appropriate, exceptional children should be educated with

nonexceptional children; and that special classes, separate schooling, or other removal of an exceptional child from education with
nonexceptional children should occur only when the intensity of
the child's special education and related needs is such that they
cannot be satisfied in an environment including nonexceptional
children, even with the provision of supplementary aids and services.

Clearly, the term that is used is not as important as the basic provision
and how it is implemented. The primary consideration must be the delivery
of a free appropriate public education.

A CONTINUUM OF ALTERNATIVE PLACEMENTS

To be sure that handicapped children are educated in the least restrictive
environment, the law requires the school system to have available a range
of services to meet the unique educational needs of each pupil. The regulations state that:

(a) Each public agency shall ensure that a continuum of alternative
placements is available to meet the needs of handicapped children
for special education and related services.
(b) The continuum required under paragraph (a) of this section
must:
(1) Include the alternative placements listed in the definition of
special education [instruction in regular classes, special classes,
and instruction in hospitals and institutions], and
(2) Make provision for supplementary services (such as resource
room or itinerant instruction) to be provided in conjunction with
regular class placement. (§ 121a.551)

and

The various alternative placements included under § 121a.551 are
available to the extent necessary to implement the individualized
education program for each handicapped child. (§ 121a.552)

The law, as well as sound special education practice, emphasizes the
importance of providing educational services to all handicapped children
according to their individual needs. These needs may require that instruction be given in varying environments, i.e., hospital, home, school, or

institution. A variety of program alternatives must be available in every agency to meet these differing needs. If the school system does not have the appropriate alternative, then it must contract for the required services from outside sources.

A 'Continuum of Services'

The term "continuum of services" simply refers to a range of educational settings and services from the least restrictive environment (a regular education program with modifications) through the most restrictive environment (a 24-hour residential program).

However, the term raises objections by many persons, just as does the term mainstreaming. The objectors feel that words other than continuum should be used (e.g., range of programs or variety of services). They believe that continuum carries negative connotations and that the concept undermines the ideals of P.L. 94-142 in that it implies best-to-worst, etc. Others feel that it discriminates against residential or private schools.

The term continuum, as with least restrictive environment (LRE), is commonly used by agencies, advocates, and parents. However, there is nothing to prohibit an agency from using other terms, such as those above, in administering these provisions.

As with LRE, the term that is used is not as important as the basic provision and how it is implemented. The purpose of a continuum is to be able to accommodate differences between handicapped children in terms of the degree of special assistance they need to receive a free appropriate public education.

A Standard Continuum of Services

A standard continuum of services (Figure 9-1) includes instruction in regular and special classes, special schools, at home, in hospitals, and in institutions. Supplementary services such as resource room or itinerant instruction, in conjunction with regular class placement, also are required by law.

Each of the placement alternatives shown on the standard continuum could include a further breakdown into different placement options. Within each type of alternative placement shown are less restrictive options. In attempting to meet the goal of least restrictive placement, the team should consider which type is appropriate, then which option within that type is the least restrictive one appropriate to the child's needs. The types of placements on the standard continuum of services and the options within each are described next.

Figure 9-1 A Standard Continuum of Services

Regular Classroom
Regular Class with Itinerant Teacher
Regular Class with Resource Room
Self-Contained Classroom
Special Day School
Residential School/Institution
Homebound and Hospital

Regular Classroom

The greatest number of handicapped students should receive appropriate services while in a regular classroom. Within this type of placement, the team might consider such options as a combination of regular classroom activities with special materials and professional consultation with the classroom teacher, or primary assignment to the regular classroom with supplementary aids and services being provided directly to the student.

Regular Class with Itinerant Teacher

In an itinerant program, the child is placed in the regular classroom but receives direct service and instruction from an itinerant teacher or specialist. These are continuing and include consultation with the classroom teacher as well as direct service to the student. The options within this type of placement are largely a function of the quantity of service to be provided by the itinerant.

Regular Class with Resource Room

In a resource room program, the child is placed in the regular classroom for the major part of the day and is scheduled into the resource room for periods of individualized instruction. The resource room could be one where the student receives direct services from a specialist or a special education class where the pupil goes for a period to receive instruction in a particular area. The options in this placement are primarily a function of time in the resource room and the particular combination of kinds of resource rooms used.

Self-Contained Classroom

Self-contained classroom programs are generally for students with severe handicapping conditions that require concentrated special education and related services. There are numerous options in this type of placement. The student could be assigned primarily to the self-contained classroom, with part-time instruction or involvement with the regular education program. The self-contained special classroom might be located in a special education day school facility. The pupil in the self-contained class could have some instruction or involvement with children at other schools or in a resource room in a regular school.

Special Day School

Removal of a student to a special education day school occurs when the handicapping condition is severe or profound. Within this type of placement there are options to enroll the pupil in outside programs or provide for a portion of instruction with less handicapped students in other special classrooms in the day school. Other options include instruction or involvement with students in a resource room program or a self-contained classroom in a regular school for a portion of the day. Where possible, the student may take part in nonacademic activities with nonhandicapped peers.

Residential School

The student placed in a residential school usually demonstrates a handicapping condition that profoundly affects educational performance. The types of options here include any combination of services that might be provided for periods of the day or school year with children in a special day school, self-contained classroom, resource room, or regular classroom who are less handicapped than the particular pupil. Since medical factors may greatly restrict the student from participating in integrated activities outside the residential setting, programs must be developed to foster some activity with nonhandicapped persons for at least a portion of the school week.

Homebound and Hospital Programs

Homebound and hospital programs are not really part of a continuum of alternative placements but are ancillary to it. That is, they supplement the types of placements such children would be assigned to normally. The content of the instruction should be the same in the homebound/hospital program as what the child normally would have received in the usual placement.

Other

If the child's unique educational needs cannot be met by an existing placement or combination of assignments, then an appropriate educational program must be devised. This may require the state and local education agencies responsible for the pupil's education to contract with private professionals, schools, or entities to develop a placement that can carry out the IEP in the least restrictive environment.

LEAST RESTRICTIVE NONACADEMIC SETTINGS

The regulations state that:

> In providing or arranging for the provision of nonacademic and extracurricular services and activities, . . . each public agency shall insure that each handicapped child participates with non-handicapped children in those services and activities to the maximum extent appropriate to the needs of that child. (§ 121a.553)

They add that those nonacademic and extracurricular services and activities may include meals, recess periods,

> counseling services, athletics, transportation, health services, recreational activities, special interest groups or clubs sponsored by the public agency, referrals to agencies which provide assistance to handicapped persons, and employment of students, including both employment by the public agency and assistance in making outside employment available. (§ 121a.306(b))

These provisions mean that handicapped children also must be provided with nonacademic services in as integrated a setting as possible. This is especially important for children whose educational needs necessitate their being solely with other handicapped pupils most of the day. To the maximum extent appropriate, even children in residential settings are to be provided opportunities for participation with other students.

REVIEW AND REEVALUATION

The regulations require that the public school system shall

> Initiate and conduct meetings to periodically review each child's individualized education program and if appropriate revise its provisions. A meeting must be held for this purpose at least once a year. (§ 121a.343(d))

They also require that the schools ensure:

> That an evaluation of the child, based on procedures which meet the requirements under § 121a.532 (Evaluation Procedures), is conducted every three years or more frequently if conditions warrant or if the child's parent or teacher requests an evaluation. (§ 121a.534(b))

A review of the IEP, yearly or more frequently, ensures that the educational services being provided continue to meet the child's needs. Periodic review by teachers and parents also is sound educational practice because they are the persons in daily contact with the student and are in the best position to determine the quality of change in performance. Therefore, their direct contact gives them the means of determining whether the program needs to be adjusted before the required annual review.

Periodic review of the IEP could occur at the schools' regular grading periods. The education agency is required to hold a meeting at least once each year to review and, if appropriate, revise each child's IEP, so those sessions could be on the anniversary date of the last IEP program session, but this is left to the agency's discretion.

Reevaluation, on the other hand, focuses on the child's total educational growth and development. The reevaluation process may occur any time the parents or education agency determine that more diagnostic information in any assessment area is necessary to meet the pupil's needs. The child's educational strengths and weaknesses must be reevaluated at least every three years.

The reevaluation provision is included in the law because it is sound special education practice. The learning process is full of kinetic energy, causing a series of changes and giving rise to new educational needs in the student. Reevaluation of needs is a mandatory part of the student's education so changes or progress can be measured and programs can be readjusted or redeveloped because needs may change before the end of the three-year period. Reevaluation can be conducted whenever parents or the school system determine it is needed.

The school system must assure that the reevaluation process:

- is conducted by qualified personnel
- uses tests and evaluation materials that focus on the specific educational needs of the student
- is multifaceted and uses a multidisciplinary approach
- is administered in the language that the child understands

The same regulations apply to the reevaluation process as involve the earlier evaluation. Parents may initiate the reevaluation and must be included in the proceedings.

The reevaluation may reinforce the fact that the student is in the appropriate place on the continuum of services or may show that the IEP needs to be redeveloped or readjusted and the child placed in the appropriate learning situation that meets the perceived needs.

CONCERNS ABOUT MISUSE

Many parents and professionals have raised concerns regarding the possible misuse of the principle of least restrictive environment in making placement decisions. For example, many persons are concerned that there may be an overzealous implementation of the LRE provision without regard to the needs of individual handicapped or nonhandicapped children.

The law includes safeguards to ensure protection against the possible misuse of the principle. The overriding rule is that each child's placement must be determined annually and be based on the IEP.

The school system must be prepared to demonstrate the appropriateness of its recommendations. Individuals with handicaps in the mildly, moderately, severely, profoundly, or multiply handicapped range might well require a resource room or self-contained classroom. However, the least restrictive settings should be determined on the basis of skill deficit rather than on labels or categories.

As for concerns about the harmful effect of placing handicapped children in regular classes, the analysis of the Section 504 regulations indicates:

> it should be stressed that, where a handicapped child is so disruptive in a regular classroom that the education of other students is significantly impaired, the needs of the handicapped child can-

not be met in that environment. Therefore, regular placement would not be appropriate to his or her needs. . . . (45 CFR 84, Analysis, Page 22687, *Federal Register* May 4, 1977)

When it is clear that because of the nature or severity of a handicap the child must be educated in a setting other than the regular class, it is appropriate to implement such a placement.

However, the LRE provision also is designed as a rights provision to protect against indiscriminate placement in a separate facility solely because the child is handicapped and not because special education is needed in that type of setting. Even with respect to severely handicapped children, it may be possible to meet the "regular education setting" goal by having a separate class or separate wing in a regular school building.

GUIDELINES ON PROPOSED PLACEMENT

The legal requirement is clear that a handicapped child's placement must be appropriate and in the least restrictive environment. The requirement consists of two basic elements: (1) that the educational placement be appropriate and (2) that it be one that can integrate the handicapped pupil with those who are not handicapped to the maximum extent possible and still provide the child with the IEP.

What are not clear are the procedures and criteria, standards, or guidelines by which a person, committee, or agency implements this requirement. Specific criteria that could have general application in placement decision making are neither widely known nor utilized in any standard fashion.

The fundamental question is: Given a handicapped child and a continuum of alternative placements, how can it be decided which placement is appropriate and in the least restrictive environment for this pupil? (Guidelines to help in reaching this decision are listed in Exhibit 9-1.)

Persons concerned with the answer must familiarize themselves first with the range of services available to handicapped children in the geographic area. Before recommending or accepting a particular placement, it is a good idea to visit the classroom and observe the program in action.

PLACEMENT MUST BE AT NO COST TO PARENTS

As discussed, the law requires that the public school system assure that each handicapped student's educational placement is able to provide the

Exhibit 9-1 Guidelines for Proposed Placement

FACTORS IN DETERMINING PLACEMENT IN THE LEAST RESTRICTIVE ENVIRON-MENT
Following are guidelines for use in considering a placement. They have been distilled from several actual cases concerning appropriate placement of handicapped children in the least restrictive environment. They are not hard-and-fast criteria but are questions to help users weigh the factors involved. Most of the points on this checklist can be used for either public or private placements.
FACTORS IN DETERMINING WHETHER PROPER PLACEMENT PROCEDURES ARE BEING FOLLOWED
• Was the placement decision made by a group of persons knowledgeable about the child, the meaning of the evaluation data, and the placement options?
• Does the proposed placement reflect a decision based upon information from a variety of sources, including aptitude and achievement tests, teacher recommendations, physical condition, social or cultural background, and adaptive behavior?
• Does the proposed placement appear to be related sequentially to the identification, evaluation, and programming decisions that preceded it?
• Was consideration given to any potential harmful effect on the child or on the quality of services needed?
FACTORS IN DETERMINING WHETHER THE PLACEMENT CAN CARRY OUT THE IEP
• Can the handicapped child's individualized education program be carried out effectively in the proposed placement?
• Is the proposed placement based on specific services needed rather than on the child's categorical label?
• Is the proposed placement flexible enough to allow for changes in the services required by the IEP?
• Are staff members in this proposed placement trained, willing, ready, and able to receive and properly provide for this child?
• Can this proposed placement, if it removes the child to a more restrictive setting, be justified by the fact that the intervention is needed for a relatively short time and the pupil then can be returned to a less restrictive environment?
• Could the child actually learn better in a setting significantly farther removed from the regular classroom than this proposed placement?

Exhibit 9-1 continued

	• Does the proposed placement match the child's level of functioning at the time of placement?
FACTORS IN DETERMINING WHETHER THE PLACEMENT AFFORDS THE MAXIMUM EDUCATIONAL AND SOCIAL INTEGRATION	
	• Does the proposed placement fully integrate the handicapped child with those who are not disabled?
	• Does the nature and/or severity of the handicap necessitate removal from the regular class if the proposed placement does not fully integrate the child?
	• Is this proposed placement compatible with the child's self-perception and the type of population with which the pupil identifies?
	• Are class activities in this placement designed to allow the child to participate without the handicap's dictating the nature of every activity or the extent of involvement in every activity?
	• Does the child's adjustment and preference in past and present placements indicate success in the proposed placement?
	• Does this placement seem to respect the child as a whole person in that it could fulfill the normal psychological/social, as well as educational, needs?
	• Does the proposal in effect overprotect the child and perhaps fail to provide a more realistic appraisal of how the pupil fits into the scheme of things?
	• Does the proposed placement reinforce the development of personality so that the child can become an integral part of the community?
	• Could the child actually be more restricted in a proposed setting that appears to be the least restrictive environment because the handicap would isolate the pupil from the others? For example, a moderately hearing impaired child might be able to function in a class of hearing students but may be more isolated by the communication deficit in that setting than in one for hearing impaired students.
	• Will this proposed educational placement adversely affect the child's familial interaction?
	• Will it contribute to the handicapped child's being lazy, aggressive, or a clown because such behavior will be tolerated?

Exhibit 9-1 continued

	● Is the placement decision that would remove the child from a setting with nonhandicapped peers based on a bona fide educational reason?
	● Are the other pupils, already in the setting, prepared for this child to enter their program?
	● Will the child's presence be so disruptive as to significantly impair the education of other students?
FACTORS IN DETERMINING WHETHER AN ALTERNATIVE PLACEMENT IS MORE SUITABLE	
	● Could the handicapped child have been placed in a regular class with the use of supplementary aids and services if the proposed placement removes the pupil from the regular class entirely?
	● Would the placement have been recommended if the school system had provided for supplementary services in conjunction with regular class placement of handicapped children?
	● Would the proposal have been recommended if the schools were to have had a more complete continuum of alternative placements available to meet the needs of handicapped children for special education and related services?
	● Were a number of alternative placements considered before selecting the proposed one?
	● Is the proposed placement the closest possible one to the child's home?
FACTORS IN DETERMINING WHETHER THE PARENTS ARE INVOLVED IN THE DECISION-MAKING PROCESS	
	● Were the child's parents involved in the decision-making process that resulted in this proposed placement?
	● Were they provided with a number of alternative placements before the selection of this one?
	● Is the proposed placement the one the parents prefer?
	● Does this proposed placement reflect the parental priorities for the handicapped child, e.g., greater academic achievement over socialization with nonhandicapped peers?
	● Does the proposal require the parents to become de facto employees of the school if the assignment is to work?

Exhibit 9-1 continued

FACTORS IN DETERMINING WHETHER FINANCIAL AND LOGISTICAL ISSUES PLAYED A CONTROLLING ROLE IN THE DECISION	
	• Has this proposed placement been recommended primarily because of the limitations inherent in the child's handicap or because of those in the school system's budget?
	• Even if the proposed placement theoretically could accommodate this child's learning needs, is it currently crowded or overcrowded?

required special education and related services "at public expense, under public supervision and direction, and without charge." (§ 121a.4(a))

Once a handicapped child has been evaluated and determined to need special education, the pupil must be provided a free appropriate public education. The right to a free education has been found by many courts to be grounded in the Constitution. In a case captioned *In Re Downey* (340 N.Y.S. 2d 687, 1973), the judge found that "to order a parent to contribute to the education of his handicapped child when free education is supplied to all other children would be a denial of the constitutional right of equal protection."

The right to a free education also is now firmly established by P.L. 94-142 and Section 504 of the Rehabilitation Act of 1973. Free education includes special education and related services at no cost to child or parents. The regulations state that:

> "At no cost" means that all specially designed instruction is provided without charge, but does not preclude incidental fees which are normally charged to non-handicapped students or their parents as a part of the regular education program. (§ 121a.14b(1))

The schools may charge fees to nonhandicapped persons or their parents or guardian (e.g., lunch money, standard transportation, etc.). The free education may consist either of free services or, if a school system places the child in a program it does not operate as its means of carrying out the legal requirements, of payment for the costs of the outside program. In other words, if a system places a handicapped student in a program other than its own, it remains financially responsible for the services provided. In no other case may a school system refuse to provide services to a handicapped child in its jurisdiction because of another person's or entity's failure to assume financial responsibility for all or part of the services.

Nevertheless, some school administrators have argued against having to assume the totality of the financial burden. The following arguments are put forth in support of not having to bear the full burden:

1. *The school system does not have sufficient funds.*

Nowhere in the law is there a provision that could be construed as relieving a school system of its responsibility to provide a free appropriate public education if sufficient funds are not available. Both P.L. 94-142 and Section 504 generally conform to the standards for the education of handicapped children set forth in such landmark cases as *Mills v. Board of Education of the District of Columbia* (348 F. Supp. 866, D.D.C. 1972). In *Mills*, the school board argued that it simply could not afford to appropriately educate all of its handicapped children. The court responded:

> Their failure to fulfill this clear duty to include and retain these children in the public school system, or otherwise provide them with publicly supported education, cannot be excused by the claim that there are insufficient funds. If sufficient funds are not available to finance all of the services and programs that are needed and desirable in the system then the available funds must be expended equitably in such a manner that no child is entirely excluded from a publicly supported education consistent with his needs and ability to benefit therefrom. The inadequacies of the District of Columbia Public School System, whether occasioned by insufficient funding or administrative inefficiency, certainly cannot be permitted to bear more heavily on the "exceptional" or handicapped child than on the normal child.

2. *The federal financial support is insufficient for the state and local education agencies to meet the requirements imposed by federal law and regulation.*

This argument posits that compliance with the regulations can be lessened because the federal financial support is less than adequate to help the localities meet those requirements. The legislative history of P.L. 94-142 clearly rejects this argument. The U.S. Senate Committee on Labor and Public Welfare in its Committee Report 94-168 states:

> The Committee rejects the argument that the Federal Government should only mandate services to handicapped children if, in fact, funds are appropriated in sufficient amounts to cover the

full cost of the education. The Committee recognizes the States' primary responsibility to uphold the Constitution of the United States and their own State constitutions and State laws as well as the Congress' own responsibility under the Fourteenth Amendment to assure equal protection of the law.

3. *The state and local education agencies need only pay their fixed per capita amount to cover the cost of educating a handicapped child.*

The argument suggests that the total contributions by state and local education agencies might not meet the cost of the education. In such a case, the difference or excess cost would have to be paid by the parents or the services would have to be withdrawn. Such a result clearly would be discriminatory on the basis of the child's handicap and therefore illegal under Section 504 and P.L. 94-142.

Funding for Residential Placement

The regulations provide that:

> If placement in a public or private residential program is necessary to provide special education and related services to a handicapped child, the program, including non-medical care and room and board, must be at no cost to the parents of the child. (§ 121a.302)

This requirement applies to placements made by public agencies for educational purposes and includes those in state-operated schools for the handicapped, such as a state school for the deaf or blind. However, when residential care is necessitated not by the handicap but by factors such as the student's home conditions, the school system is not required to pay the cost of room and board.

It is discriminatory, and therefore illegal, for an education agency to enter into a shared-burden financial arrangement with parents who can afford residential placement of their child. However, if parents independently place the handicapped child in a private school, they may not require the public school system to absorb the costs.

Funding for Placements by Parents

If a school system has made available a free appropriate public education in accordance with the law, and the parents choose to place the child in a private school, the public school system is not required to pay for the education there. Disagreements between parents and schools regarding whether the system has made such a program available or on other aspects of financial responsibility are proper subjects for a due process hearing.

Funding for Evaluation and Other Services in the IEP

Schools face various financial obligations when evaluation personnel and other staff members make recommendations for services to individual handicapped children. These can include a psychologist's recommending psychotherapy, an audiologist's proposing a hearing aid, a resource teacher's urging a service not available in the district, a social worker's supporting visual motor exercises provided by an optometrist, and a pupil personnel worker's referral of a student for a neurological evaluation.

There is a distinction between what occurs as part of the evaluation process and what results from an IEP meeting. The evaluation process is the first step in determining a child's need for special education and related services.

The law imposes only general or minimum standards for evaluation. Implementation procedures are left to each state and local educational agency. For example, such matters as who will chair the team, how recommendations will be made for further evaluation, what areas of evaluation are to be covered, and who does the evaluation, all are left to the discretion of the states.

If it is determined through this that a handicapped child needs to be evaluated in a particular area (e.g., to receive a neurological examination), that analysis must be carried out at no cost to the parents.

If a handicapped child already is in a special education program and a recommendation is made for further evaluation, this would be similar to the reevaluation requirement. However, the actual process for referring a child is left to each state and can vary from case to case. For example, a teacher might refer a child for reevaluation directly to the special education coordinator, or this determination could be made at an IEP meeting.

Once the evaluation is completed, an IEP meeting is conducted to develop a written statement for each handicapped child, including a statement of the specific general education and related services to be provided. The special education and related services listed in the IEP must be provided at no cost to the parents; financial responsibility is determined by state statute or regulation.

Since the parents participate in the development of the IEP for their child, they have the option of accepting or rejecting the proposed services. If they are not satisfied, they may protest and must be provided an opportunity for an impartial due process hearing.

The exact nature and extent of services to be provided to individual handicapped children are educational judgment questions that must be determined through the IEP process and, where necessary, through the due process procedures.

The law lists possible related services that a handicapped child might require to benefit from special education:

- specially trained teachers and teachers' aides
- speech and language therapy
- special materials and equipment
- counseling
- psychological services
- school health services
- medical services for diagnostic or evaluation purposes only
- physical therapy
- occupational therapy
- special transportation to school and activities within the school
- vocational education
- college placement services
- parent counseling and special homemaker services that teach natural and foster parents how to care for handicapped children

Certain kinds of services might be provided by persons with varying professional backgrounds and operational titles, depending upon requirements in individual states. For example, counseling services might be provided by social workers, psychologists, or guidance counselors; psychological testing might be done by qualified psychological examiners, psychometrists, or psychologists, depending upon state standards.

The list of related services is not exhaustive and may include other developmental, corrective, or supportive assistance (such as artistic and cultural programs, and art, music, and dance therapy) if they are required to help a handicapped child benefit from special education. This is the main criterion for funding by the school system. The state or local education agency has an obligation to provide a related service at no cost to the parents if the related service is necessary for the child to benefit from special education.

Funding for Psychiatric or Psychotherapy Services

The preceding general discussion on funding for related services is applicable to this section on psychiatric or psychotherapy services. Again, the state or local education agency is responsible for such services only if they can be shown to be necessary for the child to benefit from special education.

However, these particular related services carry an additional problem. Medical services are not reimbursable under the federal law as "related services" except for diagnostic purposes. Therefore, once diagnosed, a handicapped child is not entitled to receive medical services as part of a continuing program. If psychotherapy is interpreted in a state as a medical service (i.e., administered by a licensed physician), it would not be required. On the other hand, some states interpret psychotherapy as "counseling," which is included as a related service under the act. In such a case, the services would have to be provided at no cost to the parents if they were listed in the child's IEP.

Funding for Transportation

If, to carry out its obligations under the law, a school system places a handicapped child in a program it does not operate, it must ensure that adequate transportation to and from the activity is provided. The system may charge the parents an amount no greater than would be incurred if the child were placed in a program operated by the school.

As a general rule, if the public agency arranges for a parent to transport a handicapped child to a nonpublic school, that agreement brings with it the responsibility to reimburse reasonable transportation expenses. The costs to a distant facility (such as plane fare, rental car, meals, and lodging) should be covered in some fair and equitable manner according to normal state travel reimbursement policies.

Transportation must be provided as a "related service" if a child needs transportation in order to benefit from special education. The law does not set a reimbursement schedule for state and local education agencies to follow.

Generally, transportation issues would be a necessary part of an IEP developed with parent participation. Should the parents disagree with the IEP (i.e., the adequacy of the reimbursement allowance, source of the transportation, etc.), this dispute could be resolved through a due process hearing.

The law also does not set an absolute minimum number of trips home when a handicapped child is placed in a distant residential facility for educational purposes. Generally, however, transportation should be provided, at a minimum, at the beginning and end of the school term and for scheduled school holidays and recesses. Individual states' policies should at least permit case-by-case determination when a child needs more home contact. Again, disputes in this area could be resolved through the hearing process.

Of course, transportation fees normally charged to nondisabled students or their parents as part of the regular education program could be charged to parents of handicapped students without violating the law.

Funding beyond the Regular School Day

The law and its implementing regulations do not specify the length of a school day or the number of months of school. However, decisions on such factors must be a part of the development and implementation of an IEP. If parents disagree with the program the school district proposes (including any dispute over the number of months it will run), they have a right to a due process hearing. The law requires that the IEP describe the services to be made available, recognizing that they are not to be restricted to those available in the school district.

FUNDING HANDICAPPED EDUCATION PROGRAMS

Each state is obligated to provide a free appropriate public education for its handicapped children at no cost to their parents. The regulations add that:

> (a) Each State may use whatever State, local, Federal, and private sources of support are available in the State to meet the requirements of this part. For example, when it is necessary to place a handicapped child in a residential facility, a State could use joint agreements between the agencies involved for sharing the cost of that placement.
>
> (b) Nothing in this part relieves an insurer or similar third party from an otherwise valid obligation to provide or to pay for services provided to a handicapped child. (§ 121a.301)

P.L. 94-142 does not either impose or remove funding responsibilities from state education agencies, except insofar as they are responsible for seeing that all handicapped children in the state receive a free appropriate public education (FAPE). FAPE includes both special education and related services. To meet the FAPE obligation, the state may assign the burden of funding to any of its agencies or, through interagency agreements, to any combination of them in order to meet its own particular needs. The only restriction on this right in P.L. 94-142 is that the state may not use federal funds to replace ("supplant") state monies in financing a particular program or service. The act is designed to supplement, not replace, state efforts to provide FAPE.

The question of the responsibility of third party payers is self-explanatory.

Use of Insurance Proceeds to Fund Services

Both P.L. 94-142 and Section 504 prohibit a public agency from requiring parents, where they would incur a financial cost, to use insurance proceeds to pay for services that must be provided to a handicapped child under the "free appropriate public education" requirements of those statutes. The use of parents' insurance proceeds to pay for services in these circumstances must be voluntary on the part of the parents.

The U.S. Department of Education published an official interpretation in the *Federal Register* on December 30, 1980, which became effective March 30, 1981, pertaining to the use of insurance proceeds. The department interpreted the requirement that a free appropriate public education be provided "without charge" or "without cost" to mean that an agency may not compel parents to file an insurance claim when filing the claim would pose a realistic threat that the parents of handicapped children would suffer a financial loss not incurred by similarly situated parents of non-handicapped children. Financial losses include, but are not limited to, the following:

1. A decrease in available lifetime coverage or any other benefit under an insurance policy
2. An increase in premiums or the discontinuation of the policy or
3. An out-of-pocket expense such as the payment of a deductible amount incurred in filing a claim

Financial losses do not include incidental costs such as the time needed to file an insurance claim or the postage needed to mail the claim.

The statutory and regulatory provisions relating to a free appropriate public education guarantee freedom only from financial loss as described previously. Therefore, when the educational agency pays the financial costs related to filing a claim and no other cost (such as those listed above) is imposed, the parents suffer no financial loss. In addition, an agency may insist that parents file a claim when they would incur only minor incidental costs such as the time required to complete the form. The agency may require the parents to file a claim if it ensures that parents do not have to bear even a short-term financial loss. For example, if benefits begin only after a $50.00 deductible, the agency may insist that the parents file a claim if it pays for the services and the deductible in advance.

The responsibility to make available a free appropriate public education does not mean that a public educational agency must use only its own funds for that purpose. An agency may use whatever state, local, federal, and private sources of support are available to pay for required services. Moreover, nothing in the regulations relieves an insurer or similar third party from an otherwise valid obligation to provide or pay for services to a handicapped child.

PUBLIC SUPERVISION OF PLACEMENTS REQUIRED

The schools must ensure that each handicapped student's placement can provide the required special education and related services "at public expense, under public supervision and direction, and without charge" (emphasis added). (§ 121a.4(a)) This means that the state agency is responsible for making sure that all public and private entities it certifies to provide a free appropriate public education meet state standards.

Specifically, regulations provide that:

(a) The State educational agency is responsible for insuring:
(1) That the requirements of this part are carried out; and
(2) That each educational program for handicapped children administered within the State, including each program administered by any other public agency:
(i) Is under the general supervision of the persons responsible for educational programs for handicapped children in the State educational agency, and
(ii) Meets education standards of the State educational agency (including the requirements of this part).
(b) The State must comply with paragraph (a) of this section through State statute, State regulation, signed agreement between respective agency officials, or other documents. (§ 121a.600)

This provision reflects the desire of Congress for a central point of responsibility and accountability in the education of handicapped children in each state. With respect to state educational agency responsibility, the Senate Report on P.L. 94-142 says:

> This provision is included specifically to assure a single line of responsibility with regard to the education of handicapped children, and to assure that in the implementation of all provisions of this Act and in carrying out the right to education for handicapped children, the State educational agency shall be the responsible agency. . . .
>
> Without this requirement, there is an abdication of responsibility for the education of handicapped children. Presently, in many States, responsibility is divided, depending upon the age of the handicapped child, sources of funding, and type of services delivered. While the Committee understands that different agencies may, in fact, deliver services, the responsibility must remain in a central agency overseeing the education of handicapped children is squarely the responsibility of one agency. (Senate Report No. 94-168, p. 24 (1975).)

In meeting the requirements of this section, a number of acceptable options may be adopted, including the following:

1. Written agreements may be developed between various state entities concerning state educational agency standards and monitoring. These agreements would be binding on the local or regional counterparts of each state agency.
2. The governor's office may issue an administrative directive establishing the state educational agency's responsibility.
3. State law, regulation, or policy may designate the state educational agency as responsible for establishing standards for all educational programs for the handicapped and may include responsibility for monitoring.
4. State law may mandate that the state educational agency is responsible for all educational programs.

Problems in the Provision of Related Services

Since the enactment of P.L. 94-142, the federal government, states, and localities have wrestled with a number of problems in providing handicapped children with related services as required under the law. It is not likely that most of these problems will be resolved for many years to come.

The following is a shorthand list of the various areas and problems that have emerged:

1. *Costs/Resources*

   - Fiscal constraints of LEAs/SEAs limit the services they are prepared to offer.

   - Shortage of personnel, especially in urban and rural areas, makes the related services provision difficult even when there is agreement about a child's needs.

   - School officials cite instances where health agencies and insurers have refused to pay for or otherwise provide related services such as physical and occupational therapy since the enactment of P.L. 94-142. There has been a shifting of costs to educational agencies from other human services agencies.

2. *Nature of Services Required*

   - School authorities maintain that the traditional role of school to provide instructional services should be all that is expected; required provision of health-related or social services is an unwarranted expansion of their functions.

   - Some concerns have been raised about the expanded role of schools in providing health-related services listed in the act (e.g., OT, PT, counseling, and psychological services).

   - Some concerns have been raised about related services which are not mentioned in either the act or the regulations (e.g., clean intermittent catheterization (CIC) and psychotherapy).

3. *Responsibility for Provision of Services*

   - Related service providers in schools assert that administrative directives sometimes curtail their responsibility to recommend appropriate services which children require.

4. *Complaints from Parents*

   - Parents and advocates claim that schools ignore children's evaluation data and obvious needs for provision of necessary related services. Failure of school officials to indicate duration of related services on IEPs has been noted.

5. *Services Characterized as "Noneducational"*

- Issues have been raised regarding educational vs. noneducational needs relative to 1) the definition of "at no cost" as contained in the regulations and 2) a child's right to "special education" when the severity of the child's handicapping condition dictates the need for custodial care. Also, questions have been raised as to whether custodial care would be considered "special education" as it is defined in the statute and the regulations. Parents have filed complaints or initiated litigation, alleging that they are being charged for services that should be provided without cost because states have characterized such services and placements as "noneducational." Some states or districts have even required that parents relinquish custody or children be adjudged "neglected" before declaring the children to be eligible for services at no cost in residential facilities.

6. *Courts as An Enforcement Mechanism for Related Services*

- Courts have been viewed as an enforcement mechanism for related services through the use of due process procedures. Numerous related services cases have arisen. In the litigation areas (such as mental health services), judicial developments have expanded the term "education" to include self-sufficiency and broadened the concept of related services.

7. *Difficulties in Compliance*

- Monitoring visits by the federal government to states sometimes has resulted in findings that related services were not provided despite being listed on children's IEPs.

- Despite free appropriate public education requirements, monitoring by the federal government has revealed instances of parents being charged for related services that were noted on the IEP.

8. *Related Services, by Nature of Services*

- Concerns have been expressed as to how to determine when a particular related service is required by a child to assist him or her to benefit from special education.

- There is the issue of how it would be determined that a given related service is "required to assist . . ." as opposed to a general life need.

- Some states place a limitation on the nature of the service, i.e., only consultative services (rather than direct services) would be offered as physical therapy.

9. *Medical Services: Defined by Nature of Services and Qualifications of Service Provider*

- The statute limits "medical services" to those provided for diagnostic and evaluative purposes only, but does not define the term further. There is confusion and controversy as to whether services traditionally provided in health agencies or by health personnel fall outside of the "medical services" limitation. Questions have arisen in terms of the use of a licensed physician and the provision of related vs. medical services, particularly with regard to psychotherapy.

- School officials object to interpretations of P.L. 94-142 that would require them to provide "life support" services such as catheterization or psychotherapy. Court decisions indicate some services which schools characterize as medical treatment are "educationally related" when required for a child to receive a free appropriate education in the least restrictive environment (*North v. D.C. Board of Education*, 471 F. Supp. 136, 141 (1979); *Tatro v. State of Texas*, 625 F.2d. 557 (5th Cir. 1980); *Gary B. v. Cronin*, No. 79-C5383 (N.D. Ill. 1980); *In the Matter of the "A" Family*, 602 P.2d 157 (Mont. Sup. Ct. 1979).

Chapter 10

Special Requirements for Specific Handicaps

This book as a whole discusses the law as it applies generally to all handicapped children regardless of their individual impairment. This chapter addresses the factors that must be considered within each handicapping category. For each disability, the discussion begins with an examination of the definition of that handicap and who may be classified under it. The analysis then looks at the different identification, evaluation, programming, and placement factors for that condition that deserve particular attention.

It should be kept in mind that the handicapping categories provide nothing more than convenient classifications for counting children for government distribution of funds. They also establish guides for personnel development. The categories represent clusters of hundreds of behaviors.

However, the definitional categories (or labels) are not meant to serve as a basis for the development of IEPs. No child exhibits all possible behaviors inferred by the definition of any category. The heterogeneity of the children within the various classifications precludes the possibility of developing programs based solely upon a categorical approach. IEPs are required by law and sound educational practice to be based on the specific educational needs of each handicapped child individually, regardless of the handicapping label.

HEARING IMPAIRED

Definitional Factors

The regulations provide the following definitions under the category of hearing impaired:

> "Deaf" means a hearing impairment which is so severe that the child is impaired in processing linguistic information through hear-

ing, with or without amplification, which adversely affects educational performance (§ 121a.5(b)(1))

"Hard of hearing" means a hearing impairment, whether permanent or fluctuating, which adversely affects a child's educational performance but which is not included under the definition of "deaf" in this section. (§ 121a.5(b)(3))

Many states do not provide separate definitions for the deaf and the hard of hearing but use a single category—hearing impaired. Children in this category are those whose residual hearing is not sufficient to enable them to understand the spoken word and to develop language, thus causing deprivation in learning and communication.

Some state definitions focus on the hearing loss that prevents full awareness of environmental sounds and spoken language, thus limiting the child's normal language acquisition and learning achievement. Although individual state definitions may differ from those above, they still are consistent with the federal law if:

1. they are based on the child's ability to function in the educational setting
2. they include all children who meet the criteria of deaf or hard of hearing as those terms are defined in the regulations

Identification

Educators place great emphasis on the earliest possible identification of hearing impaired children because of the severe impact this disability has on language acquisition. Most states require auditory screenings as part of their identification program. Screening should be most frequent in the primary school grades. If one or more of the following characteristics are noted, the child should be referred for an evaluation:

1. Audiological: A screening indicates a possible hearing level between 10 and 20 decibels.
2. Behavioral: The child (a) has difficulty following verbal directions or fails to respond at all; (b) appears to lack full understanding of conversation, needs things repeated constantly, is confused in noisy situations, or is inattentive in group activities; (c) exhibits speech problems such as omitting plurals, e.g., "The boy has five flower;" (d) has difficulty discriminating between different sounds such as a siren and a horn or is unable to recognize where a sound is coming from.

3. Physical: The child's ear may not appear normal or there is a history of ear-related problems such as earaches, nasal obstruction, etc. There may be frequent dizziness or balance problems.
4. Speech and Language: The child's pitch, rhythm, or volume in speech may appear inappropriate compared to that of others in the peer group. The child may exhibit a number of difficulties in using spoken or written language, such as omitting sounds from words, omitting words or mixing up word order in sentences, and not using or understanding idioms, metaphors, etc.
5. School Achievement: The child's academic achievement is below the expectancy level, with the academic gap increasing with age. The ability to perform in reading, listening, speaking, etc., is impaired. Verbal skills generally are lower than nonverbal performance skills.

Evaluation

The appropriate evaluation of hearing impaired children is extremely important and difficult. Historically, such children as a class have been the unfortunate victims of discriminatory assessment. They frequently have been classified incorrectly as mentally retarded or emotionally disturbed. Therefore, it is particularly important to adhere closely to evaluation procedures that comport with sound educational practice, P.L. 94-142, the regulations, and Section 504 regarding nondiscriminatory evaluation.

In assessing a child suspected of being hearing impaired, an appropriate evaluation should include at a minimum the following:

Audiometric Assessment

This assessment should evaluate the child's air conduction, bone conduction, speech audiometry, and hearing aid value functioning. It should be noted that the regulations specifically require that:

> Each public agency shall insure that the hearing aids worn by deaf and hard of hearing children in school are functioning properly. (§ 121a.303)

The report of the House of Representatives on the 1978 appropriation bill includes the following on hearing aids:

> In its report on the 1976 appropriation bill the Committee expressed concern about the condition of hearing aids worn by children in public schools. A study done at the Committee's direction

by the Bureau of Education for the Handicapped reveals that up to one-third of the hearing aids are malfunctioning. Obviously, the Committee expects the Office of Education will ensure that hearing impaired school children are receiving adequate professional assessment, follow-up and services.

Otological Examination

The examination of the hearing disability should yield data regarding the etiology and prognosis of the impairment.

Educational Assessment

Once again it is important to emphasize that any test in this area of evaluation must be carefully selected and administered so the results are not skewed by the child's hearing impairment. In addition to standard academic achievement assessments, it is critical that the evaluation include expressive and receptive language competency, both oral and written, and speech intelligibility.

It also is critical that expert evaluators who are experienced in assessing such children conduct the analysis because the effects of hearing loss on communication and language abilities often are very subtle.

Programming

The primary qualifying factor for eligibility for special education is at least a mild degree of auditory impairment. Severity levels generally are classified according to the decibel hearing level in the better ear:

Mild: 20–40 in the speech range
Moderate: 40–65
Severe: 65–90
Profound: 90+

Programming should not be determined by the degree of hearing loss alone. The most important factor is the child's ability to use (receive and express) language, both spoken and written. Thus, the history of language instruction and enrichment are variables that directly affect the child's educational prognosis.

Another important factor involves abilities with other modes of communication such as cued speech, lip reading, finger spelling, the oral method, the manual method, the total method, sign language, or some combination of these. Other special considerations include the ability to discriminate auditorily, the nature of the hearing loss, the child's voice quality, etc. Finally, it is extremely important to consider the age of onset of the hearing loss, i.e., whether it occurred before or after acquiring language.

The IEP for the hearing impaired should include services and a program of instruction to help a child attain a broad array of communicative and language competencies.

Placement

Again, the most important factor in determining program and placement is the degree to which the hearing loss has affected the child's language development. The decision as to whether to mainstream such a child or provide a more segregated placement is not an easy one. Frequently, professionals for the hearing impaired have unusually strong differing feelings about methodology and philosophy of teaching these children. Traditionally, rather rigid educational camps have developed around the adherence to the oral and manual methods of teaching.

However, these hard-and-fast lines are becoming less influential as the concept of individualized program and placement gains greater acceptance. Moreover, the law requires adherence to the principle of placement in the least restrictive environment appropriate to meet the child's educational needs, which has succeeded in breaking down some of the rigidity. The placement decision should depend on the child's language development, intelligence, learning disabilities, emotional development, social maturity, communicative abilities, and academic skills.

To carry out the IEP of a hearing impaired child appropriately, the placement facility should have good sound properties, especially in rooms where the student spends the largest portions of the day. Resource rooms and self-contained classrooms for the hearing impaired should be treated acoustically, with consideration for carpeting, drapery, soundproofing of the walls, etc.

The facility also should be equipped with an amplification system, with individual earphones for each student that are adjustable to meet each one's needs. There also should be several developmental language kits and programs at the applicable levels. Audiovisual equipment should be available to the staff at all times.

MENTALLY RETARDED

Definitional Factors

The regulations provide the following definition for mentally retarded:

> "Mentally retarded" means significantly subaverage general intellectual functioning existing concurrently with deficits in

adaptive behavior and manifested during the developmental period, which adversely affects a child's educational performance. (§ 121a.5(4))

The definition is taken almost exactly from the one developed by the American Association on Mental Deficiency, with the exception of the added clause "which adversely affects a child's educational performance." The AAMD definition is used widely in special education and in state laws.

To be classified as mentally retarded under federal law, the child's condition must contain the following four components:

1. Subaverage General Intellectual Functioning: This is measured primarily by standard intelligence tests, resulting in an Intelligence Quotient (IQ), a standard deviance, or a fraction of normal development level.

2. Deficits in Adaptive Behavior: This is defined as the effectiveness of degree with which the individual meets the standards of personal independence and social responsibility expected of the same age and cultural group. These deficits in adaptive behavior must exist concurrently with subaverage general intellectual functioning for the individual to be classified as mentally retarded. If the adaptive behavior falls within the normal range, the child's problem may be an educational handicap resulting primarily from environmental deprivation, learning disabilities, language problems, hearing impairment, or cultural differences—not mental retardation. The problem may very well not lie with the student at all but rather with the testing that suggests a problem.

3. Developmental Period: The subaverage intellectual functioning and adaptive behavior deficits must have been manifested during the developmental period. The age limit for that period is not specified. However, the inclusion of this phrase generally is considered to mean that the law does not intend to classify children who become functionally retarded because of an injury after the developmental period.

4. Educational Performance: If the child can function in the regular classroom with services that are available in the context of the general education program, the law does not permit inclusion of the pupil in the mentally retarded category. Historically, a number of states defined mentally retarded in terms of whether or not the child could benefit from an educational program offered by the school system. Such a criterion is totally rejected under current federal law. That law guarantees to all handicapped children the right to a free appro-

priate public education regardless of the severity of their disability if their handicap adversely affects their educational performance.

Identification

There is considerable controversy in the field of special education as to the value of identifying, evaluating, and classifying mildly mentally retarded children at a very young age. This concern is related to the potential negative effects of labeling, particularly in the absence of follow-up services. It also is based on the difficulty in identifying mental retardation in the very young. Current techniques are not always reliable. However, educators generally agree that early identification of moderately and severely mentally retarded is very important, especially where the mental dysfunction is accompanied by sensory or orthopedic impairment.

With appropriate intervention at early ages, preferably preschool, the severity of such conditions can be less incapacitating. The following identification characteristics should suggest referral for further evaluation:

1. Behavioral: The child appears to have difficulty following directions, comprehending social situations, acting appropriately in social contacts, comprehending tasks. The pupil may exhibit a fear of failure and become inappropriately aggressive or highly excitable.
2. Physical: The child shows certain physical anomalies usually associated with mental retardation, a delayed physical development, or a history of severe illness or injury.
3. Speech and Language: The child appears to have a limited vocabulary, delayed speech and language, or articulation disorders.
4. School Achievement: The child achieves at less than 75 percent of expectancy of the peer group and appears to have difficulty with abstract processes and written communication.

Evaluation

The use of standardized intelligence tests with minority children as a measure of intellectual functioning is one of the main problems in the realm of education and law. It has been established clearly that children of black and other minority groups are disproportionately represented in classes for the mentally retarded. Again, the law regarding nondiscriminatory evaluation, as well as sound evaluation practices, must be followed closely to ensure accurate results.

In general, testing and evaluation materials and procedures are to be selected and administered so as not to be racially or culturally discrimi-

natory (§ 121a.530) Another important safeguard is that no single procedure may be used as the sole criterion for determining an appropriate
educational program for a child. (§ 121a.532(e)) Only children who have
deficits in both intellectual function and adaptive behavior are to be considered retarded. Both areas must be given equal weight in making a
diagnosis.

As noted above, intellectual functioning is determined by one or more
of the standardized tests developed for this purpose. To be considered
mentally retarded, a child must score two or more standard deviations from
the mean on such tests. In addition, the child must show deficits in adaptive
behavior that will vary for different age groups. Adaptive behavior is not
easily tested or measured. There is a need in the field of special education
for objective measures and standardized tests of deficits in adaptive behavior for the person to be considered mentally retarded.

Programming

The four criteria for eligibility for special education are discussed above
in the section on definitional factors. The severity levels commonly used
for classification purposes within the mentally retarded category are as
follows:

Mild: IQ 52–67
Moderate: IQ 36–51
Severe: IQ 20–35
Profound: IQ below 20

The types of programming possible vary widely, depending on the individual child. Exhibit 10-1 suggests some of the goals and objectives that
generally are considered when developing an IEP for a mentally retarded
child at different levels. The overall goal of the program for all such pupils
is to develop the ability to integrate into their environment and to achieve
their maximum intellectual potential.

Placement

Because of the widely varying abilities and needs among children classified as mentally retarded, the requirement for a range or continuum of
placement alternatives takes on special importance. The placement should
be part of a regular public school with possible exception for the most
profoundly mentally retarded. Another important factor is the ease of

Exhibit 10-1 Developmental Characteristics of Mentally Retarded Persons

Degree of Mental Retardation	Preschool Age 0–5 Maturation and Development	School Age 6–20 Training and Education	Adult and Over Social and Vocational Adequacy
Mild	Can develop social and communication skills; minimal retardation in sensorimotor areas; often not distinguished from normal until later age.	Can learn academic skills up to approximately sixth grade level by late teens. Can be guided toward social conformity. "Educable."	Can usually achieve social and vocational skills adequate to minimum self-support but may need guidance and assistance when under unusual social or economic stress.
Moderate	Can talk or learn to communicate; poor social awareness; fair motor development; profits from training in self-help; can be managed with moderate supervision.	Can profit from training in social and occupational skills; unlikely to progress beyond second grade level in academic subjects; may learn to travel alone in familiar places.	May achieve self-maintenance in unskilled or semiskilled work under sheltered conditions; needs supervision and guidance when under mild social or economic stress.
Severe	Poor motor development; speech minimal; generally unable to profit from training in self-help; little or no communication skills.	Can talk or learn to communicate; can be trained in elemental health habits; profits from systematic habit training.	May contribute partially to self-maintenance under complete supervision; can develop self-protection skills to minimal useful level in controlled environment.
Profound	Gross retardation; minimal capacity for functioning in sensorimotor areas; needs nursing care.	Some motor development; may respond to minimal or limited training in self-help.	Some motor and speech development; may achieve very limited self-care; needs nursing care.

Source: Office of Handicapped Individuals, 1975.

access to vocational training facilities and equipment. This becomes especially important above the elementary level.

The review and reevaluation also carry special importance. A mentally retarded child's adaptive behavior and intellectual function will develop regularly, even though it may be subaverage with respect to normal growth. Therefore, the placement can be considered appropriate only in terms of present needs and characteristics and may need to be changed as the child grows older. It should be flexible to allow for such changes and for the pupil's increased integration in the general education program.

MULTIHANDICAPPED AND DEAF-BLIND

Definitional Factors

The regulations provide the following definitions for the multihandicapped:

> "Multihandicapped" means concomitant impairments (such as mentally retarded-blind, mentally retarded-orthopedically impaired, etc.), the combination of which causes such severe educational problems that they cannot be accommodated in special education programs solely for one of the impairments. The term does not include deaf-blind children (§ 121a.5(b)(5)).

To be classified as multihandicapped, a child must meet three main factors for eligibility under this definition. The first factor is concomitant impairments. The definition does not list any specific single impairment or combination that it covers. It appears that any one or a combination of dysfunctions may be included. The second factor is that the combination must cause such severe educational problems that they cannot be accommodated in special education programs solely for a single impairment. The third factor is exclusionary in that the term multihandicapped does not include deaf-blind children.

The regulations provide the following definition of deaf-blind:

> "Deaf-blind" means concomitant hearing and visual impairments, the combination of which causes such severe communication and other developmental and educational problems that they cannot be accommodated in special education programs solely for deaf or blind children (§ 121a.5(b)(2)).

Two major definitional factors are used to determine child eligibility in this category. The first is concomitant hearing and visual impairments. The second is that the combination of impairments is such that the child cannot be accommodated in a special education program solely for deaf or blind children. Most states appear to include the category of deaf-blind under the broader category of multihandicapped.

Identification

The identification program of state and local education agencies should include a component that brings together information about handicapped children from other public entities such as hospitals, family health clinics, and social service groups. Children who fall within the classifications of multihandicapped and deaf-blind are likely to be known to such noneducation agencies before they reach school age. A referral for a child suspected of being multihandicapped or deaf-blind is indicated if there is an acute combination of characteristics that suggests the presence of two or more handicapping conditions.

Evaluation

The evaluation of a child referred as possibly being multihandicapped or deaf-blind should be conducted in accordance with the procedures and requirements for each suspected handicap.

Program and Placement

Obviously, the requirement of individually designed programming and placements is particularly important with this population because of the complexities and variety of combinations possible. In programming, it is important to note whether one handicap is somewhat secondary to the other or whether the combination of impairments requires a totally unique program design. Many educators emphasize that the adverse effect on a multihandicapped student's educational performance is greater than the sum of the individual impairments. A general goal for these children is to develop the ability to cope with one handicap to facilitate placement in a program for a single impairment.

The population is a low incidence group and as such has all the attendant problems in obtaining specialized services and placements. Group programming may not even be possible because of the often unique learning needs. Implementation of the principle of least restrictive environment is very difficult because there are distinct educational advantages to clustering these children together at some centralized placement. Most of these children require intensive services that cannot be delivered easily if they are dispersed throughout the school district.

ORTHOPEDICALLY AND OTHER HEALTH IMPAIRED

Definitional Factors

The regulations define orthopedically impaired and other health impaired as follows:

> "Orthopedically impaired" means a severe orthopedic impairment which adversely affects a child's educational performance. The term includes impairments caused by congenital anomaly (e.g., clubfoot, absence of some member, etc.), impairments caused by disease (e.g., poliomyelitis, bone tuberculosis, etc.) and impairments from other causes (e.g., cerebral palsy, amputations, and fractures or burns which cause contractures). (§ 121a.5(b)(6))

> "Other health impaired" means limited strength, vitality or alertness, due to chronic or acute health problems such as a heart condition, tuberculosis, rheumatic fever, nephritis, asthma, sickle cell anemia, hemophilia, epilepsy, lead poisoning, leukemia, or diabetes, which adversely affects a child's educational performance (§ 121a.5(b)(7)).*

Most states do not use two separate definitions for orthopedically impaired and other health impaired but prefer a single category that applies to all physically handicapped children. Such a category generally includes those whose bodily functions are impaired because of congenital or acquired defects in physical structure or function or who have chronic illnesses that prevent them from functioning in the regular classroom.

The most important criterion in this definition is that the handicapping condition must adversely affect the child's educational performance. To be classified as handicapped, the impairment must necessitate special education and related services. Some children who are physically handicapped may not need a special education program. Their problem may simply be one of access to a regular education program, e.g., a child in a wheelchair.

---

* In January 1981, the U.S. Department of Education amended § 121a.5 "handicapped children" definitions to transfer the definition of autism from "seriously emotionally disturbed" to "other health impaired."

Federal law does not specifically address pregnancy as to whether or not it is included under these definitions. Individual states treat this issue differently, some including pregnant students in this category, others not.

Identification

Early identification in this category is critical because it can result in prompt treatment and increased possibility of limiting the effect of the condition on the child's body and ability to learn. The family and medical services are the primary resources for early identification of physically handicapped children. This fact again emphasizes the importance of the educational entity's including community survey techniques and inter-agency coordination activities as part of the overall identification program.

However, in a preschool or school program, the teacher should consider referring a child for an evaluation if one or more of the following characteristics are observed repeatedly:

- gagging or inability to swallow
- limping, a history of falling easily, unsteady gait, tremors, spasticity of the extremities, convulsions, or seizures
- temporary or chronic lack of strength, vitality, or alertness

Evaluation

Assessment procedures cannot be developed specifically for physically handicapped children because of the heterogeneity of this population. Generally, the same evaluative instruments and techniques should be used with the physically handicapped as with other children. Of course, some adjustments would be necessary, taking into account such factors as the kind of physical or neurologic impairment, its degree, its manifestations, the age of the child, the objectives of the particular assessment, the facilities, etc.

The length of the testing session is one example of such an adjustment. Certain modifications, such as shortening each session or alternating different types of assessments, might be required if the child tires easily. Assessment instruments that largely reflect or require manipulative skills may not be appropriate.

Obviously, the medical assessment is of primary importance. It is critical that the doctor and other medical personnel report their findings and recommendation as to the child's physical capabilities and limitations in terms that are educationally useful. For example, a diagnosis of hemophilia, without more information, tells the educator and parent little about what the child can do in terms of education or possible effects of the impairment on the ability to attend school.

Programming and Placement

Educators emphasize making every attempt to alter the physical environment or classroom setting to accommodate physically handicapped children rather than resorting to special education programs. As noted, the law emphasizes placing children in the least restrictive educational environments. It also requires that special classes, separate schooling, or other removal of impaired children from the regular school environment occur only when the nature or severity of the handicap is such that education in regular classes, even with the use of supplementary aids and services, cannot be achieved satisfactorily. Even if it is necessary to remove the child from the regular classroom for part of the day, the IEP should reflect the extent to which the pupil can be integrated with nonhandicapped peers during the rest of the day.

In developing the physically impaired child's program it is important to review such factors as the severity and type of handicap, the assistance and prostheses that may be necessary to permit mobility, and the general ability to function in various programs with supportive or adaptive assistance. Placements for the physically impaired may require special tables and chairs designed for specific handicapping conditions. It also may be necessary to have special typewriters or other adaptive instructional equipment and materials to promote the fullest participation of these children.

SERIOUSLY EMOTIONALLY DISTURBED

Definitional Factors

The regulations define seriously emotionally disturbed as follows:

> (i) The term means a condition exhibiting one or more of the following characteristics over a long period of time and to a marked degree, which adversely affects educational performance:
> (A) An inability to learn which cannot be explained by intellectual, sensory, or health factors;
> (B) An inability to build or maintain satisfactory interpersonal relationships with peers and teachers;
> (C) Inappropriate types of behavior or feelings under normal circumstances;

(D) A general pervasive mood of unhappiness or depression; or
(E) A tendency to develop physical symptoms or fears associated
with personal or school problems.
(ii) The term includes children who are schizophrenic or autistic.*
The term does not include children who are socially maladjusted,
unless it is determined that they are seriously emotionally disturbed. (§ 121a.5(b)(8))

This definition essentially requires that a child's condition meet three
criteria in order to be classified as seriously emotionally disturbed.

The first criterion is that the child's condition must exhibit one or more
of the characteristics listed in the body of the definition over a long period
of time and to a marked degree. Behaviors related to passing adjustment
problems or temporary home crises usually would not be sufficient to
require special education under this definition.

The second criterion is that this condition must adversely affect educational performance. The performance referred to is that of the child with
a serious emotional disturbance. If a pupil is hindering the others or generally disrupts the learning atmosphere, the child is not necessarily emotionally disturbed under the federal definition.

The third criterion is exclusionary: the term "seriously emotionally disturbed" does not include children who are socially maladjusted unless it
is determined that they are seriously emotionally disturbed.

Educators have long struggled with developing a definition that describes
emotionally disturbed children adequately. The federal definition is but
one attempt at that task. Some states' definitions differ from the federal
in terms of who they include and exclude. The major difficulties in developing such a definition are:

- How can the level of severity of the emotional problem be described
  that will make a child eligible?

- How can a list of characteristics be developed that reflects emotional
  disturbance *and* that does not apply to all chidren at some times and
  to some degree?

- How can emotional disturbance be differentiated from other conditions such as learning disability or social maladjustment?

---

* In January 1981, the U.S. Department of Education amended § 121a.5 "handicapped
children" definitions to transfer the definition of autism from "seriously emotionally disturbed" to "other health impaired."

Identification and Evaluation

The federal description of seriously emotionally disturbed is more a list of referral characteristics than a true definition. A child who exhibits one or more of the characteristics to a marked degree and over a long period clearly should be identified as possibly handicapped. Disturbed children are identified most often as such by teachers and parents because they have the opportunity to observe the pupils in a variety of settings and situations.

In addition to the basic findings in a multifaceted assessment, a psychiatric or clinical psychological evaluation should be conducted on children suspected of being emotionally disturbed. Formal and informal behavioral measures intended to gather a precise data based description of the conduct patterns of concern also are helpful. Other tests such as an informal self-concept checklist, the Vineland Social Maturity Scale, The Human Figure Drawing-Koppitz Scoring, and the California Test of Personality can contribute useful information to the overall evaluation. The task of assessing personality, adjustment, anxiety, and psychological makeup is extremely difficult because a child's internal states cannot be measured directly. It also is difficult to define or develop a clear model of what normality is.

With all the difficulty in defining and evaluating children suspected of being emotionally disturbed, it is no wonder that establishing eligibility criteria for this classification also is a problem. However, some salient points are worth noting.

The fact that a behavior is disturbing does not necessarily mean that a child is disturbed. A disturbed child must demonstrate some internal conflict, disorganization, turmoil—a disturbance. The behavior problem must have its roots within the child rather than in the family or environment. If the problem is inherent in the child, it will manifest itself not only in the classroom but also in other spheres of the pupil's life.

Generally, the emotionally disturbed child feels anxiety, guilt, or intense concern over some problem that has been internalized. There may be trouble relating to others because of discomfort within the child. One with serious emotional disturbance is unable to respond appropriately to the environment. Such children frequently manifest difficulty in their thought processes, show reality contact difficulties, and are likely to be depressed and to internalize anger. The anger is self-directed and robs the pupil of energy to achieve.

The seriously emotionally disturbed child is likely to withdraw or lash out in a number of spheres of life. The behavior of such a child is not a matter of choice but of necessity because the disturbance controls the pupil, rather than the other way around.

It is important to remember that the law excludes socially maladjusted children from the classification of seriously emotionally disturbed. Such behavior is indeed disturbing but it is likely to be rooted in the child's environment. The behavior might respond to a different code of conduct or set of mores. Those beliefs might not be acceptable in the school but that does not necessarily mean that the child is disturbed and struggling with great inner conflict.

There is a danger inherent in the process of identifying as emotionally disturbed those children who choose to behave somewhat differently from their peers. Is the child a person whose behavioral deviation is caused by emotional problems? Or is the behavior simply different? Behavior that is strange, inadequately socialized, unconventional, immature, unwise, or deviant cannot in and of itself be regarded as a sign of an emotional disturbance. If it were, every juvenile delinquent, runaway, willful, incorrigible, truant, or other child brought before the juvenile courts would be labeled as seriously emotionally disturbed.

The juvenile courts throughout the nation take jurisdiction over children every day who are beyond the control of their parents, are law violators, or are incorrigible for one reason or another. They may indeed have problems in conforming to the rules of school, family, or society but that does not mean that they are necessarily seriously emotionally disturbed. The law clearly states that such socially maladjusted children are not eligible for special education and related services under the classification of seriously emotionally disturbed.

Program and Placement

As with the other handicapped populations, there is a broad range of severity within the category of seriously emotionally disturbed. Such a child's IEP often is more a function of educational setting and of teacher/student ratio than it is of curriculum. It is related more to the child's behavior than to academic achievement. Therefore, the general goals are to establish acceptable behavior to maximize academic achievement and adaptation to the educational environment.

The individualized education program may require counseling as a related service. The highly charged issue of psychiatric or psychological therapy as a related service is discussed in Chapter 9 on placement.

The placement decisions are important in carrying out IEPs for the seriously emotionally disturbed, particularly in developing appropriate educational intervention strategies. The placement facility should consider such factors as the need for private bathrooms, an isolation or time-out area, and a telephone for easy access to emergency assistance.

SPECIFIC LEARNING DISABILITY

Definitional Factors

The regulations define the term as follows:

> "Specific learning disability" means a disorder in one or more of the basic psychological processes involved in understanding or in using language, spoken or written, which may manifest itself in an imperfect ability to listen, think, speak, read, write, spell, or to do mathematical calculations. The term includes such conditions as perceptual handicaps, brain injury, minimal brain dysfunction, dyslexia, and developmental aphasia. The term does not include children who have learning problems which are primarily the result of visual, hearing, or motor handicaps, of mental retardation, of emotional disturbance, or of environmental, cultural, or economic disadvantage. (§ 121a.5(b)(9))

This definitional category of a handicapping condition is different from the others. It is perhaps the most difficult to define. It also is difficult to determine which students are eligible for its classification. Section 5 (b) of P.L. 94-142 required the Office of Education to develop procedures for evaluating children identified as possibly having a specific learning disability (SLD). These special SLD regulations were not a part of the original P.L. 94-142 regulations that have been referred to throughout this book. These were published in the *Federal Register* on December 29, 1977, and were incorporated into the original P.L. 94-142 regulations. Therefore, any discussion regarding what the law requires in terms of learning disabilities must be based on both the P.L. 94-142 regulations and the later SLD regulations.

Three basic factors must be considered for a child to be classified as having an SLD under federal law. The first is the process factor. It must be established that the child has a process disorder in expressive, receptive, or integrative functions that results in a severe discrepancy between ability and achievement.

The second is the academic factor. It must be established that there is a severe achievement problem in one or more of seven areas—the ability to listen, think, speak, read, write, spell, or do mathematical calculations.

The third is the exclusion factor. It must be established that the discrepancy between the child's ability and achievement is *not* the result of other known handicapping conditions or of environmental, cultural, or economic disadvantages. The original P.L. 94-142 regulations list these other handicapping conditions in the definition of specific learning disability. The new SLD regulations inserted emotional disturbance as one of the handicapping conditions in the exclusion factor.

Because of the concerns with the definition of specific learning disability, Congress in P.L. 94-142 limited the number of children eligible to be counted as learning disabled for the purpose of generating the funding entitlement. The 1977 revision removed that cap. However, some of the reviewers of the proposed SLD revisions suggested that (1) since specific learning disabilities were difficult to define based on current knowledge and (2) because of the need for extensive research before a universally accepted definition could be created, the requirement limiting the number of children eligible to be counted should be extended. They proposed retaining the cap on counting these children for allocation purposes until it was possible to differentiate all of the specific learning disabilities.

The cap was removed when the SLD regulations became effective. Parents and professionals alike generally agree that the labels used by different theorists overlap. The labels (e.g., minimal brain dysfunction) also represent assumptions about conditions that cannot, with current technology, be successfully determined or discretely categorized. Other categories of handicapping conditions have no cap. Since more than 2 percent of the school age population in some states may in fact be handicapped by SLDs, such a limitation as the 2 percent cap would be inequitable. In addition, limiting the number of children eligible to be counted as learning disabled does not help provide a basis for the determination of whether a child has a specific learning disability or resolve questions of appropriate diagnosis or placement in the event of due process hearings. For all of these reasons, the Bureau for Education of the Handicapped decided that it was better to lift, rather than maintain, the cap on the number of children who could be counted as learning disabled.

Identification

This handicapping condition is the one most defined in educationally oriented terms. The disability manifests itself in terms of an imperfect ability to perform academic tasks. Consequently, most children are not identified as possibly having such a problem until they enter school. The major source of identification of suspected SLD pupils is referrals by the classroom teacher and from parents who observe their child's performance on academic tasks.

Referral should occur if persistent behavioral characteristics are observed, such as when a child:

- demands attention to an inappropriate degree, frequently speaks out of turn, and cannot control responses

- seems disorganized in appearance and use of materials

- has a very short attention span and has difficulty completing work and following oral instructions

- seems inattentive, has a poor sense of time, has difficulty remembering what is heard and seen

A suspected SLD child is likely to exhibit a number of physical characteristics as well. For example, general coordination is likely to be poor such as difficulty with tasks involving balance or requiring differentiation between right and left.

In speech and language, the suspected SLD child may fail to grasp simple word meanings or be unable to comprehend a word in connected speech even if the pupil can understand it in isolation. The child may be unable to relate a story or experience in a proper sequence. The ability to organize and express ideas is impaired. Verbal expression may be echolalic or may be choppy because of incomplete sentences and inappropriate syntax.

In the academic area, a suspected SLD child is likely to have scores that indicate inconsistence and great variability between expectancy and performance. The pupil may write words using mirror writing, reversals, inversions, and rotations of letters and numerals. The child may be at grade level in one subject and significantly below that in another subject or have a discrepancy within one academic area. For example, the child may have good comprehension skills when material is read aloud but perform significantly lower in silent reading.

Evaluation

Eligibility for an SLD program is determined by a review of the assessment data, which must indicate something more than just "problems in school." There must be an impairment in the basic psychological processes even though the child is of average or above average intelligence and performance in most areas. An SLD child will exhibit normal intelligence with severe discrepancies between verbal and performance scores and extreme scatters of scores on subtracts.

The P.L. 94-142 regulations, as noted earlier, set out basic procedures that public agencies are required to use in evaluating all handicapped children, including, for example, the following: (1) that tests and other evaluation materials are provided and administered in the child's native language or other mode of communication (§ 121a.532(a)(1)); (2) that no single procedure is used as the sole criterion for determining an appropriate educational program (§ 121a.532(d)); and (3) that the evaluation is made by a multidisciplinary team, including at least one teacher or other specialist with knowledge in the area of suspected disability (§121a.532(e)).

The SLD regulations include additional procedures that apply only to the evaluation of children suspected of having a specific learning disability. Following is a discussion of these additional requirements.

First, the multidisciplinary team must include the child's regular teacher. If the pupil lacks one, a person qualified to teach a youngster of that age should be assigned to the team. The team also must include a person qualified to conduct individual diagnostic examinations. Within the SLD population are children who primarily display language development problems. For this population, qualified specialists in speech and language disorders represent an appropriate professional resource.

Specifically, the regulations state:

Additional Team Members

In evaluating a child suspected of having a specific learning disability, in addition to the requirements of § 121a.532, each public agency shall include on the multidisciplinary evaluation team:

(a)(1) The child's regular teacher; or

(2) If the child does not have a regular teacher, a regular classroom teacher qualified to teach a child of his or her age; or

(3) For a child of less than school age, an individual qualified by the State educational agency to teach a child of his or her age; and

(b) At least one person qualified to conduct individual diagnostic examinations of children, such as a school psychologist, speech-language pathologist, or remedial reading teacher. (§ 121a.540)

Second, criteria are established for use by the team in determining the existence of a specific learning disability. This determination is based on whether a child (1) does not achieve commensurate with age and ability when provided with appropriate educational experiences, and (2) has a severe discrepancy between achievement and intellectual ability in one or more of seven areas relating to communication skills and mathematical abilities. The regulations state:

Criteria for determining the existence of a specific learning disability.

(a) A team may determine that a child has a specific learning disability if:

(1) The child does not àchieve commensurate with his or her age and ability levels in one or more of the areas listed in paragraph (a)(2) of this section, when provided with learning experiences appropriate for the child's age and ability levels; and

(2) The team finds that a child has a severe discrepancy between achievement and intellectual ability in one or more of the following areas:

(i) Oral expression;

(ii) Listening comprehension;

(iii) Written expression;

(iv) Basic reading skill;

(v) Reading comprehension;

(vi) Mathematics calculation; or

(vii) Mathematics reasoning.

(b) The team may not identify a child as having a specific learning disability if the severe discrepancy between ability and achievement is primarily the result of:

(1) A visual, hearing, or motor handicap;

(2) Mental retardation;

(3) Emotional disturbance;

(4) Environmental, cultural, or economic disadvantage. (§ 121a.541)

Third, these concepts are to be interpreted on a case-by-case basis by the qualified evaluation team members.

Fourth, the SLD regulations include procedures for observing the child's performance and for preparing a written report of the results of the evaluation.

The regulations on observing the performance state:

Observation

(a) At least one team member other than the child's regular teacher shall observe the child's academic performance in the regular classroom setting.

(b) In the case of a child of less than school age or out of school, a team member shall observe the child in an environment appropriate for a child of that age. (§ 121a.542)

The regulations on preparation of a written report state:

Written Report

(a) The team shall prepare a written report of the results of the evaluation.

(b) The report must include a statement of:

(1) Whether the child has a specific learning disability;

(2) The basis for making the determination;

(3) The relevant behavior noted during the observation of the child;

(4) The relationship of that behavior to the child's academic functioning;

(5) The educationally relevant medical findings, if any;

(6) Whether there is a severe discrepancy between achievement and ability which is not correctable without special education and related services; and

(7) The determination of the team concerning the effects of environmental, cultural, or economic disadvantage.

(c) Each team member shall certify in writing whether the report reflects his or her conclusion. If it does not reflect his or her conclusion, the team member must submit a separate statement presenting his or her conclusions. (§ 121a.543)

In establishing the existence of a severe discrepancy, the team must assess the significance of any difference between expected and actual achievement. A mathematical formula alone should not be used to determine the significance because a discrepancy score by itself should not be the sole criterion for SLD classification. For example, a two-year difference between achievement and intellectual ability at age 7 has a different meaning from that of a two-year difference at age 16. If the assessment team determines that a child has a specific learning disability, even though the application of the formula indicates that there is not a severe discrepancy between expected achievement and actual achievement, the team judgment must prevail. Generally educators recognize four major problems in using a formula to determine the existence of an SLD:

1. the inappropriateness of attempting to reduce the behavior of children to numbers
2. the psychometric and statistical inadequacy of the procedure
3. the fear that use of the formula might easily lend itself to inappropriate use to the detriment of handicapped children
4. the inappropriateness of using a single formula for children of all ages, particularly preschoolers

If a state elects to use a formula as a guide, in instances where its application would indicate there is no severe discrepancy but the team judges that a child is learning disabled, it is permissible for the state to require that the evaluators explain why they made that decision. Clearly, the intent of the regulations is to ensure that each child is measured against an individual expected performance and not against some arbitrary general standard. This procedure places great responsibility on the assessment team.

Program and Placement

In the case of a child with learning disabilities, the evaluation is perhaps the most critical step in the overall special education decision-making process. When the child has been properly assessed in accordance with the law, an appropriate intervention program can be designed based on the severity of learning process deficits, general intelligence, actual achievement in comparison with expectancy, and the percentage of the day that the pupil can succeed in the regular program.

A particularly important component of any SLD child's IEP is a continuing evaluation designed to refine the understanding of the disability and pinpoint the most effective intervention strategies. This process is crucial in the goal of alleviating the student's learning disability and achieving successful integration into all of the regular education program.

Considerations in the selection of an appropriate placement for an SLD child center on equipment and the least restrictive educational environment in which to deliver the IEP. The placement should be equipped with the necessary multisensory materials based on developmental levels and readiness for learning. It should provide group, team, and individual stations for conducive learning activities for specific disabilities. The initial placement decision should include careful consideration of all alternatives and options for delivering the IEP and maximizing the child's integration with nonhandicapped peers. This consideration should be coordinated closely with the continuing evaluation of the IEP.

Problems with the SLD Regulations

The SLD regulations provide specific criteria for determining the existence of a learning disability. Since the enactment of these regulations a number of problems have emerged which are unlikely to be resolved for many years. The following is a list of the major problems which have arisen:

- There is no universally accepted definition of specific learning disabilities among special education administrators, parents, advocates, and educators.

- The federal evaluation criteria are flexible to the extent that non-learning disabled children are perhaps being inappropriately labeled as learning disabled in order to make those nonlearning disabled students eligible for educational assistance not available in the regular program.

- There have been many due process hearings initiated by parents over eligibility for placement in learning disabilities programs.

- The number of children counted as learning disabled has steadily increased since the implementation of the regulations.

- The General Accounting Office issued a report in 1981 which expressed concern about the classification of nonhandicapped children as learning disabled. The apparent overclassification of learning disabled children appears to be widespread.

- Parents have complained that federal learning disability procedures are not being followed by SEAs and LEAs.

- Administrators have complained that the assessment procedures are too time consuming and thus costly.

- Complaints have been raised concerning the lack of specificity in the learning disability definition, criteria, and evaluation procedures.

SPEECH IMPAIRED

Definitional Factors

The regulations define this term as follows:

> "Speech impaired" means a communication disorder, such as stuttering, impaired articulation, a language impairment, or a voice impairment, which adversely affects a child's educational performance. (§ 121a.5(b)(10))

This definition has been criticized in special education as overly broad. It could easily include most hearing impaired children and many with specific learning disabilities. Nevertheless, the federal definition applies to any child with a communication disorder causing speech to deviate so far from that of others in the pupil's environment that it calls attention to itself, interferes with communication, and is inconsistent with the youngster's age. To be classified in this category, the speech impairment must adversely affect the child's educational performance. There are four types of such speech impairments:

1. Articulation Disorder: the defective production of speech sounds (phonemes) that interfere with the intelligibility of speech.
2. Voice Disorder: an abnormality in pitch, loudness, or quality resulting from pathological conditions or inappropriate use of the vocal mechanism that interferes with communication.
3. Fluency Disorder: disruptions in the normal rhythmic flow of verbal expressions that occur frequently or are markedly noticeable and are not readily controllable.
4. Language Disorder: a disability in verbal learning resulting in markedly impaired ability to acquire, use, or comprehend spoken or written language, even where no other handicapping condition or impairment is present as the primary dysfunction.

In February 1981, the Comptroller General of the U.S. General Accounting Office issued a report in which he raised questions about whether the language in P.L. 94-142 is sufficiently clear concerning the eligibility of children with minor impairments that may not require special education. Although these eligibility questions affect children with various types of impairments, they are especially applicable to children with a minor impairment who require only speech therapy. According to the report, of the 3.7 million school children counted for funding and served under the P.L. 94-142 program as of December 1, 1978, the largest single group, about 1.2 million, were classified as "speech impaired" and were receiving only speech therapy. The report stated that for such children the states received about $253 million in federal grant funds for fiscal year 1980.

The Comptroller General also stated that the law and its legislative history are unclear on whether children receiving only speech therapy, or other services cited in the act as "related services," should be counted as handicapped for federal funding. Nevertheless, the regulations permit children receiving only speech therapy to qualify for federal funds if a child's impairment has an "adverse effect" on his or her "educational performance." As of June 30, 1980, the U.S. Department of Education had not defined these terms or issued guidance for applying them. Most local education agencies visited by the GAO in preparation for the February 1981 report, disregarded the adverse effect requirement in counting children for federal funding. Many of these LEA officials told GAO that applying an "adverse effect on educational performance" test would likely reduce their counts of speech-impaired children by 33 to 75 percent.

In July 1980, the department issued guidance to states which provided, in essence, that any child meets the "adverse effect" test if he or she is receiving speech therapy. This guidance was based on the premise that such children have not yet mastered the basic skill of effective oral communication and may be considered as handicapped without any further determination that the speech impairment adversely affects educational performance.

Undoubtedly, further clarification of such eligibility issues for the speech impaired will be made in coming years. The GAO report recommended to the U.S. Congress that clarification is necessary to determine whether, and under what conditions, children receiving only speech therapy or other related services are eligible for coverage under the P.L. 94-142 program. The Department of Education believes that such children are eligible. But, GAO made its recommendation that the Act be clarified because the department's rationale is not clearly supported by the law or its legislative history.

Identification

Identification activities for speech impairments frequently include mass screening tests. Typically, these involve such tasks as the naming of objects or pictures that include the whole range of speech sounds, the repetition of sentences designed to catch errors in a particular sound, serial speech responses such as counting, the repeating of specially selected nonsense syllables, and normal conversation.

The other primary mechanism for identifying suspected speech impaired children is teacher and parent referral. A child who persistently exhibits certain communication characteristics should be referred for an evaluation. These characteristics include marked difficulty with language, following directions in class, inattention, reluctance to engage in verbal activities, embarassment or frustration at the child's own speech. Some speech impairments might be reflected in physical characteristics such as abnormal orthodontal structure, oral muscular coordination problems, cleft palate, or other pathology of the vocal mechanism.

In the developmental speech and language area, a suspected impaired child might exhibit a voice pitch that is inappropriate to that pupil, is unusually loud or soft, or is breathy or a monotone. The child may always sound congested. There may be low or inappropriate vocabulary and a general reluctance to talk. The rhythm rate or inflection of speech may be abnormal. Speech may be unintelligible, mix the order of sounds in words, or be ineffective in communicating ideas orally. The child may stammer or stutter and have difficulty articulating isolated sounds.

In academic achievement, the child suspected of having a speech impairment generally will not exhibit speech or language commensurate with that pupil's age. Test scores will indicate that verbal areas are significantly lower than those in nonverbal areas. Academic achievement will be below expectancy.

Evaluation

In determining eligibility for classification as speech impaired, the type of disorder is not as important as the severity of its effect on educational performance. Articulation and fluency disorders are considered significant only when they are outside of the range of acceptable variation in the child's environment and inconsistent with the age. A voice problem is considered significant only when it distracts from the child's ability to communicate effectively, a language disorder only when language process and academic test results are below the age expectancy.

The law requires that each child identified as possibly handicapped be assessed in all areas related to the suspected disability, including, where appropriate, health, vision, hearing, social and emotional status, general intelligence, academic performance, communicative status, and motor abilities. Children who have a speech impairment as their primary handicap may not need a complete battery of assessments (such as on psychological, physical, or adaptive behavior). However, a qualified speech-language pathologist would (1) evaluate each such child using procedures appropriate for the diagnosis and appraisal of disorders, and (2) where necessary, make referrals for additional assessments needed to develop an appropriate placement decision.

Program and Placement

The type and extent of services in a speech-impaired child's IEP is largely a function of how great the deviation from the norm of peers may be and how well (or poorly) the pupil succeeds in the regular education program. The general goal of the IEP for speech-impaired children is to habilitate the specific speech, voice, fluency, or language disorder and integrate them in the regular program.

Traditionally, the placement alternative for speech-impaired children was in a regular class, with periodic removal to a resource room for speech therapy sessions. This approach still is the most widely used today even with children who essentially are nonverbal and who are attending special day schools or residential schools.

Other modes of delivering speech services include providing consultation and materials to the teacher of a self-contained class of hearing impaired, autistic, or other communication disordered children. The speech professional may provide direct services to such students in their classes. These pupils are likely to have other primary handicapping conditions that are complicated by speech impairments. Students with mild speech impairments make up the vast majority of the population whose primary handicapping condition involves speaking. They are served through some variation of the regular classroom and resource room combination.

The placement for speech-impaired children should consider certain facility and equipment factors to ensure that the IEP is carried out appropriately. For example, if a room is used to provide speech therapy, it should be as free as possible from noise and interruption and have good sound properties. The speech professional should have ready access to record players, records, tape recorder and tapes, mirrors, educational speech games, construction paper, crayons, scissors, etc.

VISUALLY HANDICAPPED

Definitional Factors

The regulations define the term as follows:

"Visually handicapped" means a visual impairment which, even with correction, adversely affects a child's educational performance. The term includes both partially seeing and blind children. (§ 121a.5(b)(11))

This differs from the more traditional forms of defining visual handicaps exclusively in terms of visual acuity standards. This defines the disability in terms of the child's ability to perform in the educational setting or function in everyday life experiences. The traditional definition describes *blindness* as visual acuity with correction in the better eye of not more than 20/200, or a defect in the visual field so that the widest diameter of vision subtends an angle no greater than 20 degrees. However, educators recognize that there is considerable variance among children with the same measured acuity in terms of how each one functions individually in the classroom. To be classified as visually handicapped under federal law, the major factor is whether or not the visual impairment adversely affects educational performance.

Identification

Most state and local identification programs include a mass vision screening. The field of special education for the visually handicapped has raised concerns regarding the types of tests used and the standards followed. Good screening programs, as measured solely by high rates of confirmation of true positives by diagnosticians, have trained and certified visual-technician specialists either closely supervising or actually conducting the tests.

Parent and teacher referrals are another source of identifying suspected visually handicapped children. Such referrals usually are initiated when the adult notices that the child appears clumsy in certain situations or has difficulty seeing things at certain times of the day, depending on the kind of sunlight. The child may hold the head in an awkward position to look at something, or consistently ask someone to describe what is occurring.

Other persistent characteristics can include a child's rubbing the eyes excessively and having a pronounced squint. Social adjustment is poor and the pupil frequently withdraws from activities. Academic achievement comes only with great effort and, of course, abilities requiring visual experience are likely to be reflected in lower performance scores.

Evaluation

The evaluation of visually handicapped children is a more complex undertaking than it may appear at first. The basic problem is not only that they have difficulty seeing but that they are likely to lack much of the background of normal life experience that sighted pupils have. Visual handicaps often separate children from their environment. In assessing those suspected of having visual handicaps, it is important to establish whether or not they have had the opportunity to learn things expected of normal children the same age. Educators are using more evaluation techniques that assess learning aptitude rather than traditional intelligence tests. The idea is to assess the ability to learn rather than the product of the child's previous learning.

Another problem is that the incidence of this population is low and many evaluators are inadequately experienced in administering and interpreting assessment results with such children.

The evaluation of a child suspected of having a visual handicap should include a thorough examination by an ophthalmologist. The examination and report should include information regarding the pupil's visual acuity, refractive errors, prescription correction where indicated, etiology, prognosis, and an evaluation of low vision aids where appropriate.

As noted earlier, the law does not require that any specific medical criteria be met for eligibility for a program for the visually handicapped. However, most classifications use a visual acuity of 20/70 or less in the better eye with the best possible correction or a restriction in the field of vision to an angle subtending an arc of 20 degrees or less, as criteria for eligibility as visually handicapped.

The evaluation data should be organized in terms that are relevant educationally. Conclusions that the child is blind, partially sighted, or visually handicapped say little about what the subject actually can do. In terms of program development, it is more useful to know the functional ability. Visually handicapped children can be classified in such terms at four basic levels—that they are:

1. able to read and write with or without special aids, able to identify objects visually, and able to maneuver safely through an unfamiliar environment without assistance
2. able to read or write with or without special aids, able to identify objects visually, but unable to move safely through an unfamiliar environment without help
3. unable to read or write even with special aids, unable to identify familiar objects, but able to move safely through an unfamiliar environment without assistance
4. unable to read or write even with the aid of optical or visual enlarging devices, unable to identify familiar objects, and unable to maneuver safely through an unfamiliar environment without the aid of a dog, cane, or sighted person.

Program Placement

The development of an appropriate IEP for the visually handicapped child depends largely upon the severity of the vision loss and how it affects the pupil's ability to function in the classroom. In cases of a mild impairment, assistance from an itinerant or resource person in the regular classroom may be all that is needed. Children with a greater impairment may need to learn special skills to supplement their regular programs with aids such as Braille, typing, or the use of an abacus. Those with a severe loss may require considerable help with adaptive techniques before they can function in a regular classroom. The more severely impaired will demonstrate academic achievement and social development extensively behind their peer group—problems that also must be addressed.

Placement decisions must be reviewed carefully for adherence to the principle of least restrictive environment. An assessment of degree of vision loss by itself never can be totally sufficient to make a determination. Each student must be considered carefully in terms of individual educational needs, level of development and maturation, and extent of compensation skills. Many visually impaired children need only special orientation, mobility training, and some modifications in instruction such as the use of large print to function effectively in the regular class.

Chapter 11

How to Determine Whether an IEP/Placement Is Appropriate

The regulations provide that the term "free appropriate public education" means special education and related services that:

> Are provided in conformity with an individualized education program which meets the requirements under §§ 121a.340–121a.349 of Subpart C [the provisions governing the development of individualized education programs]. (§ 121a.4(d))

Section 504 expands that somewhat by defining as "appropriate" the provision of educational services to a handicapped child that:

> (i) are designed to meet individual educational needs of handicapped persons as adequately as the needs of nonhandicapped persons are met and (ii) are based upon adherence to procedures that satisfy the requirements of §§ 84.34, 84.35, and 84.36 [governing educational setting, least restrictive environment, evaluation and placement, and procedural safeguards]. (§ 84.33(b))

The legal definitions of "appropriate" are different from most others in special education law. Most other definitions are expressed in terms of a set of factors found—or not present—in the subject or that are characteristic of the child. However, the law defines appropriate in terms of a process rather than any set of factors. The definition includes other provisions concerning procedures to be followed in arriving at an educational program for the pupil. It also incorporates those other provisions by reference. In other words, if the proper procedures specified in the law for arriving at an educational program were followed, that program is "appropriate." An IEP that is developed in accordance with the law, and is agreed to by all persons involved, is the operational definition of an "appropriate" program.

This chapter is designed to organize the definitional process of the term appropriate. The process is divided into a sequence of steps. To reach the end objective of an appropriate program, it is necessary to follow each step, complete the tasks, obtain the necessary information, and fulfill the legal requirements at that particular level. The process can be likened to a train travelling along tracks. If the tracks are not sound, or a railroad car is derailed at one point, it is unlikely that riders will reach their destination until the defect is corrected. It does not matter how good the rails may be from the breakdown point to the destination; if the train is stopped at a weak spot, it simply cannot move on and the condition of the rest of the track is irrelevant.

The process of determining appropriateness of a special education program is similar. It is related sequentially, with each step dependent upon the one that precedes it. For example, it is not possible to reach an appropriate placement unless the child first has had an appropriate evaluation. The proposed placement may be one of the finest available but cannot be determined to be the proper one for a particular child unless there has been an appropriate evaluation that shows that this child requires a certain type of program that can be provided in that setting.

The process for determining appropriateness is divided into five major steps, explained in detail below. However, there is one principle that applies to every step. The law requires the school system to provide a handicapped child with an appropriate program and the parents with an opportunity to be involved at every point of the decision-making process (indeed, it mandates their participation at several points). Without parental involvement, it is unlikely that a special education program could be determined to be appropriate. If it were so regarded, it would only be after a decision in a due process hearing.

The importance of parents' involvement cannot be overemphasized. They have a unique understanding of their child. Because handicapped children often are moved from program to program and professional to professional, parents become the single source of continuity in the pupils' lives and a source of information for the professionals as new interventions are tried. Parents also can be valuable aids to the professionals by following through on program components outside of school hours. That is why every effort must be made to involve parents in the processes of identification, evaluation, program development, and placement of their child.

The school staff can recommend, for example, that parents be allowed to observe the testing process and medical examinations. Evaluation results should be clearly explained to them and their input must be sought when developing the IEP. Moreover, they always should be encouraged to observe the programs being offered to their children. If parents can see what is occurring and if the results are communicated in a clear and understandable fashion, tensions will be reduced, they will be more supportive of the programs, and the efficacy of the efforts is likely to be enhanced.

The right, value, extent, and quality of parental involvement are factors that must be considered in proceeding step by step to determine the appropriateness of a proposed program. A truly appropriate program is one in which the parents have been equal partners with educators in exchanging opinions and evaluating what is proposed at each step.

STEP 1: IDENTIFICATION

How Did This Child Come to the Attention of the School System As Potentially Having Special Needs?

The first step in providing an appropriate educational program is that the handicapped child be identified. The term "identification" refers to the phase in the special education process in which the child first comes to the attention of professionals. They are responsible for assuring that the pupil then is channeled toward an appropriate evaluation, program, and placement. The term identification itself does not include those three factors; it simply means that the child is suspected (identified) of having some special educational needs. There may be a handicapping condition that is adversely affecting the ability to learn.

The responsibility for this identification is shared by parents, state agencies, school officials, teachers, social workers, doctors, and community workers. States and local school districts actually are required by law to prepare plans detailing exactly how they will go about identifying children with special needs. All sorts of methods have been employed to accomplish this task, including newspaper advertisements, television and radio spots, pamphlets, and other public informational materials.

However, most children with special needs were identified originally as such by their parents or teachers. These adults are the persons in closest contact with the child. They have the opportunity to notice subtleties in performance that may escape other persons less familiar with the child. The pupil may exhibit characteristics such as having persistent trouble with schoolwork, a physical complaint, failing to respond when spoken to, or squinting at a television show. Characteristics such as these may cause the parents or teacher to refer the child for an evaluation.

Identification is important because it sets the stage for the evaluation. Frequently, the nature and scope of an evaluation is determined largely by what kind of handicapping condition is suggested by the referral characteristics. Many school systems set evaluation procedures to be followed regardless of what type of handicap seems to be present but many others tailor the assessment, depending on the presenting problem.

An evaluation will not be appropriate unless it addresses every actual or potential problem area presented. That is why a proper understanding of how the child first came to be identified as possibly in need of special education is so important. Unless the evaluators have that understanding, they are likely to miss the target. The resulting program also is likely to be deficient. The placement designed to carry out the program would then be of little value. Hence, the process will have yielded an inappropriate education program that is unlikely to meet the needs of this particular child.

Understanding identification is important even if the child has been receiving special education services for several years. Almost every special educator is able to recall a horror story of a misdiagnosed handicapped child who has spent a number of months or years in an institution needlessly and to the detriment of his education.

STEP 2: EVALUATION

What Are This Child's Strengths and Weaknesses?

The second step in providing an appropriate education program is to evaluate the child. The term "evaluation" refers to the phase in the special education process in which the child, having been identified by certain characteristics as potentially in need of services, is assessed for two purposes:

1. to determine whether or not the pupil is indeed handicapped
2. to obtain the necessary information to design a program, if the student is indeed in need of special education services

When the child is identified, the question is raised of whether the pupil is handicapped and in need of special education services. If the answer is "yes," the evaluation also should yield the information necessary to develop a program to meet the pupil's needs. If the answer is "no," the special education process is completed for this child. Students who do not have handicapping conditions that adversely affect their ability to learn are not entitled to special education programs under the law.

The first procedure at the evaluation step is that the school system must obtain the consent of the parents before conducting the assessment. (This is fully addressed in Chapter 16 in Part IV.) After obtaining that consent, the other procedures at this step are required to ensure that the evaluation produces a full and fair picture of the child's strengths and weaknesses.

The starting point is the list of referral characteristics from the original identification. What type of disability is suggested? Could these characteristics be suggestive of another disability? Does one or more of them seem to suggest something different from, or in addition to the others? The law requires that the child be assessed in all areas related to the suspected disability. If an evaluation overlooks any characteristics, or fails to address the possibility of a particular disability that they suggest, it cannot be considered appropriate.

To protect against errors and omissions, the law further requires that no single procedure be used as the sole criterion; instead, it emphasizes the importance of making the evaluation as comprehensive as possible.

Data on health, vision, hearing, social and emotional status, general intelligence, academic performance, communicative status, and motor abilities, as appropriate, must be gathered to get a complete picture of the child. Moreover, the evaluation must be made by a multidisciplinary team or group of persons, including at least one teacher or other specialist with knowledge in the area of the suspected disability. It must be thorough in order to determine the child's unique needs for which an appropriate special education program must be developed.

The evaluation information is obtained by professionals from a variety of tests and assessment procedures, including:

- diagnostic tests
- aptitude, achievement, or IQ tests
- interviews with parents and teachers about the child's performance and development in and out of school
- psychological testing of functioning and behavior
- observations of the child in school and home
- medical examinations

However, even if the evaluation is comprehensive and uses one or more of these tests and procedures, mistakes and omissions are possible if those tools are not applied properly. To protect against such errors, the law requires that:

1. tests and procedures accommodate the child's native language or other mode of communication

2. tests and materials be validated for the specific purpose for which they are used
3. tests and materials be administered by trained personnel in conformance with the instructions provided by their producer
4. tests and materials be selected and administered to best ensure that when a test is given to a child with impaired sensory, manual, or speaking skills, the results accurately denote the pupil's aptitude or achievement level or whatever other factors it is intended to measure, rather than simply reflecting the handicap (except where those skills are the factors that are to be tested)

The law does not require that every child who is referred have a complete battery of assessments in every possible area by a full team of evaluators. It requires only that such tests and procedures be completed in areas related to whatever suspected disability or disabilities the pupil appears to manifest and that those tools be selected and administered in such a way as to protect against any form of discrimination.

For example, children who have a speech impairment as their primary handicapping condition may not need a complete battery of assessments. In such a case, a qualified speech-language pathologist would (1) evaluate the child using procedures that are appropriate for the diagnosis and appraisal of speech and language disorders, and (2) make referrals for additional assessments when needed to develop an appropriate program.

Evaluation is the second step in the special education decision-making process. It relates both backward and forward to the other steps in that process. It relates backward to Step 1 (Identification) in that it answers the question posed by the referral characteristics as to whether or not the child is handicapped. It relates forward to Step 3 (Translation of Data Into Specific Educational Needs) because it provides the raw data necessary to determine exactly what the needs are.

The goal of the evaluation is to provide all the necessary information about all facets of development so that a decision can be made as to whether the child is handicapped and, if so, what the pupil's strengths and weaknesses are. When an evaluation accomplishes this goal, it is appropriate, and the process can move on to the next step.

STEP 3: TRANSLATION OF DATA INTO SPECIFIC EDUCATIONAL NEEDS

What Do All the Evaluation Data Mean in Terms of This Child's Education?

The third step in developing an appropriate education program is to translate the evaluation data into the child's specific needs. The previous step, evaluation, should have provided all the information necessary to complete this step from several sources involving a number of different persons. But wide range achievement test (WRAT) scores, visual tracking measures, decibel levels, achievement scores, etc., are only raw data. What does all this mean in terms of the child's educational needs?

The law requires that the school system provide the child with an appropriate public education. It takes notice of a handicapping condition that adversely affects this education by requiring school systems to offer special instruction and related services to meet the child's unique educational needs.

The purpose of Step 3 is to now translate the raw data and professional opinions about the child's strengths and weaknesses into a list of specific educational needs. The following questions can help organize the evaluation data in meaningful educational terms:

- Does this child manifest characteristics that establish the existence of a handicapping condition? If so, the evaluation should describe them and the criteria used to so establish the condition.

- Does this child's performance deviate from normal developmental and educational milestones? If so, the evaluation should describe how it does and what criteria were used to establish the performance as deviant.

If these two items are answered affirmatively, then the child probably is handicapped and requires special education and related services. The following items help translate the evaluation data into specific educational needs:

- What curriculum level is appropriate for this child in the different academic subjects, considering the expected, as compared with actual, performance?

- Would the child benefit from itinerant or remedial assistance in one or more subjects?

- Should the child's program be adjusted, considering the level of receptive and expressive language?

- Does the program require the use of adaptive equipment and materials?

- What percentage of the school day could this child function within the regular program?

- What teacher/pupil ratio is necessary to permit the student to function within the group?

- Does this child need a certain seating arrangement in the classroom for optimum performance?

- Will the child who requires removal from the regular classroom have transportation needs?

- What conferences and consultations are necessary with other school personnel regarding the educational implications of this child's handicap?

- What conferences and training with parents are necessary regarding the educational implications of the handicap?

- Does the child require medicine or medical attention during school hours?

- What does this child need in terms of relationships and social interactions with other students and teachers?

- Are therapy or other consultation with the teacher or other professionals required to help the child more fully understand the disability, its effects on academic achievement and general school performance, or the management of its effects?

- What specific self-help skills does the child need to learn or practice?

- What specific sensorimotor skills should be learned or practiced?

- What specific sensory perception skills should the child learn or practice?

- What aspects of social emotional growth should be enhanced or developed?

- Does this pupil need to learn or practice any prevocational or vocational skills?

These guidelines provide a framework for organizing the evaluation data in terms of the child's educational needs. It would be difficult to prepare an appropriate program directly from the raw data. A special education program is supposed to be designed to meet unique needs, which must be clear before a plan can be developed to meet them.

The raw data assessment provides a great deal of information about all aspects of the child's strengths and weaknesses. Step 3 translates that information into a set of specific educational needs. This step is necessary so that attention can be refocused on developing an educational program.

The raw data might suggest beneficial interventions for the needs of the child's family and for nutrition, recreation, religious, physical, etc. However, that would broaden the task to something unwieldy, and certainly not required by law. The law requires only that the school system provide an appropriate program to meet the child's *educational* needs. Step 3 is the point in the process of determining appropriateness where those needs are defined clearly. It relates backward because the needs are based on the data gathered through Step 2 (Evaluation) and forward because they provide the basis for developing a responsive program in Step 4 (Program Development).

STEP 4: PROGRAM DEVELOPMENT

What Program Components Are Required to Meet the Educational Needs?

The fourth step in providing a handicapped child with an appropriate education is to develop the program. The pupil already has been identified as possibly in need of special education services and has been referred for an evaluation in all areas related to the suspected disability. The evaluation determined that the child was indeed handicapped and in need of special education. It also provided a great deal of raw data on all areas of the pupil's strengths and weaknesses. The data then were translated into specific educational needs that must be addressed. Now, Step 4 focuses on the elements of the program that must be provided to address those needs appropriately.

Every handicapped pupil receiving special education must be provided with an IEP that specifies what instruction and related services actually will be provided to meet the child's unique needs. The IEP must be written and must:

1. Describe Present Levels of Educational Performance

This information should have been obtained already at Steps 1 and 2, Identification and Evaluation.

2. State Annual Goals and Short-Term Instructional Objectives

Annual goals are best estimates of what the child will be able to do within one year. There should be a realistic relationship between the annual goals set and the present level of performance. The annual goals then should be broken into smaller component parts, which become the short-term instructional objectives.

The short-term objectives should be written in measurable terms so that progress can be noted and revisions made accordingly (at least annually). They also should provide a time span in which it is anticipated that they will be accomplished. It is difficult to ascertain whether or not objectives are being met if they are stated in ambiguous or subjective terms such as "the child will make progress." Following are some examples of annual goals and short-term objectives:

- Annual Goal: The child will demonstrate readiness to learn basic sight vocabulary.

- Short-Term Objectives: The child will be able to determine which alphabet letter comes before or after another given letter (two months); the child will be able to name six uppercase letters presented one at a time in random order (two months).

3. State Special Services and Extent of Participation in Regular Programs

Most children who receive special education and related services do so as only a part of their total program. The other part of their school day is devoted to participation in the regular educational program. The services and time spent in each vary from child to child. Whatever the nature and amount of special education programming, it must relate directly to the goals and short-term objectives in the IEP. The services should correspond in such a way that it is readily apparent from the IEP itself what particular educational tools will be used to build toward each goal.

For example, let the following be a short-term instructional objective:

John will say the sounds for the following letters in isolation and write the symbols when the sounds are dictated: Consonants, *ch, sh, th, wh, qu,* and all short vowels. John will perform at 100 percent accuracy by mid-October.

The special education programming for such an objective might be:

"Recipe for Reading" by Traub and Bloom
"Programmed Phonics" by Lucy Carroll
"Structural Reading Series" by Catherine Stern

The learning disabilities teacher will use these materials in combination with Orton-Gillingham techniques at least two hours each week in the resource classroom. A "token economy" will be used consistently in all activities when John is in the resource classroom. The tests in the "Recipe for Reading" will be used to measure competence. "Mastery" will be the criterion for completion and progression to the next step in the sequence.

4. Projected Dates for Initiation of Services, and Their Duration

This component is self-explanatory. However, in some cases a special service may be unavailable at the time the child is to begin the program. In such a case, it should be clearly stated in writing when the school system will provide it and what will be done in the meantime. Other considerations regarding the projected dates on services might depend on the particular placement where the child is to receive such assistance. All such factors should be reviewed so that the stated dates will be realistic.

5. Achieving Short-Term Instructional Objectives

If the short-term objectives are written initially in measurable form, as discussed above, this requirement already will have been largely satisfied. What remains to be stated is when and how the child's performance and the effectiveness of the IEP will be evaluated.

These five components are the basic elements the law requires if the program is to be considered appropriate. The IEP should contain all of the information necessary for teachers and parents to know exactly what changes in behavior, academic achievement, and development to expect, and how each program, service, or instruction will help children reach their potential.

The IEP should give a clear idea of the child's expected progress under that particular plan. It should not leave a question as to how a certain objective is to be accomplished, who will provide a particular service, when the progress will be reviewed, etc. Everything the child needs should be carefully put down in writing in the IEP so that it is clear and so that misunderstandings can be avoided. Finally, the parents' consent to the IEP must be obtained before it can be put into action unless that requirement is waived by a hearing officer.

STEP 5: PLACEMENT

How Will This Program Be Carried Out?

The fifth step in providing a handicapped child with an appropriate education program is to determine how and where the plan will be carried out. An IEP has been developed to meet the child's unique needs. Now, Step 5 focuses on how and where it can be implemented and the legal considerations in determining the appropriateness of the proposed placement. (Placement is discussed in detail in Part II, Chapter 9.)

The first consideration is that the placement decision must be made by a variety of persons, including those knowledgeable about the child, the meaning of the evaluation data, and the location options. This provision again indicates the sequential relationship of the special education process in that persons from the earliest steps must be included in this final level. Having developed the program, the major concern is finding the right vehicle for delivering it to the child.

The second consideration is the capacity of the proposed placement to carry out the IEP. The law requires that the placement decision be based on the student's IEP because it is the major factor in determining what special education services and program components will be provided to meet the needs. If the placement is not designed to carry out the IEP effectively, then the child will not receive the appropriate education. The IEP may be excellent as drafted, but its value will be diminished if the placement is not designed to deliver it properly.

The benefit the child receives from the IEP obviously is determined by how well the placement can deliver on the promise. One placement may be better equipped than another to implement the program. As discussed in Chapter 9, many factors must be considered when making a placement: student population, supplemental services, facilities and physical plant design, materials and equipment, types of support personnel, professional personnel available, etc. For example, special education services for an emotionally disturbed child might require: (1) a student-teacher ratio of no greater than 7 to 1; (2) a facility with provisions for an isolation area and access to emergency assistance for staff; and (3) the services of a speech therapist.

Another related concern is the flexibility of the proposed placement to adapt to changes in the child's program. An IEP will specify certain services, objectives, curricula, etc., that when implemented may turn out not to be appropriate or to be in need of modifications. The law requires periodic reviews of the IEP and reevaluations of the child if they are not requested earlier. Such procedures might well yield information suggesting revisions in the program.

The third consideration is whether the proposed placement is the least restrictive environment in which to provide the special education services. An IEP may be carried out in a number of different placements because most special education services can be provided in a variety of settings. For example, a child probably could be taught to read Braille in a regular classroom, a resource room, a day school, or a residential school.

The placement decision impacts upon the child's life in a broader way than just educational development—it affects the whole person. Personality growth and development are influenced strongly by the range of everyday experiences and opportunities to which the child is exposed in the surrounding environment. It follows that the best environment in which to provide an educational program is the one that is the "most normal" or the "least restrictive" setting appropriate to the child's learning needs. That is why the regulations require:

(1) That to the maximum extent appropriate, handicapped children, including children in public or private institutions or other care facilities, are educated with children who are not handicapped, and
(2) That special classes, separate schooling or other removal of handicapped children from the regular educational environment occurs only when the nature or severity of the handicap is such that education in regular classes with the use of supplementary aids and services cannot be achieved satisfactorily. (§ 121a.550(b))

As discussed in Chapter 9, the principle of placement in the least restrictive environment primarily focuses on with whom rather than where the child is to be educated. Usually, the restrictiveness of a particular placement is considered in terms of its degree of isolation or security. In special education, however, the concept of restrictiveness focuses on the extent or degree to which it is appropriate to educate a handicapped student with nonhandicapped peers.

The fourth and final consideration is that parental consent must be obtained before an initial placement of their handicapped child in a program providing special education and related services unless that requirement is waived by a hearing officer.

These four considerations are the basic requirements that must be met if the proposed placement is to be deemed appropriate. A placement must be designed so it can fulfill its purpose of carrying out the individualized education program. This again demonstrates that the special education process consists of a series of sequential steps. The law requires that Step 5 (Placement) relate back to the specifications of the IEP at Step 4 (Program Development).

CONCLUSION

Is the Proposed Program 'Appropriate' for This Child?

The process for determining appropriateness of the proposed program now is concluded. At this point it is possible to make the final determination: is the proposed program "appropriate" for this child?

The law provides that the term "appropriate" may be defined by reference to the provisions concerning the special education decision-making process. At each point in that process, the law specifies certain requirements that the parties must meet. If they have done so, the program is appropriate. If some of the requirements are ignored or not fully complied with, the end product is likely to be something less than appropriate.

To recapitulate:

Step 1, Identification, asks: "How did this child come to the attention of the school system as potentially having special needs?" After that initial information is learned, the rest should follow in logical sequence, each step building on the one before it.

Step 2, Evaluation, asks: "What are this child's strengths and weaknesses?" This step evaluates the referral characteristics from identification and produces the finding as to whether or not the child is handicapped. If that is the case, the evaluation provides a variety of data about the child.

Step 3, Translation of Data Into Specific Educational Needs, asks: "What do all the evaluation data mean in terms of this child's education?" This step makes the evaluation data meaningful in terms of specific needs that must be addressed when developing a program.

Step 4, Program Development, asks: "What program components are required to meet the child's educational needs?" This step takes the list of specific needs from the prior step and develops a program component to respond to each and every one of them. This step is not completed until every need on the list can be checked off as being covered by one portion or another of the program.

Step 5, Placement, asks: "How will this program be carried out?" This step concerns itself with where and how to deliver that program to the child. It assesses practical considerations about the capacity of the proposed placement to carry out the program and whether or not it is the least restrictive environment in which to implement it.

If each step was followed in order, the tasks completed, the necessary information obtained, and the legal requirements fulfilled, then the total proposed program is appropriate. If there was a breakdown at some point along the way, it is necessary to go back to that point, correct the problem, and then proceed to the conclusion. The process will help decide the appropriateness of actions taken and decisions made at each step, as well as assist in making the overall determination of appropriateness. The process also will help all parties in a special education due process hearing present their positions more confidently and effectively.

GUIDELINES FOR SPECIAL EDUCATION PROGRAM

The law requires that (1) a handicapped child's educational program must be appropriate and in the least restrictive environment and (2) the placement must be one that can integrate the impaired pupil with others who are not disabled to the maximum extent possible and still provide the proper curriculum.

The law is not as clear about the procedures and criteria, standards, or guidelines by which a person, committee, or agency implements this requirement. Specific criteria that could have general application in special education decision making are neither widely known nor utilized in any standard fashion.

The fundamental question is: Given a handicapped child and a continuum of alternative placements, how can it be determined which program and placement is appropriate and in the least restrictive environment for this pupil?

The preceding portion of the chapter provided a process for making that determination of appropriateness. This section distills that process down to a checklist of guidelines for making that appropriateness decision (see Exhibit 11–1). The guidelines, taken from actual cases, are not hard-and-fast criteria but are questions to help in weighing the various factors involved.

Exhibit 11-1 Checklist of Appropriateness of Program Elements

FACTORS IN DETERMINING WHETHER PROPER IDENTIFICATION PROCEDURES WERE FOLLOWED	
	Does the school system have a policy and program to ensure that all children who are handicapped and potentially in need of special education and related services are identified?
	Is it understood how a particular child came to the attention of the school system as potentially having special needs?
	Can the referral characteristics be listed?
	Is it known who identified the child as potentially in need of special education and related services?
	What possible handicapping conditions were suggested by the referral characteristics?
FACTORS IN DETERMINING WHETHER PROPER EVALUATION PROCEDURES WERE BEING FOLLOWED	
	Was consent for the assessments obtained from the parents?
	Is it possible that the referral characteristics suggest another disability or one different from that for which the child was assessed?
	Were the tests and other evaluation materials provided and administered in the child's native language or other mode of communication, unless clearly not feasible to do so?
	Were the tests and other materials validated for the specific purpose for which they were used?
	Were the tests and other materials administered by trained personnel in conformance with the instructions provided by their producer?
	Did the tests and other materials include those tailored to assess specific areas of educational need and not merely those designed to provide a single general intelligence quotient?
	Were tests selected and administered so as to best ensure that when they were given to a child with impaired sensory, manual, or speaking skills, the results accurately reflected the pupil's aptitude or achievement level or whatever other factors they purport to measure, rather than indicating the impaired sensory, manual, or speaking skills (except where those are the factors the tests purport to measure)?
	Is it certain that no single procedure was used as the sole criterion for determining an appropriate educational program for the child?

Exhibit 11-1 continued

	Was the evaluation made by a multidisciplinary team or group of persons, including at least one teacher or other specialist with knowledge in the area of suspected disability?
	Was the child assessed in all areas related to the suspected disability including, where appropriate, health, vision, hearing, social and emotional status, general intelligence, academic performance, communicative status, and motor abilities?
	Were the parents informed of their right to an independent educational evaluation?
	Were the parents provided, on request, with information about where such an independent evaluation may be obtained?
	Did the school system consider such an independent evaluation, if the parents obtained one, in any decision on providing a free appropriate public education to the child?

FACTORS IN DETERMINING WHETHER THE EVALUATION DATA WERE TRANSLATED PROPERLY INTO SPECIFIC EDUCATIONAL NEEDS

	Does this child manifest characteristics that establish the existence of a handicapping condition? If so, have they and the criteria used to so establish the handicapping condition been described?
	Does this child's performance deviate from normal developmental and educational milestones? If so, have that variance and the criteria used to establish the performance as deviant been described?
	What curriculum level is appropriate for this child in the different academic subjects, considering expected performance as compared with actual performance?
	Would the child benefit from itinerant or remedial assistance in one or more of the subjects?
	Should the program be adjusted considering the level of receptive and expressive language?
	Does the program require the use of adaptive equipment and materials?
	What percentage of the school day could this child function in the regular program?
	What teacher/pupil ratio is necessary to permit the student to function within the group?

Exhibit 11-1 continued

	Does this child need a certain seating arrangement in the classroom for optimum performance?
	Will the child have transportation needs if removal from the regular classroom is required?
	What conferences and consultations are necessary with other school personnel regarding the educational implications of this hanjdicap?
	What conferences and training with the parents are necessary as to the educational implications of this child's handicap?
	Does the child require medicine or medical attention during school hours?
	What does this child need in terms of relationships and social interactions with the other students and teachers in the school?
	Are therapy or other consultations with the teacher or other professionals required to help the child more fully understand the disability, its effects on academic achievement and general school performance, or the management of its effects?
	What specific self-help skills does the child need to learn or practice?
	What specific sensorimotor skills does the child need to learn or practice?
	What specific sensory perception skills does the child need to learn or practice?
	What aspects of social emotional growth does the child need to enhance or develop?
	Are there any prevocational or vocational skills this child needs to learn or practice?
FACTORS IN DETERMINING WHETHER A PROPER PROGRAM WAS DEVELOPED TO MEET THE CHILD'S SPECIFIC NEEDS	
	Was an individualized education program (IEP) written?
	Was an IEP meeting held about which the parents were notified and given an opportunity to attend?
	Did the parents attend the IEP meeting?
	Did the parents indicate their acceptance of the IEP by signing it?
	Does the IEP describe the child's present levels of educational performance?

Exhibit 11-1 continued

	Does the IEP state annual goals and short-term instructional objectives?
	Does the IEP contain a statement of the specific special education and related services to be provided and the extent to which the child will be able to participate in regular educational programs?
	Does the IEP contain the projected dates for initiation of services and their anticipated duration?
	Does the IEP contain objective criteria and evaluation procedures and schedules for determining, at least annually, whether the short-term instructional objectives are being achieved?
	Does the IEP contain a program component to address each and every specific educational need of the child?
FACTORS IN DETERMINING WHETHER PROPER PLACEMENT PROCEDURES WERE FOLLOWED	
	Was the placement decision made by a group of persons who were knowledgeable about the child, the meaning of the evaluation data, and the placement options?
	Does the proposed placement reflect a decision based upon information from a variety of sources, including aptitude and achievement tests, teacher recommendations, physical condition, social or cultural background, and adaptive behavior?
	Does the proposed placement appear to be related sequentially to the identification, evaluation, and programming decisions that preceded it?
	Was consideration given, in selecting this proposed placement, to any potential harmful effect on the child or on the quality of services needed?
FACTORS IN DETERMINING WHETHER THE PROPOSED PLACEMENT CAN CARRY OUT THE IEP SUITABLY	
	Can the handicapped child's IEP be carried out effectively in the proposed placement?
	Is the proposed placement based on specific services needed by the handicapped child rather than on the categorical label?
	Is the placement flexible enough to allow for changes in the services required by the IEP?
	Are the staff members in this proposed placement trained, willing, ready, and able to receive and properly provide for this child?

Exhibit 11-1 continued

	Can a proposed placement that removes the child to a more restrictive setting be justified by the fact that the intervention is needed for a relatively short time, so that the pupil can be returned to a less restrictive environment?
	Could the child actually learn better in a setting significantly farther removed from the regular classroom than this proposed placement, even if the pupil could function in the latter?
	Does the proposed placement match the child's level of functioning at the time of placement?
FACTORS IN DETERMINING WHETHER THE PROPOSED PLACEMENT AFFORDS THE STUDENT THE MAXIMUM EXTENT OF EDUCATIONAL AND SOCIAL INTEGRATION	
	Does the proposed placement fully integrate the handicapped child with others who are not handicapped?
	Why does the nature and/or severity of the handicap necessitate removal from the regular class if the placement does not fully integrate the child?
	Is this placement compatible with the child's self-perception and the type of population with which the pupil identifies?
	Are class activities in this placement designed to allow the handicapped child to participate without the limitations having to dictate the nature of, or extent of involvement in, every activity?
	What does the child's adjustment and preference in past and present placements indicate for success in the proposed location?
	Does this placement seem to respect the child as a whole person in that it could fulfill the normal psychological/social as well as educational needs?
	Does the placement in effect overprotect the child, and, perhaps, fail to provide a more realistic appraisal of how the pupil fits into the scheme of things?
	Does the placement reinforce the development of personality so the child can become an integral part of the community?
	Could the child actually be more restricted in the proposed least restrictive environment because the handicap would create isolation from the others? For example, a moderately hearing impaired child might be able to function in a class of hearing students but might be more isolated by the communication deficit there than in one for hearing impaired students.

Exhibit 11-1 continued

	Will this proposed educational placement adversely affect the child's familial interaction?
	Will this placement contribute to the handicapped child's being lazy, aggressive, or a clown because such behavior will be tolerated?
	Is the proposed placement that would remove the child from a setting with nonhandicapped peers based on a bona fide educational reason?
	Are the other pupils, already in the setting, prepared for this child to enter their program?
	Will the child's presence in this proposed location be so disruptive that the education of other students will be significantly impaired?
FACTORS IN DETERMINING WHETHER AN ALTERNATIVE PLACEMENT WOULD BE MORE SUITABLE	
	Could the handicapped pupil have been placed in a regular class with the use of supplementary aids and services if the proposed placement removes the child from the regular class?
	Would the assignment have been recommended if the school system had provided for supplementary services in conjunction with regular class placement of handicapped children?
	Would the placement have been recommended if the school system had had a more complete continuum of alternative situations available to meet the needs of handicapped children for special education and related services?
	Were a number of alternative placements considered before selecting the proposed one?
	Is the proposed placement the closest possible one to the child's home?
FACTORS IN DETERMINING WHETHER FINANCIAL AND LOGISTICAL ISSUES HAVE PLAYED A CONTROLLING ROLE IN THE DECISION	
	Has this proposed placement been recommended primarily because of the limitations inherent in the child's handicap or because of those in the school system's budget?
	Even if the proposed placement theoretically could accommodate this child's learning needs, is it currently crowded or overcrowded?

Part III

Roles, Rights, and Responsibilities

Almost every special education due process hearing involves many persons. All have different roles, rights, and responsibilities. To participate effectively in this system, all participants must understand their roles, as well as those of the other persons involved. This part discusses the roles, rights, and responsibilities of the student, parents, surrogate parents, school system staff, and hearing officer.

These persons come together from different perspectives. All declare that their objective is to reach special education decisions that serve the best interests of the handicapped students. However, invoking of the due process procedures means that a dispute exists among these persons as to exactly what those pupils' best interests are.

All of these individuals must deal with certain concerns and pressures that inevitably affect their judgment of what constitutes a free appropriate public education for the student. All contribute to the decision-making process from their own particular vantage points. No one person has an all-knowing perspective on the child.

The purpose of the special education due process hearing is to bring together as many of these perspectives, and to gather as much information as possible so that an informed decision can be made to resolve the dispute.

The lists of rights and responsibilities for each participant are intended to be comprehensive but not necessarily exhaustive. The various rights and responsibilities are taken directly from Public Law 94-142 regulations, Section 504 regulations, court cases, and policy statements from federal agencies. In most cases, the rights and responsibilities are explicitly provided in the legal sources, in some cases they are implicit.

This part is divided into four chapters, each of which presents the place of one of the participants in a special education due process hearing. If the concepts behind the law's inclusion of certain roles, rights, and responsibilities are understood, participation in the hearing process will be more effective.

Chapter 12

Students and Parents

ROLE OF THE STUDENT

Obviously, the handicapped student is the focus of the educational decision-making process. The pupil also is the focus of due process procedures when a dispute arises between the parents and the school system. However, Public Law 94-142 provides little, if any, guidance as to any active role for the student in the decision-making process or in the due process procedures when a dispute arises.

The law does provide that students should be included, where appropriate, in the meeting in which the individualized education program (IEP) is developed. Presumably, they would be expected to provide input into the various components of their IEPs. Other than that, their role is simply to be the subject around which the decision-making activity swirls.

RIGHTS OF THE STUDENT

P.L. 94-142 does not address student rights or responsibilities. Instead, it repeatedly states that ". . . the parents have a right to. . . ." It appears that the fundamental right to a free appropriate public education, and the other rights the law provides, inure to the student through the parents. In other words, the law seems to be saying that parents have a right to have their child receive a free appropriate public education and a right to invoke due process procedures if they do not feel their child is receiving such an education. The law does not speak directly to the child's rights.

However, the Section 504 regulations (the May 1977 expansion of the Rehabilitation Act of 1973) are phrased differently from P.L. 94-142 in such a way as to impose obligations on the "recipient(s)" of federal aid. Providers of elementary and secondary education are recipients under the regulations. Section 504 also provides for many of the same rights to special education as does P.L. 94-142. Therefore, handicapped students, through Section 504, have a direct right to a free appropriate public education and a right to invoke due process procedures if they do not feel they are receiving such an education.

When P.L. 94-142 and Section 504 are read together, handicapped students' rights substantially coincide with those of their parents. The handicapped student has a right to:

- a free appropriate public education in the least restrictive environment
- if placed there by a public agency that same education even if enrolled in a private or parochial school
- a residential educational placement if it is necessary to provide a free appropriate public education
- the same variety of educational programs as are provided to the non-handicapped
- extracurricular and nonacademic programs
- physical education, especially designed if necessary
- an IEP, whether in a private or a public school
- an IEP at the beginning of the school year
- review and revision of the IEP as necessary, and at least annually
- meetings to review and evaluate the educational program
- the presence of certain critical persons at the IEP meetings, placement, and review
- parental participation at all phases of the provision of special education, including the initial evaluation, IEP development and review, and placement
- attendance at the IEP meeting if appropriate
- special education with maximum integration with nonhandicapped children
- an independent evaluation if necessary
- the delivery of services regardless of parental consent (except for a preplacement evaluation and initial placement)

- communication in a language or mode the pupil understands, such as sign language

- a due process hearing, a review/appeal to the state department of education, and court appeal

- a surrogate parent under certain conditions

- tests and evaluation materials that are nondiscriminatory and properly designed and used

- a complete multifaceted evaluation in all areas of disability

- a placement decision based on a variety of sources and provided by knowledgeable persons familiar with the pupil and the evaluation materials

- the availability of a continuum of alternative placements in the school system

- supplementary services as may be necessary to help the student benefit from the special education

- a placement made on an individual basis rather than on a categorical label

- a placement as close as possible to home

- a placement that is reviewed annually

- education in a school the pupil ordinarily would attend if not handicapped unless it clearly is not feasible to do so

- access to all educational information gathered by the state or local education agency

- the amendment or correction of records that are misleading or false

- a hearing if necessary to have records amended or corrected

- inclusion of statements in the records to counter or explain the material

- protection of information from disclosure unless authorized

- a private right of action for violations of the law

- investigation of complaints or assistance regarding violations of the law

- freedom from retaliatory action if the pupil is a complainant

RESPONSIBILITIES OF THE STUDENT

As noted, it does not seem that any legal responsibilities are imposed on students, either by act, regulation, or judicial authority. However, common sense dictates that they do have some responsibilities or should be expected to cooperate with parents and school employees so far as possible considering their disability. No sanction can be imposed for simple non-cooperation. While children can be disciplined, punishment must occur pursuant to proper procedures and must take into account any disability that affects their behavior.

WHO IS CONSIDERED A PARENT?

The law defines the term "parent" to mean "a parent, a guardian, a person acting as a parent of a child, or a surrogate parent who has been appointed in accordance with" [the section on surrogate parents]. "The term does not include the state if the child is a ward of the state." (§ 121a.10)

Parent is defined to include persons acting in the place of a parent, such as a grandmother or stepparent with whom a child lives, as well as persons legally responsible for a pupil's welfare. (For further discussion, see Chapter 15 on surrogate parents.)

ROLE OF THE PARENTS

When it comes to raising a handicapped child, parents often feel that they are almost entirely on their own. Helpful friends and professionals come and go. But the parents always have the fundamental role of providing continuity. They also have the basic responsibility of finding and fighting for the services their child needs. Their role takes courage, assertiveness, commitment, determination, ingenuity, and humor. It is an extremely difficult job.

Sometimes it may seem overwhelming. It involves searching for schools, programs, treatment, the right professionals, job training, proper materials, and a variety of support services. Parents also must manage difficult problems at home. They have to encourage their child, who may suffer repeated disappointments, to keep trying and to press forward.

The law formally recognizes the role of parents in the special education decision-making process. For years, parents practically went begging for services for their impaired child. Now, state and federal laws provide that every handicapped child has a right to a free appropriate public education.

The laws also provide new and effective means for assuring that the child receives such a program. At every step in the special education decision-making process, from identification through placement, the parents' rights to take action are protected.

But no law or set of regulations is the total answer. Laws do not automatically relieve parents of their frustrations with school systems that only recently have begun to include them. It still takes hard and determined effort by the parents to make sure that a handicapped child gets the education needed. Parents need to support other parents. They need to join together and exercise good political judgment to make sure that the laws are backed by the funding necessary to implement their promise.

Parents also must educate themselves. The role that the laws provide them should be utilized to its greatest potential. Parents must learn about the steps to take to obtain services and about the staff that has the responsibility for providing them. They have to become more familiar with tests and diagnostic procedures used in evaluating their child's strengths and weaknesses.

Parents know their child best. They can offer vitally important help to professionals who work with their child. To carry out their role effectively, parents must see themselves as equal partners with professionals in planning educational programs and helping carry them out. As parents become more aware, confident, and assertive, they will help foster independence and growth in, and healthy attitudes among others toward, their child.

RIGHTS OF THE PARENTS

The parents or guardians of a handicapped child have a right to:

In General

- a free appropriate public education for their child with maximum integration with nonhandicapped peers
- information and assistance from school officials about their child, special education, their rights, etc., in language or in a mode of communication they can understand
- be provided with written notification at a reasonable time before the school system:
  1. proposes to initiate or change the child's identification, evaluation, program, placement, or free appropriate public education or
  2. refuses to initiate or change any of those elements

- be involved in every decision affecting the education of their handicapped child

- complete due process hearings and procedures to challenge the school system's actions or refusals to act regarding their child's free appropriate public education

In Identification

- insist that the state and local school systems prepare plans detailing exactly how they will go about locating children with special education needs; this may include screening all children for certain problems at different grade levels, as well as outreach efforts to inform people of their rights and other public awareness activities through the media

- notice whether their child has been identified as possibly needing special education and has been referred for an evaluation

In Evaluation

- have an evaluation conducted if they refer their child to the school as possibly needing special education and related services

- have an evaluation conducted before the school system may initially remove their child from the regular classroom program

- be notified in writing before the school system conducts any evaluation of their child

- receive a written notification containing:
    1. a full explanation of all procedural safeguards available
    2. a description of the action proposed by the school system
    3. an explanation of why the school proposes to take the action
    4. a description of any options the system considered and the reasons why they were rejected
    5. a description of each evaluation procedure, test, record, or report the school is using as the basis for its belief that the child requires a full evaluation
    6. a description of any other reasons or factors relevant to why the school proposes to evaluate the child

- have the written notification to explain why the school system refuses to evaluate their child if referred as possibly in need of special education; the notice must contain the same items as those listed above

- require that the school system obtain their consent to a preplacement evaluation before conducting one

- have all of the communications from the school system about the evaluation:
  1. written in language understandable to the general public
  2. provided in the native language or other mode of communication used by the parents unless it clearly is not feasible to do so
  3. translated orally or by other means in the parents' native language or other mode of communication if they do not use written language, in which case there must be evidence that the parents understood the content of the notice and consent

- have tests and other materials used in the evaluation of their child that:
  1. are designed to measure aptitude/achievement and not the handicap unless that is the purpose of the test
  2. are validated for the specific purpose for which they are being used
  3. are administered by trained personnel
  4. measure specific areas of need and not just one element of intelligence
  5. are not racially or culturally biased

- have an evaluation that assesses all areas related to the suspected disability

- have an evaluation conducted by a multidisciplinary team including at least one person familiar with the suspected disability

- have information provided by the school system, when the parents request it, about where an independent educational evaluation may be obtained

- have an independent educational evaluation at public expense if they disagree with one obtained by the school system; however, the school may initiate a hearing under the law to show that its evaluation is appropriate; if it is, the parents still have the right to an independent evaluation but not at public expense

- have an independent evaluation considered by the school system in any decision made as to a free appropriate public education for their child

- have an independent evaluation that they have obtained presented as evidence at a due process hearing

- have the school system conduct a reevaluation of the child, based on the same rights and procedures discussed above, every three years—or more frequently if conditions warrant or if the parents or teacher request it

In Programming

- have the school system develop and implement an IEP for their child if it is determined that special education and related services are needed

- have the system ensure that an IEP is developed and implemented if their child is placed in or referred to a private school or facility by the public schools or is enrolled in a parochial or other private school and receives special education or related services from the public system

- require that the school system have in effect an IEP for their child at the beginning of each school year

- have an IEP in effect before any special education and related services are provided for their child

- have the school system initiate and conduct meetings to develop, review, and revise the IEP

- participate in the IEP meetings

- receive a copy of the IEP

- have the following persons in attendance at the IEP meetings:
  1. a representative of the school system, other than the child's teacher, who is qualified to provide, or supervise the provision of, special education
  2. the child's teacher
  3. one or both of the parents
  4. the child, where appropriate
  5. other individuals at the discretion of the parents or school system

- have the school system ensure, for a handicapped child who has been evaluated for the first time, that at the IEP meeting there also will be present:
  1. a member of the evaluation team
  2. a representative of the school system, the teacher, or some other person who is knowledgeable about the evaluation procedures used with the child and is familiar with the results

- notification of the IEP meeting early enough so that they will have an opportunity to attend

- have the school system use other methods to ensure the parents' participation, including individual or conference telephone calls, if neither parent can attend the IEP meeting

- understand what is happening at, and participate in, the IEP meeting; if the parents require an interpreter, they have a right to have one present

- bring an experienced parent advocate or lawyer to the IEP meetings

- have the school system initiate and conduct an IEP meeting within 30 calendar days of a decision that the child needs special education and related services

- expect that their child's IEP will be implemented immediately following the meeting, with these exceptions:
  1. when the meetings occur during the summer or a vacation period, or
  2. when circumstances require a short delay (e.g., working out transportation arrangements); however, no undue delay is permitted

- have the school system initiate and conduct periodic IEP review meetings and, if appropriate, revise the document; such a meeting must be held at least once a year

- receive a written IEP that contains information on the following:
  1. the child's present level of performance
  2. the short-term and annual goals that give an idea how much the child is expected to learn over certain periods of time
  3. the specific special education and related services to be provided to help accomplish the goals
  4. how much the child will be able to participate in the regular school program with nonhandicapped peers
  5. when the special services will begin and how long each service or special program will be provided
  6. when and how the child's progress and the effectiveness of the IEP will be evaluated

- obtain programs, services, and other educational opportunities for their child comparable to those offered the nonhandicapped

In Placement

- have placement decisions based on information drawn from a variety of sources, including aptitude and achievement tests, teacher recommendations, physical condition, social or cultural background, and adaptive behavior

• have placement decisions based on information that is documented and carefully considered

• have placement decisions made by a group of persons (rather than only one individual), including those knowledgeable about the child, the meaning of the evaluation data, and the placement options

• have the school system obtain the parents' consent before placing a child initially in a special education and related services program

• have the placement determined at least annually

• have the placement based on the child's IEP

• have the placement as close as possible to home

• have the classes in the school the child would attend if not handicapped unless the IEP requires some other arrangements

• have a continuum of alternative placements available to meet the needs of their child for special education and related services, including instruction in regular classes, special classrooms for part of the school day, full-time special classrooms, special schools, residential facilities, instruction at home and in hospitals and institutions, and placements in programs outside of the system at school expense if necessary

• have the school system provide supplementary services such as resource room or itinerant instruction in conjunction with regular class placement

• have their child educated with the nonhandicapped to the maximum extent appropriate; this includes impaired children in public or private institutions or other care facilities

• have their child removed from the regular educational environment only when the nature or severity of the handicap is such that instruction in regular classes with the use of supplementary aids and services cannot be achieved satisfactorily

• have placement decisions and concerns about assigning the child to the least restrictive environment consider any potential harmful effect on the pupil or on the quality of services needed

In Due Process Hearings and Appeals

- request a special education due process hearing whenever the school system proposes to change the identification, evaluation, program, or placements of their child—or refuses to do so

- request such a hearing to resolve any dispute on the provision of a free appropriate public education to their child

- have the hearing conducted by the state or local educational agency or by whatever public entity is directly responsible for the education of their child

- have the school system inform the parents of any free or low-cost legal and other services available in the area if they request such information, or if the school is the party requesting the hearing

- have the hearing conducted by an impartial hearing officer:
  1. who is not an employee of a public agency involved in the education or care of the child, or
  2. who has a personal or professional interest that would conflict with objectivity in the hearing

- be accompanied to the hearing and advised by counsel and by individuals with special knowledge or training on the problems of handicapped children

- present evidence and confront, cross-examine, and compel the attendance of witnesses at the hearing

- prohibit the introduction of any evidence that has not been disclosed to them at least five days before the hearing

- obtain a written or electronic verbatim record of the hearing

- open the hearing to the public

- obtain from the hearing officer written findings of fact and decisions

- have the child who is the subject of the hearing present at the hearing if appropriate

- appeal the decision of the hearing officer; if the hearing was conducted by a public entity other than the SEA, the appeal is taken to the state agency; however, if the state agency was the one responsible for holding the initial hearing, then the parties have a right of appeal to a court of competent jurisdiction

- have the state educational agency conduct an impartial review of the hearing, if there is an appeal, and have the official conducting the review:
  1. examine the entire hearing record
  2. ensure that the hearing procedures were consistent with due process requirements
  3. seek additional evidence if necessary
  4. afford the parties an opportunity for oral or written argument, or both, at the discretion of the reviewing official
  5. make an independent decision on completion of the review
  6. give a copy of written findings and the decision to the parties

- have a final decision reached in the hearing not later than 45 days after the receipt of a request for such a session

- have a copy of the decision mailed to them

- have a final decision from the state educational agency, if the initial decision is appealed, not later than 30 days after receipt of a request for a review

- have a copy of the state agency's decision mailed to them

- have the hearing and state appeal conducted at a time and place reasonably convenient to them and their child

- bring a civil action in a court of competent jurisdiction if they had no appeal to the state educational agency or continue to be dissatisfied after that entity issues its review decision

- have their child remain in the present placement during the pendency of any administrative or judicial proceeding regarding the pupil's special education

- have their child placed in the public school program until the completion of all proceedings, if the complaint that is the subject of the hearing involves an initial admission to public school

In Confidentiality of Information

- receive adequate notice that fully informs them about the types of information the state educational agency must collect and maintain on handicapped children; that notice must include:
  1. a description of the extent to which the notice is given in the native language of the various population groups in the state

2. a description of the children on whom personally identifiable information is maintained, the types of information sought, the methods the state intends to use in gathering the information (including the sources from whom it is gathered), and the uses to be made of it
3. a summary of the policies and procedures that participating agencies must follow regarding storage, disclosure to third parties, retention, and destruction of personally identifiable information
4. a description of all of the rights of parents and children regarding this information, including the rights under 20 U.S.C. § 1232 G of the Family Educational Rights and Privacy Act of 1974 (FERPA), and its implementing regulations, 34 CFR, Part 99

- have a right to inspect and review any education records relating to their child that are collected, maintained, or used by the agency responsible for that pupil's education; the agency must comply without unnecessary delay and before any meeting regarding an IEP, hearing, or placement of the child, and in no case more than 45 days after the request has been made

- have the agency respond to reasonable requests for explanations and interpretations of the records

- request that the agency provide copies of the records containing the information, if failure to provide those copies would effectively prevent the parents from exercising the right to inspect and review the information

- have a representative of the parents inspect and review the records

- receive a list of the types and locations of education records collected, maintained, or used by the agency

- request the agency that maintains the information to amend it if the parents believe it is inaccurate or misleading or violates the privacy or other rights of the child

- have the agency decide whether or not to amend the information in accordance with the request within a reasonable time after receipt of such a request

- have a hearing to challenge information in education records to ensure that it is not inaccurate, misleading, or otherwise in violation of the privacy or other rights of the child

- place in the records the agency maintains on the child a statement commenting on the information if, as a result of the hearing, the entity decides that the material is not inaccurate, misleading, or otherwise in violation of the pupil's privacy or other rights

- have any such explanation placed in the child's records:
  1. be maintained by the agency as part of the dossier as long as it holds the record or contested portion
  2. have the pupil's records, or the contested portion, if disclosed by the agency to any party, also disclose the explanation

- have the agency obtain their consent before personally identifiable information is:
  1. disclosed to anyone other than officials of participating agencies collecting or using the information
  2. used for any purpose other than meeting a requirement under P.L. 94-142

- notice when personally identifiable information collected, maintained, or used under this part no longer is needed to provide educational services to the child

RESPONSIBILITIES OF THE PARENTS

The parents or guardians of a handicapped child have the responsibility to:

In General

- keep written records with copies of all of their letters to and from officials and school personnel, dates and topics of all conversations and meetings with such persons, and their own observations about their child's growth and development and difficulties

- communicate with other parents of handicapped children and participate actively in parent organizations

- join with others in the community to advocate for the budgets and range of services to comprehensively meet the needs of the school-aged population that is handicapped

- insist on explanations of actions, decisions, programs, etc., in language they can understand completely; parents should not be shy or embarrassed to insist that professionals use jargon-free language, bilingual or sign language interpreters, or whatever is necessary to facilitate their communication with school system officials and staff

- help teachers and others in the school and the community learn more about handicaps

- become aware of and utilize respite opportunities for themselves

- become politically aware of how city councils, state legislatures, local boards of education, federal agencies, the courts, etc., work and how they can be used to better meet the needs of handicapped citizens

- increase their familiarity with tests and diagnostic procedures used in special education decision making

- be informed and assertive in fulfilling their role in school conferences on evaluation, program, and placement, and in follow-up procedures that ensure that the programs continue to be effective

- get emotional support from other parents or professionals and recognize that feelings of despair, fatigue, and guilt are common to all parents

- refuse to settle for poor or inadequate services for their child, regardless of the excuses given for the shortcomings

- adopt a positive attitude toward the persons who work with their child and communicate fully and openly with them

- keep in mind that their child is not a composite of test scores, grade levels, and assessment measures, but rather is a person with the same needs as the nonhandicapped for fun, friends, achievement, disappointments and successes, physical contact, affection, adventure, recognition, privacy, and self-fulfillment

- have confidence in working with school personnel and other professionals and not be intimidated, put down, or ignored, or become unreasonable; parents also have a responsibility to give professionals room to do their job (those who become overly aggressive and interfering quickly damage their relationships with the very persons with whom they must work)

- understand that nearly every program will require some compromise and that no program, regardless of how excellent it might be, can be successful without active parental support and participation

- be active participants who stay aware of what is going on, who continue to discuss progress and problems with the teacher, who find ways that home and school can work together, who listen with sensitivity to their child's reactions, and who are alert to changing needs

In Identification

- contact the local superintendent of schools immediately if their child has a handicap and is not in school, or has been suspended from classes for an extremely long period, or repeatedly has been suspended, or for some other reason is not in school and thus not receiving an education

- contact the principal of the local school district and the special education director if the parents suspect the child has a special problem, especially if it is not obvious or severe

- request an evaluation if they think their child might have a handicap that is interfering with the ability to learn in or out of school

- follow up with telephone calls and letters to be sure that their request for an evaluation is being processed as quickly as possible

- insist that the school system use screenings and similar identification procedures at several different levels of the school-aged population to find children who may require special education and related services

In Evaluation

- insist upon receiving written notice when the school system proposes or refuses to evaluate their child

- insist that their consent be obtained before a preplacement evaluation is conducted

- insist upon a full description of the evaluation proposed or refused by the school system, an explanation of why the school proposes or refuses to evaluate their child, and a description of any options the system considered and why they were rejected

- insist upon a full description of each evaluation procedure, test, and other assessment instruments that will be used

- understand the nature of and reason for the evaluation before permitting the school to proceed

- understand and agree in writing to the implementation of the evaluation and understand that their granting of consent is voluntary and may be revoked at any time

- insist that a full and individual evaluation of the child's needs be conducted before any action is taken on initial placement in a special education program

- monitor the evaluation as much as possible to ensure that tests and other evaluation materials:
  1. are provided and administered in the child's native language or other mode of communication
  2. have been validated for the specific purpose for which they are used
  3. are administered by trained personnel in conformance with the instructions provided by their producer
  4. include those tailored to assess specific areas of educational need and not merely instruments that are designed to provide a single general intelligence quotient
  5. are selected and administered so as best to ensure that when a test is administered to a child with impaired sensory, manual, or speaking skills, the results accurately reflect the pupil's aptitude or achievement level or whatever other factors the test purports to measure, rather than indicating the impaired sensory, manual, or speaking skills (except when they are the factors the test purports to measure)

- monitor the evaluation as much as possible to also ensure that
  1. no single procedure is used as the sole criterion for determining an appropriate educational program for a child
  2. the evaluation is made by a multidisciplinary team or group of persons, including at least one teacher or other specialist with knowledge in the area of suspected disability
  3. the child is assessed in all areas related to the suspected disability including, where appropriate, health, vision, hearing, social and emotional status, general intelligence, academic performance, communicative status, and motor abilities

- participate in the evaluation as much as possible by observing the procedures, asking questions about test results, providing information, etc.

- speak frankly with the diagnosticians and other professionals and be sure to explain concerns fully

- obtain a clear and complete interpretation of all diagnostic reports, assessment results, and other evaluation data

- ask all the questions they feel they need to

- obtain copies of the reports from the evaluations and the follow-up on the recommendations

- become the leading experts on their child's special needs and problems by thoroughly reading and understanding the reports and explanations and maintaining them in an organized file

- insist that a diagnosis indicate, as far as possible, what kinds of help, in terms of educational programs, special treatment, etc., their child needs to develop to the fullest potential

- insist that an evaluation process yield more than a label or recommendation for some simple placement in a categorical program

- insist that the evaluation describe more than the disabilities; it should yield information about the child's abilities so that a program can be developed that also focuses on the capabilities and the ways the pupil can grow

- request a reevaluation if their child already is in a special education program that they feel is based on old, inaccurate, or incomplete evaluation procedures or if it does not seem to meet the pupil's needs

- seek an independent evaluation if they feel additional data are necessary or the school system's assessment was not appropriate

- be sure that any independent evaluation is received by the school personnel responsible for making decisions about the child's program and placement

- avail themselves of their due process rights if they do not feel the school's evaluation is appropriate, complete, or accurate, or that the information in the independent evaluation was not properly considered when making program and placement decisions about their child

- insist that the results of all testing and evaluations are explained to them in clear, jargon-free terms, and copies are provided to them

- be certain that the testing and evaluation results show that their child is indeed handicapped before discussing any special education program at all; if the parents disagree with the findings, they have the responsibility to avail themselves of their due process rights to resolve the issue

In Programming

- insist upon receiving written notice before the school proposes to initiate or change a special education program for their child

- insist that a meeting be held within 30 calendar days of a determination that their child needs special education and related services to formulate an IEP for the pupil

- insist that such an IEP meeting be held well before the beginning of school in September if their child already is receiving special education

- insist that the participants at the meeting include:
  1. a representative of the school system, other than the child's teacher, who is qualified to provide or supervise the special education programming
  2. the child's teacher
  3. the parents
  4. the child where appropriate
  5. whoever else the parent or school system thinks would be helpful

- insist that the IEP meeting also include a member of the evaluation team who is knowledgeable about the procedures used with the child and with their results

- insist that they be notified of the IEP meeting early enough and that it be set at a convenient time to ensure that they have an opportunity to attend

- insist that other methods be used to ensure their participation if they cannot attend

- make every effort to attend all meetings held to plan or review their child's IEP

- prepare as well as possible for the IEP meeting by reviewing their file on the testing and evaluation of their child as well as requesting and reviewing the school system's records

- bring friends, advocates, or professionals to the IEP meeting if it will help the parents feel more comfortable

- think through, ahead of time, what kinds of things they believe their child is ready to learn

- prepare an outline of key items and concerns that they wish to raise at the IEP meeting

- contribute real-life information at the IEP meeting that they feel is relevant about their child and education or gives a fuller picture than simple test scores

- discuss, at the IEP meeting, their impressions of past programs or services

- find out how the professionals feel the parents can carry over the program from school to home

- be open to new ideas or suggestions made by the other participants

- try not to be overly defensive or protective of their child or of their role

- be wary of any suggestion to place (or leave) their child in a program that has a label; a program for the "mentally retarded," "learning disabled," "physically handicapped," etc., may not be appropriate simply because the child may have that handicap; rather, a plan must be individually designed to meet the unique needs of the child—the program must be made to fit the child, rather than the reverse

- be careful to fully understand the issue of mainstreaming or least restrictive environment; if the pupil is to receive most or part of the education with nonhandicapped children, the type and extent of that mainstreaming become an issue

- urge that their child be mainstreamed to the greatest extent possible because it is essential to educational growth and development; however, parents have an equal responsibility not to push for, or allow others to push for, mainstreaming to the extent that the pupil cannot keep up with nonhandicapped peers

- be assertive of their role in decision making but at the same time recognize that other participants have valuable contributions to make from which the parents can learn, even if they disagree with the professionals' statements

- be certain that architectural barriers are not a primary reason for excluding their child from a particular education program

- have a complete understanding of the IEP that is developed and obtain a copy of the final version in writing

- be sure that the IEP is not drafted in general terms such as: "The child will make progress;" rather, the IEP should include clear-cut objectives that can be measured

- be sure that the IEP specifies how much time the child will spend in the mainstream, what special education services and related services will be received, from whom, how often, starting when, where, etc.

- understand exactly what changes in behavior and development to expect for the year and how each program, service, or teacher will help the child reach the potential

- learn about the training and experience of the staff that will be working with their child

- determine how and when their child will be tested again and reevaluated at regular intervals to see whether the original assessments and program still are appropriate

- be sure that the IEP is flexible enough to accommodate modifications to meet their child's changing needs

- understand how the program will involve them and how regularly they will be required to communicate with the staff

- communicate with other parents of children who are receiving similar program services

In Placement

- insist on notice when the school proposes to initiate or change the placement of their child, or refuses to do so

- insist that their consent be obtained before the school initially places their child in a program providing special education and related services

- insist that the notice fully explain the action (and reasons for it) proposed or refused by the school and describe any options the system considered and why they were rejected

- insist that before any action is taken on the initial placement of their child in a special program there be a full and individual evaluation of the pupil's educational needs

- be assured that the placement is based upon information from a variety of sources, including aptitude and achievement tests, teacher recommendations, physical condition, social or cultural background, and adaptive behavior

- be assured that the information upon which the placement decision is based is documented and was considered carefully

- be assured that the placement decision was made by a group (not a single individual), including persons knowledgeable about the child, the meaning of the evaluation data, and the placement options

- understand the maximum appropriate extent to which their child can be educated with nonhandicapped peers

- understand that special classes, separate schooling, or other removal of their child from the regular educational environment should occur only when the nature or severity of the handicap is such that instruction in regular classes, even with the use of supplementary aids and services, cannot be achieved satisfactorily

- insist that the educational placement fit the child, rather than the pupil's simply being put in a situation or facility because that is what is available

- insist that their child be educated in the least restrictive environment possible

- insist that the school system maintain a continuum of alternative placements, including instruction in regular classes, special classes, resource rooms, special schools, residential schools, at home, and in hospitals and institutions

- be assured that such alternative placements are available to the extent necessary to implement their child's IEP

- be assured that their child's educational placement is as close as possible to the home

- be assured that their child is educated in the school that would be attended if not handicapped unless the IEP requires some other arrangement

- visit the proposed placement before giving their permission for their child to be assigned there

- communicate with the parents of other children who are at the same placement

- be assured that the placement has the capacity to carry out the agreed-upon IEP and has the right staff, special instructional material and equipment, and adequate opportunities for integration with nonhandicapped peers to the extent called for in the program

- be comfortable with the proposed placement as being compatible with the child's self-perception and the type of population with which the pupil identifies

- be assured that class activities in the proposed placement are designed to allow the handicapped child to participate without the impairment's dictating the nature of every activity or the extent of the pupil's involvement

- be assured that the placement seems to respect their child as a whole person in that it could fulfill the normal social/emotional as well as educational needs

- be assured that the placement has been recommended primarily because of the limitations inherent in the child's handicap rather than because of school budgetary constraints

In Due Process Hearings and Appeals

- attempt to resolve disputes between themselves and the school system over issues of identification, evaluation, program, or placement of their child

- initiate due process procedures when such disputes cannot be resolved otherwise

- understand the nature and process of a special education due process hearing

- understand the roles of the hearing officer, school system, parents, child, attorneys, advocates, expert witnesses, teachers, etc., in a due process hearing

- prepare their presentation for the hearing and seek assistance if necessary

- disclose to the school system, at least five days before the hearing, the evidence they intend to introduce

- insist that they be provided with written findings of fact and decisions from the hearing officer as soon as possible

- follow through with their complaint by appealing to the state education agency or court if they feel the hearing officer did not address their concerns fairly

- attempt to reach an agreement with the school system as to the least disruptive placement for the child during the pendency of any administrative or judicial proceeding regarding their complaint

- insist that the child remain in the current placement if an agreement cannot be reached for the pendency of the proceedings

- pursue only complaints that they truly believe have merit and are in the best interests of their child

Confidentiality of Information

- be aware of and informed about the education records maintained on their child by the school system or other agency responsible for such instruction

- avail themselves of their rights to amend or delete information in those records if they believe that the material collected, maintained, or used is inaccurate or misleading or violates the privacy or other rights of their child

- place in the school or agency records a statement commenting on the information or stating any reasons for disagreeing with the agency decision if that entity decides after a hearing that the material is not inaccurate, misleading or otherwise in violation of the child's privacy or other rights

- insist that their consent be obtained before personally identifiable information about their child is disclosed to anyone other than authorized persons collecting or using the information for carrying out their responsibilities under P.L. 94-142

Chapter 13

Schools and Professionals

THE ROLE OF SCHOOL PERSONNEL

[The fundamental requirement of the law is that every state and its localities must make available a free appropriate public education for all handicapped children aged 3 to 21. However, the mere passage of this law does not ensure that its mandate will be implemented. The role of school system personnel is to shoulder that responsibility for implementation. The schools are required to deliver the entitlements to the handicapped children and their parents. Basically, the role of school personnel is to operationalize the law's promise.]

The law also contains a whole spectrum of requirements stemming from the fundamental mandate to provide a free appropriate public education. To carry out all of these, the law requires a series of interlocking responsibilities among state and local education agencies and the U.S. Department of Education.

The state must develop and adhere to a state plan. That plan must be approved by the Department of Education and no federal funds may be allocated to a state until its program is accepted. Similarly, local (and intermediate) education agencies must make formal application to the state, outlining the services they will provide in return for a portion of the federal monies. No funds may pass through to the local agency until it provides assurances and evidence of conforming to the state plan and receives state approval.

The state plan and local applications are detailed blueprints of how the education agencies propose to carry out their roles under the law. Each consists of three main components that require:

1. certain assurances, such as a guarantee that the agency will ensure due process rights and protections for children and their parents

2. a detailing of certain procedures, such as for child-find and screening of students for possible handicapping conditions
3. a detailed resource plan that must include a description of the kind and number of services, personnel, and facilities necessary to fully meet the needs of all handicapped children in their respective jurisdictions

State plans and local applications must be made available to the public at least 30 days before submission to Washington. The public then has an opportunity to comment and receive responses from the agencies. Copies of the plan and applications must be made available to parents and others upon request.

The roles of the school system personnel are so broad that the law requires states and localities to develop plans detailing how they are to be carried out. If the plans are not approved, or there is a failure to adhere to a program once it is accepted, the federal monies can be cut off. The role of school system professionals at all levels is to implement the requirement for providing a free appropriate public education for all handicapped children, and they are held accountable for how they fill that role.

RIGHTS OF SCHOOL PERSONNEL

School system personnel have a right to:

- not be held legally accountable if an individual handicapped child does not progress at the rate, or achieve the growth, projected in the individualized education program (IEP); agencies and teachers must make good faith efforts to assist each pupil in achieving the listed objective and goals but the IEP does not constitute a guarantee that a student will advance at any specified rate

- refuse to place a student in a private program at public expense if a free appropriate public education is made available

- initiate a special education due process hearing on any matter relating to the identification, evaluation, program, placement, review, or reevaluation of the child

- initiate such a hearing on any matter relating to the cost or provision of a free appropriate public education

- initiate such a hearing on the appropriateness of the school system's evaluation of the child; if the hearing officer determines that the evaluation is appropriate, then the school system need not pay for an independent analysis

- initiate a hearing on any matter related to the parents' refusal to give their consent to actions that school personnel believe are necessary to assist their child

- be accompanied and advised at the hearing by lawyers and by individuals with special knowledge or training on the problems of handicapped children

- present evidence and confront, cross-examine, and compel the attendance of witnesses at the hearing

- prohibit the introduction of any evidence that has not been disclosed to them at least five days before the hearing

- obtain a written or electronic verbatim record of the hearing

- request extensions of time as necessary in the hearing and appeals

- obtain written findings of fact and decisions from the hearing officer

- consider the hearing officer's decision as being final and act accordingly unless one of the parties chooses to appeal

- appeal the decision of the hearing officer if the professionals choose by bringing a civil action in a court of competent jurisdiction

- conduct a state level review of the hearing officer's decision (unless, of course, the initial hearing was held at the state level)

- have the state level official conducting the review:
  1. examine the entire hearing record
  2. ensure that the procedures at the hearing were consistent with the requirements of due process
  3. seek additional evidence if necessary
  4. afford the parties an opportunity for oral or written argument, or both, at the discretion of the reviewing official
  5. make an independent decision upon completion of the review
  6. provide a copy of written findings and the decision to the parties

- receive a final decision from the hearing officer not later than 45 days after receipt of the request for the session

- receive a final decision from the state level review not later than 30 days after receipt of the request for the session

- use their normal procedures on alternative service provision or suspension to deal with the child during the pendency of any administrative or judicial proceeding if the pupil is endangering self or others or is so disruptive in a regular classroom that the education of other students is significantly impaired

- provide special education and related services to private school handicapped children that are different from those offered to public school children if:
  1. the differences are necessary to meet the special needs of the private school handicapped children, and
  2. the special education and related services are comparable in quality, scope, and opportunity for participation to those provided to public school children with needs of equal importance

- conduct IEP meetings without parents present if unable to convince them they should attend; in that case, the school personnel must have a record of their attempts to arrange a mutually agreed-upon time and place such as:
  1. detailed records of telephone calls made or attempted and the results
  2. copies of correspondence to the parents and any responses received
  3. detailed records of visits to the parents' home or place of employment and the results

RESPONSIBILITIES OF SCHOOL PERSONNEL

School system personnel have a responsibility to:

In General

- make available a free appropriate public education for all handicapped children aged 3 to 21

- approach the provision of services with a view of the child as a total human being rather than by specific handicapping condition

- view the child in terms of educational needs, as opposed to labelling the pupil and fitting the label to a program

- provide the parents with written notice of a reasonable time before they:

    1. initiate or change the identification, evaluation, program, or place-
ment of the child or the provision of a free appropriate public
education
    2. refuse to initiate or change the identification, evaluation, program
or placement of the child, or the provision of a free appropriate
public education to the child

- include in the notice to parents:
    1. a full explanation of all of the procedural safeguards available to
    them
    2. a description of the action proposed or refused by the agency, an
    explanation of this position, and a description of any options con-
    sidered and why they were rejected
    3. a description of each evaluation procedure, test, record, or report
    the agency uses as a basis for the proposal or refusal
    4. a description of any other factors relevant to the agency's proposal
    or refusal

- ensure that the notice of the child's parents is:
    1. written in language understandable to the general public
    2. provided in the parents' native language or other mode of com-
    munication unless it is clearly not feasible to do so

- be certain that, if the native language or other mode of communication
is not written, the state or local educational agency will take steps to
assure that:
    1. the notice is translated orally or by other means to the parents in
    their native language or other mode of communication
    2. the parents understand the content of the notice
    3. there is written evidence that the requirements have been met

- assume leadership at the state level to carry out their expanded administrative role, which includes allocating new resources, assessing
the effectiveness of delivery systems, designing staff development programs, and monitoring private school programs for handicapped children

- monitor the distribution of federal funds; state level administrators
must assume fiscal responsibilities in providing for all handicapped
children because the state is directly accountable to the U.S. Department of Education for all funds that flow through to intermediate and
local education agencies

- cut off federal funds to intermediate and local education agencies that
do not comply with the overall state plan or to their own application
requirements

- ensure that federal funds are not commingled with, or used to supplant, state funds in educating handicapped children

- reassess priorities in state school finance formulas to fulfill the mandates of the law if the flow of federal dollars were to be cut back

- modernize recordkeeping systems in order to keep a constant tally of the number of handicapped children being served throughout the state and to monitor the effectiveness of all delivery systems

- conduct a needs assessment on the state level to determine which persons are inadequately trained and what staff development is necessary

- design at the state level inservice staff development programs on a continuing basis for all persons engaged in the education of handicapped children

- provide options to their staff members such as released time, stipends, academic credit, salary step credit, or certification renewal to create incentives for teacher participation in staff development programs

- work with universities and teacher colleges to redesign teacher preparation programs so that general elementary and secondary education majors gain more knowledge and skills necessary for dealing with various types of handicapped children in their classrooms

- make provisions for public school personnel and equipment to be used in private schools or facilities to properly implement the IEPs of children enrolled or placed in such programs

In Identification

- identify, locate, and evaluate all children who are handicapped and need special education regardless of the severity of their impairment

- develop and implement a practical method to determine which children are receiving needed special education and related services and which are not

- take steps to notify handicapped children and their parents or guardians of the school system's duty to identify, locate, evaluate all of the impaired who need special education, regardless of the severity of their dysfunction

- conduct child-find activities on a continuing basis, including use of newspapers, radio, television, and magazines

- establish working relationships with other human service agencies in the same jurisdiction to identify, locate, and evaluate all handicapped children

- conduct surveys in the community to locate and identify handicapped children; such surveys could be door-to-door interviews, telephone interviews, mailed questionnaires, church or synagogue bulletins, notices in public utility bills, etc.

- screen all kindergarten children annually for health, vision, hearing, motor functioning, language development, and social/emotional development

- screen all school-aged children regularly by school, grade, or class to identify those who may have special education needs

- establish a standard procedure for receiving and routing referrals of children who are possibly in need of special education and related services

- notify the parents of the child who is referred for an evaluation by any source

In Evaluation

- ensure that, before any action is taken on the initial placement of a handicapped child in a special education program, a full and individual needs evaluation is conducted

- ensure that if a handicapped child already is receiving special education, an evaluation is conducted every three years (or more frequently if conditions warrant or if the parents or teacher requests it)

- obtain parental consent before conducting a preplacement evaluation

- initiate a special education due process hearing, or petition a court of competent jurisdiction, to override parents' refusal to consent to an evaluation if the school specialists strongly believe such an assessment is warranted

- ensure that testing and evaluation materials and procedures used for assessment and placement of handicapped children are selected and administered so as not to be racially or culturally discriminatory

- ensure specifically that tests and other evaluation materials:

1. are provided and administered in the child's native language or other mode of communication, unless it clearly is not feasible to do so
2. have been validated for the specific purpose for which they are used
3. are administered by trained personnel in conformance with the instructions provided by their producer
4. include those tailored to assess specific areas of educational need and not merely those designed to provide a single general intelligence quotient
5. are selected and administered so as best to ensure that when a test is administered to a child with impaired sensory, manual, or speaking skills, the results accurately appraise the aptitude, achievement level, or whatever other factors it purports to measure, rather than reflecting the impaired skills (except where they are the factors the test is intended to evaluate)
6. are administered by specialists familiar with local cultural, language, and social patterns and practices
7. incorporate established local community norms when norm-referenced tests are used

- ensure that no single procedure is used as the sole criterion for determining an appropriate educational program for a child
- ensure that the evaluation is made by a multidisciplinary team or group, including at least one teacher or other specialist with knowledge in the area of suspected disability
- ensure that the child is assessed in all areas related to the suspected disability including, where appropriate, health, vision, hearing, social and emotional status, general intelligence, academic performance, communicative status, and motor abilities
- inform parents that they have the right to obtain an independent educational evaluation of their child
- provide to the parents, upon their request, information about where such an independent evaluation may be obtained
- consider the results of any independent evaluation obtained by the parents in any decision made about providing a free appropriate public education to the child

In Developing the IEP

- develop and implement an IEP for every handicapped child if it is determined that the child's needs require special education and related services

- develop and implement an IEP for every child who is handicapped and in need of special education, even if the system places or refers the pupil to a private school or facility or even if the student is enrolled in a parochial or other private school and receives special education or related services from the public school system

- have an IEP in effect at the beginning of each school year for each handicapped child who already is receiving special education

- have an IEP in effect before providing any special education and related services to a child

- initiate and conduct meetings to develop, review, and revise each child's IEP as often as needed, but at least once a year

- conduct such an IEP meeting within 30 calendar days of when a child is initially determined to need special education and related services

- take steps to ensure that one or both of the parents are present at each meeting, or are afforded the opportunity to participate, by:
  1. notifying them of the meeting early enough to assure that they will have an opportunity to attend
  2. scheduling the session at a mutually agreed-upon time and place

- make sure the notice indicates the purpose, time, and location of the meeting and who will attend

- ensure that if neither parent can attend, other methods to assure their participation, including individual or conference telephone calls, are used

- take whatever action is necessary to ensure that the parents understand the proceedings at a meeting, including arranging for an interpreter for those who are deaf or whose native language is other than English

- give the parents, on request, a copy of the IEP

- ensure that each meeting to develop the IEP includes the following participants:
  1. a representative of the school system, other than the child's teacher, who is qualified to provide, or supervise the provision of, special education
  2. the child's teacher
  3. one or both of the parents
  4. the child, where appropriate
  5. other individuals at the discretion of the parent or school system

- have the evaluation personnel, for a handicapped child who has been assessed for the first time, ensure that:
  1. a member of the evaluation team participates
  2. the representative of the school system, the teacher, or some other person is present who is knowledgeable about the evaluation procedures used with the child and is familiar with the results

- ensure that the parents understand and participate in what is happening at the IEP meeting

- implement the IEP immediately following the meeting; an exception would be (1) when the meetings occur during the summer or a vacation period, or (2) where circumstances require a short delay, such as working out transportation arrangements; however, there can be no undue delay

- provide a written IEP that contains information on the following:
  1. the child's present level of performance and strengths as well as weaknesses
  2. the short-term and annual goals that indicate clearly how much the child is expected to learn over certain periods of time; these goals should be stated in objective or measurable terms
  3. the specific special education and related services to be provided to help accomplish the goals
  4. how much the child will be able to participate in the regular school program with those who are not handicapped
  5. when the special services will begin and how long each service or special program will be provided
  6. when and how the child's progress and the effectiveness of the IEP will be evaluated
  7. a justification for the type of educational placement chosen
  8. a list of the specific individuals responsible for implementing the IEP

- offer programs, services, and other educational opportunities to the handicapped child that are comparable to those offered the nonimpaired

In Placement

- make placement decisions based on information from a variety of sources, including aptitude and achievement tests, teacher recommendations, physical condition, social or cultural background, and adaptive behavior

- ensure that placement decisions are based on information that is documented and carefully considered

- ensure that placement decisions are made by a group, including persons knowledgeable about the child, the meaning of the evaluation data, and the options

- obtain the parents' consent before placing a child initially in a program providing special education and related services

- redetermine the placement at least once a year

- ensure that the placement is based on the IEP

- place the child in a program as close as possible to home

- educate the child in the school that would have been attended if there were no handicap unless the IEP requires some other arrangements

- ensure that a continuum of alternative placements is available; this continuum should include instruction in regular classes, itinerant assistance, special resource rooms for part of the school day, full-time special classrooms, special schools, residential facilities, instruction at home and in hospitals and institutions, and placements in programs outside of the system at the expense of the school if necessary

- make provision for supplementary services such as resource room or itinerant instruction, to be provided in conjunction with regular class

- ensure that to the maximum extent appropriate, handicapped children, including those in public or private institutions or other care facilities, are educated with the nonimpaired

- ensure that special classes, separate schooling, or other removal of handicapped children from the regular educational environment occur only when the severity of the impairment is such that participation in regular classes, even with the use of supplementary aids and services, is unsatisfactory

- ensure that in selecting the least restrictive environment, consideration is given to any potential harmful effect on the child or on the quality of services

- not place in a regular classroom a handicapped child who is so disruptive that the education of other students is impaired significantly

- be certain that the staff members in the placement are trained, willing, ready, and able to receive and provide properly for the child

ɔse a placement compatible with the child's self-perception and the type of population with which the pupil identifies

In Due Process Hearings and Appeals

- establish a system and procedures for conducting special education due process hearings and appeals

- contract with individuals to serve as independent and impartial hearing officers

- initiate a special education due process hearing whenever an impasse is reached with the parents over the child's identification, evaluation, program, or placement

- initiate such a hearing to override the parents' refusal to consent to an action the school proposed if the staff members believe the step is warranted

- inform the parents of any free or low-cost legal and other relevant services available in the area if they request such help or if school personnel are the ones requesting the hearing

- not permit any school employees to serve as hearing officers

- keep a list of those who serve as hearing officers; include a statement of the qualifications of each

- carry their case through the appeal process at the state level and to the courts if they feel their position is meritorious

- ensure that not later than 45 days after receipt of a request for a hearing:
  1. a final decision is reached
  2. a copy of the decision is mailed to each of the parties

- ensure at the state level that not later than 30 days after receipt of a request for a review or appeal:
  1. a final decision is reached in the review
  2. a copy of the decision is mailed to each of the parties

- attempt to reach agreement with the parents as to the best placement for the child during the pendency of any administrative or judicial proceeding regarding a complaint

- place the child in a public school program until the completion of all administrative or judicial proceedings if the complaint involves an application for initial admission to public school and the parties cannot reach an agreement on another temporary placement

- use normal procedures for alternative service delivery or suspension when dealing with a child who is endangering self or others, pending the outcome of the special education decision-making process

In Protecting the Confidentiality of Information

- establish written procedures for the storage, retrieval, and use of all information collected pertinent to the education of every handicapped student to assure its confidentiality
- provide notice to parents that is adequate to inform them fully about the legal requirements on confidentiality of information; the notice must include:
  1. a description of the extent to which it is given in the native languages of the various population groups in the state
  2. a description of the children on whom personally identifiable material is maintained, the types of information sought, the methods the state intends to use in gathering the material (including sources), and the use to be made of it
  3. a summary of the policies and procedures participating agencies must follow on storage, disclosure to third parties, retention, and destruction of personally identifiable information
  4. a description of all of the rights of parents and children regarding this information, including the rights under 20 U.S.C. § 1232 G, The Family Educational Rights and Privacy Act of 1974 (FERPA), and its implementing regulations, 34 CFR, Part 99
- ensure that before any major identification, location, or evaluation activity, notice must be published or announced in newspapers or other media, or both, with circulation adequate to notify parents throughout the state of the activity
- permit parents to inspect and review any education records relating to their children that are collected, maintained, or used by the agency; the agency in turn must comply with a request without unnecessary delay and before any meeting on an IEP or hearing on the identification, evaluation, or placement of the child, and in no case more than 45 days after the request has been made
- inspect and review education records, including:
  1. obtaining a response from the agency to reasonable requests for explanations and interpretations of the records

    2. obtaining from the agency copies of the records containing the information if failure to provide them would prevent parents from exercising the right to inspect and review the records '

    3. having a representative of the parents inspect and review the records

- presume that parents have authority to inspect and review records relating to their child unless the agency has been advised that they lack that right under state law governing such matters as guardianship, separation, and divorce

- keep a record of parties obtaining access to education records (except parents and authorized employees of the agency), including the name of the party, the date access was given, and the purpose for which the party is authorized to use the records

- ensure that if any education record includes information on more than one child (in other words, pupils from more than one family), the parents have the right to inspect and review only the material relating to their child or to be informed of that specific information

- provide parents on request with a list of the types and locations of education records collected, maintained, or used by the agency

- provide a procedure whereby parents who believe that the records are inaccurate or misleading or violate the privacy or other rights of the child may request the agency that maintains the information to amend it

- decide whether to amend the information in accordance with the request within a reasonable time after receipt of the request

- ensure that if the agency decides to refuse to amend the information in accordance with the request, it informs the parents of that action and advises them of the right to a hearing

- provide an opportunity for a hearing to challenge information in education records to ensure that it is not inaccurate, misleading, or otherwise in violation of the privacy or other rights of the child

- ensure that if as a result of the hearing, the agency decides that the information is inaccurate, misleading, or otherwise in violation of the child's privacy or other rights, it will amend the material accordingly and inform the parents in writing

- ensure that if, as a result of the hearing, the agency decides that the information is not inaccurate, misleading, or otherwise in violation of the child's rights, it will inform the parents of their right to place in the records a statement commenting on the material or giving reasons for disagreeing with the agency finding

- require that any explanation placed in the child's records:
  1. be maintained by the agency as long as it keeps the record or contested portion
  2. disclose to any of the parties an explanation of why the agency opened the child's records or the contested portion to anyone, if it in fact did so

- obtain parental consent before personally identifiable information is disclosed to anyone other than officials of agencies collecting or using the material to locate, identify, and evaluate children who may require special education or to fulfill other data collection requirements under the law

- ensure that the annual state program includes policies and procedures to be used if parents refuse to consent to the appropriate disclosure of confidential information

- protect the confidentiality of personally identifiable information at collection, storage, disclosure, and destruction stages

- ensure that one official at each agency assumes responsibility for assuring the confidentiality of any such information

- ensure that all persons collecting or using such information receive training or instruction regarding the state's policies and procedures on the confidentiality of such material

- maintain for public inspection a current listing of the names and positions of agency employees who may have access to personally identifiable information

- inform parents when such information no longer is needed to provide educational services to the child

- destroy such information at the parents' request; however, a permanent record of a student's name, address, and phone number, grades, attendance record, classes attended, and grade level and year completed may be maintained without time limitation

- ensure that the state educational agency annual program includes policies and procedures on the extent to which children are afforded rights of privacy similar to those given to parents, taking into consideration the age of the child and type or severity of disability

- describe in the annual state program plan the policies and procedures, including sanctions, that the state uses to ensure that they are followed and that legal requirements are met

In Dealing with Parents

- recognize the right of parents to be involved in the decisions about their child's education

- not allow themselves to be harassed or pressured by parents bent on interfering with them and other school system personnel as they carry out their responsibilities

- be sensitive to parents' feelings without labelling or judging them; society places a tremendous stigma and burden on being handicapped—a pressure that produces intense feelings in those who have the difficult job of parenting disabled children; this difficult job takes a great deal of care and consumes much physical and emotional energy

- help parents find the programs, resources, and services needed to raise a handicapped child; such assistance might well go beyond simply meeting the educational needs

Chapter 14

The Hearing Officer

THE ROLE OF THE HEARING OFFICER

The law provides that parents or the school system may initiate a due process hearing whenever there is a dispute over the provision of a free appropriate public education to a handicapped child. The hearing can involve a dispute over the child's identification, evaluation, program, or placement. When such a dispute arises and a hearing is sought, the authority to decide the issue passes from the parties themselves to the hearing officer.

The role of the hearing officer is to conduct the due process hearing in an orderly and impartial manner, then render a decision within the limits of the law and in the best interests of the child. To carry out this function, the individual must use the proceeding as a mechanism for gathering information and resolving conflicts about it. The hearing officer has only a short time for self-education about the child and the proposed program and thus must facilitate the presentation of information. The school system and the parents must have a full opportunity to be heard in an orderly fashion, to question all witnesses, and to discuss the evidence.

The hearing officer begins the role in many jurisdictions as somewhat of a coordinator, responsible for arranging the hearing and notifying all parties of the major activities or requirements leading up to it.

At the hearing, the hearing officer sets the tone. The individual's values, manner of speaking, attitudes, style, and example will permeate the proceeding. It usually is helpful to make the parties feel comfortable and relaxed, but a professional atmosphere must be maintained and the proceedings or participants must not be abused.

The hearing officer provides a structure and maintains an atmosphere that will encourage everyone to participate without sacrificing decorum. Throughout the process, the hearing officer is responsible for informing all parties of their rights before, during, and after the hearing.

After closing the hearing, the hearing officer becomes a decision maker who is responsible for making a reasonable finding based solely on the evidence and testimony presented.

SELECTION OF INDIVIDUALS TO SERVE

The hearing officer must attempt to keep the parties on the track of decision making with regard to the child's special education and must have sufficient strength and clarity of purpose to resist being diverted on side issues.

The role is limited to focusing on the case presented. The role is even narrower when it is noted that the proceeding can focus only on the child's need for special education. The role does not include such matters as the school system's budget or the parents' domestic problems. The role is to direct the due process hearing, render a decision, and maintain professional integrity as an independent arbiter.

To carry out the role of hearing officer effectively, the individuals selected should have the following qualifications or characteristics:

- ability to analyze and evaluate evidence

- ability to interpret and apply laws, rules, regulations, and legal precedents

- ability to write clear and concise statements of fact and law, recommendations, and orders

- ability to obtain facts from individuals through observation and interviews under difficult conditions

- ability to handle difficult situations when presenting or preparing cases

- ability to preside at and control meetings, conferences, or hearings

- ability to make independent decisions on important matters

- ability to be objective and free from influence of any kind

- professional standing among members of the profession

- knowledge and experience in special education fields

- demonstrated judicial temperament and poise

IMPARTIALITY AND WHO MAY SERVE

To protect the integrity of the role, the hearing officer must be an impartial party in no way involved with the child, parent, or school system. The regulations provide that:

> A hearing may not be conducted:
> (1) By a person who is an employee of a public agency which is involved in the education or care of the child, or
> (2) By any person having a personal or professional interest which would conflict with his or her objectivity in the hearing. (§ 121a.507(a))

A person who otherwise qualifies to conduct a hearing is not considered to be an employee of the agency solely because of being paid by the agency to serve as a hearing officer.

In most instances, the language of the law is adequate to determine whether a particular individual is qualified to serve as an impartial hearing officer (IHO). However, a number of questions have arisen regarding certain types of persons serving as IHOs and unfortunately, the answers have been somewhat unclear.

For example, one question has been whether a member of a board of education or a director of special education from another school district can serve as an IHO. Different states follow different policies. The U.S. Department of Education has clarified some of the problems of interpretation but has not addressed a number of others. Court decisions also have impacted on this problem. The following analysis of the overall issue of impartiality and who may serve as an IHO summarizes the various questions and answers:

Q. Can a member of a local board of education serve as an IHO at a local level hearing?
A. No.

Q. Can a director of special education or similar employee serve as an IHO at a local level hearing?
A. No.

Q. Can a member of a local board of education or a director of special education serve as an IHO at a local level hearing in another school district?
A. Yes. Although there is no clear legal barrier to this practice, it is questionable. A person such as a director of special education is likely to

have been a party in a number of disputes in this field. Such experiences increase the possibilities of partiality and conflict of interest that would put the prospective IHO within the prohibition of having a personal or professional interest that would conflict with the individual's objectivity.

Q. Can a person employed by or affiliated with a state education agency (SEA) serve as a review officer at a state level appeal?
A. Maybe. Several courts have decided that this practice is not permissible. However, the Department of Education does not prohibit the practice so long as the SEA is not the direct provider of the special education program to the student.

Q. Can an IHO's authority be limited to conducting the hearing and making recommendations to a final decision maker such as the local board of education or the superintendent of schools?
A. No. The same applies to a state level review or appeal.

THE IMPORTANCE OF TRAINING

There are three major problems that commonly arise among hearing officers:

1. Failure to control the hearing: There is a tendency for hearing officers to be intimidated by attorneys. Tactics involving noneducational matters during a hearing may tend to confuse, obstruct, and hinder a natural and orderly educational hearing process.
2. Using material not in evidence: The hearing officer may fail to ask a question since the individual already knows the answer, then in the decision, uses this material as "an already known fact" even though it was not in the evidence.
3. Basing a decision on personal ideas: The hearing officer may decide a case on the basis of a personal educational theory rather than on the evidence.

Hearing officers with special education backgrounds generally seem more susceptible to being caught in the pitfalls just described than those with no experience in the field. Lawyers who are appointed hearing officers have considerably less trouble with this sort of problem. Their training teaches them how to ask every question necessary to adduce evidence in a way that the whole story is evident without gaps to be filled in by assumptions. Lawyers also are less confident in matters of special education and therefore feel the need to ask questions even if they think they already know the answer.

Lawyers also are trained to detach themselves from the conflict. They are taught to let the evidence speak for itself or to try to put the best gloss on the evidence available. Either way, they know that the strength of their case rests on the evidence they have marshalled and not on their own personal philosophies or theories, which they might wish the evidence could show.

However, persons with special education backgrounds have the potential to be the best type of hearing officers because of their intimate experience with the subject. What they must remind themselves is that their decision should be apparent from the evidence presented. Would an observer without special education training have arrived at the same conclusion if required to write the decision from the same evidence?

The special education background of the hearing officer can be extremely helpful if used properly. The knowledge of this field can be used to probe deeper into the assertions and contentions of the hearing participants.

Why does the social worker believe that family therapy would be necessary in addition to individual therapy for the child? How does the proposed program intend to address the child's visual distractibility? What is this handicapped pupil's primary learning modality? Why wasn't a neurological assessment performed to rule out the possibility of brain damage to explain this student's behavior and performance?

The point is that a hearing officer with a special education background should use personal knowledge as an observer would: to bring out more information pertinent to this particular child.

The following outline contains suggested topics in training persons for the hearing officer role. Topics could be expanded or reduced depending on the background, experience, and training needs of the persons involved.

TRAINING WORKSHOP OUTLINE

Session I. Overview of Due Process

    A. Historical review of the right to education
    B. Public Law 94-142
    C. State public policy on the education of handicapped children

Synopsis

This component addresses the legal basis of a handicapped child's right to an education and the assurance of that right through procedural safeguards. It includes a discussion of landmark court decisions and legislation in a historical context and with regard to their current implications for special education.

Format

Audiovisual presentation, lecture, and discussion.

Session II. An Appropriate Education for the Exceptional Child

A. Who is a handicapped child under the law?
B. How might such a child come to the attention of parents or teachers?
C. How can this child's needs and abilities be measured?
D. How can such evaluation data be translated into educationally relevant terms?
E. How is a special education program developed to match the child's needs?
F. What would be an appropriate placement for this child?
   1. What does "appropriate" mean?
   2. What is the principle of "least restrictive environment"?
   3. What would implementation of this placement plan require?

Synopsis

This component provides a general overview of the process leading to an educational placement of the handicapped child. The discussion should focus on descriptions of impaired pupils in terms of educational needs, identification, evaluation, programming, and placement. In addition to providing basic information to hearing officers with limited special education background, this component should address the critical issue of "appropriateness."

Format

Audiovisual presentation, guidebook, materials, case study exercise, lecture, and discussion.

Session III. The Hearing Officer

A. Role in the due process hearing
B. Qualifications
C. Responsibilities

D. Authority
E. Ethical considerations

Synopsis

This component should help define the parameters of the hearing officer's role in due process procedures.

Format

Lecture and discussion.

Session IV. Preparation for the Due Process Hearing

A. Sequence of events leading to a due process hearing
B. Administrative details
C. Prehearing conference
D. The hearing room

Synopsis

This component should acquaint hearing officers with the preliminary matters they must attend to before a due process hearing can proceed at the appointed time.

Format

Checklist materials, training exercises, lecture, and discussion.

Session V. Conduct of the Due Process Hearing

A. Basic issues at the due process hearing
B. Hearing officer's statement
C. Order of presentations
D. Evidence and testimony
E. Burden of proof
F. Suspension of a hearing
G. Conclusion of hearing
H. Implementing the decision

Synopsis

This component should familiarize hearing officers with the conduct of a due process hearing and the issues and problems involved.

Format

Audiovisual presentation, lecture, and discussion.

Session VI. Simulated Due Process Hearing

Synopsis

This component should provide hearing officers with the opportunity to apply the information learned in a simulated setting. The exercise should use actual due process cases and materials that have been adapted slightly to protect the confidentiality of the real parties. The exercise should involve all the trainees in different roles.

Format

Simulation exercise.

A. Assign roles to participants (i.e., principal, teacher, parents, and hearing officer)
B. Review role descriptions
C. Study documents relative to role
D. Each side caucus and plan presentation
E. Role play due process hearing

Session VII. The Decision

A. Timelines
B. Arriving at a decision
C. Format of the decision
D. Writing the decision
E. The appeal process

Synopsis

This component should provide guidance to hearing officers in how to develop a sound decision. It also should explore placement considerations during the decision-making process.

Format

Continuation of simulation, exercise in writing a decision, lecture, and discussion.

MONITORING HEARING OFFICERS

Even with careful selection criteria and training, hearing officers should be monitored for fitness to serve in this important role. The following are suggested guidelines for that task.

The Hearing Officer's Impartiality

1. Does the individual make decisions based on factors other than the record?
2. Are decisions affected by the identity of lawyers or parties?
3. Does the person discuss pending matters off the record with the lawyer or party for one side without notifying all parties?
4. Is the officer influenced by personal, political, or financial pressures?

The Hearing Officer's Judicial Temperament

1. Does the individual treat attorneys, other hearing officers, and other persons patiently, respectfully, and courteously while sitting as a hearing officer?
2. Is the person reasonable and fair to attorneys and the parties?
3. Is the officer's conduct at the hearing conducive to respect for the law and the hearing forum?

The Hearing Officer's Professional Abilities

1. Does the officer understand issues in complex cases?
2. Are decisions well-reasoned and justifiable under existing law and sound educational practice?
3. Does the person keep abreast of legal developments and new theories in the field of special education?

The Hearing Officer's Diligence

1. Does the individual appear punctually for scheduled hearings and other pertinent meetings?
2. Are decisions written in a timely fashion?
3. Does the person generally seem well prepared for the hearing and decision writing?

Overall Evaluation of the Hearing Officer

1. Does the officer appear to be qualified and effective in the role overall?

LIABILITY OF HEARING OFFICERS

The liability of hearing officers may be raised in two ways. Attempts
may be made to find hearing officers liable for money damages (1) in their
official capacities or (2) in their individual capacities.

Emphasizing the functional similarity between hearing officers and judges,
the Supreme Court has held that hearing examiners for federal administrative agencies enjoy absolute immunity from damages for actions taken
in their official capacity. *Butz v. Economou*, 438 U.S. 478 (1978). The
Court stated:

> We think that adjudication within a federal administrative agency
> shares enough of the characteristics of the judicial process that
> those who participate in such adjudication should also be immune
> from suits for damages. The conflicts which federal hearing ex-
> aminers seek to resolve are every bit as fractious as those which
> come to court. . . .
>
> There can be no doubt that the role of the modern federal
> hearing examiner or administrative law judge within this frame-
> work is "functionally comparable" to that of a judge. . . . More
> importantly, the process of agency adjudication is currently struc-
> tured so as to assure that the hearing examiner exercises his in-
> dependent judgment on the evidence before him, free from pres-
> sures by the parties or other officials within the agency.
>
> In light of these safeguards, we think that the risk of an un-
> constitutional act by one presiding at an agency hearing is clearly
> outweighed by the importance of preserving the independent
> judgment of these men and women. We therefore hold that the
> persons subject to these restraints in performing adjudicatory
> functions within a federal agency are entitled to absolute immunity
> from damage liability for their judicial acts. Those who com-
> plained of error in such proceedings must seek agency or judicial
> review.

Hearing officers presiding over state and local education hearings share
the same function and play the same role as hearing examiners in any

adjudicatory administrative hearing and as such should not be liable for actions taken in their official capacity.

The purpose of providing this protective shield of absolute immunity is to preserve the independence and impartiality of hearing officers so that their decisions may be made free from intimidation or harassment. Individuals unhappy with the decisions of hearing officers, as the Court stated, have adequate redress by seeking a higher level administrative hearing or judicial review.

However, hearing officers enjoy only qualified immunity from money damages for actions taken in their individual capacities. There are two bases for finding a hearing officer liable in an individual capacity. One is if the hearing officer knew or should have known that the action taken within the sphere of official responsibility would violate the constitutional rights of the student affected. However, the hearing officer has no duty to anticipate unforeseeable constitutional developments. *Wood v. Strickland*, 420 U.S. 308 (1975).

The second basis for finding liability in an individual capacity is if the hearing officer took the action with the malicious intention to cause a deprivation of constitutional rights or other injury to the student. Malicious intent is a deliberate intent to act wrongfully.

In general, the hearing officer is not liable for money damages if sued in an individual capacity if there were reasonable grounds for the actions taken and the person acted in good faith. *Scheuer v. Rhodes*, 416 U.S. 232 (1974).

RIGHTS OF THE HEARING OFFICER

The hearing officer has a right to:

- determine a structure for the hearing and conduct the session accordingly

- require all participants to conduct themselves in an orderly manner

- rule on preliminary matters and objections raised during the proceeding

- question witnesses presented by either party and request the production of information or documents

- direct that an independent evaluation be conducted at the expense of the school system

- delay the hearing to gather more evidence or information if it is needed

- grant extensions of time upon request of any party

- issue a decision that is final and not simply a recommendation to the board of education, the superintendent of schools, or other authority

- issue an independent decision on the issues without interference or coercion by either of the parties

RESPONSIBILITIES OF THE HEARING OFFICER

The hearing officer has a responsibility to:

In Preparing for Being a Hearing Officer

- participate in the training sessions provided by the state education agency

- be familiar with state and federal legislation on the handicapped, particularly the aspects of law regarding public education due process protections

- keep up to date on litigation pertaining to the handicapped, particularly cases that originate in courts with local or state jurisdiction

- know procedures for due process adopted by the board of education

- be familiar with the procedures for survey, screening, evaluation, program development, and dismissal of children into/out of programs for the handicapped

- have a functional knowledge of the guidelines for least restrictive environment and the program models recognized by state law

- have a functional knowledge of the guidelines for nondiscriminatory testing and evaluation

- have a functional knowledge of the guidelines for confidentiality of information

- have a functional knowledge of the guidelines for individualized education programs (IEPs)

- know the procedures to follow before, during, and after a hearing

- obtain information regarding procedure/forms utilized in the local school system

In Arranging for a Hearing

- ensure that the parties have been contacted with regard to the date, time, and place of the session

- ensure that the administrative or logistical arrangements have been made to reserve the hearing room and have it properly equipped

- ensure that all of the parties are fully aware of their rights so that they may avail themselves of them before the date of the hearing, such as obtaining an independent evaluation, requesting the review of school records, disclosure of evidence at least five days before the session, etc.

In Conducting a Hearing

- make a self-introduction and explain the hearing officer's role in the case

- cite briefly the legal authority under which the proceeding is held

- explain the purpose of the hearing

- ensure that the parties are informed of their rights and had an opportunity to avail themselves of them

- explain the procedure that will be followed during the session

- preside at the hearing and ensure that all parties have a fair opportunity to present their evidence and to challenge the evidence of the other side

- administer oaths or affirmations in jurisdictions where they are required

- receive all documentary evidence submitted by the parties

- ensure that a verbatim recording of the proceeding is made

- rule on preliminary matters, procedural requests, objections, etc.

- summon witnesses or require the production of documents

- question witnesses presented by the parties if the hearing officer feels that further matters need be addressed

- present a judicious temperament by treating the participants patiently, respectfully, and courteously

- conduct the role of hearing officer in a manner conducive to respect for the law and the hearing forum
- make a complete record of the proceeding and include all relevant matters, rulings on objections, documentary evidence submitted, and verbatim record

In Issuing a Decision

- issue a decision in a timely fashion according to the rules of the jurisdiction
- determine credibility and the weight of evidence in making findings of fact and conclusions of law
- make decisions solely on the basis of the record, without being affected by factors such as the identity of the lawyers or parties, personal, political, or financial pressures
- abstain from discussing pending matters with any of the participants outside of the hearing
- produce a decision that is well-reasoned and justifiable under the law and in consideration of the evidence presented
- write a decision that includes findings of fact, conclusions of law, and the reasons for them; if the decision is to disapprove a proposed educational program, it should state what would be adequate and appropriate for the child; if the decision is to approve a plan, it should indicate why less restrictive placement alternatives could not serve the child's educational needs adequately and appropriately

In Protecting the Integrity of the Role

- be impartial and also ensure the appearance (and the fact) of impartiality
- not be an employee of a public agency involved in the education or care of the child
- not have a personal or professional interest that would conflict with objectivity in the hearing
- decline to serve as a hearing officer in a case where such a conflict exists or where it appears as though one might exist
- decline to disclose or discuss confidential information acquired in the course of a case

Chapter 15

The Surrogate Parent

THE ROLE OF THE SURROGATE PARENT

One of the fundamental provisions of the law is the right of the handicapped student's parents to be involved in the special education decision-making process. However, the law also recognizes that every such child may not have parents available to participate. Therefore, the law extends the right of parental participation by requiring that a surrogate parent be appointed to represent such children in the development of an individualized education program (IEP).

A surrogate parent is a person who is appointed to safeguard the educational rights of a handicapped child whose parents or guardians are unknown or who cannot be found by the agency after reasonable efforts, or when the pupil is a ward of the state. The surrogate parent acts as an advocate to assure that the student receives a free appropriate education in the least restrictive environment and that all educational due process guarantees are enforced.

The role of surrogate parent is limited. The regulations provide that:

> The surrogate parent may represent the child in all matters relating to:
> (1) The identification, evaluation, and educational placement of the child, and
> (2) The provision of a free appropriate public education to the child. (§ 121a.514(e))

Therefore, natural parents and legal guardians do not lose custody or parental rights in any other respect. A surrogate parent is not like a foster parent. A child lives in the home of a foster parent, who deals with most aspects of the pupil's development. The surrogate parent functions only in the educational realm. There is no overall, 24-hour-a-day responsibility for the child, as there is for a foster parent.

The surrogate parent participates in the special education decision-making process and development of the IEP as would a natural parent. The surrogate parent also takes part in other conferences and meetings with school personnel to make sure that the handicapped student receives the services set forth in the IEP. The surrogate works to see that the child receives the program components necessary for learning and for acquiring skills.

THE NEED FOR SURROGATE PARENTS

According to the regulations, each public agency with responsibility for educating the child

> shall insure that the rights of a child are protected when:
> (1) No parent . . . can be identified.
> (2) The public agency, after reasonable efforts, cannot discover the whereabouts of a parent; or
> (3) The child is a ward of the State under the laws of that State. (§ 121a.514(a))

The following questions focus on determining when a handicapped child is not represented by a parent as defined in the regulations, when a parent is not available to represent the pupil, and under what limited conditions a child is considered a ward of the state.

1. When is a child without a parent who can be identified?

The regulations define the term parent as including "a parent, a guardian, a person acting as a parent of a child, or a surrogate parent who has been appointed in accordance with [the law]. The term does not include the state if the child is a ward of the state." (§ 121a.10) Any handicapped child who is not represented by one of the above in the education decision-making process must be assigned a surrogate parent.

2. Who qualifies as a "guardian" and thus as a "parent" under this definition?

The term guardian refers to private individuals who have been given legal custody of a child. If a pupil is represented by such a person, no surrogate parent is needed.

3. Where a state or a state agency has been assigned as the legal guardian of a child, do they qualify as a "parent" under this definition?

No. Children for whom a state or local government agency is guardian still will require a surrogate parent.

4. In states where institutionalized or parentless children are assigned a legal guardian who is an employee of the state, does that employee qualify as a parent under this definition?

If the employee was assigned as the child's guardian because of the position with the state, or if the employee exercises the rights of a guardian as a part of the state job, then that person is seen as an agent of the state and is not considered a parent. For example, neither the director of an institution who is the legal guardian of the children being cared for there nor a social worker assigned to make decisions for children who are wards of an agency would qualify as a parent. Surrogate parents would have to be appointed for these children.

5. Who qualifies as a "person acting as a parent of a child" and thus as a parent under this definition?

The term refers to relatives of the child or private individuals allowed to act as parents by the pupil's natural parents or guardians. It does not include any persons or agencies supported in whole or in part by public funds to care for the child. For example, a grandparent, neighbor, governess, friend, or private individual caring for the child with the explicit or tacit approval of the natural parent or guardian would qualify as "a person acting as a parent of a child." If a child is represented by such a person, no surrogate parent is needed.

6. Would a foster parent qualify as "a person acting as a parent of a child?"

No. A foster parent is selected as custodian for a child by state or local agencies, not by the parents. While they cannot be considered parents, foster parents may volunteer to be trained and serve as surrogate parents for their foster children provided they have no conflict of interest and provided the nonemployee requirement does not apply to them.

7. What is a "reasonable effort" to locate a child's parent?

The law offers little guidance on this question and does not specifically define the phrase. The states must apply the legal "rule of reason" in determining what would constitute a reasonable effort to locate parents in their jurisdiction. Some activities that might be included would be documented telephone calls, letters, certified letters with return receipts, and visits to the parents' last known address. The certified letter is a good tool for this process, but it is not sufficient by itself. Experience indicates that many persons will not sign for certified mail, fearing summonses or collection agencies. Thus, the return of a certified letter should be followed by a visit to the last known address of the parent.

8. *If the natural parents have not been in contact with the child or custodian for a long period, is this grounds to declare them unavailable?*

No. The responsible authority must actively seek to contact the parents.

9. *Why was the term "unavailable" in the act changed in the regulations to apply only when "the public agency, after reasonable efforts, cannot discover the whereabouts of a parent"?*

The regulations applied this restrictive definition to prevent public agencies from using the surrogate parent requirement to circumvent the procedures for gaining consent from uncooperative or nonresponsive parents for the initial evaluation or placement of a child. Surrogate parents may not be used to replace this requirement, nor can they be used as part of an administrative procedure to meet it.

After these administrative or due process procedures are complete, federal regulations require only that prior notice be given to the nonresponsive parents before review or revision of a child's educational program is undertaken. However, because this leaves the pupil unrepresented by one key actor in the IEP process, the federal government is willing to allow states the option of assigning surrogate parents to these children after permission for initial placement has been obtained. The surrogate could act until a parent appeared to represent that child. This is an option available to states, and is not a federal requirement. The effect of this option on the liability of the surrogate parent or the state would depend on the laws of each individual state.

10. *Can a surrogate parent be appointed to act with the permission of the child's natural parent?*

Yes, as an option. The federal government allows states the option of letting the responsible public agency offer parents the services of a surrogate to represent their child. Some states have requested such an option to help them cope with parents who live a great distance from their child's school, or who are imprisoned, or who are unresponsive, etc. However, the parents' permission must be voluntary, explicitly stated in writing, and revokable at any time by them. This, too, is an option available to states and is not a federal requirement. The effect of this option on the liability of the surrogate parent or the state would depend on the laws of each state.

11. When is a child a "ward of the state" and thus eligible for a surrogate parent?

Under the regulations, a child is a ward when the state has assumed the legal responsibility to make decisions concerning the pupil's education under state law. However, if the state is the custodian but the parent retains the right to make decisions on education, the child is not a ward of the state and no surrogate parent is needed.

THE DUTY OF THE PUBLIC AGENCY

The regulations provide that:

> The duty of a public agency . . . includes the assignment of an individual to act as a surrogate for the parents. This must include a method (1) for determining whether a child needs a surrogate parent, and (2) for assigning a surrogate parent to the child. (§ 121a.514(b))

This section describes the public agency's responsibility to ensure that a system is in place to locate children in need of surrogate parents and to appoint surrogates. The following questions focus on this responsibility and some of the associated administrative problems:

1. Which public agency is responsible for appointing surrogate parents?

This is a matter of state discretion. States are allowed to establish and implement the surrogate parent provision in any way permitted under the laws. The program could be operated on the SEA or LEA level by the public agency or it could be contracted to a private group. The courts also could appoint surrogates. However, the SEA is ultimately responsible for seeing that all of the requirements of this section are met.

2. If a child eligible for a surrogate parent attends a school in a district away from where the pupil lives, who is responsible for appointing a surrogate parent?

This is a matter of state discretion.

3. What should be the term of a surrogate parent's appointment?

This, too, is a matter of state discretion. However, if at the end of a given term of service the surrogate parent is replaced, the individual may call for a due process hearing to attempt to gain reinstatement.

4. Can a surrogate parent be removed before the term of assignment is up?

Yes. A surrogate parent may be removed in midterm for failure to perform the duties defined by state and federal requirements, conflict of interest, or actions that threaten the well-being of the assigned child. Disagreements about the choice of surrogates may be the subject of a due process hearing, which is the proper forum for challenging qualifications to serve. A surrogate parent also would be removed if a parent as defined in the regulations appeared to represent the child, or if the pupil no longer were eligible for special education.

5. Who is responsible for monitoring surrogate parents?

Each public agency must ensure that the surrogates it appoints perform their duties, stay free from conflict of interest, and take no action that might be harmful to their child. The actual monitoring may be performed by any public agency. The SEA has the ultimate responsibility to see that monitoring is carried out effectively.

6. When may a surrogate parent resign?

This is a matter of state discretion.

7. If a handicapped child has reached the age of majority, does the student require a surrogate parent?

A handicapped child who has reached the age of majority needs a surrogate parent if the student continues to be eligible for public education and is not represented by a parent as defined in the regulations.

CRITERIA FOR SELECTION OF SURROGATES

The regulations, in prescribing the criteria for selection of persons to serve as surrogate parents, state:

(1) The public agency may select a surrogate parent in any way permitted under State law.

(2) Public agencies shall insure that a person selected as a surrogate:

(i) Has no interest that conflicts with the interests of the child he or she represents; and

(ii) Has knowledge and skills, that insure adequate representation of the child.

(d) Non-employee requirement; compensation. (1) A person assigned as a surrogate may not be an employee of a public agency which is involved in the education or care of the child.

(2) A person who otherwise qualifies to be a surrogate parent . . . is not [considered to be] an employee of the agency solely because he or she is paid by the agency to serve as a surrogate parent. (§ 121a.514(c),(d))

This section grants states the freedom to select surrogate parents by a method of their own choosing and describes the qualifications the individuals must meet. The following questions focus on the issues that arise from these qualifications:

1. What constitutes conflict of interest?

Determinations of conflict of interest must be made on a case-by-case basis. However, there are some guidelines for determining when one exists. A person would have a conflict of interest who held a job or other position (e.g., school board member) that might restrict or bias the ability to advocate for all of the services required to ensure a free appropriate public education for a handicapped child. A surrogate parent must be free from institutional bias regarding the child's education and from the possibility of administrative retaliation for the faithful execution of the rights and duties of that role.

2. What "knowledge and skills" must a surrogate parent have?

The specific "knowledge and skills" vary from state to state. However, in terms of knowledge, the surrogate parent probably will need to be familiar with state and federal requirements, the structure and procedures of the public agency educating the child, and the nature of the disability and needs. Skills involve the ability to advocate effectively for a child's educational program in a group decision-making process. However, this does not necessarily mean that the surrogate parent must be a highly trained special education and psychology professional, as some jurisdictions have interpreted the requirement. Most natural parents certainly fulfill their role adequately without being professionals. There is nothing in the law which requires a surrogate parent to have any specialized professional training.

3. Does the knowledge and skills provision require that the surrogate parent be culturally matched with the assigned child?

As far as is practical, a surrogate parent should be culturally matched with the child. If volunteers who match a child's ethnic, cultural, or linguistic background cannot be found, special attention should be given to ensuring that the surrogate parent who is appointed is sensitive to factors in the pupil's background that might affect performance during evaluation or in the classroom.

4. Could a situation arise where a child's natural parent would be appointed to serve as surrogate parent?

Yes. In some instances, the laws for a child in the custody of the state (in departments of welfare, correction, etc.) require that the state assume full legal guardianship for reasons that do not reflect on the capabilities of the natural parents. If in the judgment of the state the natural parents are capable of representing the child's educational interests, then they may be appointed to fulfill the surrogate parent requirement. Because they will be acting as surrogate parents, they must meet the knowledge and skills requirement.

5. Which employees are disqualified from serving as surrogate parents?

No employee of any state or local government agency may serve as a surrogate parent for a child as a part of the job with that entity. In assuming the duties of a surrogate, a government employee acting in an official capacity would be assuming the role of parent for a child as an agent of the government and not as a private citizen. This is forbidden. However, these persons may volunteer their own time to serve as surrogates unless they are subject to a conflict of interest or the nonemployee requirement applies.

The nonemployee requirement prohibits any "employee of a public agency which is involved in the education or care of a child" from serving as a surrogate parent. Because the phrase "which is involved in the education or care of the child" modifies the term "agency" and not "employee" in both the law and the regulations, this exclusion applies to all persons in that agency and not only to those working directly with a child. This exclusion prohibits these persons from serving as surrogates under any circumstances, even as volunteers on their own time.

6. Are foster parents disqualified from serving as surrogate parents?

No. As previously mentioned, although foster parents are not considered parents, they may volunteer to be trained and appointed as surrogate parents provided they have no conflict of interest and the nonemployee requirement does not apply.

7. What is the status of employees of private institutions educating handicapped children?

These individuals almost certainly would be disqualified from being surrogate parents for children in their institution under the conflict-of-interest provision.

8. May surrogate parents be paid for performing their duties without being disqualified under the nonemployee requirement?

Yes.

9. Must surrogate parents be paid?

Nothing in the act or regulations requires that they be reimbursed or paid for their services. The determination of whether and/or how to compensate surrogate parents is a matter of state discretion.

RIGHTS OF SURROGATE PARENTS

The surrogate parents of a handicapped child have the right to:

- review all written records regarding the child's education
- take part in the evaluation and development of the IEP
- reject, accept, or recommend changes in the IEP
- request and/or initiate a second evaluation
- initiate mediation, hearing, or appeals procedures

- receive legal help at no cost if such assistance is necessary in further-ance of the surrogates' responsibilities

- monitor the child's program

- recommend changes in the pupil's placement

- take advantage of all the rights afforded to natural parents in the special education decision-making process

RESPONSIBILITIES OF SURROGATE PARENTS

The surrogate parents of a handicapped child have the responsibility to:

- participate in whatever training program might be offered so as to ensure that they will have the knowledge and skills to provide adequate representation of the child

- be certain that they have no interest that conflicts with those of the child

- represent the child throughout the special education decision-making process of identification, evaluation, program development, initial placement, review of placement, and reevaluation as necessary

- be well acquainted with the child and the educational needs

- attempt to ascertain the child's educational wishes and concerns

- respect the confidentiality of all records and information

- become familiar with the assistance provided by other human service agencies in the community that affect the child or might be a helpful resource

- monitor the child's educational program and placement

- recommend changes in the program and/or placement of the child if they do not seem appropriate

- initiate due process procedures when a dispute arises between the surrogate parents and the public agency over the identification, eval-uation, program development, placement, review of placement, re-evaluation, or the provision of a free appropriate public education

- be especially certain that the child is receiving special education and related services in the least restrictive environment, particularly since many children who are in need of surrogate parents are institutionalized

- engage the services of an attorney or other professional on behalf of the child if it appears necessary to do so to advocate effectively for the pupil's best educational interests
- fulfill to the greatest extent possible the responsibilities natural parents would have for the child in the context of special education decision making

LEGAL PROBLEMS IN PROVIDING SURROGATES

Sometimes there is a gap between law and reality. Law may fall behind reality or become meaningless when applied to a real situation. Persons attempting to implement the surrogate parent provision of P.L. 94-142 may fall into such a gap.

As noted, the surrogate parent provision is designed to protect the interests of a handicapped child whenever the parents are not known or are unavailable, or the pupil is a ward of the state. This assumes that there are no adult protectors to represent the child. Obviously, this is a real situation that unfortunately occurs frequently. An example could be an abandoned retarded boy who has been institutionalized. However, this situation could not exist in the realm of law.

In law, there always are adult protectors to whom the child can be assigned. One of the responsibilities of those adult protectors is to provide for the child's education. This continuity of guardianship is not interrupted throughout the child's minority. When a child is born, the state, in effect, assigns the child to the natural guardians, the parents. They hold the total rights to that child for care, custody, education, and upbringing. If one parent dies, the survivor is entitled to the totality of the rights to that child.

The Development of Parental Rights

Parents' rights have grown out of their legal obligation to maintain and educate their children. Public policy historically has demanded that such rights be held inviolate and not easily controlled by other considerations. At common law, the parents' rights to custody and control of their child were sacred. A court could not interfere with those sacred rights except when the parents forfeited them by conduct so cruel as to amount to criminal assault.

Only the state has an interest in the welfare of a child, and the authority to protect the youngster, that goes beyond the parents' natural rights and authority. The state actually stands in the paramount relation to the child as parens patriae. In that capacity, the state may assume the direction, control, and custody of the child. Today, parents' rights involving the care and custody of their children are subject to considerable control and regulation by the state through legislative and judicial action. However, even though parental rights in general no longer are absolute, they may be limited or interfered with by the legislature only for the most substantial reasons. Parental rights to a specific child may be subjected to judicial control only when the interests of that individual clearly demand it.

Limitation and Transference of Parental Rights

What happens to parents' rights when it becomes necessary for the court to intervene on behalf of the child? When it does so, the court limits the exercise of parents' rights. The court also may transfer some of those rights to someone else. When the retarded boy mentioned earlier is removed from his home because of neglect or abandonment, the parental rights to legal custody are transferred to an agency or a third party relative.

That legal custodian then is vested with the responsibility for the child's physical well-being: the rights and duty to protect, train, and discipline the child, and the responsibility to provide food, shelter, education, and ordinary medical care. The parents still hold guardianship rights: authority to consent to marriage; enlistment in the armed forces; major medical, surgical, or psychiatric treatment; and to make other decisions of substantive legal significance concerning the child.

The court could limit the parents' rights more severely or terminate them completely. But when such rights are restrained, limited, or terminated, they must be shifted to someone else. The child's person and legal rights are continuously with some adult or combination of adults. If the court places a child in an agency's care, the head of that entity acts in loco parentis for the portion of parental rights given to the agency by the court. In the example of the retarded boy, the superintendent of the institution would hold the parental rights and responsibilities.

Guaranteeing Adult Guardians for Every Child

A child is always provided with an adult legal guardian through the judicial process. This is done so that the exercise of care and control over the child's person and rights will always be accountable at law. The state holds the totality of authority and responsibility, although it usually delegates these rights to the natural guardians, the parents. But if the parents are not able to discharge their duties properly, then the state, through its courts, delegates all or part of those rights to someone else. Someone always must be accountable at law for the child's care and custody.

Ideally, the system of providing court-appointed guardians assures that every child's person and rights will continuously be with competent adults, who are identified with the pupil's interests and welfare. In reality, this unfortunately is not true. Parents, legal guardians, etc., are not always willing or available to accept the full responsibility of advocating for the child's best interests. In educational decision making, many children lack adult representatives willing or able to participate in the process. In the example, here, it is unlikely that an institution that supposedly acts in loco parentis for the retarded boy actually participates in developing the IEP.

P.L. 94-142 requires that the local education agency involve the parents in the decision making. It also provides that surrogate parents be assigned to represent the child's educational best interests, if the natural parents are not known or are unavailable, or the pupil is a ward of the state.

If the parents are truly not known, the child is likely to have been adjudicated as abandoned, neglected, or dependent. The court then would have placed the child with a person (or agency) who became vested with the parental rights described above.

If the parents are truly unavailable, it also is likely that the child has been adjudicated as abandoned, neglected, or dependent and, as above, would have been placed with a person or agency vested with parental rights.

If a ward of the state, it also is likely that the child has been adjudicated as abandoned, neglected, or dependent and perhaps beyond parental control or delinquent. In any case, the court again would have placed the child with a person or agency vested with the parental rights.

In other words, in each circumstance where P.L. 94-142 prescribes that a surrogate parent be assigned to represent a child, it is likely that a court has already placed the child with a person (or agency) who became vested with the parental rights for that child.

The Legal Dichotomy

Therefore, a state or local education agency that appointed surrogate parents would be attempting to fill a position already occupied legally by someone else. Although such an appointment may be necessary in reality, it may be highly inappropriate at law.

By appointing surrogate parents the education agency in effect would be arrogating to itself the authority to name a person to take the place of a child's parents. Such an assumption of authority has no basis in law and may be contrary to the constitutional principle of separation of powers.

The constitutional system provides that the three branches of government perform their separate functions without infringing on each other's prerogatives. The legislative branch promulgates rules and criteria to determine on which children's behalf the state will intervene. The judicial branch decides whether a particular child meets those rules and criteria. The executive branch carries out the specific program needed.

The state and local education agencies structurally are part of the executive branch. The agency function in this area is to provide and administer a surrogate parent program. The agency may be acting outside its proper constitutional authority if it develops rules and criteria as to which children should be provided with surrogate parents and then decides whether a particular child meets those rules and criteria. This is because it has exceeded its executive branch function and is infringing on the prerogatives of the legislative and judicial branches.

Implementing the Surrogate Parent Provisions

Do these legal obstacles mean that a child who needs a personal representative for educational decision making must be denied one? No, but education agencies should be careful not to attempt to implement the surrogate parent provision of P.L. 94-142 in a legal vacuum. There are three basic approaches that education agencies have used to put their surrogate parent program on a sound legal foundation.

The first approach involves the state legislature's approving an explicit grant of legal authority for the surrogate program. For example, in Connecticut, the legislature passed a law titled "An Act Concerning Surrogate Parents," P.A. 76-429. This granted the State Board of Education the authority to establish a program and then petition the juvenile court for the specific appointment of surrogate parents in individual cases. This approach offers the strongest legal foundation because its parameters are developed by the legislature and the interpretation of the law is placed with the court. The special education agency's role is to execute the program, which is an appropriate function for an arm of the executive branch.

The second approach involves both the establishment and execution of the program by the education agency. The agency first establishes the rules and criteria for the program, then determines that a particular child is in need of a surrogate parent. The agency then requests the court to order the appointment of the surrogate parent for that particular child. This approach places the education agency on a legal foundation because it provides the surrogate parent with a grant of legal authority from the court to act on behalf of the particular child. This approach also ensures that there is not more than one person legally authorized to act in loco parentis with regard to the educational decision making for the child.

The third approach involves a private contract between the education agency and the custodial agency (or persons) vested with parental rights for the child. (In the example of the retarded boy, the custodial agency vested with the parental rights would be the institution where the youth lives.) The contract basically states that the education agency will provide the custodial agency with surrogate parents for children who do not have parents involved in the educational decision-making process. The education agency selects surrogate parents in accordance with P.L. 94-142; the custodial agency agrees to delegate one of the parental rights it holds—the right of educational decision making for the child—to the surrogate parents.

This third approach seems to place the education agency on the least secure legal and operational foundation. For this approach to operate successfully, the two agencies must cooperate fully. Such cooperation is difficult to depend on. The legal problems also are major. The legislature and the court have not provided the education agency with the legal authority to create the surrogate parent program, nor to decide that a specific child requires a surrogate parent, nor to appoint a surrogate to be the child's advocate. Furthermore, it is questionable whether the custodial agency may contract away part of its legal responsibilities to another person or agency without the approval of the legislature or the court.

Potential Legal Liability of Surrogate Parents

At the time the provisions of the federal law on surrogate parents were being drafted, a number of persons were concerned about the legal liability. Some felt the regulations ought to protect surrogates from any legal liability. However, no change was made. The legal liability of surrogates will be determined under state law relating to such matters as breach of fiduciary duty, negligence, and conflict of interest. The federal government has no authority to limit legal liability.

Therefore, in addition to the legal framework for the program, each education agency should address the potential legal liability of the individuals participating in the program as surrogates. There appears to be no case law in this area since the legal relationship between the surrogate parent and the child is so new.

However, there are two closely analogous situations from which the legal principles could be borrowed for the surrogate parent situation. The first is that of a trustee responsible for a legal trust created for the benefit of someone else. This is called a fiduciary relationship. The trustee as administrator must exercise the degree of care and skill reasonably prudent persons in business would exercise in dealing with their own property. It is immaterial whether the trustee is acting without pay or is being paid for those services. In the surrogate parent situation, the surrogates would be required to exercise the degree of care and skill reasonably prudent parents would exercise in dealing with their own child's education. If the surrogates represent themselves as possessing special skills or knowledge, they are under a duty to exercise those talents. They must perform up to these standards in order to avoid legal liability.

The second situation from which legal principles could be borrowed is that of professional persons acting within the scope of their particular discipline. They must possess a minimum standard of specialized knowledge and ability. These professionals are required to exercise the degree of care that a reasonable colleague, with the same specialized knowledge and ability, would exercise under the same circumstances. Applying this principle to surrogate parents, they should have received special training from the education agency and possess knowledge and skills that are adequate to represent the child's interests. They then are charged by law to conduct themselves as reasonable surrogate parents would do with the same or similar information about the child. If the surrogates perform below this standard, they could be risking legal liability.

The education agency probably will want to protect its surrogate parents from any potential liability. To ensure such protection, it should make clear in its contract that the surrogate parents will be held harmless by the state when acting in their official capacity except for acts or omissions that are found to have been wanton, reckless, or malicious. This protection from legal liability can be effectuated through the state legislation establishing the surrogate parents program, the court order appointing them to represent the child, or through the contract establishing the mutual responsibilities between them and the education agency. Regardless of the manner chosen, it is important to have it expressly agreed in advance that the surrogate parents will not be liable for the consequences of conduct that otherwise might be legally negligent.

In summary, P.L. 94-142 provides that the state or local education agency must appoint a surrogate parent for each handicapped child whose parents are unknown or unavailable, or where the pupil is a ward of the state. The purpose of the surrogate parent is to stand in the place of the child's parents in the educational decision-making process. However, it is likely that the state, through its legislature and courts, already has taken over the parents' rights and responsibilities, which include educational decision making, to another person or agency. Unfortunately, that person or agency may not, in reality, be able to serve as the child's personal educational advocate.

Thus, the child may truly need surrogate parents as provided for in P.L. 94-142. However, a surrogate parent program should not be established in a legal vacuum. It must be developed so that it can fit into the context of the child's legal status and the configuration of adults who hold parental rights to that pupil. After developing a surrogate program in relation to the legal context, the education agency probably will want to protect individual surrogate parents from any potential liability for their efforts on behalf of a handicapped child.

Part IV

Procedures of the Due Process Hearing

The concept of due process in the American legal system consists of two types of law—substantive and procedural. Special education due process, which has evolved over the last decade as a result of local, state, and federal litigation and legislation, also consists of both substantive and procedural law.

In many areas it is difficult to draw the line between substantive and procedural. Generally, the rules of substantive law govern the rights and responsibilities of people in their ordinary relations with each other or with the community as a whole. The rules of procedural law govern the means by which individuals can maintain their substantive rights when they have been violated, threatened, or ignored.

In special education matters, substantive due process means the legal requirement that a free appropriate public education be provided for all handicapped children in the least restrictive environment. This broad substantive right also involves the aspects of law related to assuring such factors as proper evaluation, program development, and placement selection. These substantive requirements are discussed throughout this book.

This part, however, deals with the procedural rights, rules, and requirements of special education due process. In such matters, procedural due process involves the procedures and timelines that must be adhered to in identification, evaluation, program development, and placement of handicapped children. It concerns the requirements regarding parental consent before evaluation and placement, the various types of notice, hearing procedures when parents and public schools disagree on matters of a substantive nature, appeal procedures when there is disagreement with the findings and decisions in hearings at the local level, etc.

Throughout this part, four principles regarding procedure should be kept in mind:

1. Procedure exists primarily to implement substantive rights, not to obstruct them.
2. Procedure should give all the parties to a dispute the feeling that they are being dealt with fairly and have a reasonable opportunity to present their side before an impartial decision maker.
3. Procedure should promote administrative efficiency.
4. Procedure should yield final and lasting decisions so that individuals can have a clear understanding of how their substantive rights apply to a specific set of circumstances.

Chapter 16

Notice Requirements and Timeliness of Proceedings

"Notice" is information, advice, or warning, in more or less formal form, that is intended to apprise individuals of some proceeding in which their interests are involved. Notice also is informing them of some fact that it is their right to know and the duty of the notifying party to communicate.

THE PURPOSE OF THE NOTICE REQUIREMENT

The U.S. Supreme Court has declared in numerous cases that the Constitution requires government agencies or officials to provide notice and a trial-type hearing before taking action that may deprive an individual citizen of liberty or property. The concepts of liberty and property as used in constitutional law go far beyond the ordinary meanings of the two words to include within their protection a child's legal interest in receiving a public education.

P.L. 94-142 AND THE NOTICE REQUIREMENT

Public Law 94-142 and the regulations require that written notice be given to the parents of a handicapped child, within a reasonable time frame, if the public education agency proposes—or refuses—to initiate or change the identification, evaluation, or educational placement of the child or the provision of a free appropriate public education to the pupil.

A basic principle found throughout P.L. 94-142 and its regulations is that parents should be involved in the education of their handicapped child as one means of protecting the youngsters' rights. The law assumes that, in most cases, parents will be committed, and provide continuity, to the advocacy of their child's educational interests. Perhaps an even more important reason for this principle is that parental involvement is likely to

279

substantially increase the efficacy of the individualized education program (IEP).

The intent of the law's notice provision is to increase parents' involvement in the identification, evaluation, program development, and placement decision making with respect to their handicapped child. The law requires the public school system to notify parents when it intends to classify a child as handicapped through such means as large-scale screening, conducting an evaluation to determine possible special education needs, or placing or changing the placement in a special education program of any type. The law further requires the system to notify parents if they request any of these services or actions and the local education agency refuses to perform them.

When notice is required, it must be given to parents within a reasonable time, which is not defined in this context. In determining what is a reasonable amount of time, two basic factors should be considered: (1) the parents' need to have adequate time to consider the local education agency's proposed actions, and (2) the child's need to receive a free appropriate public education without unnecessary delay. Standard legal procedures probably would require a minimum of one week and a maximum of two weeks for providing such a notice. An amount of time within those parameters would seem reasonable to protect the interests of the local education agency, the parents, and the child.

CONTENT OF THE NOTICE

The regulations require that the notice must include:

(1) A full explanation of all of the procedural safeguards available to the parents . . . . ;
(2) A description of the action proposed or refused by the agency, an explanation of why the agency proposes or refuses to take the action and a description of any options the agency considered and the reasons why those options were rejected;
(3) A description of each evaluation procedure, test, record, or report the agency uses as a basis for the proposal or refusal; and
(4) A description of any other factors which are relevant to the agency's proposal or refusal. (§ 121a.505(a)).

This clearly requires that the local education agency provide the parents with four major types of information whenever it proposes, or refuses, to initiate or change a handicapped child's identification, evaluation, program, or placement in special education. These four major types of information can best be shown in checklist form as follows:

1. a full explanation of procedural safeguards available to parents
2. a description of the action proposed or refused by the local education agency
3. a description of each evaluation procedure
4. a description of any other factors relevant to the LEA's proposal or refusal

1. A Full Explanation of Procedural Safeguards Available to Parents

- The parents have a right to examine, and obtain copies of, all reports, records, and files on their child involving a free appropriate education generally and the proposed action particularly.

- The parents have a right to refuse permission for the school to conduct a preplacement evaluation of their child.

- The parents have a right to refuse permission for the school to place their child initially in a program providing special education.

- The LEA has a right, if the parents refuse permission for a preplacement evaluation or for the agency to place their child initially in a program providing special education, to request a hearing to present its reasons and try to obtain approval to conduct the evaluation or make the placement.

- Parents have a right to an independent educational evaluation:
  1. the LEA will provide the evaluation at public expense if:
     a. the agency agrees to pay for an independent evaluation as requested by the parents
     b. the parents disagree with the LEA evaluation, the agency believes the assessment is appropriate, and a hearing officer decides in favor of the parents
     c. the hearing officer, conducting a session involving any issue in the provision of a free appropriate education for the child, determines that an independent educational evaluation is required
  2. the parents may obtain the evaluation at private expense if:
     a. they voluntarily seek and pay for such an evaluation

    b. they disagree with the LEA evaluation, the agency believes the assessment is appropriate, and a hearing officer decides in favor of the LEA

- The parents have a right, if they obtain an independent evaluation at their own expense, to have the results considered by the LEA or the hearing officer in relation to the provision of a free appropriate public education.

- The parents have a right to be notified of any other action the school proposes to take with regard to the identification, evaluation, programming, or placement of the child.

- The parents have a right to an impartial due process hearing if they contest the LEA's proposed action (or refusal to act) with regard to the identification, evaluation, programming, or placement of the child.

- The parents have a right, as a party to the hearing, to:
  1. be informed as to where to obtain any free or low-cost legal and other relevant services available in the community
  2. have the hearing conducted by an impartial hearing officer who is not an employee of the public agency involved in the education or care of the child or who has any personal or professional interest in the outcome of the case
  3. be accompanied and represented at the hearing by a person of their choosing, including legal counsel or individuals with special knowledge or training with respect to the child
  4. compel the attendance of any LEA official or public employee who may have evidence or testimony directly related to the subject of the hearing
  5. present evidence, including documents, reports, data, and expert medical, psychological, or educational testimony
  6. confront, question, cross-examine, and otherwise challenge witnesses
  7. prohibit the introduction of any evidence that has not been disclosed to them at least five days before the hearing
  8. obtain a written or electronic verbatim record of the hearing
  9. have their child who is the subject of the hearing present, if appropriate
  10. have the hearing open or closed to the public
  11. obtain written findings of fact and decision from the hearing officer
  12. have the final decision issued within 45 days after the LEA received their request for the hearing.

- The parents have a right to appeal the decision of the hearing officer to the State Department of Education and have the appeal heard and decided within 30 days after receipt of a request for appeal.

- The parents have a right to appeal from a decision of the State Department of Education to either a state court or the federal district court in accordance with the rules of the local jurisdiction.

- The parents have a right to have their child remain in the present educational placement until all the due process proceedings, hearings, appeals, etc., are completed. However, the parents and the LEA may agree to a different temporary placement while the proceedings are pending.

2. A Description of the Action Proposed or Refused by the Local Education Agency

- What action is the LEA proposing or refusing to take?

- Why does the LEA propose or refuse to take the action with regard to this handicapped child?

- What options did the LEA consider as alternatives to its proposed action?

- Why did the LEA reject those options?

- Who may the parents call to discuss the LEA's proposed action or refusal to act?

- How should the parents indicate their consent or refusal to consent to placement, if it is an initial placement? Is there a deadline for a response?

3. A Description of Each Evaluation Procedure

(a) Notice of intent to conduct an evaluation:

- How did the child come to be referred for an evaluation?

- What specific evaluation procedures and instruments will be used?

- What is the scope of the procedures and instruments that will be used?

- How will the procedures and instruments evaluate the child in all areas related to the suspected disability?

- How may the parents review the procedures and instruments to be used?

- How are the findings of the evaluation to be used, by whom, and under what circumstances?

- Who can the parents call to discuss the proposed evaluation or the refusal to evaluate?

- How should the parents indicate their consent or refusal to consent to the evaluation if it is a preplacement evaluation? Is there a deadline for a response?

(b) Notice proposing or refusing a placement based on an evaluation:

- How did the child come to be referred for an evaluation?

- What specific evaluation procedures and instruments were used?

- What was the scope of the procedures that were used?

- How did this evaluation assess the child in all areas of the suspected disability?

- Who conducted each part of the evaluation?

- What were the findings of the evaluation procedures and instruments used?

- What specific educational needs are indicated from these findings of the evaluators?

4. A Description of Any Other Factors Relevant to the LEA's Proposal or Refusal

Some examples of these factors might be:

- the child's age

- the location of a proposed program

- information about the child furnished by the parents or their evaluators

- the availability of openings in different programs, timing considerations, etc.

THE FORM OF THE NOTICE

The regulations require that:

(b) The notice must be:
1. Written in language understandable to the general public, and
2. Provided in the native language of the parent or other mode of communication used by the parent, unless it is clearly not feasible to do so.
(c) If the native language or other mode of communication of the parent is not a written language, the State or local educational agency shall take steps to insure:
1. That the notice is translated orally or by other means to the parent in his or her native language or other mode of communication;
2. That the parent understands the content of the notice, and
3. That there is written evidence that the requirements [above] have been met. (§ 121a.505(b),(c))

The purpose of notice is to inform. This purpose cannot be accomplished unless the notice can be comprehended by the parents. To assure that the information is communicated to the parents, the law provides these language requirements.

The first requirement is that the notice be written in language understandable to the general public. This means that the notice must avoid the use of professional jargon as much as possible. Where jargon is used, it should be explained in a manner understandable by lay persons. When discussing an evaluation, for example, a list of assessment instruments by name probably would not be meaningful to the average parents. However, a list of the instruments used, what each one is, its purpose, what data were obtained from each one, and what those data mean with regard to the child's educational needs, can provide parents with a great deal of helpful information. The law is clear that a local education agency does not discharge its responsibility to provide parents with notice simply by disseminating to them a packet of information in terms they may not comprehend.

In addition, the law requires that the notice be provided in the parents' native language or other mode of communication, such as sign language, if they are not literate in English. The term native language in this context refers to the language the parents generally use in communicating with other adults. It does not necessarily mean the language of the handicapped child, the home, or the community. If the LEA has reason to believe that the parents cannot comprehend written English, it should attempt to find out what language they use to communicate. The LEA could do this by discussing the matter with the child, calling the parents, or visiting the home.

The law does provide the qualifier that the notice must be communicated to the parents in their native language "unless it is clearly not feasible to do so." However, it is likely that at a minimum the LEA would be required to ascertain what native language or other mode of communication the parents use and then attempt to communicate with them accordingly. If the LEA must rely on the native language qualifier, it should be able to demonstrate a good faith effort to communicate the information to the parents. Without notice, parents could effectively be deprived of their basic due process rights.

The native language requirement also may mean that the LEA will have to obtain an interpreter to assist in communication with the parents. Obviously, such an interpreter must be knowledgeable in the parents' spoken and written language. However, it would greatly facilitate communication if the interpreter is someone the parents already know and trust. It would be even more effective if the interpreter is someone from the parents' family or neighborhood. The more familiar the interpreter is with the parents, the more comfortable they are likely to be and the more effective the communication.

If the parents' native language or other mode of communication is not a written language, the LEA must ensure that the notice is translated orally or by other means in their language or communication mode. Once again, the selection of an interpreter is the key to effective communication. The interpreter could be selected with the same guidelines as discussed in reference to the choice of one for parents who use a written language other than English.

The law further requires that when the parents do not communicate with a written language, the LEA must maintain written evidence that it translated the notice orally to the parents and that they understood the content. Under the circumstances, it probably is difficult enough to be sure that the notice was communicated adequately. It undoubtedly is even more difficult for the LEA to ensure that the parents actually understood the content of the notice. In these cases, the interpreter could be asked to assess whether or not that individual believes the parents understand. It is to be hoped that if the parents are comfortable with the interpreter, they will be able to indicate truthfully what they understood and what needs more clarification. Another technique would be to have the parents relate in their own terms what they understood the notice to mean.

Regardless of the means of communication, parents are likely to perceive the notice as complex, frightening, formal, unfamiliar, or overly legal. The notice must contain so much legal and educational information that the LEA should attempt to communicate the material in the simplest and clearest fashion possible. Charts, checklists, outlines, diagrams, and illustrations could be used to help communicate the contents. A cover letter explaining the purpose of the notice might facilitate the parents' understanding by providing them with an introduction to approaching the information. Another technique is to provide the names and telephone numbers of contact persons at the LEA and perhaps a parents' organization whom they might call. '

The basic principle behind this requirement is that the LEA must get the information in the notice across to the parents in a way that they are likely to understand. The burden clearly is upon the LEA. In the long run, the agency will strengthen its relationship with the parents, and thus facilitate the educational process, if it communicates effectively with them about what it proposes to do with their child.

THE MEANING OF 'NOTICE' AND 'CONSENT'

"Notice" means that one party has informed a second party of some action it proposes to take. "Consent" means that the second party has given permission to the first to carry out the proposed action. (Requirements under these two categories are shown in Exhibit 16-1.)

CONSENT IN ADDITION TO NOTICE

The regulations require that in special education matters, parental consent must be obtained before:

(i) Conducting a preplacement evaluation; and
(ii) Initial placement of a handicapped child in a program providing special education and related services.
(2) Except for preplacement evaluation and initial placement, consent may not be required as a condition of any benefit to the parent or child. (§ 121a.504(b))

Notice to the parents is only the first step the public education agency must complete before it may conduct a preplacement evaluation and initially place the handicapped child in a special program. The second step

Exhibit 16-1 Requirements of Notice and Consent for Proposed Actions by the LEA

Actions	Prior Notice Required	Consent Required
Screening of a general population for potential special needs	X	
Other identification activities focused on a general population	X	
Referral for evaluation	X	
Refusal to conduct an evaluation	X	
A preplacement evaluation consisting of individually focused assessments with the possible result that the child could be placed in a special education program	X	X
Refusal to develop an IEP and place the child	X	
Development of an IEP and initial placement of the child in a special education program	X	X
Change or refusal to change the educational program and placement of child	X	
Review of the child's IEP	X	
Reevaluation of the child	X	

is that the LEA must seek and obtain the parents' consent before carrying out the proposed action.

A preplacement evaluation means one that is focused individually on a particular child. It does not include large-scale screening of a group of children to identify those potentially in need of special education. The LEA must obtain parental consent before beginning a preplacement evaluation that contemplates the possible recommendation that the particular child be placed in a special education program. When a child becomes the focus of such an evaluation, the law requires that parental consent also be obtained for all assessments and procedures, including testing, reviewing of school records, interviewing, and observation, no matter how broad or narrow the scope of the scrutiny.

An initial placement means the removal of the handicapped child from a regular classroom program to any kind of special education program for the first time. The pupil may be in the regular classroom program for most of the day and be removed only for speech therapy for one hour a day, two days a week. When the LEA proposes to place the child initially in a special program, it first must obtain parental consent. The consent requirement is not dependent upon the type or extent of the special education services that the agency intends to provide the handicapped student.

When the P.L. 94-142 regulations were being developed, some persons commented that the consent requirements should be deleted because they made the process administratively inconvenient and because the judgments of professional educators should be final. The basic consent requirement was kept, with one modification. It was changed from requiring consent for all evaluations to approval for only the preplacement assessment.

The drafters believed there was no need to require consent for reevaluation. If a handicapped child was placed initially in accordance with the notice and consent provisions of the law, and if the IEP was reviewed annually in accordance with the review provisions, a further consent requirement was deemed not necessary.

Therefore, once the handicapped child is placed in a special education program, the law does not require parental consent for subsequent evaluations. There also is no consent requirement for implementing a change in the special education program once the child has been placed initially. Moreover, the law does not address the situation in which a family moves from one jurisdiction to another. If a handicapped child was receiving special education services in the old jurisdiction, does the provision of similar services in the new location constitute an initial placement? The law is silent.

In the situations just described, the law specifically does not require parental consent or is silent. However, it is clear that in each of those situations, the LEA must at least provide prior notice to the parents of its intention to evaluate further, to change the placement from one special program to another, or to provide a special program for the first time in that particular jurisdiction. It is recommended that parental consent also be obtained for any such action.

The proposed actions may involve evaluations or changes in programming subsequent to the initial placement. However, these subsequent actions may have a greater impact on the child's educational future than did the preplacement evaluation or initial removal from the full-time regular classroom. Parents' consent is advisable at these junctures because of the importance of their cooperation and participation in whatever program is eventually determined to be appropriate for the child.

THE ELEMENTS FOR A VALID CONSENT

As noted, when an LEA proposes to conduct a preplacement evaluation and initially place a handicapped child in a special education program, it first must obtain the parents' consent. The giving of consent is an act that often involves very important consequences. Rules on consent can be found in many areas of law. The fundamental legal principle involved is applicable to the law of special education. That principle is that consent, in order to be valid, must be (1) knowledgeable, (2) voluntary, and (3) competent.

These basic elements can be seen in the specific wording of the consent provision in the P.L. 94-142 regulations. The law requires that, before parental consent can be considered valid, the LEA must be certain that:

> (a) The parent has been fully informed of all information relevant to the activity for which consent is sought, in his or her native language, or other mode of communication;
> (b) The parent understands and agrees in writing to the carrying out of the activity for which his or her consent is sought, and the consent describes that activity and lists the records (if any) which will be released and to whom; and
> (c) The parent understands that the granting of consent is voluntary on the part of the parent and may be revoked at any time. (§ 121a.500)

These three basic elements of a valid consent have a special meaning in the context of education for handicapped children. Because of the importance of consent in special education due process, the three elements are discussed in detail.

Knowledge

This element means that the parent must have sufficient information upon which to make a decision as to whether or not to give consent. Parents must be "fully informed of all information relevant to the activity for which consent is sought." Consent may be valid only if it is given by parents who are informed about the proposed action. Without sufficient information, parents' consent is meaningless.

Moreover, the parents can only be informed if the information is provided in a manner they can comprehend. This is another reason why the notice and consent request must be written in language understandable to the general public or "in his or her native language, or other mode of communication." This consideration is more fully addressed earlier in this chapter in the section "The Form of the Notice."

It should be noted that the law does not require that parents be informed of every detail concerning the proposed action. To do so would place an unduly heavy burden upon the LEA. It also would be unnecessary. The parents do not need to read pages of explanation of technical material on the choice of a particular assessment instrument. Indeed, such information may detract from, rather than facilitate, their ability to understand the proposed action. It also would be difficult, if not impossible, for the LEA to anticipate what might occur when evaluating the child, additional objectives that might be accomplished in a particular placement, etc. The LEA is required to provide parents with all relevant information. The requirement is for relevant, rather than all, information. The question then becomes, "What is relevant information?" This determination is left largely up to the individual LEA. However, "relevant information" must at least include the information discussed earlier under "Content of the Notice."

Voluntary

This element means that the parents give their consent freely. They must not be influenced by coercion, misrepresentation, undue pressure, or inducement.

The regulations require not only that the consent be voluntary but also that "the parent understands that the granting of consent is voluntary" and "may be revoked at any time." If there is any question about its voluntariness, or if the parents have second thoughts, the consent may be retracted.

It seems unlikely that school personnel would attempt to extract consent from parents by threats of physical force and the like. However, it certainly is possible that a zealous placement professional may engage in some puffery in an attempt to sell the parents on the proposed action. This puffery could cross over into fraud if the professional began to misrepresent the services or other benefits.

Another subtle problem in this area is the undue pressure or influence the professional-parent relationship may have on the parents' ability to make a decision. The parents may be awed, enamored, or intimidated by the school professional. Undoubtedly, the professional will attempt to convince the parents of the value of the proposed action. However, it may be the parents' perception of the professional, rather than the expert's presentation, that induces them to agree to give their consent. Of course, school professionals cannot determine how they will be perceived by each individual parent. Nor should they refrain from enthusiastically presenting the LEA's point of view on the child's educational interests. But they also should be sure that the parents' ability to make an independent decision, after considering the information, is not overwhelmed.

The LEA can take some precautionary measures to protect the parents' ability to give consent freely. For example, the professionals should be instructed not to overstate the services and benefits that will be provided if the parents agree to the proposed action. The professionals might even point out some of the possible deficiencies or weaknesses. They can give the parents time to think over the proposal. The parents might have time to consult with other parents or professionals to obtain independent advice. The LEA should encourage the parents in this and perhaps provide the names and telephone numbers of persons they can consult.

Finally, it is important that the LEA not deprive the student or parents of any other right or benefit because of their decision on consent. The hint of any quid pro quo or reprisals is inconsistent with voluntariness. The LEA must be straightforward and present the proposed action and its merits for the child's educational agenda. If the professionals present the proposal with even subtle threats or for hidden agendas, then they obviously are not receiving voluntary consent. Consent is not given if it is not voluntary.

Competent

This element means that the parents must have the capacity to give consent—at least to be able to know what is being asked of them, basically understand what the proposed action is about, and indicate a decision regarding the request for approval.

The regulations require that if consent is to be valid, the "parent understands and agrees in writing to the carrying out of the activity for which" consent is sought. The ability to understand what is being proposed, and what is being asked of the parents, underlies the whole concept of consent.

All persons are presumed by law to be competent to manage their own affairs. There are two exceptions to this principle that are relevant to this discussion of competency: (1) persons who are children before the law, i.e., under the legal age of majority, are considered incompetent to make legal binding decisions and commitments; (2) this also is true of adults who have been adjudicated as being incompetent by an appropriate court. If the parent from whom approval is sought falls into one of those categories, then the consent automatically is invalid.

In most cases, the LEA will be seeking to obtain the consent of parents who are presumed to be competent. Some parents, however, may have language difficulties that impair their ability to give their consent in a competent fashion. This has been addressed at numerous points in the discussion of notice and consent but the problem here is somewhat different from that presented by the notice requirements.

With notice, the concern is in communicating the content; with consent, the concern is in understanding the content of the notice and making an appropriate decision regarding consent. As mentioned before, it is much more difficult to ensure understanding than communication. In such cases, the LEA must employ an interpreter (as discussed in the sections on notice requirements). The same guidelines regarding closeness to the family are applicable here.

The LEA also should use techniques that enable a person to ascertain another's level of understanding of a subject matter. For example, the parents might be asked to indicate whether they understood the information conveyed or to repeat informally their understanding of it. This could be done in written or oral form. The idea is to obtain an indication that they understand the information and that they are being asked to give their consent.

Many parents may seem unreasonable or even irrational to LEA personnel. But such an appearance or demeanor alone is not a sufficient reason to avoid obtaining their valid consent. Where a parent actually has been adjudicated incompetent, the court must appoint a guardian of that individual to act as a substitute decision maker. If the parent has not been so adjudicated but is unknown or unavailable, surrogate parents may be appointed to represent the educational interests of the child.

If the parents fall into none of these categories, but clearly cannot comprehend and respond appropriately, the LEA must seek alternative means of obtaining approval. For example, the agency might initiate legal procedures for the appointment of surrogate parents for the child or a guardian for the parents. It also might treat the parents' inability to respond as a refusal to consent to the proposed action. It then could initiate due process proceedings to obtain a decision from a hearing officer.

The purpose of the consent provision is to increase parent involvement in the child's educational decision making. Most parents are competent to participate. The LEA is required to involve them despite possible extreme difficulties because of language barriers, minor emotional or intellectual problems, inaccessibility, unreceptiveness, etc. However, some situations will require that the agency seek to have a person other than the parent appointed if the student's interests are to be represented meaningfully. If parents genuinely cannot comprehend and respond to the request for consent, then the LEA must seek to have someone appointed who has the capacity to make the necessary decisions. Consent from incompetent parents is incompetent.

WHEN PARENTS REFUSE CONSENT

The public agency is put in a difficult position when it is required to obtain consent, before taking action, and the parents refuse to grant such approval. In such a situation, the regulations provide that:

(1) Where State law requires parental consent before a handicapped child is evaluated or initially provided special education and related services, State procedures govern the public agency in overriding a parent's refusal to consent.

(2) (i) Where there is no State law requiring consent before a handicapped child is evaluated or initially provided special education and related services, the public agency may use the hearing procedures [in a later section] to determine if the child may be evaluated or initially provided special education and related services without parental consent.

(ii) If the hearing officer upholds the agency, the agency may evaluate or initially provide special education and related services to the child without the parent's consent, subject to the parent's rights [to appeal]. (§ 121a.504(c))

This means that where state law requires consent before evaluation or before special education and related services are initially provided, and the parents refuse (or otherwise withhold) consent, state procedures such as obtaining a court order authorizing the agency to conduct the evaluation or provide the education and related services, must be followed.

If, however, there is no legal requirement for consent outside of the regulations, the agency may use the act's due process procedures to obtain a decision to allow the evaluation or services without parental approval. The agency must notify the parents of its actions and they have appeal rights as well as rights at the hearing itself.

The procedures are designed not to interfere with existing state laws that may require consent. Where the state does not require consent, the school system is afforded a special education due process hearing. These rules, and the consent requirements generally, are designed to provide protection to the parents, the child, and the public education agency. They also are intended to foster the participation of everyone concerned in the educational decision-making process.

Chapter 17

Invoking the Hearing

RIGHT TO IMPARTIAL DUE PROCESS HEARING

The regulations provide that:

> A parent or a public educational agency may initiate a hearing on any of the matters described [related to the LEA's proposal or refusal to initiate or change the identification, evaluation, or educational placement of the child or the provision of a free appropriate public education]. (§ 121a.506(a))

The two most basic aspects of procedural due process are (1) the right to receive notice before a public agency takes action that will affect a person's property or liberty, and (2) the opportunity of the person affected to be heard by an impartial decision maker.

In special education matters, parents have the right to know what action the local education agency (LEA) proposes or refuses to take with regard to the identification, evaluation, program development, and educational placement for their handicapped child. As noted earlier, if they disagree with the LEA's proposals, they may initiate a hearing and have an opportunity to be heard, confront school personnel, present their own evidence, and receive a decision from an impartial hearing officer.

Chapter 16 discusses the requirements of notice and some of the issues that may arise with respect to those requirements. This chapter discusses how the hearing process is invoked and what rights each party has.

It is clear from the wording of the above provision of the law that the right to initiate a hearing belongs to both the parents and the LEA. There are numerous situations in which the agency may propose an action such as placement of a child in a special education program to which the parents will object. The LEA may persist in its belief that the proposed program is appropriate as indicated by a multifaceted evaluation. Under such circumstances it would be the agency's right and responsibility to initiate a hearing at which LEA personnel and the parents will have an opportunity to be heard, present and confront witnesses, and introduce evidence.

THE AGENCY RESPONSIBLE FOR THE HEARING

The regulations provide that:

> The hearing must be conducted by the State educational agency or the public agency directly responsible for the education of the child, as determined under State statute, State regulation, or a written policy of the State educational agency. (§ 121a.506(b))

Each state may determine which education agency will be responsible for conducting the hearing. There are three basic choices:

1. the state education agency
2. the intermediate education agency, an administrative unit that usually consists of a number of local education agencies that have joined together to share resources
3. the local education agency

Any one of these options would satisfy the requirements of the law. The determination of which arrangement will be used normally is influenced by the size of the state and the administrative structures already in place. Some states place the responsibility for hearings at the state education agency level but actually provide the hearings at the local level rather than at the capital.

It seems most advisable that the hearings actually be conducted at the local level, regardless of which agency has the legal responsibility for administering them. Frequently, the hearing issues are narrow and clear and simply require an objective adjudicator to resolve the different positions. The hearing itself may be exceptionally brief. Under such circumstances it would be unnecessarily burdensome upon the parents and the school personnel to travel a great distance away from their locality for the session.

Another reason for conducting hearings at the local level is for the accommodation of witnesses. The resolution of issues presented may require the participation of one or more school professionals or private experts. It is difficult enough to get some of these persons to take time out of their busy schedules to attend a hearing in the local community. It would be more difficult to get them to travel to a hearing outside of the local area.

Even if the professionals were willing to travel, they would be likely to request payment for the time spent, travel costs, and other expenses. These costs must be covered by the parents if a witness is a private professional whom they requested. The costs might become prohibitive if the professionals must travel outside of the local area. In the case of school professionals such as classroom teachers, the school system might have to hire substitutes for the entire day if the experts are required to travel. If the hearing were held locally, the professionals would have to leave their posts for perhaps only a few hours rather than a whole day. The school system also would not have to bear the expense of the professionals' travel and meals if the hearing were held locally.

Finally, a local hearing is easier to arrange in terms of the other logistics. Convenience in terms of the parties, witnesses, and administrative logistics can facilitate the whole process. Arrangements for a local hearing generally are made more easily than those for out-of-town sessions.

INITIATING A DUE PROCESS HEARING

Parents may initiate a hearing, as discussed, on any matter related to the school's proposed action or refusal to act with regard to the identification, evaluation, programming, and placement of their handicapped child. If they request the school to take some action and it refuses, the parents may initiate a hearing. If the school notifies the parents that it intends to start or change a program for their child, and the parents object, they again may call for a hearing.

Regardless of how the decision to ask for a hearing develops, the parents may request one by contacting the appropriate person or office designated to administer special education due process proceedings. As noted, this person or office may be located at the state, intermediate, or local education agency depending on the administrative system of the state. At the very least, the LEA should be able to direct the parents to the proper person or office.

If the school sends the parents a notice on a proposed action or refusal to act, it also must inform them of their right to an impartial hearing should they disagree with the school's recommendation. The notice also should contain the name of the person or office whom the parents may call to arrange for a hearing.

Many school systems have a "Student Hearing Office," or "Office of Hearings and Appeals," or "Division of Special Services," etc., that are likely choices to administer such hearings. School personnel such as the principal, legal counsel, director of special education, superintendent, etc., are likely to be familiar with such hearings' requirements. When in doubt, these officials probably could provide information.

The process begins as soon as the appropriate person or office in the agency responsible for administering the hearings receives an oral or written request from either party. It is advisable that the request be in writing so there can be no mistake that the party intended to initiate the process. The date of receipt of the request also should be recorded carefully. The parties are entitled to receive a final decision not later than 45 days after receipt of the request.

INFORMING PARENTS WHERE TO OBTAIN HELP

The regulations provide that:

(c) The public agency shall inform the parent of any free or low-cost legal and other relevant services available in the area if:
1. The parent requests the information; or
2. The parent or the agency initiates a hearing under this section.
(§ 121a.506(c))

The school's obligation goes beyond providing the parents with notice and opportunity for a hearing. The public agency responsible for administering such proceedings also must assist parents in locating free or low-cost legal and other relevant services in their community.

However, the agency is not obligated to obtain these services for the parents or to pay for them. There is one possible exception—the independent educational evaluation, which is discussed in detail in Part II, Chapter 7. It simply is noted here that parents have the right to obtain an independent educational evaluation of their child. Each public agency responsible for the education of the pupil is obligated to provide to the parents, on request, information about where they can obtain an independent evaluation. The agency must provide this evaluation at public expense if the parents disagree with the one the entity obtained. However, the agency may initiate a hearing to show that its evaluation is appropriate. If the final decision upholds that position, the parents still have the right to an independent evaluation, but no longer at public expense.

ADMINISTRATIVE REVIEWS AND MEDIATION

Several states require parents and school personnel to attempt to resolve their differences through an administrative review panel or a mediator.

The idea is to settle the conflict without having to resort to a hearing. Some states offer this as an intervening step that is optional at the election of one or both of the parties. Other states require it as a precondition to a hearing.

Administrative reviews or mediation are not required by P.L. 94-142 or Section 504. However, many states have pointed to the success of mediation in making a formal hearing unnecessary. An agency may suggest mediation.

Mediation and administrative reviews have been conducted by members of state educational agencies or local educational personnel not previously involved in a particular case. In many situations, mediation or administrative reviews have led to resolution of differences without the development of an adversarial relationship and with minimal emotional stress.

However, mediation or administrative reviews may not be used to deny or delay parents' rights under the law. Again it should be emphasized that the public agency must ensure that the parents receive a final decision not later than 45 days after receipt of their request for a hearing.

Chapter 18

Prehearing Activities

Before the special education due process hearing begins, a number of activities must be carried out. These activities, described below, are important to assure that the case is in a procedural posture for being heard at the time the session is to be held. If these tasks, arrangements, and notifications are not completed properly before the hearing, it might contain a number of needless procedural obstacles and might even have to be postponed.

RESPONSIBILITY FOR PREHEARING COORDINATION

In several state and local education agencies, the hearing officer assigned to a case is responsible for coordinating the prehearing activities. In many other jurisdictions, the coordination responsibility lies with an administrative employee of the office responsible for arranging and conducting special education due process hearings. Still other jurisdictions distribute the responsibility somewhere between those two levels.

It is highly advisable to keep the hearing officer out of the coordination responsibility as much as possible since prehearing activities necessarily involve contact with the parties before the case actually is heard. Ideally, the prehearing activities simply attempt to complete procedural requirements so that the case can be heard with fairness at the appointed time.

Nothing of any substance is to be addressed before the session because the law provides that the hearing officer's decision must be based solely on evidence presented at the hearing. Impressions or information obtained inadvertently before the hearing through telephone calls or visits to the school or family home are not factors the hearing officer may consider in reaching the decision. No information can legally be offered ex parte, i.e., by one side without knowledge or out of hearing of the other. All information and evidence must be offered formally in the hearing.

However, it probably is just human nature for the parties to try to put in a good word for their side, given the opportunity to talk with the decision maker alone before the actual confrontation. Special education due process hearings often occur only after the parties have fully exhausted their patience with each other. The issues involved are emotionally charged and high cost. It is hoped that the hearing officer is an individual who is detached from the facts of the case. Such a person must be completely impartial and have no conflicting professional or financial interest in the outcome.

The hearing officer may have contacts with the parties before the hearing but must limit inquiries to matters of procedure rather than substance. Manuals for hearing officers in jurisdictions where they are involved in prehearing activities caution them that the purpose of such contacts is to provide and elicit information required for the preparation of the session— nothing more. Frequently the manuals counsel them that "You *MUST NOT* discuss any information pertaining to the case."

However, these manuals do not offer guidance as to how a hearing officer can stop a frustrated father from discussing in no uncertain terms exactly what the "no-good school professionals" have been doing. It is equally difficult to protect against an exasperated school official's condescending attempt to reach a sympathetic understanding with the officer about the "unfortunate mental instability of the parent." The point is that assigning hearing officers to complete advance activities only exposes them to possible inadvertent impressionistic or substantive information about the case outside of the session that may affect the decision.

RECEIPT OF THE REQUEST FOR A HEARING

The date of receipt of a written request for an impartial due process hearing must be noted because the decision must be released within 45 days. If the request is oral, the date of receipt still must be noted. However, it also might be suggested to the party that it be put in writing just to be clear or a form request could be sent with instructions to sign and return it promptly.

At this point, the coordinator (hearing officer or administrative employee) will want to determine whether all the basic information about the child has been received, such as: What are the full names and addresses of the child and the parents or guardians? Are telephone numbers included? What school program is the child enrolled in? What school personnel will be the contacts for this case? If the coordinator does not have this information from the formal hearing request, it should be obtained in a follow-up.

It is a good idea at this point to begin to assemble a list of the persons who must receive all further information regarding the hearing and/or who will be required to be present. If a party indicates that that side will be represented by an attorney or other advocate, all correspondence should be directed to that representative at the business address.

ARRANGING HEARING DATES AND LOGISTICS

After obtaining the information on contacting the parties, the coordinator should begin to arrange for a hearing date and one or two alternatives. Then it will be necessary to obtain a confirmed reservation for the hearing room on the chosen date(s). The dates should be pinned down with the hearing officer, parents, and school personnel.

The coordinator also should arrange for support services such as copying machines, telephones, mail services, typewriters, clerical assistance, interpreters, etc., if they will be needed.

PROVIDING A VERBATIM RECORD

The coordinator must arrange for a verbatim record of the hearing. The regulations provide that any party to a hearing has the right to

Obtain a written or electronic verbatim record of the hearing. (§ 121a.508(a)(4))

The hearing record can be produced by a court stenographer or a tape recorder. A stenographer's recording and transcribing can be extremely expensive but the product will be clear and highly accurate. A tape recording is much more convenient and inexpensive but it often is difficult to make out some passages and to know to whom some comments should be attributed.

If a stenographer is used, the coordinator should notify that individual well in advance. It is also a good idea for the stenographer to arrive a little early to set up the equipment and obtain the correct names of all participants. If a tape recorder is used, it must be checked first to make sure it is functioning properly. The coordinator should supply the hearing officer with an ample supply of blank tapes because the sessions may run longer than expected.

The coordinator also should consider how to duplicate the verbatim record. The law does not require that each party must receive a copy; it says only that a party has the right to obtain one. It is recommended that copies be provided only upon request because of the expense. It also is not clear from the law whether a party requesting a copy must be provided one at no cost. A reasonable charge probably could be assessed for each copy unless the party making the request cannot afford to pay the cost. In such a case, the indigent party should receive one free.

Copies do not necessarily have to be a full written transcript of the proceeding. If the hearing was recorded on tape, a copy of the tape may be furnished. If the session was recorded by a stenographer, it need not actually be transcribed unless a request is made. Even if there is a request, the party may be interested in only a portion of the record, such as the testimony of a particular witness. The stenographer then could be asked to transcribe only that portion.

DETERMINING THE NEED FOR AN INTERPRETER

When the parents of the child are deaf or when their native language is not English, the hearing coordinator must arrange for an interpreter. The best type of interpreter is a person who is familiar with individuals from the parents' community as well as with their native language. It is even better if the interpreter is a person familiar to the parents and trusted by them.

A list of interpreters should be maintained by the office responsible for administering special education due process hearings. Another resource might be the agency's special services office. Local government and court agencies also maintain such lists. If preferred, a family member or neighbor or a community organization that deals extensively with people from the parents' neighborhood could function as interpreter. When selecting an interpreter it must be remembered that the person must be someone totally acceptable to the parents, if not suggested by them.

The coordinator should establish contact with the interpreter before the hearing and develop a list of dates and times when the individual will be needed. The coordinator may need the interpreter to translate all pre-hearing correspondence for the parents.

THE INDEPENDENT EDUCATIONAL EVALUATION

At the outset of the process, the coordinator should determine whether or not the parents will be seeking an independent educational evaluation of their child. If so, it may affect the timing of the hearing. Frequently it is difficult for parents to schedule the various professional appointments for the evaluation within a short time. After the evaluation is completed, they must wait for the written report. They may wish to provide copies to school personnel.

Another consideration is who will pay for the independent evaluation. The law provides that parents have the right to an independent evaluation at public expense if they disagree with the one obtained by the schools. However, the schools may initiate a hearing to show that their evaluation is appropriate. If the final decision finds that evaluation is appropriate, the parents still have the right to an independent assessment but not at public expense.

Therefore, the hearing coordinator must first determine whether the parents plan to seek an independent evaluation and, if so, whether they intend to request the school system to pay for it. If they want the school system to pay, it may very well object. This scenario could necessitate a full due process hearing on the independent evaluation issue before a session on the original issue may be scheduled.

PLACEMENT DURING THE PROCEEDINGS

The hearing coordinator must determine the child's current educational placement and where the pupil will be placed during the proceedings. The regulations state that:

> (a) During the pendency of any administrative or judicial pro-
> ceeding regarding a complaint, unless the public agency and the
> parents of the child agree otherwise, the child involved in the
> complaint must remain in his or her present educational place-
> ment.
> (b) If the complaint involves an application for initial admission
> to public school, the child, with the consent of the parents, must
> be placed in the public school program until the completion of
> all the proceedings. (§ 121a.513)

This procedural safeguard is commonly misunderstood or overstated. For example, the following erroneous statement was taken from a brochure regarding P.L. 94-142 disseminated by a leading state advocacy organization:

> Regardless of the kind of hearing that is offered, the *child is to
> remain in his or her educational placement pending final resolution
> of the hearings and appeals procedures.*

This rule is applicable in most cases but there also are a number of situations that need analysis. They arise because of the requirement that the parents of the handicapped child must give their consent before a preplacement evaluation may be conducted or an initial placement made. As a result of the interfacing of the consent requirement with the mandate that the child remain in the present educational placement pending the proceedings, the following hypothetical situations could develop:

1. The child is in a private placement paid for by the parents and they are seeking, through due process procedures, to have the public school system pick up the expense.

In this situation, the parents would like the child to remain at public expense in the present placement pending final resolution of the proceeding. They will be contending in the hearing that the school system does not have a placement that can appropriately meet the needs of their child. They will argue that the schools should be required to pay their child's tuition to attend a private facility like the one in which they have placed the pupil on the ground that it is the system's responsibility to provide an appropriate education at no cost to them.

The parents plan to claim that they had to enroll their child in the private school because the public schools had no appropriate program. They will assert that, while the issue is being determined, they have a right to have the child provided with a public education and to remain in the current placement. Therefore, the parents will contend that the school system must pay for the child's education in the private facility at least during the hearing and appeals.

These circumstances come under the heading of an application for initial admission to public school as stated in § 121a.513(b) above. The parents in this situation would be entitled to have their child remain in the private facility during the pendency of the proceedings but not at public expense. The law requires that the school system make available free appropriate public education but does not require parents to accept it if they wish to provide a private education at their own expense.

Here, the parents declined a public education, for whatever reason, and enrolled their child in a private facility. Now they are seeking through the due process procedures to have the public schools pay for the private education. The hearing officer may decide that the placement proposed by the public schools is not appropriate to meet the child's needs. The public schools then may try to develop another program and placement in their system to meet the child's needs more appropriately, or they may determine that they have no placement available and pay tuition for a private facility that can meet the needs.

However, the public schools do not have to cross that bridge until the proceedings; they need only offer to have the child placed in their proposed program or other public school on a temporary basis. If the parents refuse, they are entitled to maintain the child in the current private school program at their own expense.

2. The child is in a private facility paid for by the public schools, which have proposed a change to the public system. The parents object and are challenging the move through a due process hearing.

This situation is different from the previous one because in this case the placement at a private facility actually was made by the public schools. It was they that prepared the IEP and recommended the private placement. The parents consented to the placement and the public schools enrolled the child at public expense. Now the public schools propose a change for the coming year that would entail moving the child to their system. The parents object.

These circumstances fall under the main requirement that the child remain in the current educational placement pending the outcome of the proceedings. The parents are entitled to have the child remain in the private facility at public expense. This situation essentially is no different from one involving a change from one placement to another in the public schools.

3. The child is in a private placement paid for by the public schools. The private school determines that it no longer can serve the child's needs or that the pupil no longer meets their eligibility requirements. The public schools propose a new educational placement. The parents oppose it and are challenging it through a due process hearing.

This situation poses the problem of a change in educational placement necessitated by circumstances beyond the control of either the public schools or the parents. Neither party wants the child removed from the present placement. However, the public schools are forced to come up with an alternative placement because the private facility refuses to continue providing service.

These circumstances fall under neither of the two requirements regarding placement during the proceedings. Neither party has the power to insist that the child remain at the private facility if it refuses to allow the pupil to remain. Fortunately, when this situation arises, the private facility usually gives the public schools and the parents some advance notice. However, that advance notice may not be sufficient. When it is not, the parents probably are entitled to an alternative placement that is substantially identical to the facility that refuses to continue service.

A factor that might be taken into consideration is how promptly the public schools responded after having been made aware of the development. If they did not act expeditiously and the child is not in a program or will be terminated from one imminently, the parents might be entitled to reimbursement for funds they might have expended to place the child in another facility substantially identical to the one that halted service.

If the public schools did act expeditiously but were unsuccessful in getting the child admitted to another facility, they still have a duty to provide some kind of education. In this case, the parents and public schools would have to negotiate a compromise at least for the temporary placement of the child during the proceedings.

4. The child was placed in a regular classroom or special education program in the public schools that was totally unsuccessful from the point of view of both the parents and school. The public schools propose a new special educational placement. The parents object and are challenging it through the due process procedures. During the pendency of the proceedings, the parents refuse to enroll the child in any public school program and cannot afford a private facility.

These circumstances are particularly difficult because they could involve legal proceedings against the parents based on violation of compulsory education or child neglect laws. The requirements discussed earlier regarding the child's placement during the pendency of the proceedings are not really applicable. The parents do not want their child in the proposed placement even temporarily. The previous placement was an unmitigated disaster according to the parents and admitted by school personnel. The parents do not want the child placed inappropriately even on a temporary basis because they do not want to risk another failure.

This is a situation that calls for sensitive negotiations. If the hearing process appears to be moving rapidly and the child does not seem to be suffering too much from the missed days, perhaps school officials could allow the pupil to remain with the parents with assigned homework and home-bound instruction even if the circumstances do not quite meet education agency regulations.

If the circumstances appear to be damaging to the child, and the proceedings are likely to be protracted, the school may want to consider filing a neglect action through the local district attorney. School officials ought to approach this alternative warily because instigating such a proceeding is likely to alienate the parents further. In addition, the action may not be successful. Judges are very reluctant to substitute their own judgment or to order parents to do something against their will when, as here, they seem to have their child's best interests in mind. The recalcitrance of the parents is based on their concern rather than on neglect of their child's educational needs.

An action by school officials based on a violation of compulsory education laws, if the parents are failing to provide any education at all, would run the same risks as a neglect action. But a judge is likely to order the parents to enroll the child in some educational program at least temporarily pending the resolution of their differences with the schools.

5. The child was placed in a regular classroom or special education program in the public schools that was unacceptable from the point of view of school professionals. They believe the child is a danger to self or others. They propose a new special placement. The parents object and are challenging it through the due process procedures. During the pendency of the proceedings the public schools refuse to admit the child.

In this situation, the public schools must provide some kind of education. They cannot totally refuse the obviously handicapped child access to a public education. If the professionals feel so strongly that this child cannot be maintained in any public school program, then they must at the very least provide some homebound instruction during the proceedings. They should be prepared to prove that their extreme concern is valid and based on solid evidence as opposed to mere conjecture.

Explanatory comments to the regulations of both P.L. 94-142 and Section 504 make it clear that "where a handicapped student is so disruptive in the regular classroom that the education of other students is significantly impaired, the needs of the handicapped child cannot be met in that environment." Presumably this caveat also could be extended to a special education program in which the child is very disruptive.

Another alternative is for the public schools to take a chance and admit the child to the regular classroom or special education program. This may be advisable if the school professionals do not really have hard evidence that the child would present a substantial danger or disruption. They may feel that the situation might work out in the particular program in which they wish to enroll the pupil even though the child presented a danger or substantial disruption in the previous placement. If the parents consent, the schools could give this approach a try.

If the child does not make it in the program, the explanatory comment to this regulation regarding the pupil's status during the proceedings states that school officials may use their "normal procedures for dealing with children who are endangering themselves or others." This generally means that the child may be suspended from school. School officials may do this under the proper circumstances without affording the parents the notice and due process protections that normally would accompany a change in their child's placement.

Technically, such a suspension is not considered a "change in educational placement;" rather, it is regarded as only a temporary removal for the safety of the child and the school community. The removal is truly only a stop-gap measure because the length of such a suspension usually is limited by school regulations and state law. It should be remembered that suspension also is subject to other due process requirements that may require full notice and an opportunity to be heard on the school professionals' allegations as the basis for the suspension.

In these four problem situations, it is strongly advised that the parties attempt to resolve their differences through negotiation and compromise, at least for a temporary placement. If circumstances are exacerbated to the extent that they proceed to the "worst case" version, they enter a gray area in which no one is likely to benefit—least of all the child. The nature of special education programs requires particularly close cooperation between parents and schools. The potential for such cooperation is diminished severely early if the parties become intransigent over the placement during the proceedings, thus making it even more difficult to resolve their differences for a long-term solution.

CURRENT PLACEMENT REPRESENTATION

At the outset, the hearing coordinator ascertained the child's current placement. If a school district other than the one of present residence (or a private school) is providing the current program, the coordinator might wish to ask the superintendent of that district whether it wishes to be involved in the hearing. A similar situation could exist where the local education agency is proposing an action (or refusing to act) and the child is attending a state-operated facility such as a school for the blind. In such a case, the coordinator might ask the superintendent or director of that facility whether it wants to be involved.

Such contact by the hearing coordinator should be handled with sensitivity and diplomacy. The LEA might object to any such unilateral contact on the ground that the LEA, not the state school or private facility, has the responsibility to provide a free appropriate public education for the child. This agency should be prepared at the hearing to prove that its proposal is appropriate to meet the child's needs for the coming year. The child's current placement is irrelevant.

The individuals providing the child's current program have no place at the hearing as separate parties. They may, of course, be asked to be witnesses by either the parents or school officials. However, the coordinator may wish to contact the individuals providing the current placement because they may have an independent interest to protect. For example, the facility might be under certain legal mandates not to accept or contribute to the cost of educating certain types of children. These types of interests may legitimately need to be voiced in the context of the hearing.

PROVIDING HEARING INFORMATION TO PARENTS

The hearing coordinator will need to obtain certain information from the parents in advance, such as: whether they will need an interpreter, what dates and times are convenient for them to attend the hearing, and their address and telephone numbers or those of their representative. This information should be obtained shortly after receipt of the request for a hearing but no later than 10 days to two weeks before the session.

The coordinator also will need to provide certain information to the parents or at least be sure the school already has given them such material. The primary information is a full explanation of the procedural safeguards afforded them as part of this hearing process. If there is any doubt that the information has been provided to the parents, it would be best to send them an additional packet explaining their due process rights. These rights are listed early in Chapter 17 under the heading "Content of the Notice."

The coordinator might also remind the parents that they must be given full access to their child's educational records before the hearing. The regulations clearly state that the parents must be afforded an opportunity to inspect and review all education records with respect to:

(a) The identification, evaluation, and educational placement of the child, and
(b) The provision of a free appropriate public education to the child. (§ 121a.502)

OPEN OR CLOSED MEETING, CHILD'S PRESENCE

The regulations state that:

(b) Parents involved in hearings must be given the right to:

(1) Have the child who is the subject of the hearing present; and
(2) Open the hearing to the public. (§ 121a.508(b))

The hearing coordinator must inform the parents of these rights and determine their wishes. These issues usually do not present major problems. The parents request to have their child present if of suitable age and discretion so that the pupil could contribute or gain something from the hearing. The hearings generally are closed unless the parents specifically request that they be open. In most cases, the issues are of interest only to the parties.

Generally, there are no crowds of spectators standing outside the hearing room awaiting the decision as to whether they will be admitted. However, the parents frequently bring observers to provide moral support. Schools also engage in this practice. Sometimes a person who may have to participate in future hearings will ask to sit in and observe the proceedings. The parents should be asked if they object to the person's observing for the purpose of learning about the process. In most cases there will be no objection.

OBTAINING A WITNESS LIST AND WRITTEN EVIDENCE

The hearing coordinator should obtain each side's list of witnesses and should be sure that the parties have provided each other with the written evidence they intend to submit. The regulations provide that any party has the right to:

(3) Prohibit the introduction of any evidence at the hearing that has not been disclosed to that party at least five days before the hearing. (§ 121a.508(a)(3))

The coordinator must obtain this information well in advance in order to assure that the five-day requirement is met. The written documents include all reports, evaluations, records, etc., that will be submitted to the hearing officer for consideration in arriving at a decision. Each side needs to know what the other will present so that no one is surprised by a document and unable to respond because of a lack of opportunity to prepare a proper reply. The same principle applies to the testimony of witnesses. Each party should furnish the other with a list of those it intends to present, including the full name, title, occupation, and place of employment of each. It also should provide a capsule summary of the witnesses' testimony.

This rule is designed to encourage the sharing of information between the parties by providing a penalty if they do not. The penalty is that information, documents, or witnesses not disclosed at least five days before the hearing may not be submitted into evidence. There are a number of sound reasons for this rule.

First, a special education due process hearing is intended to be a forum for obtaining information, not for winning contests. Everyone involved is presumed to be acting in the best interest of the child. Clever strategy, surprise, or trickery do not serve that purpose. The role of the attorney or advocate is not to win a contest by some unexpected maneuver such as introducing a critical report or witness in the manner of Perry Mason. To allow such tactics would put a premium on style and strategy rather than on persuasiveness of the evidence.

A party who is surprised by the introduction of an uninspected report or witness cannot respond properly, not having had a fair opportunity to consider the contents of the document or the gist of the testimony. Indeed, the second party would have brought additional documents or witnesses had there been timely notice of the unexpected evidence.

Because the surprised party would not be ready to respond the hearing officer would lack the benefit of the other side of the story so far as that item of evidence was concerned. That also would make such evidence less reliable because the surprised party would not have had an opportunity to test its value, accuracy, truthfulness, etc. The policy requiring that all information be shared in advance increases the hearing officer's ability to reach a fair and reliable decision on the true merits of the case.

Second, sharing of evidence by the parties narrows the issues to be heard. With all the evidence in hand, the parties can better recognize which points involve serious differences and which do not.

Third, advance sharing of evidence gives the parties an opportunity to become familiar with it so that the actual hearing will run more smoothly. The presentation of evidence will be facilitated because the parties could perhaps agree to the admission of certain documents, etc., without having to read through them at the hearing.

Fourth, if the parties have all the evidence in hand before the hearing, they are more likely to resolve their differences by negotiation and compromise. The strengths and weaknesses of their respective positions will be more apparent so both sides may then wish to settle in a more amicable fashion rather than continue with an adversarial procedure.

However, there will be instances in which certain documents or the presence of a witness could not have been obtained except at the last minute. A critical report or expert might inadvertently have been left off the advance list. In such situations, the party wishing to present such evidence or witness may ask the other side if it would allow the unshared information into evidence. The decision is up to the opposing party because it is its right to have the information in advance—a right it now is being asked to waive. The hearing officer is not allowed to make that decision but may recess the hearing to give the opposing party an opportunity to review the new information and consider whether or not to waive the right to have it excluded. In most cases, the opposing party will allow the information to be introduced. If it does not, the hearing officer may set another date when that information can be introduced, after the opposing party will have had sufficient time to prepare a response.

COMPELLING THE ATTENDANCE OF WITNESSES

Frequently a party will want to present the testimony of a person but has been unable to get that potential witness to the hearing by a simple request for an appearance. Under such a circumstance, the coordinator must determine the appropriate means of compelling the attendance of the witness. The regulations provide that any party to a hearing has the right to:

> Present evidence and confront, cross-examine, and compel the attendance of witnesses. (§ 121a.508(a)(2))

If the witness is a school system employee, it is presumed that such a person will not refuse to attend. The witness might require an official letter from the hearing coordinator or someone acting in the name of the superintendent that the individual's appearance has been requested and that the person was required to attend. The employee then could take this notice to a supervisor and be properly excused to meet the obligation. Refusal to appear after the school employee's presence has been properly requested is tantamount to insubordination because the hearings are likely held under the authority of state or local education agency regulations that the local superintendent is obligated to enforce.

The procedure for compelling attendance by witnesses other than school personnel generally is governed by laws and regulations of the individual state. The coordinator may find it helpful to check with the schools' legal counsel or the local district attorney to determine the correct procedure.

If witnesses are beyond the reach of legal compulsion, are inconveniently far away, or otherwise are unable to be present, the coordinator might suggest that the party use an alternate procedure to obtain the testimony. This could be by a written affidavit, a deposition, or interrogatories sworn to before a notary public. Finally, a simple written statement or proffer of what would have been testified to had the witness been able to be present might be accepted if there are no strenuous objections from the other side.

FINAL NOTICE TO THE PARTIES

At least five days before the hearing, the coordinator must send to the parties a formal notice that should include the following:

1. a comprehensive list of all participants and witnesses, including names and titles or relationships to the child
2. a reminder of the date, time, and location of the hearing
3. a summary of the main items determined during the prehearing contacts with the parties (written evidence to be presented, open/closed hearing, etc.)
4. an agenda and/or a set of procedures to be followed during the hearing

If the prehearing activities (see Exhibit 18-1) have been completed and the final notice sent out, the case is ready to proceed to a hearing.

Exhibit 18-1 Checklist of Prehearing Activities

	1. Who is the prehearing coordinator?
	2. Was the date of the request for the impartial due process hearing logged? (A decision must be issued 45 days after the request is made.)
	3. Does the LEA have an impartial due process hearing form? The form must include basic information such as: ● the names, addresses, and telephone numbers of the parents or guardians ● the names of school personnel who are serving as contact persons ● a statement describing the current school program of the child
	4. Have the safeguards governing the placement of the child been thought out and arranged?
	5. Has the prehearing coordinator developed a list of names and addresses of persons who must receive information about the hearing?

Exhibit 18-1 continued

	6. Has the prehearing coordinator notified all persons involved that their attendance is required? Have arrangements been made to receive notarized testimony?
	7. Have all persons been informed of the hearing date?
	8. Has the prehearing coordinator established alternate dates?
	9. Has the hearing room been reserved?
	10. Does the prehearing coordinator know where to get support services such as copying machines, telephones, mail services, typewriters, clerical assistance, interpreters?
	11. Have arrangements been made for the recording of a verbatim transcript? Are tape recorders working? Are there enough tapes or has a court stenographer been hired?
	12. How will a copy of the transcript be made available to a party that requests one?
	13. Have parents desiring an independent evaluation made all the arrangements for it before they requested the hearing? If not, will all evaluations by different professionals be completed before the agreed-upon hearing date?
	14. Have the parents been informed of their due process rights?
	15. Has each side provided the other with the written evidence it intends to submit at the hearing? (Written evidence must be submitted to the parties at least five days before the hearing.)
	16. Has a list of witnesses, their titles or relationships to the child, occupation, and a capsule summary of their testimony been shared with the parties?
	17. Has an agenda and set of procedures for the hearing been mailed to all participants at least five days before the session?

Chapter 19

Conducting the Hearing

The purpose of the special education due process hearing is to provide a forum in which the parties can have a fair opportunity to be heard and the hearing officer can obtain the information necessary to hand down a decision on the issue(s) presented. To accomplish this purpose, it is critical that the proceeding be conducted in a professional and orderly manner. An informal atmosphere should be maintained to facilitate the full participation of everyone present.

However, from the outset, there is a need for clear structure so that everyone understands that the proceeding will allow each participant an opportunity to provide input. It also should be apparent to everyone that the hearing officer is the person who will control the session. The hearing officer then must exercise this control when appropriate. The informality should not become a license for any participant to abuse the process or for the hearing to be reduced to acrimonious exchanges between the parties.

This chapter discusses the manner in which the special education due process hearing should be conducted to facilitate its objective.

HEARING ROOM SEATING ARRANGEMENT

The hearing room should be arranged in a manner conducive to an orderly presentation so as to allow all participants to hear and see each other easily. Figure 19-1 illustrates two preferred arrangements using conference tables. Both place the hearing officer at a central position, with the school participants on one side and the parents on the other. The witness testifies from a chair directly opposite the hearing officer. Alternate arrangements may be required depending on the number of participants, acoustics of the room, and other such factors.

Figure 19-1 Suggested Seating Arrangements for a Hearing

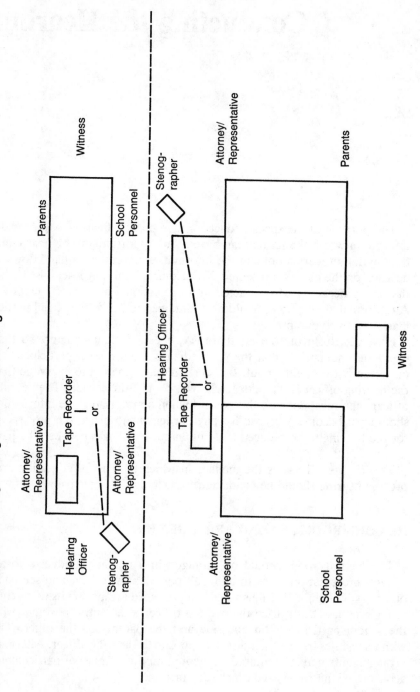

The hearing officer should arrive before the appointed time to organize the room and have an opportunity to greet and direct the participants as they arrive. If the hearing officer arrives after others, the individual still should organize the hearing room and direct the participants to their places.

The hearing room arrangement is important for reasons other than simple practical considerations. The physical layout conveys the message to everyone that the hearing officer is controlling the proceeding and that it has structure. The hearing will not be a totally informal and open-ended meeting; it must be organized for the accomplishment of a purpose.

RECORDING EQUIPMENT

Most hearings use tape recorders to comply with the legal requirement that a verbatim record be made. The hearing officer should check the tape recorder and microphones at the outset to be sure they are functioning properly. The microphones might need to be better arranged to facilitate the recording of everyone's presentation. A check must be made to assure there are sufficient tapes even if the session is prolonged. The hearing officer also should instruct the participants to state their name and role before they begin to speak. This will be helpful if a written transcript must be made from the recording. If a court reporter (stenographer) is used instead of a tape recorder, the participants should be similarly instructed.

The participants should be asked not to use gestures such as nodding when indicating yes or no answers, or pointing. Gestures will not be reflected on the tape.

The hearing officer must carefully monitor the recording equipment throughout the session. If a tape must be changed in the recorder or on the court reporter's machine, the participants must be instructed to refrain from talking for the necessary few moments.

The verbatim record is important so what was said or agreed to by the participants can be reviewed later. This information is essential to the hearing officer who must write a decision solely on the evidence presented. It also is important if the decision is appealed.

Frequently, an appellate body will review only a specific part of the evidence rather than rehear the whole case. That body usually obtains a copy of the verbatim record below and examines that without taking any further evidence or testimony. Therefore, a complete and accurate verbatim record is essential. The hearing should not proceed if the recording equipment is not functioning. If there is a breakdown, the session should be recessed until later. Legally, if no verbatim record is available, the case must be reheard.

STARTING THE HEARING

The hearing officer has the responsibility of starting and conducting the proceeding. This responsibility begins when the individual calls it to order at the appointed time, starting the recording at that point. The hearing officer then presents an introductory statement that ought to include the following basic components:

1. Introduction of the Hearing Officer and the Case

This component consists of a short greeting by the hearing officer welcoming the participants and with self-identification as (*name of hearing officer*), the hearing officer in this matter of (*name of child*).

2. Statement of the Legal Authority for the Hearing

The hearing officer should indicate the legal authority for conducting the proceeding. It generally is held under the authority of state law or regulations of the state's department of education, depending on the individual state. The authority also might be found in the local board of education rules or a court decree. Some jurisdictions cite the legal authority as the federal law, P.L. 94-142, the Education for all Handicapped Children Act.

The hearing officer and the participants should be clear what single or combination of legal authorities govern the proceedings so they can prepare and present their positions accordingly. The statement of legal authority also serves to remind the participants that the hearing is not an ad hoc meeting but rather a legal proceeding governed by legal regulations and having legal consequences.

3. Explanation of the Hearing's General Purpose

Many of the participants will not be familiar with a special education due process hearing. The hearing officer should explain that the purpose is to resolve an impasse between the parents and the school system about the student's educational program. The hearing does this by providing an opportunity for both sides to present their positions and evidence before an impartial individual. That individual is the hearing officer, who receives the information on any matter relating to the identification, evaluation, programming, or placement of the student that cannot be resolved through informal school procedures.

4. Explanation of the Specific Purpose of This Hearing

The hearing officer should then clearly articulate the specific purpose of the particular hearing. For example, the purpose might be to determine whether the evaluation of the student, (*name*), is appropriate, or whether a further educational evaluation or an independent assessment might be necessary. As another example, it might be to determine whether the proposed placement of the student, (*name*), at the (*name of school or program*) is adequate and appropriate to meet that pupil's educational needs.

5. Explanation of the Hearing Officer's Role

Since many of the participants will be unfamiliar with this proceeding, they should be provided with an explanation of the hearing officer's role. It should be pointed out that the hearing officer is selected to serve as an impartial individual who is prepared to hear all sides of the matter.

The hearing officer is responsible for conducting the hearing in an orderly manner and for providing an opportunity for a full presentation of the evidence. This responsibility requires that the hearing officer ask questions of a witness or party to elicit further information. It may be necessary to have certain statements clarified and areas explored that have not been sufficiently developed. In addition, the hearing officer will rule on procedural matters and objections raised by the parties. After the session, the hearing officer will arrive at a decision based solely on the testimony and evidence presented during the proceeding.

6. Acknowledgment of Persons Present

The hearing officer should pass around a sheet of paper for all persons present to sign. It should indicate their names, addresses, titles, and roles. The list should be made part of the record. It also will help clarify all participants' relationships to the case. The hearing officer then may introduce each person so that everyone is familiar with who they are and their relationships to the case.

7. Informing Parents of Due Process Rights

Once again, the parents are informed of their rights and asked whether they had an opportunity to avail themselves of them before the hearing. (The rights are enumerated in Chapter 16 under "Notice and Consent.")

The hearing officer should proceed down the list of rights and question the parents or their representatives on each one.

In addition, it might be deemed wise to ask the parents whether they were able to read and understand the written notice (as discussed in earlier chapters). They may desire the assistance of a reader or interpreter—which the coordinator should have arranged for earlier.

This process can be expedited if the school system uses a standard written notice containing the parents' rights. The hearing officer then could simply ask the parents if they received that notice, if they were able to read and understand it, and if they had had an opportunity to avail themselves of the rights as was their option. If the parents are represented by an attorney or an advocate familiar with these proceedings, the hearing officer can ask that representative whether the clients would waive a formal reading of the rights. Usually the representative will accede. The representative undoubtedly will have fully discussed the rights with the parents previously.

Frequently, the hearing officer does learn of a defect in the provision of notice and the opportunity for the parents to exercise their rights. Such a defect does not necessarily mean that the hearing must be adjourned to a later date to allow for correction of the defect. Frequently, it can be corrected at the hearing without the need for a continuance, or the parents may waive the particular right so the proceeding can get to the main issue. This situation is discussed further under the heading "Ruling on Objections During the Hearing."

8. Open or Closed Hearing

This should have been determined before the hearing, as discussed in Chapter 17. Usually the hearing is closed and all matters discussed are strictly confidential. The issues are high cost and emotionally charged. However, the persons primarily interested in a particular case are the participants. There normally are no throngs attempting to gain access; occasionally, one or two persons may wish to observe for professional reasons. The parents' permission is sought and generally is received.

However, if the case is of high public interest, the parents probably will have requested an open hearing in advance. The hearing officer or person responsible for completing the prehearing activities should have arranged for a room that could accommodate spectators as well as participants. If there is a large crowd, the hearing officer should conduct the session no differently from any other. However, the hearing officer may need to assert control more firmly. Persons present as observers may do just that—observe. Unless they have some information relevant to the specific case, they generally do not participate. The hearing officer may need to remind those present that the task is to gather evidence regarding this specific student's educational needs and provide a decision based solely on that evidence. The proceeding should not be turned into a forum for public complaints on problems with the school system and its programs for handicapped children.

9. Instructions on Proper Decorum

Another step is to direct the participants to make all comments to the hearing officer. This is to ensure that they all have an opportunity to present their testimony in a clear, rational way. There is no need for the participants to argue and attempt to convince each other of the validity of their positions—they had that opportunity before the hearing process was invoked, and it does not serve the child's educational interests. Now they must convince the hearing officer of the validity of their case by means of facts, statements of chronological events, interpretations of test results, testimony of witnesses, and other evidence.

The hearing officer reserves the right to exclude from the room any person whose behavior substantially interferes with the orderly procedure of the hearing.

10. The Procedure during the Hearing

The preferred order of procedure during the hearing is as follows:

- An opening statement is made on behalf of the schools.
- An opening statement is made on behalf of the parents.
- The public schools present their evidence.
- The parents may cross-examine the witnesses presented by the public schools.
- The parents present their evidence.
- The public schools may cross-examine the witnesses presented by the parents.
- A closing statement is made on behalf of the public schools.
- A closing statement is made on behalf of the parents.

After the opening statement by the hearing officer, the witnesses may be directed to leave the hearing room until they are called to testify. This way a more objective presentation of the case can be developed because it ensures that the testimony presented by each witness will be free from influence by what the other witnesses say. If, however, neither party requests the exclusion of the witnesses and the hearing officer doesn't think it necessary, the witnesses may remain in the hearing room.

ADMINISTRATION OF THE OATH

Many jurisdictions require that an oath be administered to those who will give testimony. If this is required or preferred, the hearing officer may swear a witness individually before giving testimony, or swear all the witnesses collectively at the beginning of the session.

The attorneys or advocates representing the parents or public schools generally do not take an oath because they will not be presenting evidence so their statements are not testimony. Their role is to give opening and closing statements to summarize the evidence and contentions of the party they represent.

They also organize their party's case by calling witnesses and eliciting testimony from them and by submitting documents. If they also are personally involved in the case and have information to offer for the hearing officer's consideration, then of course they also are witnesses and should be sworn as such.

There are a number of statements for an oath. Two suggested versions are:

1. "Do you solemnly swear or affirm that the testimony you are about to give will be the truth, the whole truth, and nothing but the truth?"
2. "Do you affirm that your statements will be true and accurate to the best of your knowledge?"

ORDER OF PRESENTATION

To maintain decorum and fairness, the hearing officer follows an ordered format that should be outlined in the introductory remarks. The following is a suggested order:

1. Preliminary Matters

One party or the other usually has a question, problem, or objection to raise before the presentations begin. These usually involve the absence of a witness, the need to have a certain witness heard out of order, a request that the witnesses be excused from the hearing room until they are called to present evidence, a need for a continuance, an objection to holding the session because prehearing steps have not been completed, etc.

These matters may be heard at this time and disposed of as appropriate. The hearing officer may feel it is premature to raise certain matters at that point and instruct the party to reserve the issue until the proper time later in the hearing.

2. Opening Statements by Both Sides

It is helpful to have the representative of each party present a brief, clear opening statement before the presentation of evidence. These statements summarize the main contentions of the parties and the supporting evidence. Opening statements are not evidence and cannot be used by the hearing officer as a basis for the decision. They may discuss what evidence the party intends to submit but they are not evidence.

The purpose of the opening statements is to outline what course each presenting party intends to take, what propositions it intends to prove, what evidence it believes to be important, etc., in a context or a perspective it will urge the hearing officer to adopt. The statements allow the parties to begin their presentation on a less formal basis and argue their positions before they are confined to the structured task of proof.

3. The Public Schools Present Their Evidence

The school system presents its case first because it is legally responsible for the child's educational program and placement. It also bears the burden of proof as to the appropriateness of its identification, evaluation, programming, and placement of the child.

Usually in a court or administrative hearing, those who initiate the hearing present their case first because they have the responsibility of proving that their contentions are true. They have the burden of establishing in the mind of the decision maker that their position is the right one. However, the burden of proof is allocated differently in a special education due process hearing. It is the responsibility of the public schools to provide a handicapped child with a free appropriate public education so they always must stand ready to prove that their conduct on behalf of the student meets this fundamental legal requirement. They must establish that their actions at every stage are intended to provide the child with an appropriate educational program. Therefore, it does not matter in these proceedings which party initiated the hearing.

The responsibility of proof rests with the school system as another protection for the handicapped pupil. The child, who ostensibly is the focus of the proceeding, may not even be at the hearing. That is why it is not adversarial in the usual sense. If one party fails to make out its case, the other side does not automatically win, such as in a criminal trial. The hearing officer's responsibility is to issue a decision on the appropriateness of the child's educational program. A hearing officer who does not feel that either the parents or the public schools have presented a position that is appropriate may reject both and adopt a third course.

Two examples illustrate this point further.

In the first example, the schools initiate a hearing to demonstrate that their evaluation of a suspected handicapped child was appropriate. The parents contend that the evaluation was not appropriate and seek to have the schools pay for an independent educational evaluation. Here, the schools have initiated the hearing—they have the responsibility of proof. However, this is not because they initiated the hearing but because the law requires that a child suspected of being handicapped be provided with an appropriate evaluation by the public schools.

It does not matter who raises the question as to the appropriateness of the evaluation. The bottom line is that the school system must provide one. The schools could fail to prove that their evaluation was appropriate and the hearing officer would not necessarily be constrained to order that they pay for an independent evaluation as requested by the parents. The hearing officer might find that the evaluation was slightly defective and order that it be corrected by completing a certain additional assessment component. The hearing officer might not believe that a full independent evaluation is necessary, based on the evidence.

In the second example, the parents may initiate a hearing to prove that their child should be placed in a private residential facility at the expense of the public schools. The schools oppose such a move because they contend they have an appropriate placement within their system. Here, the parents have initiated the hearing but the responsibility of proof still is on the schools. Again, this is because the law requires that they provide a handicapped child with a free appropriate education. And again, it does not matter who raised the question as to the appropriateness of the placement. The bottom line still is that the public schools must provide an appropriate placement.

The parents, who initiated the hearing, could fail to prove that the child should be placed in a particular private residential facility but, again, that would not necessarily mean that the hearing officer would be constrained to find that the placement recommended by the public schools was appropriate. The hearing officer could find that neither placement—the one recommended by the public schools or the parents' choice—was appropriate.

After the schools' presentation of their case, the parents then have their opportunity to challenge the system and present their own contentions. If the schools fail to at least demonstrate on its face that their program is appropriate, the hearing officer may order them to develop such a plan in accordance with their legal responsibility without even hearing the parents' side.

During their presentation, the public school system presents its documentary and testimonial evidence. The documents and witnesses should correspond with the lists of such materials and persons furnished to the parents before the hearing.

4. Parents May Cross-Examine Schools' Witnesses

The parents may cross-examine the school personnel after each testifies or after the entire opposing case has been presented. This questioning should be limited to the testimony or to the contents of any documents submitted into evidence. The parents should not attempt to present new or contradictory evidence at this time through their questioning.

5. The Parents Present Their Evidence

This is the opportunity for the parents to prove their case and rebut the public schools. The parents (or the schools) should present their case in an organized manner, directed by one advocate or representative, who involves the others on that side by calling each in a logical order to offer information. Another way to organize the presentation is for the advocate to direct specific questions to each person to elicit information.

A structured argument is necessary to acquaint the hearing officer with the background and current circumstances of the case. It must be kept in mind that the hearing officer may have just become aware of this problem when assigned to the case while both parties may have been involved for months and even years.

6. Schools May Cross-Examine Parents' Witnesses

The public schools have the opportunity to cross-examine the parents and their witnesses in the same manner as the parents did.

7. Reexamination and Additional Evidence

After its witnesses have been cross-examined, either party may wish to reexamine them to clarify earlier statements or to elicit further information. The opposing party then also has the opportunity to recross-examine. A party also may have additional evidence to rebut or clarify earlier statements or evidence. This is the appropriate time for the hearing officer to receive such information.

8. Closing Statements by Both Sides

Both parties conclude with a closing statement. This is closely related to the opening statement and is treated in the same fashion. It summarizes each side's contentions and what it believes its evidence has proved.

THE PRESENTATION OF WITNESSES

The role of a witness is to present testimony that becomes evidence in the case. The witness testifies to information learned by direct observation of the child or other similar involvement with the pupil's school or home life. If the witness is a professional who is testifying as an expert in a particular field, the person may give an expert opinion as to what the assessment data mean or what the individual would recommend as an appropriate placement to meet the child's special educational needs.

The witness may or may not be asked to attest to reports, recommendations, evaluations, or other documents as part of the testimony. The documents themselves may then also become evidence. But essentially it is what witnesses say that is the evidence they offer.

Because the exact testimony is not certain until a witness says it, many jurisdictions require that such individuals be allowed into the hearing room only when testifying, as noted earlier in this chapter in Item 10, on "The Procedure During the Hearing." Other jurisdictions adopt this principle as sound practice to ensure fairness.

An attorney or representative for a party may formally request such a rule at the outset. This is a precautionary measure to guard against one witness's being influenced by the statements of another. Even the brightest, most secure persons are susceptible to such influence. Three witnesses in a row might suggest that the child exhibited violent and dangerous behaviors in their presence at one time or another. The fourth witness might have observed the child on several occasions and felt that the pupil acted up frequently because of determined provocation by the other students who had targeted this individual for such harrassment. After hearing several other witnesses, the fourth may feel less sure of those observations and be inclined to have second thoughts, to vacillate, or to modify testimony so that it does not seem so out of line with the others.

Many other examples could be offered to show how a witness might be influenced in testifying by hearing the other witnesses and the proceedings before taking the stand. For this reason, witnesses might be asked to remain outside the hearing room until they are called to testify. However, in many cases all of the witnesses and participants know each other, are familiar with each other's involvement and positions on the issues, and have no objection to all witnesses being present in the hearing room.

If the public schools present their case first, as recommended above, then their witnesses should be called first. The hearing officer should direct the witnesses to the appropriate chair. They then should be asked to state for the record their name and address; position, title, and relationship to the child; and reason for appearing in the case.

The public school attorney will question the witness first. The questioning should be in what is called direct examination. The questions should be simple, open-ended, and not suggest a particular answer.

Depending on the procedure agreed to at the outset, the attorney either will present all the schools' witnesses first or allow the parents the opportunity to cross-examine each one after direct examination. After both sides have had an opportunity to examine the witness fully, the hearing officer should ask whether either will require further testimony from that individual later. If not, the witness may be excused with thanks for appearing.

The parents introduce their case in similar fashion at the conclusion of the schools' presentation.

The hearing officer should not hesitate to control or limit the questioning of witnesses where appropriate. A party should be permitted to question a witness only through its attorney or representative. If questioning by others is allowed, the hearing officer should be careful to keep it orderly and should step in immediately if it becomes hostile or irrelevant. Frequently, a party will offer several witnesses, all of whom have the same information. The hearing officer may decide that the testimony is becoming redundant and the additional witnesses are not necessary.

If a party or other witness fails to appear, the hearing officer may use discretion in deciding whether to continue the session to another date. This judgment can depend on how critical the witness is to the proceeding. If the missing witness is a party, the case may proceed if the hearing officer believes that adequate notice was provided to missing persons before the session.

If a witness for a party does not appear, the hearing officer may proceed, setting another date for that person to testify. Another way to handle this problem is for the hearing officer to ask the opposing party if it will accept a written statement, affidavit, or deposition from the witness in lieu of a personal appearance. In many cases such an alternative is acceptable because there may not be any real disagreement about what that particular witness would testify to if present.

The parties to a special education due process hearing have the right to compel the appearance of witnesses. As noted earlier, this procedure generally is governed by state regulations. The hearing officer should consult the schools' lawyer or the local district attorney for further information. If a school employee fails to appear, the hearing officer may have another course available. Since the hearings generally are conducted under the authority of state and local education agencies, the failure of a public school employee to appear may amount to insubordination.

INTRODUCING DOCUMENTS INTO EVIDENCE

The attorney or representative for each party may decide how and when to introduce a document into evidence. When this is done, the document should be identified by number and described orally so that everyone will know which one is being discussed and so the tape recording will contain its specifics.

The proper way to introduce a document is through a witness. The representative takes up a document and asks the hearing officer to mark it in some way for identification. The representative then takes the labeled paper to the witness and asks if the person recognizes the document marked "Exhibit 1." The representative asks the witness to describe the document, how the individual came to be familiar with it, etc. A copy of the document should already have been furnished to the opposing party before the hearing. If it was not, it may be subject to exclusion at the hearing. If it is not excluded, a copy should be furnished to both the opposing party and the hearing officer. In this way, everyone may follow along with the presentation.

The hearing officer should keep a file of all documents entered into evidence. Before the hearing ends, the hearing officer may wish to review the documents with the parties to be sure there have been no misunderstandings or omissions.

CONTINUANCE OR POSTPONEMENT OF A HEARING

Frequently, a party will request that the hearing be postponed or continued to another date or the hearing officer may so determine. This issue could arise before the scheduled date, at the outset of the hearing, or during the session. The decision whether or not to postpone or continue rests with the hearing officer, not with the parties. If the postponement request comes before the session starts, the hearing officer may not yet be involved in the case. In such a situation, the decision would rest with the hearing coordinator or that person's supervisor.

There are a number of reasons why a party might request a continuance or postponement. Some of the most frequently cited ones are:

1. the absence of a person who was expected to be a witness
2. the failure of the attorney or representative of a party to appear at the appointed time for the hearing
3. a failure to finish the assessments or to receive the reports of the evaluators in time
4. the unavailability of a document that can be obtained later
5. the progress of negotiations or mediation on the issues that are to be decided at the hearing
6. an emergency or other unforeseen circumstance preventing a party from appearing
7. the illness of one of the parties, witnesses, or hearing officer
8. a substantial defect in the notice provided to the parents or in the provision of their rights

The granting of a continuance is essentially a judgment call left to the discretion of the hearing officer. However, the interests of the child in the speedy provision of a free appropriate public education should be weighed carefully when considering such a request. Both parties may agree to continue or postpone the hearing but that continues the child in an uncertain educational situation. A request for such a continuance also may be a stalling tactic by one of the parties. The hearing officer should grant continuances and postponements when appropriate but only after careful considerations of the reasons offered.

The following guidelines will assist the hearing officer in determining whether or not to grant the request for a postponement or continuance:

1. Was the Request Made before the Hearing?

If the request came in before the hearing, it is less likely to disrupt the process because the participants have not yet assembled. The request in such a case would be for a postponement rather than a continuance—that the hearing be deferred before it starts rather than continued after it begins.

2. Who Is Making the Request?

If both parties agree to postpone or continue, the hearing officer generally will grant the request, provided that a sound reason is shown. In this situation, the parties will have waived their right to have a final decision within 45 days.

3. Why Is the Request Being Made?

If the request is being made for a reason beyond the control of the party, the hearing officer will generally grant it. Such reasons might include the failure of a representative or witness to appear, the unavailability of important documents or reports through no fault of the requesting side, etc.

4. Could the Problem Be Corrected by Less Disruptive Means?

Often a party will request a continuance when the problem is not really compelling enough to merit one. However, if a report or document is missing, the parties might stipulate to what it would say if it were available. The same goes for a witness. The hearing could proceed in the absence of the witness or report and a written statement or document could be furnished to everyone later. Even though there might be a substantial defect in the notice provided to the parents, they may be prepared to proceed with the hearing anyway. A short recess could be offered for them to review documents and rethink the matter before they proceed.

5. Will a Delay Be in the Child's Best Interests?

As noted, the hearing officer's responsibility is to conduct the proceeding and to issue a decision in such a way as to ensure the child's educational interests. The focus of concern is neither the parents or the school, it is the child. Yet it is the parents or school who may request a postponement or continuance. Nevertheless, the hearing officer must keep in mind the ramifications that granting a request will have for the child.

For example, a party may be requesting a postponement or continuance as a delaying tactic. The school may wish to avoid the issue of whether the child should receive summer instruction by delaying a hearing until well after the summer program has begun. The parents may prefer the child's current placement to the one being proposed by the school so, to delay a possible adverse ruling as long as possible, they resort to various legal maneuvers to postpone or continue the hearing as long as they can.

Such tactics subvert the lawful mission of the hearing process and do not contribute to providing the child with an appropriate education.

If a hearing officer determines that the request for postponement or continuance should be granted, the reasoning behind that decision should be made clear to everyone. Generally, the hearing should be continued to a time and place certain, convenient to all participants, and as soon as possible. The hearing officer also should make clear what each participant is to do during the interim.

For example, the parents may be required to obtain a psychological report from the private school the child is attending and send it to the placement specialist at the public schools. The specialist may be told to review the report and decide whether or not to modify the recommendation for therapy services. The hearing officer may wish to clarify what the child's status should be during the interim and what services are to be provided.

If the situation merits a postponement or continuance, and neither party makes such a request, then it may be done on the hearing officer's own accord.

Postponements and continuances disrupt the process, impose a burden on parties and witnesses, and delay the child's appropriate education. The hearing officer should consider these guidelines in deciding whether or not to grant one. These considerations can be summed up in the question:

When weighed against the child's interests for a speedy resolution of the issues, is a postponement or continuance really necessary?

RULING ON OBJECTIONS DURING THE HEARING

In addition to ruling on requests for continuances or postponements, the hearing officer may also be required to decide on objections raised by the parties as the session progresses.

A party, through its representative, may raise an objection to (1) admission of a document, (2) testimony by a witness, or (3) some other procedural matter that the advocate feels is unfairly affecting the rights of the side. Following are three examples:

1. Admission of a Document

The school professionals introduce a physician's report and recommendation that the child be placed in a special school that has a medical support capacity for the orthopedically handicapped or otherwise health impaired. The school experts also are proposing just such a placement. The physician who wrote the report is not present at the hearing.

The parents' representative objects strenuously to the introduction of the report, contending that it simply states conclusions without a clear explanation for the underlying reasoning. The representative charges that the parents in effect are being deprived of their right of cross-examination because the author of the report is not available for questioning.

2. Testimony by a Witness

The parents wish to present a social worker from the private school where their child is enrolled in their attempt to prove that the placement proposed by the public school is not appropriate. They believe the social worker will testify favorably to them about the handicapping condition and what type of educational program would be appropriate to meet the child's needs.

The public school representative objects, declaring that the witness is trained as a social worker and is not professionally qualified to diagnose the child's learning and emotional disorders. Moreover, the social worker's testimony would not be reliable because the person is employed by the private school at which the parents are hoping to have their child placed at public expense. The representative contends that the social worker's testimony would be "incompetent" and biased.

3. A Procedural Matter

The school personnel introduce a psychologist's report concerning the child that unfortunately was not shared with the parents before the hearing. The parents' representative objects to the admission of the document, asserting that the parents have a right to prohibit any evidence that has not been disclosed to them at least five days before the hearing.

Most objections involve these types of concerns. The hearing officer has three options in making a decision on an objection:

1. Sustain the Objection: The hearing officer agrees with the person raising the objection.
2. Overrule the Objection: The hearing officer disagrees with the person raising the objection.
3. Restrict or Modify the Evidence Objected To: The hearing officer agrees in part with the person raising the objection but believes that the problem at issue can be corrected without excluding the entire bit of evidence.

Generally, the hearing officer should take the third option, largely because in administrative proceedings such as the special education due process hearing, the policy usually is to admit all relevant evidence. The hearing officer may take into consideration the points raised by the objecting party after admitting the evidence and while preparing to decide the case. Just because certain evidence is accepted does not mean that the hearing officer will necessarily give it much weight and credibility or be persuaded by it. For example, a hearing officer may accept contradictory statements from two witnesses. The first witness may have reviewed numerous reports on the child, the second may have worked directly with the pupil. If the two are otherwise equal in qualifications, the hearing officer may give more weight and credibility to the statement by the witness who worked directly with the child. Thus, the hearing officer may admit both statements for consideration but in the end be more persuaded by one of them.

Returning to the three earlier examples, a hearing officer probably would exercise the third option unless the objection were frivolous because of a desire to be fair to both parties. The hearing officer would want to be responsive to the objecting party's concerns while also protecting the right of the other side to present its evidence. Of course, evidence that is not relevant or is overly repetitious may be excluded because it tends to obscure the central issue in the case.

In the first example—the physician's report—the hearing officer probably should admit the document but may want to provide another time at which the parents can question the doctor about it. As one alternative, the doctor could answer written questions submitted by the parents. The parents may wish to have the child examined by another doctor of their own choosing. Or the hearing officer may simply admit the document and give it little weight in reaching a decision. After all, even an expert's conclusions may not be very convincing if the reasoning behind them is not apparent.

In the second example—the social worker—the hearing officer should allow the witness to testify but possibly under restrictions. The first point on this objection is that it is premature. The person objecting is anticipating what the social worker may wish to testify to before the witness's mouth is even open. However, if the social worker does begin to testify to matters beyond the scope of the person's professional training, the witness should be stopped and redirected. Even though the social worker may not be able to testify to the diagnosis of the child's emotional disturbance, it may be possible to report specific behaviors that were observed.

Professionals usually are aware of what they are legally "competent" to discuss as "expert" witnesses. Any witness may testify to what actually was seen or heard but persons presented as "experts" may give professional opinions only in the area in which they are "competent" because of proper training, certification, and experience.

As for bias by the social worker, the hearing officer can take this into consideration in later evaluating the evidence and assessing the weight and credibility of each witness' testimony. In the example, the social worker was employed by the private school the child was attending. This expert's testimony could be extremely valuable to the hearing officer in reaching a decision. The social worker may have an interest in the outcome because of the employer but that does not mean the person is biased in favor of the parents. The individual may have an interest in the case and still be able to communicate information in a professionally responsible manner. It is doubtful that the social worker would lie because of place of employment but might tend to advocate zealously for a particular position.

Therefore, the hearing officer would not want to exclude this testimony but would want to keep in mind the employment association when assessing the weight and credibility to be accorded to it.

In the third example—the psychologist—the hearing officer is confronted with a common objection based on a procedural ground: to exclude what may be an important piece of evidence because the school failed to share the document with the parents. The sharing of evidence before the hearing is an important right guaranteed by law, as discussed in Chapter 18. But the right to present relevant evidence also is an important right guaranteed by law to both parties.

How can the hearing officer resolve this conflict between two equally important rights? In such a situation, the sense of fairness and finesse must be used. It should be made clear to both parties that the document should not be excluded from evidence even though the other side did not have an opportunity to review it before the hearing and prepare to rebut its contents if necessary.

Such a problem usually is resolved by the hearing officer's having the cake and eating it too. The hearing officer could admit the document then or at a later session when the other party might have had a better opportunity to prepare its response. If it is admitted at the present hearing, the other party could be granted a short recess in which to review its contents and see if there is any problem. If there is no problem, the other party may be asked to waive its right to advance inspection of the document. If there is a problem, the hearing officer may proceed with the session and provide for an alternative way of receiving the other party's rebuttal evidence. The alternative may include holding a follow-up session for the sole purpose of examining and cross-examining the persons involved with the document, etc.

In general, a hearing officer in a special education due process hearing is not required to observe the strict rules concerning the admission or exclusion of evidence as in a.regular court proceeding. All evidence that bears on the issue at hand should be admitted. The hearing officer usually should resolve objections by attempting to settle the underlying concerns rather than by excluding evidence. If unable to resolve the objection satisfactorily, the hearing officer should overrule or sustain it and allow the losing party to put on the record a statement of the substance and purpose of the excluded evidence or the reasons why the challenge should have been upheld.

The hearing officer should keep in mind that procedure is supposed to facilitate, not obstruct, a proceeding, and should not allow legal maneuvers to dominate the process. There should be a quick ruling on the objection so the case could continue to move along.

CLOSING THE HEARING

At the conclusion of the presentations by the parties, the hearing officer should ask if anyone has anything further to contribute, then request that one person from each side present a closing statement as discussed earlier under "Order of Presentation." The hearing officer then should make a brief statement to formally conclude the session. This closing statement should cover the following points:

1. What Will Happen Next?

The hearing officer should explain that the evidence presented at the hearing will be considered and a decision issued within whatever number of days are stipulated in that jurisdiction. If the hearing has been recessed for a continuance, the hearing officer will want to instruct the participants as to what is to be done during the interim.

2. Requests for a Verbatim Record

The hearing officer should mention briefly how the parties may obtain copies of the record if they choose.

3. Limits on Holding the Record Open

If the hearing officer said the record would be held open to receive further documents, a date and certain time should be established by which the materials must be submitted if they are to be considered. The documents or their nature should be clarified and reviewed. The hearing officer should instruct a party submitting documents to be sure to provide copies to the opposing side. As an alternative, the opposing party should be informed that the hearing officer will see to it that copies of any such documents are provided to it.

4. Explanation of Appeal Procedures

The hearing officer should review and explain the appeal procedures available to the parties should they disagree with the decision. Appeal procedures are discussed in detail in Chapter 20.

5. Thanking Participants and Closing the Hearing

Finally, the hearing officer will want to thank the participants for attending and contributing their input on behalf of the child, then conclude with a clear statement that the hearing is over or adjourned. Such a statement rounds out the hearing and conveys the message once again that the hearing is a legal proceeding with a specific task and a clear beginning and end.

Chapter 20

After the Hearing: Alternatives and Procedures

Regardless of the outcome of the special education due process hearing, one or both parties may be dissatisfied with the decision and decide to appeal. This chapter discusses the procedures for appeal as provided by law. It also analyzes the problem that arises when one party chooses to ignore all or part of the hearing officer's decision. This occurs when a decision has been issued and neither party appeals but one fails to comply with its directions. The question then is:

How can the hearing officer's decision be enforced?

THE RIGHT TO APPEAL

The regulations provide that:

> A decision made in a hearing . . . is final, unless a party to the hearing appeals the decision . . . (§ 121a.509)

This requires little explanation. It clearly states two points: (1) that the hearing officer's decision is final, unless appealed, and (2) who may appeal.

On the first point, the adjudication of the dispute and the various rights of the parties become fixed unless one side acts to have that decision reviewed. Unfortunately, P.L. 94-142 and its accompanying regulations do not provide a time limit for indicating an intention to appeal. They do permit only 30 days after the state agency's receipt of an appeal for the reviewing authority to issue a decision. (See § 121a.512 and the final portion of this chapter.) However, there is a gap as to how much time can elapse between the hearing officer's decision and the filing of an appeal. It is suggested that a reasonable time limit be adopted by the LEA, if applicable state regulations do not cover this contingency.

A reasonable time limit probably would be between one and two weeks after receipt of the hearing officer's decision. Any longer period might impair the child's right to receive a free appropriate public education in the least restrictive environment. The hearing officer's decision must become final at some point if the due process hearing is to accomplish its purpose. If no time limits are provided by state or local regulation, then the hearing officer might specifically state a time frame within which parties could appeal as an element of assuring fairness to all parties, especially to the child, so the pendency situation would not be prolonged more than necessary.

The second point clearly states that only "a party to the hearing" may appeal. If the decision has ramifications beyond the facts and parties of the case, others (such as a parent advocacy group or a different education agency) may want to make the issue a class action or test case, but the actual parties involved may not wish to appeal.

'APPEAL' DEFINED

The law provides that a party may appeal the hearing officer's decision. This raises the question of what it means to appeal a decision.

An appeal is an administrative or judicial hearing that reviews the proceedings in a lower forum to determine whether errors were made. An appeal usually is not a new hearing in which the parties and witnesses present their information all over again. The panel, judge, or official conducting the review will respect and uphold the previous decision unless a party can demonstrate that an error was committed and the rights of that side are significantly affected.

An appeal focuses only on alleged errors in the lower authority's decision, not on the whole controversy. An appeal is not simply another hearing conducted by a different authority. If it were, the parties probably would bypass the lower authorities and present their case directly to the U.S. Supreme Court, the highest appellate authority in the country. The parties also might start at the local special education due process hearing and continue up the ladder to the Supreme Court, presenting their whole case over again at each level, until they obtained a favorable ruling.

Obviously such a system would be ludicrous. It would be many years before any child's individualized education program could be determined with finality, and the nation's court system would collapse from the incredible burden. That is why appeals are limited to reviews of the previous hearing records to see whether or not errors were committed that interfered significantly with the rights of one or both of the parties.

WHAT IS AN 'ERROR'?

When a party challenges a hearing officer's decision, the official, panel, or judge conducting the appeal will review the previous hearing record to determine whether, as noted, any errors were committed that interfered with any party's rights. An error is an action by a hearing officer that is not supported by, or is based on an incorrect application of, the law.

A hearing officer's decision that favors a program proposed by the public schools, because it is the best the system has to offer, is an example of a ruling that is not supported by the law. The parents in such a case may appeal, citing as error the hearing officer's basis for upholding the school system's proposed program.

The law does not require the parents to accept the school system's best possible program if they do not believe it is adequate and appropriate to meet their child's needs. Indeed, the fundamental principle of the law is that all handicapped children are entitled to receive an individually designed education program that meets their particular needs. The idea is that programs are to be fitted to needs rather than the needs being fitted into a program because it is most convenient for the school system.

If the proposed program is not appropriate, the hearing officer should order the school system to develop a different plan using its existing resources, design a new one with different resources, or arrange for the child to attend one outside the system at no cost to the parents. To uphold the schools' proposed program simply because it is the best the system has to offer the child would be an error.

An error based on an incorrect application of the law occurs when the hearing officer rejects the school system's proposed program because the independent educational evaluation dictates a different plan. The school system may appeal the hearing officer's total reliance upon the recommendations in the independent evaluation. It could argue that the law requires it to consider the evaluation when making decisions about the child and that the assessment also may be presented as evidence at a hearing.

However, the law does not require that the results of the independent evaluation necessarily dictate the outcome of the hearing. The hearing officer also must weigh the schools' evidence in arriving at the decision. To allow the independent evaluation to determine the issue, to the exclusion of other evidence, would be considered an error because it is an incorrect application of the law requiring that such evaluations be considered.

INITIATING AN APPEAL

In most jurisdictions the procedure for initiating an appeal appears in the regulations of the state or local education agencies and the rules of the court. The process begins with the filing of a notice of appeal with the administrative agency responsible for conducting the hearing. The notice must be filed shortly after the party receives a copy of the decision. A time limit should be stated clearly in the applicable regulations of the state or local education agencies or rules of court.

A notice of appeal is a simple document that should specify the following items:

1. the name and address of the party taking the appeal
2. the forum (administrative agency or court) to and from which the appeal is taken
3. the name and address of the other parties in the case
4. the decision or order being challenged and whether the appeal is from all or only part of that decision (if it is from only part, the specific part should be indicated)
5. the decree or relief desired from the appellate body

A copy of the notice of appeal should then be served upon each party to the hearing.

FILING APPEAL WITH ADMINISTRATIVE AGENCY

The regulations provide that:

> If the hearing is conducted by a public agency other than the State educational agency, any party aggrieved by the findings and decision in the hearing may appeal to the State educational agency. (§ 121a.510(a))

As discussed earlier, there are differences from state to state as to which administrative agency has the responsibility for conducting the initial due process hearing. That responsibility could be delegated to a local, intermediate, or state educational agency. The provision here specifies which administrative agency may be appealed to, depending on which entity heard the initial case.

Simply stated, the regulations provide that if the initial hearing is held at the local or intermediate level, a party dissatisfied with the decision may appeal it to the state level. But if the hearing is at the state level, then the act provides that a dissatisfied party may appeal it to the proper state or federal court. (§ 615(e)(2))

The hearing officer at the close of a special education due process hearing should clearly state the proper procedures for an appeal and the agency to which it should be directed. The information also could be included in the body of the decision. Literature provided to the parents regarding their due process rights also should contain this important information.

When a party brings an administrative appeal, the state educational agency (SEA) may conduct its review either directly or through another state entity that acts on its behalf. However, the SEA remains responsible for the final decision if it is appealed to the courts.

Of course, all parties have the right to continue to be represented by counsel at the state administrative review level, whether or not the reviewing official determines that a further hearing is necessary. If the reviewing official decides to hold a hearing to receive additional evidence, the other hearing rights discussed earlier also apply.

PROCEDURES FOR AN ADMINISTRATIVE APPEAL

The regulations provide that:

> If there is an appeal, the State educational agency shall conduct an impartial review of the hearing. The official conducting the review shall:
> (1) Examine the entire hearing record;
> (2) Insure that the procedures at the hearing were consistent with the requirements of due process;
> (3) Seek additional evidence if necessary. If a hearing is held to receive additional evidence, the rights in 121a.508 [hearing rights] apply;
> (4) Afford the parties an opportunity for oral or written argument, or both, at the discretion of the reviewing official;
> (5) Make an independent decision on completion of the review; and
> (6) Give a copy of written findings and the decision to the parties. (§ 121a.510(b))

The procedures and format of an administrative appeal may not be as clearly defined as they are for the initial due process hearing. The reviewing official has considerable discretion in determining what type of presentation will be required to assist in arriving at a decision and may structure the proceeding as desired. But the official at minimum has procedural responsibilities to:

Examine the Entire Hearing Record

The record includes the verbatim recording of the initial hearing and all documentary evidence submitted by the parties. If the hearing is tape recorded, the reviewing official may either have a transcript made or listen to the tapes and take notes.

Ensure That Due Process Requirements Were Met

Procedural safeguards are listed in Chapter 16. The same list can be used by the reviewing official to ensure that those safeguards met the requirements of due process.

The reviewing official will want to be sure that both parties were treated fairly, given ample and complete notice, and afforded a full opportunity to be heard at the initial hearing. These factors are the essence of procedural safeguards. If a party was not provided with one or more of these essentials, the decision would be likely to be tainted because it would rest on a foundation that was incomplete, incorrect, or misleading.

The reviewing official should ensure that the parties obtain the full measure of their procedural safeguards by using one of the following options:

1. Choosing to reverse any decision unfavorable to the appealing party and require the local school system to hold a new hearing. However, the reviewing official should judiciously use discretion in requiring the agency to conduct a new hearing because of the additional time the child may remain in an inappropriate educational program.
2. Allowing the party to exercise any rights during the appeal that were not fully afforded at the initial hearing. An example would be if the official allowed the party to introduce documents at the review that might have been excluded by the hearing officer at the initial hearing. (See the section later in this chapter on "Decision Options of the Appellate Official" for a fuller treatment of the subject.)

Seek Additional Evidence If Necessary

The reviewing official may determine that additional evidence is needed to decide the issue presented by the appeal. The parties could be requested to present that material in oral or written form. This provision states, however, that if a hearing is held to receive additional evidence, the parties must be afforded the same rights they had at the initial hearing, e.g., to know what witnesses will be present, to be represented by an attorney, etc.

Make Discretionary Use of Oral or Written Argument

Oral or written argument may be used in conjunction with the procedures stated above to assist the reviewing official in arriving at a final decision. This is traditional practice before appellate courts. Each party prepares its own argument and presents it to the reviewing official. The reviewing official's procedure could involve the following:

1. Each side prepares a written argument called a brief. The brief of the party bringing the appeal will attempt to convince the reviewing official that the decision below was incorrect for certain specified reasons. The brief of the party opposing the appeal will attempt to convince the official that the initial decision was correct. Occasionally both parties will appeal the hearing officer's decision. This occurs when the decision is based on grounds different from those urged by either side. In such a case, both parties will prepare individual briefs seeking to convince the reviewer that the initial decision was correct in some respects and incorrect in others.
2. The party preparing a brief for appellate review should use a concise format that includes a statement of each of the following items:
   a. the issues to be determined by the reviewing official
   b. the facts pertinent to the issues
   c. the specific provisions of the law applicable to the issues on appeal
   d. the relationship of the facts to the applicable law
   e. the logical, legal, and educational reasons why this particular view of the relationship of the facts should be adopted by the reviewing official
   f. legal precedents that are pertinent to the issues on appeal
   g. legal and educational literature pertinent to the issues on appeal
   h. a closing summary of the argument and requests for the action the party wishes the reviewing official to take
3. Briefs are most effective when they are well reasoned and well organized. They should be written in a simple, grammatical style. They should avoid hyperbole, flamboyant language, and personal attacks. Briefs are most persuasive when they communicate the party's position through a clear and honest argument.

4. Each party presents its argument orally, relying on the briefs. Frequently a case is balanced so evenly that the oral presentation can clarify questions and emphasize arguments enough to affect the outcome. The following guidelines should be helpful in presenting an oral argument:
   a. A time limit often is provided. Learn what the limit is for each side and stick to it. It usually is brief so it is necessary to carefully edit the written argument to be presented.
   b. The format of the brief should be followed without actually reading from it. Emphasize the strong points and give only passing (or no) attention to the others. On some points it is possible simply to refer the official to the applicable portion of the brief.
   c. The reviewing official may ask questions; they should be answered promptly, forthrightly, and respectfully.
   d. A conversational tone of voice should be maintained. It is acceptable to give strong emphasis to certain major points. However, exaggeration, shouting, or negative remarks about personalities should be avoided.
   e. It is very important to be thoroughly familiar with the initial record since this is the essence of an appeal. It is smart to respond to questions from the reviewing official with references to the initial record. Even if no questions are asked, significant points from the record can be highlighted where possible.

Arrive at an Independent Decision

After completing the review, the official must issue a decision. This official is not bound by the finding of the hearing officer below or the representations of the parties at the appeal. The official may adopt a completely independent course. In most cases, the reviewer will choose one of the decision options discussed in the later section titled "Decision Options of the Appellate Official."

Issue the Decision and Written Findings of Fact

The responsibility of the reviewing official is the same as that of the hearing officer in reporting the decision in the initial hearing. It is particularly important for the reviewer to include a full description of the case and the reasoning behind the new conclusions. A party dissatisfied with a reviewing official's decision may appeal to the proper state or federal court. The court will need a complete record and clear decision in order to perform its function of judicial review of the administrative agency's actions.

RIGHT TO SUE IN STATE OR FEDERAL COURT

The regulations provide that:

> The decision made [in an administrative appeal] by the reviewing official is final, unless a party brings a civil action. (§ 121a.510(c))

The regulations add that:

> Any party aggrieved by the findings and decision made in a hearing who does not have the right to appeal under § 121a.510 of this subpart, and any party aggrieved by the decision of a reviewing officer under § 121a.510 has the right to bring a civil action under section 615(e)(2) of the Act. (§ 121a.511)

These provisions appear complex and somewhat confusing. The gist of what they are saying is that any party may bring a civil action in the proper state or federal court. To explain further, if a special education due process hearing has been held and a decision issued by the hearing officer, any party has the right to appeal that finding. However, the party aggrieved by the decision must follow the proper appeal channels, which basically are as follows:

Channel of Appeal 1

    a. special education due process hearing held under the auspices of the local or intermediate education agency
    b. appeal to the state education agency for administrative review
    c. appeal to the proper state or federal court

Channel of Appeal 2

    a. special education due process hearing held under the auspices of the state education agency
    b. appeal to the proper state or federal court

Thus, any party may bring a civil action in the proper state or federal court, the only difference in the two channels of appeal being that the first includes the intermediate step of an administrative appeal and the second does not.

A party wishing to appeal must first determine which channel its case is following. This depends on which administrative agency is responsible for conducting the initial hearing. If it is the state agency, then the party must follow the second channel and file a civil action in court. The reason for this difference is that it would be inappropriate to have an initial hearing conducted by a state agency followed by an administrative review, also by the state agency.

It is important for the appellant party to know which channel of appeal it must follow and the steps it must take within that channel. This information should come from the hearing officer. It also could come from the director of special education, the legal counsel for the schools, the local district attorney's office, those in charge of the office responsible for conducting the hearings, a local parent advocacy center, or a local private attorney. Every state, and many subjurisdictions, have different procedures to fill out the bare outlines of the channels of appeal. The appellant party will have to research and investigate the different requirements and factors involved in deciding where to file a civil action. The rules of the jurisdiction also will determine which court is proper for such an appeal.

If a party appeals to a court for review, the judge is likely to follow one or more of the same procedures as discussed above for the reviewing official in an administrative appeal. The major difference between the appeal procedures before a reviewing official and a judge are more of form than of substance. However, the proceeding before a judge probably would be much more formalistic and rigid. The reviewing official at the state agency level has wide discretion to determine the manner in which the appeal will proceed. The judge also has wide discretion but there are numerous rules of court, laws, and case precedents that impact on court proceedings. Again, it is imperative to review pertinent state and local statutes, regulations, administrative procedures acts, and court rules before attempting to appeal. If the party is not familiar with these types of references, it must seek guidance from someone who is. It would be unfortunate indeed to suffer a delay or dismissal of a meritorious appeal because of failure to comply with the correct procedures.

DECISION OPTIONS OF THE APPELLATE OFFICIAL

After reviewing the hearing record and the actions taken by the lower authority, the state agency official (or judge) conducting the appeal will hand down an independent decision. The appellate official and judge are not limited by the lower authority's decision or by the positions presented by the parties on appeal. In some jurisdictions the review, at the state level and in certain courts, is conducted by a panel of officials or judges. In such a situation, the panel will issue a single independent decision that has been reached by a majority of its members.

Regardless of what type of appellate body (state agency reviewing official, judge, or panel) conducts the review, that entity may order any relief deemed appropriate. It can reclassify the child; change or restructure the pupil's identification, evaluation, program, or placement; and/or affirm or overturn the decision of the lower authority.

Following are the basic options available to the appellate body in reaching its decision:

Affirm the Decision of a Lower Authority

If a decision is affirmed, it means that the appellate body did not agree with the appellant party. It found no error in the proceedings below or, if it did, did not believe it significantly interfered with the rights of the party as claimed.

An example of an error that might not significantly interfere with the rights of the appealing party would occur when a hearing officer allowed documents to be introduced that had not been disclosed to the other side before the hearing. The appellate body might indeed acknowledge such action as an error. However, it might regard the error as not significant if the document only added to the already substantial evidence supporting the decision, if the contents already had been known to the other party even if that side had not actually seen it, or if the document had not been relevant to the issue being appealed. Therefore, the appellate body could affirm a lower decision if it determined that any errors that might have been made did not interfere significantly with the rights of the appealing party.

Modify the Decision of a Lower Authority

An appellate body may modify or change a decision if this would remove the effects of a significant error. The example above also could be determined to have been a significant error, depending on the nature of the document. For example, if the schools had introduced a document stating that counseling services were required one day a week to help the child benefit from the special education program, the parents might appeal on that issue. They could contend that it had been a significant error for the hearing officer to allow that document to be presented since it had not been disclosed to them before the hearing. The parents might claim that, had they known about the document's recommendations in advance, they would have obtained evidence to show that their child required counseling services daily to benefit from the proposed program.

If the parents were to have obtained such evidence subsequently and presented it with their appeal, the appellate body might be persuaded by their contention. In such a case, the appellate entity might leave most of the decision of the lower authority intact but modify the portion dealing with the quantity of counseling services required to help the child benefit from the special education program. On that particular point, the appellate body could modify the decision of the lower authority to increase the amount of counseling services from once a week to once a day.

Reverse the Decision of the Lower Authority

If the errors by the lower authority interfere with the rights of the appealing party in a significant way, the appellate body may reverse the decision. A reversal means that the appellate body set aside the entire decision of the lower authority.

The example above could be used here again. If the document had been introduced by the parents, and had been a report by an expert stating that the child required residential placement in order to function, the school system might have appealed on that particular issue. The schools could contend that it had been a significant error for the hearing officer to allow into evidence a document that had not been disclosed before the hearing.

The schools might claim that, had they known about the recommendation in advance, they would have obtained evidence to show that the child's needs could be appropriately met in a special day school. If the schools were to have obtained such evidence subsequently and presented it with their appeal, the appellate body might be persuaded by their contention. In such a case, the appellate body might reverse the whole decision and its premises. In doing so, the appellate body is saying that the whole decision is so defective, by reason of the error committed in the hearing, that the decision cannot be allowed to stand.

Remand All or Part of the Lower Decision

If the errors committed by the lower authority interfere with the rights of the appealing party, the appellate body may remand all or part of the decision. If a decision is remanded, it means that the lower authority is ordered to conduct further proceedings in accordance with the appellate body's instructions.

The examples above could be used here again. In the example about counseling services for the child, the appellate body could remand, rather than modify, the lower authority's decision. In such a case, the appellate body would require that further evidence be presented (and heard) regarding the amount of counseling services required to help the child benefit from the program.

In the example about the expert testimony regarding residential placement, the appellate body could remand, rather than reverse, the decision below. In such a case it probably would direct that further evidence be presented and heard as to the least restrictive educational environment appropriate to meet the child's special needs.

When the appellate body remands a decision, it is acknowledging that an error has been committed in the proceedings conducted by the lower authority and that the error is significant. However, the appellate body has not been sufficiently persuaded that it ought to correct the error by ordering something different from what is set forth in the lower decision. The appellate body is indicating that it recognizes that the lower decision is in error on the particular appeal issue but it is not as clear on what would be the correct solution. It needs further information to make an intelligent determination.

The appellate body also is indicating, by ordering a remand, that it is reluctant to substitute its judgment on matters in which it does not have the necessary expertise. It feels that the issue could be resolved best if the lower authority could gather more information from additional witnesses and documents.

THE ENFORCEMENT OF DECISIONS

In some special education due process hearings, a decision is issued and becomes final because there is no appeal but a party fails to comply with the ruling. In such a case the party that wants the decision enforced may take further action. Such action is not an appeal of the decision because the party bringing the complaint is not dissatisfied with the outcome but with the other side's compliance.

Decisions are enforced differently depending on which party appears to be in noncompliance. If the parents are dissatisfied, they may fail to comply. They always retain the right to remove the child completely from the public schools and provide a private educational program of their own choice and at their own expense.

The school system cannot enforce a hearing officer's decision against the parents if they opt out by removing their child. In fact, it is difficult for the school system to get any legal leverage over the parents in terms of compliance. If the parents leave their child in the program but fail to follow through with their responsibilities under that plan, there is little the schools can do. They cannot refuse to provide the child with an education program, because that is guaranteed by law. However, the parents' credibility would be severely impaired if they later contended at a hearing that the school program was inappropriate to meet their child's needs.

Enforcement actions are largely brought by parents against the schools. It is the school system that has the legal responsibility to provide an appropriate program. The parents' legal responsibility is limited to assuring that their child attends some education program. Only if they totally refuse to allow their child to attend any program do they become susceptible to legal sanctions.

The regulations provide that:

> The State educational agency shall describe in its annual program plan the policies and procedures, including sanctions, which the State uses to insure that its policies and procedures are followed and that the requirements of the Act and the regulations in this part are met. (§ 121a.575)

The law does not specify any particular way a party may seek to enforce a decision. However, every jurisdiction has one or more standard ways of doing so in an administrative proceeding such as a special education due process hearing. The following are types of actions usually available to a party wishing to enforce a decision:

Administrative Compliance or Show Cause Hearing

The party contending that the other side is not complying with the hearing officer's decision notifies the superintendent of schools of specific points of noncompliance. If the matter is not resolved, the party may invoke the hearing process again for investigating the allegations of noncompliance. It is recommended that the same hearing officer who heard the case initially be assigned to the compliance hearing, which also is referred to as a show cause hearing. This is because the party alleged to be in noncompliance must show cause as to why it acted or did not act.

At the compliance or show cause hearing, the scope of inquiry should be limited to the following:

1. evidence relating to the issue of compliance or noncompliance
2. evidence relating to factors that may excuse performance

The hearing officer must refrain from rehearing the whole case. The only issues at this point are compliance with the decision and the merit of the reasons for noncompliance if it is found that the second party failed to comply.

The hearing officer who finds that a party has failed to comply, and there are no substantial mitigating factors to excuse performance, may refer the case to the legal office of the school system or the local district attorney for enforcement. If the schools are found not in compliance, the hearing officer may allow the parents to place the child in a comparable private program and order the system to reimburse them for as long as it remains in noncompliance.

Judicial Intervention

The United States Administrative Procedures Act provides that a party to an administrative proceeding may seek enforcement of a decision through the courts. That act states that the courts shall "compel agency action unlawfully withheld or unreasonably delayed." (5 U.S.C.A. 706). Similar provisions are contained in the administrative procedures acts of state and local jurisdictions and thus apply to special education due process hearings.

Administrative actions such as those at issue in special education proceedings depend for enforcement, either immediately or ultimately, upon sanctions imposed by courts. Courts have a number of mechanisms at their disposal for the compulsion of agency action. They may force administrative action through fines, awards of money damages to the injured party, injunctions, and mandatory orders.

Injunctions and mandatory orders are the steps most likely to be employed for enforcement of decisions in special education hearings. These mechanisms are orders to an agency or officer to take whatever action is directed. If the agency continues to fail to respond, it now is disobeying the court and therefore is in contempt of court. A person or party in contempt may have property seized, authority to administer subordinated to a court-appointed expert, or be imprisoned.

A party may invoke judicial intervention by proceeding privately to sue the other side for noncompliance or may bring the nonaction to the attention of the local district attorney's office and have it prosecute. If a party wishes to invoke judicial intervention to enforce a decision, it should consult with a local attorney to obtain advice on the rules for such proceedings and the most advisable steps to take.

Intervention by Chief State School Officer or the U.S.

If a party to a special education hearing believes the noncompliance is serious enough or widespread enough, it may wish to formally apprise the chief state school officer. This officer has the overall responsibility for monitoring the state's compliance with P.L. 94-142.

If that officer sees there is sufficient cause to believe a local or intermediate jurisdiction is not in compliance with the law, investigation of the matter may ensue. The investigation may lead to a hearing in which the jurisdiction will be required to defend what appears to be serious or widespread noncompliance with the law. The chief state school officer ultimately may decide to withhold state or federal payments as a sanction until the jurisdiction comes into compliance.

If the matter still is not resolved satisfactorily, it may be brought to the attention of the U.S. Secretary of Education. That official may follow essentially the same procedures, at the federal level, as discussed above on the state level. The secretary may move to withhold federal payments to a state that is in noncompliance with the law or that has a local jurisdiction in noncompliance.

TIMELINES IN DUE PROCESS PROCEEDINGS

In addition to proper procedures in special education due process hearings, it is important that an effective system maintain timelines for completion of the procedures. Without timelines, the process gets bogged down or derailed altogether when the parties fail to perform the required tasks within a reasonable period. This section discusses the timelines required by the law and suggests areas that may call for deadlines to be developed.

Initial Hearings and State Level Reviews

The regulations provide that:

(a) The public agency shall insure that not later than 45 days after the receipt of a request for a hearing:
1. A final decision is reached in the hearing; and
2. A copy of the decision is mailed to each of the parties.
(b) The State educational agency shall insure that not later than 30 days after the receipt of a request for a review:
1. A final decision is reached in the review; and
2. A copy of the decision is mailed to each of the parties.
(c) A hearing or reviewing officer may grant specific extensions of time beyond the periods set out in paragraphs (a) and (b) of this section at the request of either party.

(d) Each hearing and each review involving oral arguments must be conducted at a time and place which is reasonably convenient to the parents and child involved. (§ 121a.512)

Simply stated, this means that a hearing officer's decision must be mailed to the parties within 45 days after receipt of a request for a hearing. If the parties appeal the decision to a state agency, the reviewing official's decision must be mailed to the parties within 30 days after receipt of a request for a review.

Many school officials have complained that these timelines are very restrictive. However, other school officials state that with proper organization and preparation the timelines can be met. Regardless of these comments and opinions, the law is clear as to what is required. A hearing or reviewing officer may grant specific time extensions to help parties prepare for the hearing if either side so requests. However, such discretion should be exercised judiciously. Guidelines for the exercise of this discretion are discussed in Chapter 19.

This provision also requires the hearings be held at a time reasonably convenient to the parents and child. This does not mean that all hearings must be conducted at odd hours, because that would not be reasonable. However, it does mean that they may need to be scheduled in the evening or on weekends if parents genuinely cannot arrange to appear in regular business hours during the week.

The point is that the primary consideration is the convenience of the parents and child. The law does not say that a hearing should be scheduled at mutually convenient times. It is, of course, best to schedule it at a time convenient for all participants, but this is not always possible. When it is not, the convenience of parents and child take priority.

OTHER TIMELINES TO BE ESTABLISHED

The law provides only those two timelines for hearings and reviews. However, they themselves suggest the necessity for others to ensure that the overall hearing and review timelines can be met. Suggested additional timelines to help the public agency meet the 45/30 day deadlines follow in Exhibit 20-1.

Policies also should be adopted to establish timelines on the completion of procedures at each stage of the special education process. These policies should include deadlines for the completion of tasks and procedures for identification, education, program development, and placement, as well as the hearings and reviews.

Exhibit 20-1 Timeline for Special Education Due Process Tasks and Procedures

Tasks and Procedures	Number of Days	Timelines Required by Law
Child is identified as possibly in need of special education services. A referral is received and further procedures are deemed warranted.	3–5	
Parents are notified and perhaps a conference is scheduled.	2–7	
Parents consider whether or not to give consent for a multifaceted evaluation of the child (preplacement).	3–14	
Evaluation is scheduled and conducted. Child is determined to be in need of special education and related services.	20–30	
Meetings are initiated and conducted to develop, review, and revise the child's IEP and placement. Parents receive formal notice of evaluation recommendations and participate in process of program development and placement.	20–30	At least one such meeting, including the parents, must be held within 30 calendar days.
Parents consider whether or not to give consent for the initial placement of the child in a program providing special education and related services. If parents request an independent evaluation, the same amount of time should be afforded to them to obtain independent evaluation as was afforded to public schools to obtain their evaluation.	3–14	
If hearing is required to resolve any dispute arising out of the above process, the prehearing activities are completed and a hearing is held after receiving the request.	20–30	The total hearing process must be completed no later than 45 days after receipt of a request for a hearing.
Hearing officer issues decision and copies are mailed to the parties.	10–15	
Parties consider whether or not to request review by state agency official.	5–10	

Exhibit 20-1 continued

Tasks and Procedures	Number of Days	Timelines Required by Law
If a review is requested, the necessary procedures are completed after receiving the request for review.	15–20	The total review process must be completed no later than 30 days after receipt of a request for a review.
Reviewing official issues decision and copies are mailed to parties.	7–10	
Parties consider whether or not to appeal decision of reviewing official by filing civil action in proper court.	5–10	

Exhibit 20-1 provides a suggested timeline for the special education due process sequence that includes the tasks and procedures that must be completed and recommended deadlines for their completion.

Effective Presentation at the Hearing

The purpose of the special education due process hearing is to gather information impartially from the parties involved. Public Law 94-142 requires that the decision be based solely on the evidence presented at the hearing. Because of this requirement, it is critical that each participant approach the proceeding as though the hearing officer had absolutely no knowledge or understanding of the facts being presented. The participants must provide information to support each and every contention that they make.

Part V provides an overview of evidence, what it is, and how to use it effectively. Understanding the concept of evidence will help the participants present their information and assist the hearing officer in evaluating it so that the best interests of the student will be served.

Chapter 21

Evidence and Burden of Proof

This chapter provides an overview of evidence in the context of the special education due process hearing. It covers the basic concepts of what evidence is about and how it is used. Different types of evidence are explained as well as admissibility.

EVIDENCE DEFINED

Evidence is simply any relevant information submitted to a person who must decide on the truth of a matter in a contested issue.

THE USE OF EVIDENCE IN A HEARING

The basic purpose of the special education due process hearing is to gather information to determine the appropriateness of the public school agency's individualized education program (IEP) for a handicapped child. When the hearing process is invoked, it is because of a dispute between the parents and the agency over critical facts in the IEP.

Evidence submitted by participants is the material from which inferences are drawn as the basis for proof of facts in dispute. A hearing officer may draw inferences from the words or gestures or inflections or demeanor of a particular witness and may infer an ultimate fact from undisputed basic facts or from an entire record of conflicting evidence.

For example, a teacher might testify to the child's lack of friends in the classroom, inability to participate in group activities, failure to interact with the other pupils, etc. The teacher's testimony is evidence. It is material from which inferences may be drawn as the basis for proof of facts in dispute. In this example, the fact of whether or not the child is seriously emotionally disturbed is in dispute. The hearing officer may use the teacher's testimonial evidence to infer the basic fact that the child has difficulty building or maintaining satisfactory interpersonal relationships with peers. The hearing officer may then go on to infer the ultimate fact that the child suffers from serious emotional disturbance.

DIFFERENT FORMS OF EVIDENCE

Evidence may be provided to the hearing officer in four basic forms:

1. Real Evidence: Tangible objects presented to the hearing officer for inspection. This type of evidence speaks for itself. It usually is the most trustworthy type. Real evidence might include actual examples of a student's schoolwork, the chair the child threw at another, the eyeglasses the pupil wears, etc.
2. Documentary Evidence: This is similar to real evidence but consists of a written rather than a tangible object. The written contents are able to speak for themselves. Documentary evidence might include an evaluation report, a letter to a parent, school records, etc.
3. Testimonial Evidence: This type involves oral statements made at the hearing by a witness. It may be either factual or opinion testimony. Examples of testimonial evidence might be a parent's observations of the child at home, a school administrator's statements about the benefits the school offers, the professional opinion of a physical therapist about a program to strengthen the child's leg muscles.
4. Judicial or Official Notice: Judicial notice is a type of evidence whereby the hearing officer accepts certain indisputable facts as true without the necessity for formal proof. Judicial notice actually is a substitute for evidence. It involves facts that are matters of common knowledge or easily verified. For example, a hearing officer might take judicial notice of the fact that the Martha Saunders School is a school for the physically disabled, if that is generally known in the community. Another example: the placement of a pupil in a residential setting would mean that the facility would be responsible for providing for the child's basic life needs as well as educational requirements. Other examples of judicial notice might be information already in the official record of the case, May 5 is a Monday, there are nine months in the school year, etc.

ADMISSIBLE AND NONADMISSIBLE EVIDENCE

The term "admissible" refers to whether or not a particular piece of information may be used as evidence by the hearing officer in reaching a decision. A hearing officer has a great deal of discretion in determining what evidence will be admitted. Generally, most evidence will be allowed into the record. However, the hearing officer need not admit everything and should be careful not to accept certain evidence presented by the parties.

For example, the hearing officer should admit only evidence that bears a significant relationship to the matters in dispute. This relationship usually is stated in terms of "relevancy" and "competency." A rule of thumb to determine whether evidence should be submitted might be stated in one sentence: Relevant evidence is admissible, if competent.

Relevant Evidence

Relevant evidence relates to one or more of the substantive issues in the proceeding. An item of evidence is relevant if it tends to make the essential issue more probably true or untrue than would be the case without the evidence.

Generally, to be considered relevant, there must be a significant relationship between the evidence and what is at issue in the hearing. For example, testimony by the parents about their difficulty in caring for their physically handicapped child in the home may be irrelevant to the issue of the pupil's academic program. For another example, testimony by the vice principal that a hearing impaired student had adjusted socially in the regular classroom may be irrelevant to the number of hours per week of speech therapy that the pupil needs.

Competent Evidence

Competent evidence is what is legally qualified to be presented and is reliable.

For example, testimony by an expert witness such as a psychologist that the handicapped pupil would be appropriately placed in a program for health impaired students because it could better meet the child's medical needs may be incompetent. This is because the witness probably was qualified as an expert in psychology rather than medicine.

The hearing officer would be likely to be interested in the psychologist's testimony only about the area in which the individual has had the necessary professional training and experience to provide an expert opinion. Testimony outside the psychologist's area of expertise probably is incompetent because that is not a field in which the individual qualifies as an authority.

OTHER FACTORS IN ADMITTING EVIDENCE

The hearing officer has the discretion to decide whether certain factors or principles outweigh the need to admit otherwise proper evidence. Such limitations might be concerned with:

- undue physical and mental inconvenience of bringing evidence into the hearing room

- indecency or impropriety, especially the casting of a witness in undue bad light

- undue and unfair prejudice to the parties

- collateral issues and minor details

- unduly cumulative and repetitious evidence

ASSESSING WEIGHT AND CREDIBILITY

Each witness and each document submitted into evidence is different. One witness might present testimony that shows a great depth of understanding of the student who is the subject of the hearing. Another witness might present testimony based on a review of the pupil's records. One document might be a comprehensive evaluation of the student's abilities, another might focus on the child's academic abilities only.

At the conclusion of the hearing, the hearing officer will have to weigh all of the evidence submitted. Certain witnesses will seem more credible than others, certain documents weightier than others. Ultimately, the hearing officer's perception of the different pieces of evidence will total up to a decision for one party or the other.

Almost certainly, some of the evidence presented by the two parties will be contradictory. The hearing officer must decide how much weight, if any, each piece merits. In making these decisions, various factors must be considered. They relate generally to the witness' qualifications to give the type of evidence offered. Such qualifications, and past experiences working with similar types of children, is relevant, as is the nature and extent of involvement with the pupil who is the subject of the hearing.

Another general consideration in assessing evidence is the distinction between "lay" and "expert" witnesses. Lay witnesses usually testify about matters within their own observation, knowledge, or recollection. For example, the parents, based on observation and knowledge of their handicapped child, may testify as to the developmental history, how the pupil relates to others, the family, what the student does when not in school, and what types of activities the child is involved in at home and in the community. In addition, based on their involvement with the school, they may testify as to their child's experience there and the meetings and discussions they have been involved in with the personnel.

Expert witnesses, because of their special knowledge and competence in a particular area, in addition to testifying about their own observations, knowledge, and recollections, may present their opinions. An example of an expert witness would be a psychologist who, based on an evaluation and assessment and various tests administered to the child, could testify as to the handicapping condition, as well as present an opinion as to what type of activities or programs would meet the pupil's needs.

The fact that a witness has been allowed to testify as an expert does not automatically mean that such testimony should be given greater weight in the decision-making process than that of a lay witness. Rather, the expert's testimony should be given only the weight that the hearing officer believes it merits, after considering the witness' qualifications, past experience, and involvement with the present parties. For example, if the lay witness has had more extensive involvement with the handicapped child than the expert has, it is entirely legitimate for the former's testimony to be given greater weight than the latter's.

It is important that each participant understand some specific factors the hearing officer will consider in weighing the evidence. The participants will be able to present testimony or documents more effectively if they are aware of these points. Exhibit 21-1 lists factors commonly considered when assessing the weight and credibility of a witness or writer of a document.

THE BURDEN OF PROOF

In a special education due process hearing or any legal proceeding, one party or the other has the burden of presenting evidence on the issues in the case as discussed in earlier chapters. But which party is obligated to present the evidence? How much evidence must be presented? What are the consequences of the party's meeting or not meeting the burden of proof?

"Burden of proof" is a legal phrase used loosely to refer to two separate concepts: (1) The burden of persuading the hearing officer as to which party is correct and (2) the burden of producing evidence.

The Persuasion Burden

The party must establish a belief in the mind of the hearing officer that its version of the facts is the correct one to adopt. The burden of proof in

Exhibit 21-1 Checklist for Assessing Witnesses and Documents

	• What is the individual's interest in this case?
	• How objective does that person's presentation of information seem to be in light of that interest?
	• Did the witness have a particular expertise that was used to support an expert opinion in that area?
	• How well did the person seem to know the child?
	• What degree of first-hand knowledge of the child did the individual have?
	• Was the person familiar with the pupil's history, other records, or the work of other persons with this child?
	• Did the witness show an understanding of the child beyond the handicapping characteristics?
	• Was the reasoning behind the witness' conclusions or recommendations articulated clearly?
	• How recent is the information upon which these conclusions or recommendations were based?
	• Did the witness seem candid and able to answer specific questions with specific answers?
	• Was the writer of a document submitted in evidence present at the hearing to explain its conclusions and recommendations and answer further questions?
	• Did the writer seem easily annoyed or defensive when questioned about the conclusions and recommendations?
	• Did the writer seem to be knowledgeable about specific aspects of the IEP proposed by the school or the parents?
	• Did this individual seem to be knowledgeable about specific features of the placement proposed by the school or the parents?
	• Did the witness seem to have a sound grasp of the assessments used to evaluate the student?
	• Did the writer seem able to analyze the information gleaned from the assessments and translate it into what it means in terms of the child's specific educational needs?
	• Were the conclusions and recommendations corroborated by other evidence at the hearing?
	• Did the witness seem less clear or less sure of recommendations and conclusions when being cross-examined?

this sense basically means producing the degree of evidence required to win the case. This concept is called the persuasion burden. It is an obligation that is fixed. One of the parties has the original and continuing duty to persuade the hearing officer that its position is more correct than the other.

If both parties produce equally weighty evidence and the scales of evidence are perfectly balanced, then the side with the persuasion burden loses because it had the obligation to establish by evidence that its position was more well-founded than the other. If that party can only prove that it is a toss-up between its position and that of the other side, the first party must lose.

The Production Burden

The production burden is different from the persuasion burden. The persuasion burden is concerned with the weight or force of the evidence to persuade the hearing officer. The production burden is concerned with who must produce what evidence and when.

The production burden is not fixed on either party; rather, it shifts during the course of the hearing. The production burden is first allocated to the party that also has the persuasion burden. That side must produce evidence to persuade the hearing officer that its version of the facts is the correct version to adopt. It must produce sufficient evidence from which a reasonable person could infer that these are the facts to accept.

If the party does not produce sufficient evidence in that regard, it will lose before the other side even begins. If it does produce sufficient evidence, this burden shifts to the other party. The latter then has the burden to produce sufficient evidence in rebuttal and in support of its own position. If the second party does not meet its production burden, it, too, would be in danger of losing automatically. The party with the production burden must produce evidence when it is at bat or risk losing automatically.

How the Two Concepts Work in Practice

The following example illustrates the two concepts of burden of proof discussed.

The parents of a learning disabled boy are hoping to persuade the hearing officer that the school system's proposed placement is not appropriate. They want the hearing officer to order the system to place the child in a private residential school.

It must be determined at the outset by the hearing officer that the parents have the persuasion burden on the central issue of appropriateness. This burden of proof is fixed with the parents.

At the conclusion of the hearing, the hearing officer must have been persuaded that the parents' position is more well-founded than that of the school system. The weight and force of the evidence must be in favor of the parents' position. The parents must "win" in the mind of the hearing officer. If they fail to meet their persuasion burden, the school system's proposed placement will stand as being appropriate.

Since the parents have the persuasion burden, they also initially have the production burden—producing sufficient evidence from which a reasonable hearing officer could infer that the school system's proposed placement is not appropriate.

The parents present their case through documents and witnesses. It is assumed in this instance that they produce rather weighty evidence. While they continue to bear the persuasion burden, the production burden now has shifted to the school system. If the school does not counter the parents' evidence with some of its own, at least to the point of making it equally convincing, the system will lose. It must produce enough evidence to bring the scales back to a position of parity. If it fails to do so, it fails to meet its burden of producing evidence and will lose automatically.

Now, it is assumed that the parents produce no actual evidence other than a simple expression of their feelings about the proposed placement. From that presentation, a reasonable hearing officer probably cannot infer that the proposed placement is not appropriate. The parents have not met their production burden and consequently they lose automatically. Even if they produced an expert who could not testify clearly to the appropriateness of the placement, they probably have failed to meet their production burden.

If both sides produce evidence when they are required to do so, both have met the production burden. Then the hearing officer will weigh the evidence. For the parents to win, that weight must come down on their side. They have the persuasion burden. If in the hearing officer's mind both sides have produced equally weighty evidence, or the weight comes down on the side of the school system, it will win. Any other assessment of the evidence will result in the ultimate finding that the proposed placement is appropriate.

Whoever has the production burden must produce or automatically lose. If both sides bore the production burden when they had it, the proceeding will run its full course. The side that ultimately will prevail is then decided by the persuasion burden. If the party that has the persuasion burden meets it, that side wins; if it does not meet that burden of proof, it loses.

How is it determined which side will have the persuasion burden in a special education due process hearing? No federal statutes relevant to the topic (i.e., P.L. 94-142; P.L. 93-380, the Educational Amendments of 1974;

P.L. 93-112, the Rehabilitation Act of 1973) specifically address themselves to the issue of who will bear the persuasion burden in all hearings brought under § 121a.506 and § 121a.500.

There is, however, one instance in which the federal government has made it clear on whom the persuasion burden falls. Section 84.34 of the regulations implementing § 504 of the Rehabilitation Act of 1973 states:

> A recipient [the school system] shall place a handicapped person in the regular educational environment operated by the recipient unless it is demonstrated by the recipient that the education of the person in the regular environment with the use of supplementary aids and services cannot be achieved satisfactorily.

The quoted sentence indicates that when the school proposes to place a child out of the mainstream, the burden is on it to prove that removal is warranted. This principle probably is applicable in the majority of special education hearings.

While the persuasion burden, by regulation, is on the school in the circumstance described above, there is no general explicit rule on this point. However, on November 11, 1974, the Aid to States Branch of the then Bureau for Education of the Handicapped offered guidelines to states that were attempting to implement P.L. 93-380. Although they do not have the weight of law, these guidelines assert:

> The burden of proof as to the appropriateness of any proposed placement, as to why more normalized placements could not adequately and appropriately serve the child's educational needs, and as to the adequacy and appropriateness of any test or evaluation procedure, will be upon the local agency.

Many states have voluntarily enacted legislation putting the burden of persuasion on the school in hearings, as have all courts that have considered the matter. Aside from considerations of statutory authority and legal precedent, practical considerations dictate that the burden of proof be borne by the party that has at its disposal greater resources and easier access to verification of the issues in question. In the case of hearings on the identification, evaluation, or placement of handicapped children or the provision of a free appropriate public education, the party with the greater resources and easier access to the pertinent data is certainly the school system.

Chapter 22

Presenting Evidence

The previous chapter discussed the role, types, and limitations of evidence in the special education due process hearing. This chapter focuses on how to present evidence at the hearing and the various considerations involved in so doing.

The primary function of participants in such a hearing is to provide relevant evidence to assist the hearing officer in deciding the case. The attorney or advocate for each party presents the evidence for one side or the other. It is important that both advocates and participants understand how evidence is presented so they all can perform their functions more effectively. This chapter assumes that the reader has the function of an advocate.

PLANNING FOR THE HEARING

The key to successful planning for a special education due process hearing is to find the theme of the advocate's case. What is the central, unifying point? It should be possible to state the theme in only a few words. Everything the advocate does at the hearing should relate back to the case theme or central point.

Special education hearings frequently involve a number of emotionally charged issues and a history of conflicts. However, the hearing officer has not been involved in the case throughout its existence and probably is not really interested in old complaints and tangential problems. The amount of information presented at hearings usually is voluminous. The hearing officer will need a framework to help organize the material in a meaningful way.

If the advocate for one of the parties offers a central point or theme underlying all of the evidence, it is likely that such a presentation will be more persuasive to the hearing officer. A presentation that attempts to place every issue, every piece of information, every encounter, etc., into the record is likely to overwhelm, confuse, or incorrectly focus the hearing officer.

As noted, the hearing officer does not know the case before the session. By its conclusion, the effective advocate should have helped the presiding officer to understand the case the same way as the advocate understands it. If the central theme is that this child can receive an appropriate special program to meet the educational needs only in a residential setting, then all the evidence presented by that party should focus on or come back to that point.

In addition to conceptualizing the case, the effective advocate should prepare a hearing notebook. It should contain everything that will be necessary during the hearing. It should be loose-leaf so information can be inserted. If documents will be used in questioning witnesses, the materials should be inserted next to a page of questions and notes for particular individuals who will testify.

The order of the witnesses also should be planned. There may not be any special way of presenting them but one sequence should be decided upon in advance. They could be presented in chronological order of their involvement or one who is expected to have a major impact could be heard first. Whatever is decided, it is important to give the hearing officer and other participants the impression that the advocate knows the case thoroughly and is presenting it in a definite and controlled manner.

PREPARING WITNESSES FOR THE HEARING

The advocate should review, discuss, and rehearse the testimony of everyone expected to be called as witnesses. Most persons do not have much experience being witnesses and are somewhat uncomfortable in the role. It is the advocate's responsibility to prepare them as best as possible so that the most effective presentation can be derived from their testimony. The advocate should brief the parents or professionals regarding the following points and procedures:

Preparation for a Special Education Hearing

1. Careful preparation is the key to effective testimony. As a general rule, whenever a parent or professional suspects a case may involve a hearing, the individual should record findings in detail, with complete descriptions of each manifestation and of all conversations with the parents, child, and professionals.

2. The parents and professionals should review their notes and records carefully before testifying. The parents should be prepared to present the child's developmental and social history. The professionals often will be asked to describe their involvement with the case chronologically. They should be prepared to testify as to when their association with the child began and what specifically occurred thereafter.

3. Medical and academic records frequently are presented as documentary evidence. The parents and professionals should expect careful examination and cross-examination on information in the records.

4. Parents and professionals should meet with the attorney or advocate before the hearing to review the case, evaluate the need for certain witnesses or documents, discuss the types of questions that will be asked, and "role-play" questions and answers for both direct and cross-examination.

5. Many parents and professionals are uncertain as to whether they are allowed to talk with the attorney or advocate for the other side before the hearing. There is no prohibition against such conversations; all are free to act as they choose. The parents or professionals should be aware, however, that the attorney for the other side will cross-examine them on any inconsistencies between what they say informally and what they testify at the hearing.

6. The professionals usually can arrange to be placed on stand by or on call so they can remain at their work until telephoned, thus avoiding long delays at the hearing while waiting to testify.

Direct Examination

1. The parents and professionals may be asked to present evidence establishing the nature, extent, and seriousness of the child's disability as well as their knowledge of its cause and the educational needs arising from it.

2. Parents and professionals should state their knowledge of the case objectively and avoid becoming emotionally involved while testifying.

3. Witnesses are allowed to use the educational and medical records, or any other notes, to refresh their memory while testifying. Because the opposing attorney or advocate has the right during cross-examination to see such reports and notes and ask questions based on them, witnesses should be warned against unsupported opinions, inaccurate information, or inconsistencies between their testimony and the records or notes.

4. The witnesses, in order to testify accurately and authoritatively about the case, should know these basic principles of appearances on the stand:

a. They should answer only the questions asked, and should not volunteer information.

b. They should ask to have questions they do not understand repeated. They never should guess at what a question means.

c. They should say so if they do not know the answer to a question. They never should guess an answer. If not certain of an answer, they should say so.

d. They never should get angry or defensive with the opposing attorney or advocate. They must be calm, cool, objective, honest, and concerned about the handicapped child.

e. They should request the hearing officer to allow them to explain a response properly or fully if asked to give a yes or no answer and feel that this would be misleading without an explanation. They also can indicate to their attorney or advocate that they want to explain the answer.

f. They should be exact in their testimony. For example, they should say "1 p.m." instead of "around noon," or "three occasions" instead of "numerous occasions."

g. They should take time in answering questions and think before they reply. They should not let themselves be hurried by the opposing attorney or advocate.

h. They should use lay terms when testifying and be careful to explain all terms so that the hearing officer and attorneys can understand the testimony.

5. Parents and professionals should review such terms as the following and consider how they would explain them while testifying:

fluency of speech	self-concept
childhood adjustment reaction	hearing loss
emotionally disturbed	isolate
neurosis	multidisciplinary evaluation
socially maladjusted	primary language
retarded	culture-free test
visual acuity	support services
mildly retarded	regression
psychiatric social worker	withdrawn behavior
least restrictive	autistic-like manifestations
milieu therapy	social history
environment	developmentally disabled
learning disability	minimal brain dysfunction
hyperactive	

Cross-Examination

1. Cross-examination usually is the most difficult part of testifying for parents and professionals. The key to an effective presentation during cross-examination is adequate preparation. The attorney/advocate for each side should be able to assist the participants in preparing for cross-examination by pointing out questions likely to be asked and by role-playing the situation.

2. Witnesses should remain calm on cross-examination and not become defensive, angry, or condescending. This will diminish credibility with the hearing officer and will detract from the ability to respond competently to the questions asked.

3. Professionals often are cross-examined on the degree of certainty with which they are able to diagnose or ascertain special needs. Professionals may not be in a position to be 100 percent certain of the diagnosis or recommendation but can articulate reasons why, in their best professional judgment, they believe the child requires special education.

4. The opposing attorney may question the professionals about each specific manifestation separately, trying to suggest that each one, by itself, is not so unusual. The professionals should make it clear that it may be the existence of numerous manifestations, often in different combinations, that indicates special education needs.

5. The opposing attorney often attacks the professionals' expertise by closely questioning them on their past involvement and experience with these types of cases, trying to establish that they are not specifically experienced in the particular area at issue. The attorney's strategy is designed principally to upset the witnesses. Professionals should bear in mind that in the vast majority of cases, their overall background and experience will be sufficient to qualify them as expert witnesses in the eyes of the hearing officer.

6. The opposing attorney may employ the cross-examination strategy of attempting to upset the parents when they are testifying. The objective is to confuse them or make them seem irrational. Another similar ploy is to ask the parents a series of questions to make them seem unreasonable in their requests. For example, "Isn't it true, Mrs. Smith, that you want the public schools to provide Johnny with speech therapy, academic instruction, psychiatric therapy, recreation, well balanced meals, and a place to live, too?"

7. Opposing attorneys on cross-examination of parents commonly attempt to discredit their testimony as hopelessly biased. The hearing

officer expects parents to be emotionally involved with their child but that does not mean that they should be barred from providing valuable information about the student. It does mean that the parents as witnesses should strive to present their information in an objective manner. They should refrain from editorializing on the facts or attempting to color them in a certain way. Parents and professionals will be effective witnesses on cross-examination if they simply are candid and straightforward.

THE OPENING STATEMENT AT THE HEARING

In most hearings, each party will make an opening statement before evidence is actually presented (as discussed in Part IV). This statement is a very important part of the proceeding. Its purpose is to acquaint the hearing officer with each side's view of the case. The opening statement is not evidence. It is the opportunity for the advocates to present what they regard as the theme of the case and tell the hearing officer what evidence will be forthcoming to support that concept. It is like giving a theater audience a playbill or program to acquaint them with what soon will be forthcoming before them. The opening statement is the time each side tries to hammer home its theme.

When the presentation of evidence begins, the advocate must allow that material to speak for itself, for better or for worse. But in the opening statement the advocate has the opportunity to tell the hearing officer what to be looking for in the documents to be submitted or to listen for in the testimony of the witnesses.

When preparing for the opening statement, the advocate should consider the following points:

1. The opening statement should be well prepared and rehearsed in advance.
2. The opening statement should familiarize the hearing officer with the essential facts and the advocate's theme of the case. The advocate therefore must know the case in every detail, have a total command of it, and be able to convey just that impression.
3. The opening statement should be delivered without notes. The advocate should have it so well prepared that it is not necessary to read a written statement. The advocate must convey an impression of total control of the case, especially by making confident and strong eye contact with the hearing officer and others in the room.
4. The opening statement should be clear and short. The advocate does not want to allow the attention of the hearing officer and others to

stray at this point. The opening statement should give everyone the first and lasting impression of what this case is all about. It should be delivered in a direct style, using plain English. It is not the point to argue an erudite interpretation of legal terminology or attempt to impress anyone with a command of educational jargon. Clarity communicates ideas better and gives the impression that the advocate has a real grasp of the case.

5. The opening statement should have a beginning, middle, and end. This again will give the impression that the advocate understands the case and has it all under control. The advocate demonstrates with the opening statement that it actually is possible to make some sense out of all the chaotic materials that will be presented.

6. The opening statement should not include anything that the advocate cannot prove. The advocate is trying to sell a point of view to the hearing officer and in order to sell anyone something, the seller must convey a sense of trustworthiness. If the advocate exaggerates or embellishes upon the case, and the deficiency is revealed when evidence is presented, the hearing officer's view of that side can only be diminished.

7. The opening statement also should admit any problems with the case. Again, it will enhance the hearing officer's view of the advocate and that side's case if the individual is straightforward about obvious defects or problems. For example, if the school system's advocate knows that in past years the program offered to the child was a miserable failure, this should be acknowledged at the outset. The advocate then should go on to state why the program being proposed now is appropriate.

8. The opening statement should inform the hearing officer and other participants about the basic players in the case. It should answer in a brief way who the persons in the room are and why they are there. Such basic facts as the age, sex, current placement of the child, etc., are helpful in orienting everyone and therefore making them more receptive to perceiving the evidence as the advocate wants them to.

9. The opening statement should not give away the whole case before it starts. Its purpose is to familiarize the hearing officer with the facts and the advocate's theme. If possible, the advocate should avoid undermining the impact that a particular witness or document is expected to have when that evidence is presented.

PRESENTING THE EVIDENCE

After opening statements have been completed, each party in turn presents its evidence and witnesses. Documents are introduced through the witnesses. They first present their testimony on direct examination, then are asked questions by the other party during cross-examination. When one party has finished presenting all of its witnesses for direct and cross-examination, the other side has its turn to do the same.

DIRECT EXAMINATION

Direct examination is the most common method of affirmatively presenting a case. The advocate introduces a witness, then asks certain questions to elicit the necessary information. Direct examination is more efficient then simply allowing the witness to give a narrative.

The concept of direct examination is not difficult to understand. Most people use a form of direct examination in their everyday conversations. Without some direct questioning, an inquiry about what a teacher did yesterday could take hours to relate. The teacher could dwell on minute detail from arising until going to sleep—or the conversation could end immediately with an answer such as "nothing." Obviously, the interested party must engage in direct examination through the particular questions to obtain answers about the teacher's day.

When presented at a special education due process hearing, the witness first should be asked questions about name, title, and, where necessary, credentials and qualifications to speak as an expert.

The advocate then should direct questions to help the witness explain the relationship to this case or student. For example:

> As the second grade teacher at Fillmore Elementary School, did you know Walter?

> As a therapist at the Woodlawn Mental Health Center did you have occasion to provide services to Walter?

With these introductory questions, the advocate helps the hearing officer and other participants become acquainted with the witnesses and their relationship to the student. This process is referred to as "laying a foundation" for the testimony the advocate is about to elicit.

Having laid such a foundation, the advocate then asks about the information the witness has to offer about this child. There may be as many or as few questions as the advocate deems appropriate. The advocate may ask about any subject as long as the information is likely to be relevant to the hearing issues. Of course, the advocate can ask only questions that the witness is competent to testify about. For example, an art teacher probably is not competent to testify to the child's academic performance levels in reading and mathematics.

On direct examination, the advocate usually is limited to questions calling for specific responses, such as Who? Where? When? How? etc. The following are examples of questions an advocate may ask on direct examination:

At what grade level is Walter performing in reading?

What have you observed during the last month regarding Walter's behavior?

How does Walter relate to the other children in his classroom?

With what types of students would Walter be placed under the proposed program?

Can you describe the schedule that Walter would have if he were to be placed at Fillmore?

The witness may be asked any question the advocate feels will elicit testimony in support of that side's case. However, leading questions should be avoided. A question is leading when it suggests to the witness the answer that the advocate expects and wants or calls for a predetermined "yes" or "no" answer. For example, "The teachers at your school think Johnny should be mainstreamed, isn't that true?" The question should be asked, "Do the teachers at your school have an opinion about mainstreaming Johnny? If so, what have they expressed to you in that regard?"

Hearing officers may allow leading questions on cross-examination and in noncrucial areas, such as:

- preliminary or background questioning (setting the stage)

- jogging a witness' memory

- dealing with a timid or confused witness or a child of tender years

- trying to cope with a witness who is hostile and uncooperative

The main point to remember in conducting an effective direct examination is to convey the impression that the advocate is in control. The advocate can accomplish this objective by being thoroughly prepared and having internalized that side's theme of the case. This will enable the advocate to develop a pace or rhythm and to respond adroitly during the hearing.

CROSS-EXAMINATION

After direct examination, the advocate for the other side has an opportunity to ask the witness questions. This is called cross-examination. Typically, the opposing party uses cross-examination to confront the witness with prior inconsistent statements, to cast doubt on the witness' ability to make observations and remember them accurately, to show the witness' bias or lack of qualifications, to question the truth of the witness' testimony, or to further develop the information presented by that person.

Cross-examination is the most reliable and effective way of testing the credibility and accuracy of witnesses and their testimony. The right to cross-examine in any proceeding therefore is regarded as an essential element of due process.

Just as with direct examination, most persons use a form of cross-examination in their everyday conversations. For example, if a teacher says a particular student is "awful," a skeptical coworker might "cross-examine" the instructor to obtain a fuller and more accurate disclosure of the facts behind the statement. The coworker might ask if the teacher actually knows the student or just heard about the pupil from others. If the teacher knows the student, the coworker might further cross-examine to determine how many others of this nature the instructor generally works with each year.

Does the teacher usually like or dislike this sort of student? Is the teacher disappointed in the student as a whole or really just the behavior, grooming, parents, academic performance, personality traits, or other specific features?

The cross-examination on the teacher's simple one-word statement could go on for a long time until the coworker had a better understanding of the basis of the viewpoint. When that understanding is obtained, the coworker can better make an independent decision about such a student.

The advocate might use cross-examination to make the witness appear less credible to the hearing officer. If the advocate feels that the witness has made an important impression during direct examination, it may be worthwhile to bring out points that the individual was reluctant to mention. Perhaps the advocate wishes to undermine the witness by revealing flaws in the testimony, etc.

For example, a witness testifies on direct examination that the student will require a speech component as part of the education program. On cross-examination, the advocate might ask if the witness is aware that the proposed placement does not have a speech laboratory or the services of a speech pathologist. The advocate probably knows that this witness is not aware of those facts so if the individual cannot answer the question or responds with a "no," this tactic probably has succeeded in raising doubts in the hearing officer's mind about this person.

The witness may have appeared highly knowledgeable and credible on direct examination but on cross-examination may seem unaware of critical elements involving the capacity of the proposed placement to carry out an important program component and may appear uninformed and somewhat foolish. On direct examination, the witness may have seemed to be a proponent of the proposed program but on cross-examination appear inadequately informed about the very program this person supposedly endorsed as being appropriate for the child. The witness' credibility is sharply impaired.

For another example, a witness on direct examination expressed the opinion that the student is seriously emotionally disturbed. On cross-examination, the advocate might ask how long the witness evaluated the pupil. The witness may not actually have observed the child in person but rather reviewed only the reports. Even if the witness had watched the student on several occasions, the circumstances may not have been conducive to obtaining an accurate reading. Qualifications as a school psychologist might not really qualify the witness to be making such a diagnosis.

On cross-examination, any type of question that would be proper on direct can be used, together with certain types that would not be, but some types of questions are not permitted:

- Assuming facts not in evidence. Example: "Do you still place students at only cheap facilities?"

- Compound: A question that requires a single answer to more than one question. Example: "Did you place her and the Saunders child?"

- Argumentative: A leading question that also reflects the examiner's interpretation of the facts. Example: "It was all your fault, wasn't it?"

- Conclusionary: A question calls for an opinion or conclusion that the witness is not qualified or permitted to make. Example: "Did your principal know and understand this also?" (opinion as to principal's understanding)

- Cumulative: A question that already has been asked and answered; however, more repetition is allowed than on direct.

Using Cross-Examination as a Strategy

If the advocate is simply trying to elicit from the witness more information than was brought out on direct examination, any question can be asked.

The questions can be of an open-ended nature such as those on direct examination. However, if the advocate is trying to use cross-examination as a strategy to undermine the opposition and reveal its weaknesses, the questioner should keep in mind several following points.

Brevity and Plain Words

The questions should be brief and phrased in plain words. On cross-examination, the question is as important as the answer. The advocate will want the hearing officer to remember the question clearly when considering the answer in the context of the decision-making role. The hearing officer needs to see the point the advocate is trying to make by asking the question. As always, clear and distinct questioning is the most effective because it is easily understood and remembered.

Leading, Not Open-Ended, Questions

The questions should be leading in nature rather than open ended. On cross-examination, the advocate does not want to give the witness the opportunity to expound again upon a point already made on direct examination. This can only hurt the advocate's case because it will emphasize the witness' testimony in the mind of the hearing officer. The questions on cross-examination should almost put words in the mouth of the witness. They should be structured so as to keep the witness penned in and limited to a "yes" or "no" answer.

For example, an open-ended question on cross-examination might be: "Mr. Administrator, do you believe that Urban Public School For the Retarded can carry out this program you have proposed for Cathy?"

A more effective approach might be:

"Mr. School Administrator, isn't it true that the Urban Public School For the Retarded already is woefully overcrowded?" or, "Mr. Administrator, isn't it true that every class at the Urban Public School For the Retarded is already up to the maximum allowable teacher-to-student ratio?"

Advance Knowledge of Answers

The advocate should know in advance the answers to the questions on cross-examination. An advocate who is using cross-examination as strategy is more interested in making a point with the hearing officer than truly trying to learn information. For that reason, questions on cross-examination are largely loaded in a sense. The advocate is going somewhere with the line of questioning, trying to make a point about the witness or about what the person stated on direct examination. To do this effectively, the advocate must know where the questioning will lead. If not, the loaded questions may blow up in the advocate's face.

For example, the questions above are asked with the intent of undermining the witness' credibility. They should be asked only if the advocate already knows the answer. If the advocate did not, the witness might well give an answer precisely the opposite to what was desired. Mr. School Administrator could respond by saying, "Why, no! The classes at the Urban Public School For the Retarded have unusually low enrollments that will allow our staff to give even more individual attention to Cathy than we had originally hoped." Such a response makes the advocate, rather than the witness, appear uninformed and foolish.

Abjuring Arguments with Witnesses

The advocate should not argue with the witness during cross-examination. Sometimes the witness will make a statement that is inconsistent with an earlier response or with other evidence already in the record. The advocate might raise this point later in a closing statement or when questioning another witness. But the advocate should not argue with the witness as to why a statement is wrong, inconsistent, etc.

Such argumentative questions only induce the hearing officer to sympathize with the witness. They only give the witness an opportunity to explain away the inconsistency. The advocate should save the point for later. Arguing with a witness only serves to distract everyone's attention from the main point the advocate is seeking to get across.

Staying within Bounds

The questions on cross-examination should stay within the bounds of matters that were brought out on direct examination. Any type of question may be used so long as the content or subject of the question has already been introduced by the witness during his or her direct testimony. The advocate can try to get the witness to say anything that will be helpful but generally cross-examination questioning is limited to topics discussed during direct examination.

For example, if a witness testified about the degree of the student's hearing loss, it would not be appropriate to ask about the child's academic performance unless the individual had said something about academic performance. If questions are not limited to matters brought out on direct examination and the inferences naturally drawn from them, it is likely to cause confusion in the mind of the hearing officer.

The main point for the advocate to remember in conducting an effective cross-examination is to know why certain questions are asked and what information they seek to elicit. If the advocate simply wants to obtain information for personal edification, then questions may be asked. An advocate who intends to use cross-examination as a strategy to undermine the opposing side's evidence should attempt to confine the witness to very narrow answers that fit into the point being made. The advocate never should ask a question if the answer is not known in advance.

After cross-examination, the party who originally called the witness may want to ask a few more questions to help clarify or restore the credibility of evidence damaged by cross-examination. This is known as a redirect examination and is limited to the matters discussed during cross-examination. If reasonable, a witness may be recalled later.

ADMISSION OF EVIDENCE

In a court of law the judge decides what evidence will be admitted and what will not, following the rules of evidence. These rules are a set of laws and principles that determine whether or not a particular item or piece of information can be considered. They are extensive and complex.

However, in administrative hearings such as in special education due process cases, the hearing officer need not strictly observe the rules of evidence observed by courts. The rules on the introduction of evidence are much more relaxed as compared to court proceedings so hearing officers routinely allow evidence that a court would exclude.

Parents and school systems have the right to present evidence, in the form of oral testimony, written documents, or other recordings that they believe can help to resolve the dispute. Evidence may be admitted and its value assessed if it is the kind on which reasonable persons are accustomed to rely in the conduct of serious affairs. The primary restrictions are that the parties may not submit incompetent, irrelevant, immaterial, or unduly repetitious evidence, which are defined as follows:

- Incompetent evidence: A statement by a person whom the law considers not able or qualified to make such a comment. (An example would be a physical therapist testifying as to the psychological diagnosis of a child.)

- Irrelevant evidence: Information that sheds no light on, and has no logical relation to, any material fact or issue that is in dispute.

- Immaterial evidence: Material offered to prove or disprove a fact or proposition that is not at issue (not contested).

- Repetitious evidence: Information that adds nothing new to, or more than, material produced earlier.

The hearing officer is free to admit into the record any evidence that bears on the issue at hand, and should allow witnesses to speak freely without interruption unless, as noted earlier, the testimony is incompetent, irrelevant, immaterial, or unduly repetitious. Exclusion of evidence is more likely to invalidate a decision than its inclusion. For this reason, hearing officers generally allow the introduction of more evidence than is necessary.

However, there is one other type that may not be admissible: evidence offered contrary to the five-day rule. (§ 121a.508(a)(3)) As discussed in earlier chapters, this requires that at least five days before the hearing, each party must give the other a list of all documents it plans to introduce and of all the witnesses it will call.

OBJECTIONS

An objection is the assertion by one party that an action or statement by another is unfair or improper. The person who is objecting is asking the hearing officer to rule whether that action or statement should be allowed.

If the conduct of the hearing is to be fair and workable, the hearing officer must be informed promptly of contentions that evidence should be rejected, and why. The initiative for an objection is placed on the parties, not on the hearing officer. However, the hearing officer may initiate a determination that certain evidence should not be admitted.

THE WAY TO STATE AN OBJECTION

If one party believes any question or tactic by the attorney or advocate for the other is improper, the first side must object. This is done by simply stating, "I object," then stating the reason. When an objection is made, the hearing officer may decide immediately by sustaining or overruling the objection or may ask the parties first to explain their respective positions on the challenged information or action.

If the objection is overruled, the witness is allowed to answer the question or take the action because the hearing officer disagrees with the person objecting or with the reason for the challenge. If the objection is sustained, the witness may not answer or take a particular action because the hearing officer agrees with the person objecting that the question or act is improper under the law.

THE USE OF OBJECTIONS

Objections should be used sparingly. As noted, the hearing officer generally will allow most evidence to be admitted. Moreover, technical legal maneuvers should not be allowed to dominate the proceeding. However, a person should not be reluctant to raise an objection if it is felt that certain information or a tactic by the other side is improper. The failure to object is a waiver of whatever ground for challenge there may be.

An objection is appropriate where a person feels that the other side is attempting to present evidence that is irrelevant or incompetent. For example, the parents of an emotionally disturbed child may object to the public agency attorney's submitting into evidence a report by a school counselor. The counselor's recommendation is that the child be placed in a residential program that can provide therapy for psychiatric disturbances. The parents could object because a school counselor is likely not to be "competent" to be making judgments about a child's psychiatric condition.

Another type of objection is to admission of certain documents. These objections usually center on problems of who or what caused the document to be written, or when, where, or how. For example, a public agency may object to a letter from the director of a private school asserting that the latter's program would be perfect for the student. The public agency might challenge it on the basis that the writer had such an interest in the outcome that such input could not be objective.

Another common objection is that a certain piece of evidence is hearsay. Usually the objection is made when a witness reports what someone else said or did, rather than what the witness said or did. The main characteristic of hearsay evidence is that it is secondhand.

The basic problem with secondhand evidence, or hearsay, is reliability since it is virtually impossible to ensure its accuracy and truth. It may be wrong or it may be a mistake and the witness who heard it from someone else cannot vouch for its truth.

Hearsay can be defined more precisely as a statement

1. not made in court or at the hearing
2. not made so the declarant could be cross-examined
3. offered as evidence of the truth of its content

Hearsay is a complex concept with many exceptions. However, in administrative proceedings such as a special education due process hearing, hearsay generally is admissible as long as it is relevant. However, the hearing officer may use discretion and exclude it if it is unfair to one of the parties.

It should be noted that there are many other grounds for objecting. The general principle for advocates to follow is to object sparingly but not to neglect doing so when necessary.

OPINIONS AND EXPERT WITNESSES

As a general rule, witnesses must testify to facts and not to their opinion or conclusions drawn from them. In theory, witnesses are supposed to testify to facts perceived, and the hearing officer then will draw opinions, inferences, and conclusions. However, there are exceptions that should be noted:

- Lay Witness: An ordinary witness may give an opinion on a question involving ordinary sense perceptions such as time, space, speed, intoxication, and irrational conduct. Otherwise lay opinions are not permitted.

- Expert Witness: A qualified expert witness may give an opinion on facts that are not common knowledge and are within the individual's special expertise.

An advocate may be required to offer a rationale for presenting an expert witness at a special education hearing. If so, the advocate first must establish that:

- The subject matter is appropriate for expert testimony. The facts or inferences depend upon special knowledge, skill, or training not ordinarily within the realm of the experiences or training of the general public.

- The expert is qualified with the degree of training, knowledge, and experience that will enable the person to apply the special knowledge required.

- The expert must have developed an opinion or conclusion about the subject matter. If this opinion is a mere guess or speculation, it is inadmissible as expert testimony.

- The opinion must be supported by facts that are in the evidence or that the expert knows from personal experience. The questioning of the expert should disclose the facts on which the opinion is based. This also may include facts related by another expert in documents or at the hearing.

When presenting an expert witness for direct examination, the advocate wants to accomplish two objectives: (1) to qualify the witness as an expert, and (2) to elicit the opinion of that witness. When qualifying the witness as an expert, the advocate should bring out facts in such areas as:

- education and honors
- teaching experience in the context of the profession
- experience in the profession
- publications
- professional recognition by peers

After the qualifying of the witness has been completed, the advocate should ask the hearing officer to accept this individual as an expert. The advocate then should proceed to conduct direct examination of the expert witness. On direct examination, the expert may testify to opinions based on personally observed facts, on facts introduced in evidence if the witness was present when that was done, or on a hypothetical question based on evidence in the record.

When cross-examining the expert, an advocate may attempt to:

- challenge the qualifications of the expert
- demonstrate that the expert's practice does not really encompass the issues involved in this case
- demonstrate that the expert's review of the evidence, upon which the opinion was based, was insufficient to reach that conclusion
- take the overall conclusion apart and separate it into its component parts so as to devalue it
- challenge the expert by reference to contradictory statements in authoritative writings of other known experts in the field
- pose hypothetical questions different from those on direct examination as long as the alterations are based on the evidence

THE CLOSING STATEMENT

At the conclusion of the presentation of the evidence, each side customarily makes a closing statement. The closing statement is important because it is the last chance to speak to the hearing officer before the case is decided and the final opportunity to persuade the official to decide in favor of the advocate's side.

The advocate has a fairly wide latitude concerning what to say in the closing statement, such as:

- issues in the case

- evidence in the case

- reasonable inferences from the evidence

- any argument that is fair

- matters of common knowledge

Generally, the same points discussed earlier with regard to the opening statement are applicable as well to the closing one. The advocate should review that section while preparing for the closing statement.

The advocate should remember to emphasize the theme of the case, speak in plain language, avoid overstating what the evidence has proved, and structure the closing statement so that it has a clear and concise form.

Chapter 23

The Witness: A Guide

Increasingly, special education due process hearings are becoming more like courtroom trials than informal meetings. Skilled attorneys or advocates frequently represent each side. This section reviews some of the preceding material and presents a step-by-step approach for parents, other lay persons, and professionals to be effective witnesses at a special education due process hearing. Because of the personalized nature of this "how to" advice, it is presented in the second person.*

PREPARING TO TESTIFY

When you appear at a hearing as a witness, you may be nervous in anticipation of the experience. Don't worry—such anxiety is normal.

Dress Appropriately

Your personal appearance is important. Because formal proceedings tend to be conservative, you should dress in business rather than casual attire.

Prepare Ahead of Time

You know in advance when you will be called to testify. Use the time while you are waiting to refresh your memory and recall details about

---

* This chapter is largely adapted from *The Legal Aspects of Protective Services for Abused and Neglected Children*, by Barbara A. Caulfield, published by the U.S. Department of Health, Education, and Welfare, Office of Human Development Services, 1978.

events related to the case. Review these events in your mind, go over your notes. Don't expect to use your notes extensively at the hearing, although they may be referred to if necessary to refresh your memory. A witness generally is expected to testify from memory.

Don't Memorize Your Testimony

Review your expected testimony mentally. It is not a good idea to prepare a script. Spontaneous responses are more believable and less likely to be shaken on cross-examination.

BEING NERVOUS AND NOT SHOWING IT

Expect to Feel Anxious

You probably will feel a sense of anxiety when you are called into the hearing room. It always is a bit of a shock to see the hearing officer, lawyers, advocates, and other participants sitting in their respective places—and all of them watching you as you enter.

It is important to remember that the hearing officer and participants observe all witnesses as they approach the stand. This is not unusual or because of something wrong with the individual. However, it is easy to feel stared down at this point. Just be prepared for the occurrence, making every effort to remember that this is how the participants view every witness, that it has nothing to do with any particular characteristics you may have.

Look directly back at the hearing officer and questioners, just as you would if you were speaking to them. Don't avoid their glance. You will find this approach relaxing.

Get Ready to Answer the First Question

You will feel a special kind of nervousness when you begin to testify. At this point, the most common symptoms of nervousness are: (1) perceptual problems in the hearing room (especially of sight), (2) lowering of the voice, (3) slumping in the chair, (4) speaking rapidly, (5) speaking in a monotone, and (6) inability to recognize anyone in the room.

Although you may really know the participants, you may not recognize them. To overcome these symptoms, take the following steps:

- Sit with your back straight, taking care not to allow your shoulders to slump or your body to slide down in the chair. If you begin the slumping and sliding process, your natural desire to get out of the spotlight will keep you doing that. Start out straight and you have a better chance of staying that way. A curled-up witness may not make as good an impression on the hearing officer as an erect witness.

- Look around the room to orient yourself. Look at each of the walls you can see in your line of vision without turning around. Look at each wall separately. If you are really nervous, the room may seem huge and cavernous. You may experience tunnel vision where you see only the lawyer about to question you, or unhappy participants—just as if they were at the end of a tunnel.

To avoid the nervous overemphasis of the scene, reorient yourself to the entire room and to the people in it. Therefore, any technique that serves to achieve that is helpful. A simple technique is to look at the wall to your left, to the back of the room, and to your right. Look at each person in the room separately.

Speak a Little Louder and Slower than Necessary

Participants tend to lower their voice and speed up their rate of talking when on the witness stand. What you should strive for is to speak somewhat louder and slower than you may think is necessary under the circumstances.

Concentrate on making each word heard but avoid long pauses between your words, phrases, or sentences. Moderation is the key word in your effort to overcome nervousness.

ANSWERING QUESTIONS

Be Sincere and Dignified—But Warm

Hearings are inappropriate settings in which to inject humor or comic relief. The image you want to project is one of sincerity and dignified warmth.

This case—as with all cases—is a serious matter. But it also is a human one in which you have a genuine concern for the persons involved.

Your projection of a humane attitude may assist the hearing officer in evaluating your credibility in a positive manner. A concerned appearance on the stand usually makes a better impression than does a frozen or calculating one.

Speak Clearly and Distinctly

The participants and hearing officer must hear your response, so speak clearly and distinctly and in a voice that probably is louder than the one you use in ordinary conversation.

You should give a spoken answer; nodding or shaking your head, gesturing, gasping, and other nonverbal communications should not be accepted as answers. They also do not reproduce on audiotape recordings.

Use Appropriate Language

Use ordinary English words with which you are comfortable. Slang, jargon, and words with unfamiliar meanings should be avoided. If you use technical terminology, explain its meaning. You often can check beforehand with the attorney or advocate who is calling you as a witness to identify some of the technical phrases that need to be explained.

Answer the Question That Was Asked

You must listen very carefully to each question so you know what information is appropriate. For example:

> Q. You stated that you are a licensed social worker. Where did you take your training?

That means formal schooling in social work—not the elementary and high schools you attended or the degrees you received that do not relate to your professional skills.

> Q. What did you and Mary Jones talk about during your first interview?

Give the time, date, and place of the conversation, then describe the substance of the conversation or topics discussed. Ordinarily you will not have to mention discussing such things as the weather or bus schedules or other items that have no bearing on the professional contact. You might summarize these kinds of conversations by saying you "chatted briefly" or "discussed other matters" so the advocate can explore them if they seem relevant.

Be alert to the kind of response desired. Direct examination usually calls for narrative responses, whereas cross-examination normally asks for a "yes" or "no" or other very short answer.

A common error of the witness is double-thinking or overthinking the question. To help avoid this, pause before answering a question, and try to keep your brain from overextending the questioner's meaning.

Avoid offhand responses as well as too technical ones in attempting to draw meaning from the question.

Let the Attorney Develop Your Testimony

This applies to both direct and cross-examination. For example:

> Q. Do you remember an interview with Mary Jones on Monday, April 11, at 10:15 a.m.?

The best response is "yes" or "no."

In the next question, the examining attorney or advocate may ask you to narrate the substance or circumstances of the interview. The purpose of the first question may be to prepare a foundation before introducing the significant part of your testimony. This is the attorney's or advocate's job, so don't jump ahead.

If You Don't Know, Say So

Don't guess. If you cannot remember, it is better to say so than to speculate. You may remember the answer later during your testimony; if so, the attorney or advocate questioning you may ask the question again. Do not rely, however, on the use of "I don't remember" or "I don't know" to avoid answering difficult or indelicate questions. You will not be an effective witness if you cannot remember details.

Don't Conform Your Testimony to Others'

You are called to testify regarding what you observed or what your opinion is. Different witnesses can have different impressions of the same event. You are not expected to agree with or parrot someone else's testimony; the other person may be wrong. You can discuss discrepancies with your attorney or advocate, but this is done outside the hearing.

Look at the Questioner or Hearing Officer

You are testifying in order to impart information to the hearing officer who will use it to determine the outcome. If you always look over at your attorney or advocate before answering another lawyer's question, it will look as if you are waiting to be coached.

Tell the Truth

Pure and simple, tell the truth. Let the chips fall where they may. Do not attempt to color your answers to fit the outcome of the case you believe is most fair or just.

It is natural to feel like an advocate for a certain outcome but you are a better witness if you are an impartial one.

A slight shift in emphasis on cross-examination in an attempt to advocate a certain outcome can backfire, giving opposing counsel a basis to argue that you are biased. This may put a dent in your credibility.

The lawyer or advocate is there to argue the case; you are there to report facts impartially. If a truthful answer seems to hurt the side that asked you to testify, this should not be your concern. You are there to tell the facts.

SURVIVING CROSS-EXAMINATION

Cross-examination is a necessary information-gathering technique used in the hearing process. It is effective because it helps each side throw a different light on the testimony of witnesses.

Cross-examination is not used against you personally. It is practiced on all witnesses, and the more important the witness the more vigorous the cross-examination.

Here are a few points on cross-examination.

Don't Speculate

As noted in the previous section ("Answering Questions"), don't speculate when you can't remember. Stick to what you actually do recall.

The cross-examiner may attempt to suggest details to you that you do not remember and that you did not state on direct examination. Do not follow the cross-examiner's leading question into an answer. For example, the cross-examiner may present a question in such a way that it seems eminently logical. However, if that is not what you remember, do not agree with the cross-examiner.

Be Careful What You Say and How You Say It

Even a friendly cross-examiner looks for inconsistencies by which to trip you whenever possible. Remember:

- Listen to the question.

- Make sure you understand what is being asked.

- Don't volunteer information that is not asked for. Volunteering provides the cross-examiner with additional opportunities to try to confuse you.

- Don't explain why you know something unless you are asked.

- The attorney/advocate offering your testimony has an opportunity to ask additional questions after cross-examination.

Listen to Questions; Don't Answer if Unclear

If you don't understand the question, ask the examiner to rephrase it or say you don't understand what information is being sought. This situation can arise easily on cross-examination since leading questions (that is, questions suggesting the answer) are permitted. (Leading questions, as noted earlier, are prohibited on direct examination.)

Answering Two-Part Questions

Many times, cross-examiners ask compound questions. Do not answer a partially untrue question with a yes.

When responding to a compound question, divide the question into parts and then answer it. For example:

Q. Is it not true that you drove to the Smiths' home on August 16, 1976, stormed inside, and immediately picked up their child, Mary Smith?

A. There are three parts to that question, and each part has a different answer. I did go to the Smith home, but I spoke with Mrs. Smith on the porch for 15 minutes. Then we spoke in her living room for another 15 minutes. After that, she allowed me to speak with Mary.

Do not begin your answer with "yes," because the attorney may cut you short and not allow you to complete your response, thus giving an erroneous impression of your actions.

Keep Calm

Do not lose your temper at questions you consider impertinent or offensive. Exercise absolute self-control. If you maintain your composure, you will be less likely to become confused and to be inconsistent. Outbursts of anger or temper do not enhance a witness' credibility.

If the questioning is improper, your attorney will object. Pause long enough before answering to allow the objection to be made. However, don't pause so long that you appear hesitant or unsure.

Some questions are simply nasty. These should be handled with tact and truth.

Answer Positively Rather than Doubtfully

Qualifiers such as:
"I think . . ."
"To the best of my recollection . . ."
"I guess . . ."
weaken the impact of your testimony. Be forthright if you know the answer. If you don't know the answer, say so.

Testifying on Distances

Most people have difficulty in estimating distance in feet or yards. If you are not good at this, refer to an object in the room to clarify distance in your testimony. For example:

Q. How far from the school was Johnny standing?
A. I can't say how many feet, but it was from here where I'm sitting to where Mr. Jones is sitting now.

The number of feet or yards then can be measured if necessary.

Avoiding the 'Yes or No' Problem

If on cross-examination the opposing attorney asks a question and ends it with "Answer yes or no," don't feel obliged to do so if you feel that such an answer would be misleading. Begin your answer with "Well, that needs explaining."

Admit Your Beliefs or Sympathy

Often, a witness will be asked a question regarding sympathy for one side or the other in the case. It would be absurd to deny an obvious sympathy. Honest admission of favoritism will not discredit a witness. This is very different from coloring answers because of favoritism.

An attorney/advocate who shows that a witness will change testimony because of feelings about a case is demonstrating that those feelings are affecting the testimony. This is bias that can damage credibility.

Merely stating obvious or natural feelings will not discredit you, as it has not been demonstrated that your natural feelings have affected your testimony. For example:

> Q. Do you have a feeling as to how you would like this case to come out?
> A. Yes, I'm afraid I do.
> Q. You would like the school system to place Barbara in a residential setting, wouldn't you?
> A. Yes, I feel that way. But I have answered all of your questions as honestly as I possibly could. I have told the truth.

Reconciling or Distinguishing Expert Opinions

If you have to research your professional opponent's arguments, do so ahead of time. The attorney/advocate calling an expert expects that professional to assist in the preparation of the technical part of the case.

When you are the expert, it means you must polish up your expertise. This may entail reviewing textbooks and training manuals, reading about new developments in your field with which you are unfamiliar, taking advantage of a conveniently timed workshop or internal training session, and conferring with colleagues.

Generally, do whatever is necessary to brush up your professional knowledge and skills so that when you are asked for your opinion, you can answer with authority and confidence, knowing that you are current and knowledgeable in your area of special competence.

Only thus can you reconcile or distinguish your opinion from others'.

Supplying Additional Details

Avoid ending your testimony with finality, such as, "And that's all there is." Later, if you remember something that ought to be added, you may find yourself offering excuses for your earlier lapse. It is better to offer no comment.

Don't Be Rushed

Cross-examination typically is fast paced so that the lying witness has no time to calculate an answer. However, the sincere witness may need time to make a careful and complete answer.

If the examiner interrupts your answer with a new question, it generally is better to complete the response you began before going on to something new.

As noted above, if questioning is improper, your attorney/advocate will object, and a slight pause from you will create an opportunity for that objection to be made. If an objection is made, stop, even in midword.

Don't Get Caught by a Trick Question

If you are asked, "Are you being paid to testify?" remember that it is acceptable for experts to be paid.

If you are being paid to testify, say so and explain. For example: "I am being paid a fee of $20."

If the expert is being paid the normal consultation rate, the expert should state this. Of course, if the answer is no, say "No."

To the question, "Who told you to say that?" you should state that you were told to tell the truth.

You may be asked, "Have you discussed this case with anyone?" Since you naturally have talked the case over with the attorney/advocate for your side, say so. Also, name your supervisor and anyone else with whom you have discussed the case.

PRESENTING YOUR INFORMATION EFFECTIVELY

Check with Attorney Before You Testify

The attorney/advocate offering your testimony should go over with you the information it is desired to elicit on direct examination and the information you have to offer. You should inform the attorney of any problems you see in the case or in the agency investigation. Adverse information and weaknesses should be disclosed beforehand. The witness stand is no place to spring a surprise.

Organize Your Material and Your Thoughts

Your testimony probably will fall into one or more of the categories listed below. Your preparation should be different for each of your three functions:

1. Personal Observations: Prepare to testify from memory with little, if any, reference to your notes. If the relationship with the case covered

a long period of time before the hearing, you can prepare a separate sheet, such as a chronology of events. This short summary can be used to jog your memory on the stand, plus help keep your thoughts and recollections organized. Opposing counsel/advocate and the hearing officer probably will look at your list, but it usually will not be introduced as evidence unless it differs from your oral testimony. As noted earlier, memorize the facts but avoid sounding as though you were giving a recitation from a script.

2. Expert conclusions: As an expert, you should be prepared to explain:

   - your professional qualifications, e.g., your educational degrees, length and extent of experience, special training, membership in professional associations

   - the professional theories and approaches you used in forming your opinion

   - the common theories and approaches you rejected

   - your methodology and how it is similar to, or different from, that of other similar professionals

   - what opinions you formed, and why; this will be the major portion of your testimony as an expert

3. Reading Reports: Prepare by being thoroughly familiar with the contents and organization of the file, i.e., all your written documents on the case. Make sure you can read any handwritten parts and double-check the contents to see if any correspondence or notes have been omitted. You should be able to explain briefly the method for production, transcription, and processing of the file if it was kept in the ordinary course of a professional practice.

Stop Talking When There Is an Objection

Maintain your composure when there is an objection from the attorney, but do not finish your sentence. The hearing officer will sustain or overrule the objection. If it is overruled, you can go on, but usually either the presiding officer or the examining attorney will instruct you to continue. Above all, don't worry too much about what may have been objectionable.

Choose a Simple and Logical Structure

Chronological order probably is the most common structure for organizing your material. Use an organizational format that is natural for you and clear to everyone else. The simpler the better.

Parents should relate their contacts with the public agency in a chronological manner so that the hearing officer can better understand the historical framework from which they are operating. It is best to relate this chronology in an emotionally controlled manner. After doing so, explain what you think it shows about the issues.

Finally, it is important for the parents to be clear about what they are requesting the hearing officer to do. Frequently parents come to a hearing with great frustration toward the agency. They may want the hearing officer to condemn or punish the agency's officials.

The hearing officer has no such authority or responsibility. The parents' requests should be framed carefully in terms of specific action necessary for the agency to appropriately identify, evaluate, program, and place the student in accordance with the special education needs.

This discussion on evidence is included so that all parties to the hearing can present their information more effectively. Discussions of the use and forms of evidence, the admission and nonadmission of evidence, the use of objections, the techniques of direct examination and cross-examination, and assessing the weight and credibility of evidence are presented so that parents and professionals can be effective providers of information at the hearing.

Become familiar with the step-by-step approach to being an effective witness. These techniques are used in the hearing process to help the hearing officer reach an impartial decision concerning the appropriate placement of the handicapped child.

Part VI

The Decision

It is important for all of the participants to know how the decision in a special education due process hearing is reached. If participants can understand what the hearing officer needs to know, they will be able to present their information more effectively.

At the conclusion of this proceeding, the parties are entitled to receive a written decision by the hearing officer. The decision is developed after consideration of the law, the presentations by the participants, the procedural issues, the evidence submitted, and the issues presented.

This part first addresses the process a hearing officer could use to arrive at a decision and some of the legal parameters of that process. It then provides a framework on how to write a decision.

Chapter 24

Arriving at a Decision

The special education due process hearing has been concluded. The hearing officer has thanked the participants and everyone leaves. The hearing officer packs up notes, reference materials, hearing tapes, documents submitted into evidence, etc. At this point, the individual may have a headful of thoughts about the case. The hearing officer probably is happy the hearing is over and begins to feel relaxed. Soon the mind will turn to the task that lies ahead: writing the decision.

That task is the most important and most difficult part of the proceeding. However, it will be a great deal less difficult if the hearing officer has conducted the session in an effective and efficient manner. That conduct is the key to developing a good written decision.

The hearing officer may need to experience the whole process several times before actually grasping this concept. While the session is in progress, the hearing officer must understand what will be needed later in developing the decision.

But now the hearing officer has come to the point of developing a decision. It is to be hoped that the proceeding has been conducted in accordance with its purpose, i.e., a mechanism for gathering all of the necessary information. This chapter provides the hearing officer with an approach to arriving at a decision. The following chapter covers the writing of a decision.

The writing should not begin until the hearing officer is clear on precisely what the decision is. The general idea is to have the decision jump out from the evidence, rather than the officer's having to dig into the materials to come up with the decision. The following approach is offered as a way to facilitate that process of arriving at a decision.

STEP 1. THE PERSPECTIVE OF AN OBSERVER

The hearing officer has just concluded the special education due process proceeding and may want to begin to write the decision while everything still is fresh in mind.

It is suggested that the hearing officer not begin to develop the decision shortly after the hearing. This is especially true if the individual is still new to the role. The ideas and impressions should be allowed to settle for a day or two. Perceptions that seem so important immediately following the hearing may lose some of their glitter, and be replaced by others, upon reflection.

In developing a decision, the hearing officer needs to adopt the perspective of an observer. The person cannot be caught up in the emotionally charged feelings permeating the dispute between the parents and school personnel. The law requires that the hearing officer be impartial, having no "personal or professional interest which would conflict with his or her objectivity in the hearing" process. (§ 121a.507)

The hearing officer's perspective upon entering the case should have been that of an outside observer with little or no information about the issues. The perspective should be resumed as the decision begins to develop to ensure that the fundamental principle of fairness that has been maintained throughout the process does not stop after the hearing.

Although adopting this perspective may seem axiomatic, the failure to do so is one of the most common pitfalls hearing officers encounter in developing decisions. It happens frequently without their awareness.

To avoid this pitfall and to arrive at an objective decision, the hearing officer should be careful not to make the following common mistakes:

1. Avoiding Assumptions without the Evidence

Sometimes the hearing officer does not ask a specific question at the hearing because the answer already seems apparent. In developing the decision, this assumption is used as a reason for a conclusion, even though there actually is no evidence in the record to support it.

For example, a hearing officer presides at a case involving a learning disabled child who also suffers from diabetes. The school system is recommending placement at a facility for children with health impairments. The hearing officer upholds the school's program as appropriate. One of the critical reasons for the conclusion, cited in the decision, is the "known fact of the child's diabetes which will require the attention and supervision by medical staff personnal." Such a statement is an assumption by the hearing officer. It may or may not be true, but the assumption should not be part of the findings unless the witnesses or the evaluations indicated that the diabetic condition did in fact require medical attention.

The observer perspective means that the hearing officer bases decisions only on what is observed or elicited from the participants. The hearing officer no longer is an observer when personal assumptions on testimony or documents in evidence are interjected.

2. Avoiding Personal Philosophies or Theories

A proceeding often will involve issues about which the hearing officer has professional views. In developing the decision, these personal educational philosophies or theories are used as the basis for a conclusion, even though there actually is insufficient evidence to support it.

For example, a hearing officer presides at a case involving a hearing impaired child. The school system proposes a program that involves language development through the manual method. The decision rejects that program as not appropriate. One of the critical reasons for the conclusion, cited in the decision, is that "the manual method deprives the student of the ability to communicate with hearing persons and to learn the nuances of the English language."

Such a statement is a conclusion based on the hearing officer's personal philosophy or theory about education of the hearing impaired. The conclusion may or may not be true. However, the statement should not be part of the decision unless the witnesses or the evaluations indicated that the hearing deficiency required instruction in other than the manual method.

The observer perspective means that the hearing officer's premises are based only on what is observed or elicited from the participants as to what is appropriate for this child. Even if the oral or cued-speech methods were more widely accepted among educators of the deaf, that does not mean the manual method could not be the appropriate way of teaching this child. Hearing officers no longer are observers when they interject their own notions about education of the handicapped, if such concepts cannot be found in the hearing testimony or documents.

As noted in earlier chapters, they must base their decisions solely on the evidence presented at the session. It is a violation of due process to base them on information obtained elsewhere. To do so renders the decisions defective and subject to reversal on appeal.

Why is it a violation of due process to base a decision on information obtained elsewhere? The reason is that the parties have been denied the opportunity to cross-examine and challenge that outside information. The information finds its way into the decision without being tested in the open to determine whether or not it is accurate, or even applicable to the particular case.

If the hearing officer's own opinions are the outside information, then that individual has ceased to be the impartial adjudicator and has become a witness. The parties do not have a chance to cross-examine. The hearing officer has become a witness after the hearing is finished and the decision is being developed.

To develop a decision in keeping with the principles of due process, the hearing officer should remain detached from the controversy. He or she should adopt the objective perspective of an observer.

STEP 2. THE WEIGHT AND CREDIBILITY OF EVIDENCE

After the hearing officer adopts the objective perspective of an observer, he or she should review all of the evidence. The hearing officer should take the documents and lay them out. A list of the witnesses who testified similarly should be set down. The hearing officer may refresh his or her memory regarding the testimony of the witnesses, by reviewing the record of the proceeding, by reading the transcripts or listening to the tapes. It is recommended that inexperienced hearing officers review the entire hearing record as described above. Experienced hearing officers who understand the process will need to review only portions of the record, or be able to rely on notes taken at the hearing.

As the hearing officer reviews the testimonial and documentary evidence, he or she will want to make some mental notations. Each piece of evidence should be weighed in the hearing officer's mind. Evaluation of credibility should be given to the testimony of witnesses and documents. In assessing the weight and credibility to be given to each piece of evidence, the hearing officer may wish to consider the list included in Chapter 21—Exhibit 21-1, Checklist for Assessing Witnesses and Documents.

The hearing officer should assess the weight and credibility of each piece of evidence, even if it is uncontradicted. If there are contradictory or conflicting pieces of evidence, the above mentioned list of considerations should aid the hearing officer in determining which piece should be given more weight and credibility in developing a decision.

STEP 3. IS THE CHILD HANDICAPPED?

After adopting the perspective of an observer and assessing the weight of the evidence, the hearing officer should make a series of three sequentially related determinations. The first determination is whether the child is handicapped within the meaning of the law. This may be a very simple determination.

A child is not eligible to receive special education under federal law unless he or she is "handicapped." The law defines "handicapped" children as:

> mentally retarded, hard of hearing, deaf, speech impaired, visually handicapped, seriously emotionally disturbed, orthopedically impaired, other health impaired, deaf-blind, multi-handicapped, or as having specific learning disabilities, who because of those impairments need special education and related services. (§ 121a.5)

The law does not provide a single generic category for handicapped children. Every child who is classified as being handicapped must actually have one or more of the disabilities listed in the above definition.

For example, a child may be a "slow learner" and have "behavior problems." This child may or may not qualify for an education program for the seriously emotionally disturbed, or for those with specific learning disabilities, as defined in the law. The description of a "a slow learner with behavior problems" also could mean that the child simply requires some remedial attention in the classroom but does not have one of the disabilities listed above.

The hearing officer will need to include a finding as to whether or not the child is handicapped and, if so, under which one of the specific listed disabilities the condition falls. A child who is not found to be handicapped within the definition is not entitled to receive special education and related services under the federal law.

STEP 4. THE NEED FOR SPECIAL EDUCATION

The second determination is whether or not the child requires special education and related services. This may seem to be unnecessary if the hearing officer already has determined that the child is handicapped and actually has one or more of the legal disabilities. However, not all children who have a disability require special education. Many can attend the regular classroom program without any modifications.

The "handicapped" definition discussed in Step 3 lists a number of specific disabilities of which a child must have one or more to be eligible for special education. That same definition provides an additional criterion for eligibility for special education: the child must require special education by reason of the handicapping condition. Having a disability is not enough to require special educational services; the child also must need such services to meet unique educational needs caused by the handicap.

For example, a child may be orthopedically impaired and confined to a wheelchair but may be fully able to participate in the regular education program without any modification. Another example may be a child with asthma or other health impairment that does not adversely affect educational performance and, therefore, does not require any special services.

The hearing officer will need to find whether or not the disability adversely affects educational performance. If the disability does not require special services, then the child technically is not "handicapped" under the law and is not entitled to specially designed instruction.

STEP 5. APTNESS OF PROGRAM AND PLACEMENT

Once it has been determined that the child is handicapped and by reason of that disability requires special education, the hearing officer must decide whether or not the proposed program and placement are appropriate. The law requires that the school system's proposed program be appropriate to meet the child's unique educational needs. This is the point where the greatest number of disputes arise between the parents and the school personnel. Chapter 11, "How to Determine Whether an IEP/Placement Is Appropriate," analyzes the question that also is posed here. The hearing officer should review the information provided there to assist in making the necessary determination.

STEP 6. SELECTING A DECISION OPTION

Having arrived at this final step, the hearing officer should know the answer to the question posed by the central issue of the case. If the answer is not apparent at this point, the hearing officer will need to retrace the five steps above and see where the process broke down. The answer is not easily obtained but should become clear if this process is followed carefully. If the answer is clear, the hearing officer should proceed to select one of the decision options below.

The hearing officer need not select the position urged by either the parents or the school system. As noted in earlier chapters, a special education due process hearing is not an adversarial contest in the sense of a criminal trial. In this type of proceeding, the hearing officer must resolve an impasse between parents and school personnel and issue a decision in the child's best educational interests. The proceeding is simply the forum the law provides so the hearing officer can gather the information necessary to make that decision.

It is presumed that together the parents and the school personnel will cover the spectrum of information and recommendations about the child's educational needs. The fact that the hearing may take on an intense adversarial character is unfortunate. It also is not relevant. Regardless of the degree of controversy or even hostility between the parties, the hearing officer must not lose sight of the task of gathering information on which to develop a decision.

THE TWO RESTRICTIVE REQUIREMENTS

The hearing officer is restricted by only two requirements in making a decision. The first is that the decision must be based solely on the evidence presented at the hearing. This point has been discussed earlier. Suffice it to say that while wide discretion may be possible in fashioning a decision, the hearing officer may not develop a program simply because of the belief that it is best. The decision must not be at variance with the evidence in the record. A hearing officer who is not satisfied with the evidence for any reason may direct that further information be presented.

The second limiting requirement is that the decision must focus on the school system's proposed action, or refusal to act. It is the system that has the responsibility for providing the child with a free appropriate public education.

The focus is not upon which proposal is better as between that of the parents and of the schools. If, for example, the hearing officer does not believe the school's proposed placement is appropriate for the child, the decision should not summarily direct that the child be placed in the facility proposed by the parents. The hearing officer may direct the school system to propose a different placement appropriate to carry out the IEP developed for the child. The types of characteristics the appropriate placement should have also may be described. However, the hearing officer should direct the school system to place the child in a particular facility.

If the schools' action is not appropriate, the hearing officer may specify what would be necessary to make it so. A decision that goes beyond that may exceed the hearing officer's authority to resolve disputes on the system's actions.

CHOOSING AMONG OPTIONS

In issuing the decision, the hearing officer, as discussed earlier, has several options. The official can:

Require Submission of Further Evidence

In some cases the answer to the question at issue is not apparent no matter how many times the hearing officer reviews the evidence. The reason is that the answer may very well not be in the hearing evidence, which simply may be insufficient. If that is the case, the hearing officer may issue an interim decision that requires one or both parties to provide further evidence of a certain type. An independent educational evaluation also may be ordered to help resolve the contradictory positions.

If this option is selected, the hearing officer should clearly specify the type of information needed, the persons or party responsible for obtaining it, the date by which it should be submitted, and the date by which either party may request a further hearing to discuss the additional material if they so choose.

Uphold the Schools' Proposed Action

If persuaded by the evidence that the schools' proposed action is appropriate, the hearing officer may so rule and uphold their action. If this option is chosen, it indicates that the system's proposed action is appropriate and that the schools may proceed accordingly.

Allow the Schools' Action on a Trial Basis

The schools' proposed action may appear appropriate on paper but the hearing officer may have some reservations about its implementation. This situation arises where the system is starting an action for the first time with a particular child, such as an initial placement. The hearing officer may recommend that it start for a trial period. This would enable the hearing officer to see how the school staff members follow through on their proposals and gather information on how well the child responds.

If this option is chosen, the hearing officer should clearly specify the reason for the trial basis, what the parties are expected to do in the interim, what factors will be reviewed at the conclusion of the test period, what objective criteria will be used to measure or evaluate these factors, the time frame of the trial, and the date of the hearing to review the school system's action if the parties still feel one is necessary after that period.

Uphold the School System in Part

The schools' proposal may largely be appropriate except for a few modifications. In such a case the hearing officer may uphold the action in part and reject it in part.

For example, the parents have requested that the system pay for an independent educational evaluation because they are dissatisfied with the one performed by school personnel. The schools initiate a hearing to prove that their evaluation is appropriate and thereby relieve them of having to pay for a costly independent evaluation.

The hearing officer believes the evidence shows that the schools' evaluation procedures are appropriate. However, the child's referral characteristics suggest that a neurological assessment might be helpful to determine the educational needs more precisely. If the hearing officer gives that evidence substantial weight, the schools' evaluation may be upheld as appropriate as to the procedures followed but not appropriate in its comprehensiveness.

The hearing officer may then require the schools to perform a neurological assessment rather than ordering the system to pay to have the whole evaluation done over again independently.

If this option is chosen, it is necessary to specify clearly what parts of the school system's proposed action are found to be appropriate, what parts are not, what changes in the action are necessary to make all parts appropriate, and the date by which these changes should be made.

Reject the Schools' Proposal as Inappropriate

The hearing evidence may be persuasive that the schools' proposal is not appropriate. In such a case, the hearing officer may so indicate and thereby reject the action.

If this option is chosen, the hearing officer should specify clearly the defects in the action that make it inappropriate, what the school system must do to meet its legal responsibilities to the child, and the date by which these tasks should be accomplished.

At this point, the hearing officer has arrived at a decision. Now it is time to put it in writing. The following chapter addresses that task.

Chapter 25

Writing a Decision

The writing of a decision involves two steps: (1) determining what the ruling will be (discussed in Chapter 24) and (2) actually putting it on paper (described in this chapter). No attempt should be made to write until the hearing officer determines which way the case will go. Otherwise the written decision is likely to be muddled and unclear.

The most important characteristic of the written decision is that it be self-explanatory. The reasoning should be understandable even if the reader was not present at the proceeding. There should be no gaps in the presentation of that reasoning. There should be no perplexity as to how the hearing officer reached a particular conclusion, or what evidence must have been presented to lead to the adoption of a certain argument urged by one of the parties.

When sitting down to write, the hearing officer must know what the decision is and how it was reached. Reviewing officials or judges will not know the background; they will have only the written decision before them, so it must speak for itself. The hearing officer will not be there to explain what is meant by it nor what thoughts were involved in reaching a particular conclusion.

Undoubtedly, the hearing officer carefully evaluated all of the evidence and thought through the decision. However, the written opinion must demonstrate that the decision-making process was proper by disclosing precisely how the result was arrived at—particularly that it was not reached in an incompetent, arbitrary, or capricious manner. This can best be done by taking the reader along a route that clearly shows the basis for the decision. The following sequential format is suggested for that purpose:

1. cover page
2. jurisdiction and procedural posture
3. the issues

415

4. applicable law and regulations
5. evidence considered
6. summary of the evidence
7. evaluation of the evidence
8. findings of fact
9. conclusions of law
10. order and appeal information

THE COVER PAGE

A cover page identifies a particular case and the parties involved. It includes a variety of basic information about the child and the parents. It should be written on a sheet of paper separate from the body of the decision. Its purpose is to include the "personally identifiable" information about the child that is necessary for the school system's records—material that the law requires be kept confidential.

It is strongly recommended that the hearing officer include all such personally identifiable information on the cover page and not anywhere else in the body of the written decision. The reason is so the decision may be shared with numerous persons without having to go through the entire text to delete personally identifiable information about the child.

Many persons other than those involved in the case may have a legitimate interest in wanting to read the decision. For example, other parents who are considering invoking the hearing process with regard to their handicapped child may wish to see a decision in a case similar to their own. The law also requires that the school system transmit the decisions, "after deleting any personally identifiable information, to the State advisory panel established . . ." under the law. (§ 121a.508(a)(5)) Therefore, it is much more practical to include all of the "personally identifiable" information on a single cover page that can be removed easily.

The regulations define the term "personally identifiable" information as including:

(a) The name of the child, the child's parent, or other family member;

(b) The address of the child;

(c) A personal identifier, such as the child's social security number or student number; or

(d) A list of personal characteristics or other information which would make it possible to identify the child with reasonable certainty. (§ 121a.500c)

Each individual jurisdiction will determine for its hearing officers exactly what personally identifiable information it will require on a cover page. The following list contains the most common items to be included:

- the name of the child

- the name of the child's parents

- the family's address

- the name of the family's legal counsel or representative

- the address of the family's representative

- the name of the school district

- the name of the school district's legal counsel or representative

- the address of the school's representative

- the date of the hearing

- the child's current grade level or name of program

- the child's date of birth

- the child's Social Security number or other school identification number

- the date of the request for a hearing

- the date of the written decision

- the name of the hearing officer

- the persons present at the hearing, listed with their proper names, titles, function, or relationship to the child

Throughout the text of the decision, the hearing officer should refer to the handicapped child by first name only or as "the child" or "the student" rather than by full name. The other persons should be referred to as "the parents," "the child's mother," "the school psychologist," etc., rather than by their names.

Some jurisdictions recommend that the hearing officer refer to the parties as the "petitioner" and the "respondent," with the party initiating the hearing, usually the parents, as the petitioner and the responding party, usually the school system, as the respondent. Any such method is acceptable. The point is that the written decision should read like a story with the actual names of characters omitted. The purpose of the cover page is to record the names and information that makes it possible to identify the child and participants where it is important to do so.

JURISDICTION AND PROCEDURAL POSTURE

The special education due process hearing is a legal proceeding. The hearing officer is authorized by law to conduct the session and issue a decision that sets forth the rights and responsibilities of the parties. This legal authority is called "jurisdiction." The hearing officer's jurisdiction is found under P.L. 94-142, state laws, and agency regulations. The specific jurisdiction is defined in different legal sources, depending on the individual state.

It is important for the hearing officer to set forth a statement of jurisdiction at the outset of the decision because that point is the underpinning for everything that follows. It is what makes the decision have the force of law as opposed to simply being a report. The statement also informs the participants of where the hearing officer derives the rules under which the process functions. Thus, a participant who disagreed with the decision would know what law to turn to for further information if an appeal was planned.

Procedural posture refers to the status of the case at the time of the hearing. The first few sentences of this portion should set forth how this matter came to be heard. It should briefly summarize the critical events or actions by the parties that led up to the hearing.

The procedural posture also is the place to address preliminary matters. Frequently, a procedural problem will arise at the outset of the hearing. For example, the parents may not have known they could have an independent educational evaluation performed before the hearing. The school personnel may not have been informed in advance that the parents intended to bring in an expert witness. These types of problems are addressed in Part IV. If they arise and the hearing officer is able to resolve them, the decision should include a statement of what the problem was and how it was settled.

There also should be a statement that the hearing officer asked the parents whether they had been afforded an opportunity to exercise all of their due process rights. If so, and it appears that the procedural posture of the case complies with the stated legal authorities, the hearing officer should so state.

THE ISSUES

The purpose of the hearing is very broad: to resolve an impasse between the parents and the school system about the appropriateness of the child's education. It could encompass many diverse conflicts. The hearing officer needs to state in this section the specific issue(s) presented for resolution.

The setting or framework now has been established by the jurisdiction statements. The statements on procedural posture indicate that the stage is set and the participants are ready to begin. At the hearing, each side presented an opening statement, a brief sketch of the party's perspective as to why the procedure was invoked, and what the party intended to show.

All this should enable the hearing officer to frame what specific issue(s) need to be resolved and where the parties differ. Those specific question(s) or issue(s) are to be included in this section of the written decision.

The reader now should know three points: (1) the authority under which the hearing is being held, (2) the procedural posture, and (3) what the proceeding is all about.

APPLICABLE LAW AND REGULATIONS

The hearing officer's decision must be based solely upon the evidence presented at the hearing and be within the limits of the law. What law? Under the jurisdiction section of the decision, the hearing officer states the sources of legal authority for conducting the proceeding and issuing the decision. Those sources also can identify the specific provisions that bear upon the issue of this hearing.

These specific provisions are not those that authorize the hearing in the first place. That is addressed in the earlier section on jurisdiction for the proceeding. This section consists of the specific provisions by which the hearing officer will be guided in evaluating the evidence. Following sections discuss the evidence at length. Since every legal proceeding is a mixture of facts and law, this section describes the pertinent law.

The hearing officer should simply list the specific provisions of the law under the headings of its source. For example, the applicable provisions of P.L. 94-142 would be listed under that heading, state law under its heading, and local education agency policies under their heading. It always is best to include the full text of the provision rather than simply the reference number of the particular section. The list of provisions should be brief. It usually is not necessary to list all the broad rights a child may have in special education law. What is needed is the precise provisions most applicable to the specific issue in this case.

The reader now should clearly understand the fourth point: the specific rules by which the hearing officer is being guided in developing this decision.

THE EVIDENCE CONSIDERED

The hearing officer's decision must be based solely upon the evidence. To demonstrate compliance with that requirement, the hearing officer at this point lists persons who testified and the list of documents received (evidence consists of both testimony and documents). This list clearly shows the sources from which everything that follows emanates.

The hearing officer may reach a number of different conclusions but all must have their basis in something from this list of evidence. Conclusions may not be drawn simply from the hearing officer's own background or beliefs. The list sets the parameters on the evidence and shows the origin of the hearing officer's ideas about this case. A participant who disagrees with the hearing officer thus may go back to the primary sources of the information to see whether the conclusions are reasonable.

The hearing officer should remember not to list the names of the witnesses except on the cover page. Personally identifiable information in the heading of a document also should be deleted. The documents should have been numbered at the hearing, such as "Exhibit 1." If they carry such a reference number, it should be included in this part of the decision as well. Those who need to review an actual document may seek permission to do so. The document remains with the record of the hearing and usually is not returned even after the decision is issued.

If the hearing officer for some reason does not consider a piece of evidence in that decision, that should also be indicated. For example, one document may seem completely irrelevant and therefore is not even considered. A witness may testify about an experience with the child so long ago it really could not have much bearing on the current issue. The hearing officer may state that the testimony of that witness is not considered in the decision.

The reader by now should clearly understand a fifth point: the identity of the main players and the documents.

SUMMARY OF THE EVIDENCE

Once again it is important to note that the decision must be based solely upon the evidence presented at the hearing. The hearing officer in the previous section of the decision has listed the specific pieces of evidence considered and now must explain just what they say.

The hearing officer should avoid repeating long pages of testimony or documents and instead should summarize the main points of each witness' testimony and the individual documents that were submitted. For emphasis or clarity, it may be advisable to include certain important quotations from a document or a witness' testimony.

The main characteristics of this section are that it should be clear and comprehensive. Brevity may need to be sacrificed somewhat for the sake of completeness. The hearing officer is like a reporter in this section. The individual has heard or read a piece of evidence and now is reporting a summary of it. The reporting should be objective. This is not the place where the hearing officer makes personal judgments. That will come later. This section must show exactly what the evidence is, what happened in this case, and what the participants think should be done. A witness the hearing officer did not like or believe should not be evaluated in this section nor shortchanged. The section should report fairly and accurately what occurred at the hearing and what was said and submitted.

The reader now should clearly understand a sixth point: what occurred at the hearing. This section expands on the evidence, reports the whole story in summary form, and provides all the information the reader needs to know.

EVALUATION OF THE EVIDENCE

The previous sections set everything in place for this section. Up to this point the hearing officer has been limited to reporting objectively on the evidence and laws involved in reaching this decision. Now is the point for setting forth an evaluation of the evidence within the parameters of the applicable law. This part explains what evidence the hearing officer found persuasive and why, or why not. This is where the hearing officer makes judgments and clearly shows how they were reached.

The hearing officer should use a simple narrative style to provide the rationale behind the decision. What did the hearing officer think about the school's proposals? How do the requests of the parents fit within the law? Why was the report of one evaluator more persuasive than the contradictory testimony of an expert witness? All of these questions and others like them should be answered in this section.

The reader now should clearly understand a seventh point: how the hearing officer sees the evidence stacking up.

FINDINGS OF FACT

The law requires that any party to a hearing have the right to obtain written findings of fact. These are the distillation of the evaluation of evidence. In the previous section the hearing officer has taken all the evidence and evaluated it. What was found after that evaluation? The parties have proposed a number of contentions. One side contended something was a fact, the other side disagreed and insisted something else was the fact. Which side does the hearing officer find to be true? Or does the truth lie in a different position altogether?

What does the hearing officer find to be fact? For example, the parents contend that their child manifests a psychotic disorder, the school personnel contend that the child manifests only a slight behavior problem. The conclusion will rest on what the hearing officer finds the fact to be. There is a large difference between a psychotic disorder and a behavior problem. The previous section provided an evaluation of the evidence. This section presents what the hearing officer believes are the facts in the case.

Findings of fact may simply be listed. They should be written in full sentences. They must relate back to the evaluation of evidence and be consistent with that analysis. It should be clear from the evaluation how the hearing officer is reaching each finding of fact in this section.

The reader by now should clearly understand an eighth point: what facts the hearing officer finds after weighing all the evidence.

CONCLUSIONS OF LAW

This section is closely related to the previous one on findings of fact. In that section, the hearing officer set forth the facts found after evaluating the evidence. Now the conclusions based on the findings of fact, mixed with the pertinent provisions of the law, are presented.

For example, the evidence in a case may be contradictory as to the child's emotional problem. The hearing officer evaluates the evidence and makes findings of fact, then applies the legal definition of "seriously emotionally disturbed" to the findings of fact regarding the child's condition, and reaches a conclusion as to whether or not the pupil is "seriously emotionally disturbed."

Conclusions of law are the last step of a classical syllogism structure. The syllogism of logic that many students learn in school is as follows:

1. All men are mortal. (This is the applicable law.)
2. Socrates is a man. (This is a finding of fact.)
3. Socrates is mortal. (This is a conclusion of law.)

Conclusions of law may simply be listed as such by the hearing officer. As with findings of fact, they also should be written in full sentences. They must relate back to the evaluation of evidence and be consistent with the findings of fact.

The reader should understand a ninth point: what conclusions the hearing officer reaches after applying the rules to the facts.

THE FINAL ORDER AND APPEAL INFORMATION

All the important findings and conclusions have been made in the previous sections. The written decision is clear on how the hearing officer made the findings of fact and reached the conclusions of law. The conclusions should not have been presented as though they were self-evident. The written decision has followed a logical format so that the reader can have full insight into the process and analysis used by the hearing officer and that it was consistent with the section before it and the one after it. Now the hearing officer must set forth the specific decision. The decisional options are discussed in the previous chapter.

The purpose of this decision section is to state clearly and explicitly what the parties must do now. What do the findings of fact and conclusions of law dictate must be done to provide the child with a free appropriate public education? The decision operationalizes those findings of fact and conclusions of law. It should state forthrightly what must be done, by whom, and by what date. The directives should be simple, specific, and measurable.

This section provides the final directives to the parties. If they are dissatisfied with the decision, they have rights to appeal. This section should reiterate briefly those appeal rights and provide information as to how parties might avail themselves of them.

The reader by now should clearly understand a tenth and final point: precisely what the hearing officer is ordering the parties to do to implement the conclusions and how they may appeal if they disagree with the outcome.

CASE STUDY OF PEGGY

The following is a sample decision that includes all of the sections and major points discussed in this chapter. This decision was selected because it involves a common issue. The hearing officer's style is such that every witness' testimony and every issue of the case are detailed thoroughly so that the reader can follow the train of thought easily.

FAIROAKS COUNTY PUBLIC SCHOOLS

Department of Special Services

COVER PAGE FOR HEARING OFFICER DECISION

Student's name Peggy Ouzer

Name of student's parents Robert and Joan Ouzer

Family address 120 Merrimac Street, Rochester, Ohio 65432

Name of family's legal counsel or
representative Joseph Cooperman

Address of
representative 243 Field Street, Rochester, Ohio 65429

Name of school district Fairoaks County Public Schools

Name of school district's legal counsel Thomas Chambers

Address of represen-
tative 7824 Woodland Avenue, Rochester, Ohio 65432

The student's current grade level or
school Bright Senior High School

The student's date of birth April 11, 1964

The date of the request for a hearing April 18, 1980

The date of the written decision May 12, 1980

Name of the hearing officer Michael H. Berger

The persons present at the hearing were:
Joseph Cooperman, Jr., attorney for the parents and student
Robert and Joan Ouzer, parents of the student
Katherine Tarbi, psychologist, FCPS
David R. Halpern, Jr., assistant principal, Bright High School
Rochelle Neal, principal, Community Mental Health Center
School
Edith Winograd, appeals coordinator, FCPS
Thomas Chambers, attorney for the FCPS
Miriam E. Sinken, psychologist, FCPS
Howard Smith, placement specialist, FCPS

FAIROAKS COUNTY PUBLIC SCHOOLS
Department of Special Services

In the matter of:　　　　　　)
　　　　　　　　　　　　　　)
Peggy　　　　　　　　　　　)　　　　　Case Number _____
　　　　　　　　　　　　　　)
Student　　　　　　　　　　　)

HEARING OFFICER'S DECISION

JURISDICTION AND PROCEDURAL HISTORY
In accordance with Fairoaks County Public Schools Regulation 29.88, Public Law 94-142, and other applicable laws and regulations, a hearing was held in the matter of Peggy. The hearing was held on April 17, 1980 before Hearing Officer Michael H. Berger.

This matter involved an appeal by the student's parents from a decision of the Fairoaks County Public Schools (hereinafter FCPS) Central Eligibility Committee. The decision stated that Peggy was ineligible for special education services in a program for emotionally disturbed students. The parents then formally invoked these due process procedures by their letter requesting an impartial due process hearing.

Notice of the time, date, and place of the hearing was furnished to the parties by the FCPS Department of Special Services. The notice also enumerated the due process rights which the FCPS is required to assure the parents in these proceedings.

At the outset of the hearing, the Hearing Officer determined that the parents had been fully informed of, and afforded, their due process rights as provided by law. The attorney for the parents waived the formal reading of those rights.

THE ISSUE
After hearing opening statements by both parties, the Hearing Officer determined that the issue to be resolved at this hearing was:

Was the action taken by the Fairoaks County Public Schools, of denying Peggy eligibility for special education services in a program for emotionally disturbed students, appropriate?

APPLICABLE LAW AND REGULATIONS

The laws and regulations applicable to the issue raised in this matter can be found in the Fairoaks County Public Schools Regulation 29.88; Public Law 94-142 (Section 612 of 20 U.S.C. 706); Public Law 94-142 Regulations (The Federal Register, August 23, 1977).

EVIDENCE CONSIDERED

The evidence considered by the Hearing Officer in this matter, consists of the following:

1. The testimony of Katherine Tarbi, Psychologist, FCPS.
2. The testimony of Miriam E. Sinken, Psychologist, FCPS.
3. The testimony of David R. Halpern, Jr., Assistant Principal, Bright High School.
4. The testimony of the father of the student.
5. The testimony of the mother of the student.
6. The seventy-one (71)-page document entitled *Exhibits Submitted by Fairoaks County Public Schools In the Impartial Due Process Hearing On Behalf of Peggy.*

The FCPS document contained all of the correspondence, referral information, and evaluations pertinent to this matter. The attorney for the parents stipulated to the fact that the document was complete as represented by the FCPS attorney. The attorney for the parents further stated that the document had been received by the parents sufficiently in advance of the hearing date to have allowed a thorough review of its contents.

The Hearing Officer did not consider as evidence in this matter the letter of Dr. William Rothman, dated April 15, 1980. The attorney for the FCPS objected to the admission of the letter on the following grounds:

- The letter was presented to the FCPS for the first time at the hearing. That is in contravention of the legal requirement that all documentary evidence be submitted to the opposing party at least five (5) days prior to the hearing.

- The contents of the letter were not based on any further treatment by Dr. Rothman, but were merely interpretation of contents in the earlier report prepared by Dr. Rothman. That earlier report is already part of the record because it was included in the FCPS document. The report should be allowed to "speak for itself" without further interpretation by Dr. Rothman.

- The letter is hearsay evidence bearing on significant questions in this matter. The admission of that letter would effectively deprive the FCPS of the opportunity to cross-examine Dr. Rothman on the assertions he makes therein.

The Hearing Officer sustained the objection for the reasons enumerated above. The letter was made a part of the record, but not considered by the Hearing Officer in rendering this decision.

The seventy-one-page document mentioned above is also included in the record of this matter. Its contents are incorporated in this decision by reference. The testimonial evidence presented at the hearing is summarized below.

SUMMARY OF THE TESTIMONY
Mr. Thomas Chambers, Attorney, presented the case for the FCPS. He argued that Peggy is not eligible to receive special education services in a program for emotionally disturbed students because she is not a "seriously emotionally disturbed" child, as defined in the law. Rather, this sixteen-year-old girl simply does not want to go to school.

Mr. Chambers contended that Peggy is able to learn in a regular school setting such as her current placement at Bright High School. However, the student refuses to go to school, and efforts by her parents to get her to go to school have not been effective. The student is unquestionably a serious disciplinary problem. But that does not mean that she is necessarily a "seriously emotionally disturbed" child, as her parents contend. It would be short-sighted to categorize this student as "seriously emotionally disturbed," when she is not, simply to make her eligible for special educational services. The label of "seriously emotionally disturbed" could have a negative impact on the student in the long run.

According to Mr. Chambers, Peggy may indeed benefit from a residential program, as the parents are requesting. Many students do better in different residential programs, such as a boarding school or military-style school. In such programs the student is required to function within a more structured routine than that required within a regular public school. However, that does not mean that those students, or this particular student, are handicapped by serious emotional disturbance.

Mr. Chambers further asserted that, unfortunately, many parents turn to the FCPS special education programs to solve what are essentially family or social problems, rather than true educational problems. The FCPS Central Eligibility Committee decided in this case that Peggy was ineligible for special education services in a program for emotionally disturbed students. The members of the committee believed that Peggy did not meet any of the legal criteria to qualify for such a categorical program, and to place her in that category would be inappropriate. Therefore, Mr. Chambers requested that the Hearing Officer uphold the FCPS Central Eligibility Committee's decision.

The first witness presented by the FCPS was Katherine Tarbi, Psychologist, who had sat on the FCPS Central Eligibility Committee. Ms. Tarbi testified that the most noteworthy aspect of this student's records was her extremely poor school attendance. A number of different educational programs had been offered to the student, but her failure to attend the programs rendered each one unsuccessful. Ms. Tarbi discussed some of those educational programs. They included a learning disability resource program, homebound instruction, and enrollment in a small private school (by her parents at their own expense). According to Ms. Tarbi, the Central Eligibility Committee was unanimous in its decision that this student was ineligible for special educational services in a program for the emotionally disturbed. Ms. Tarbi stated that this student manifested behaviors and attitudes which were very immature for her age. School experiences have not been satisfying for Peggy. School is extremely hard work for her, and she is unwilling to make the necessary effort to achieve. Her problems seem to reflect a characterological disturbance rather than any true emotional disturbance.

Upon cross-examination, Ms. Tarbi stated that she had never actually met Peggy and was testifying from her familiarity with the records and evaluations of Peggy. Ms. Tarbi stated that she did not believe that the student's problems were caused by emotional disturbance. She defined an emotionally disturbed child as one who feels anxiety, guilt, or intense concern about some issue. The emotionally disturbed child's problem is an internalized problem. He or she may have trouble relating to other people because he or she is so uncomfortable within his or her own skin.

Ms. Tarbi further stated that she was not only familiar with Dr. Rothman's report, but had put great weight on it in reaching her own decision about Peggy. She was aware that Dr. Rothman had recommended a residential setting for this student. However, Ms. Tarbi pointed out that there is a distinction between placing a student in a residential setting for psychiatric treatment, and placing a student in a residential setting for a structured routine. Peggy may well benefit from a residential setting where she would be required to adhere to a structured routine. But Peggy does not need a residential setting to provide treatment for emotional disturbance.

According to Ms. Tarbi, the information on Peggy does not show that she would meet any of the criteria under the legal definition of "seriously emotionally disturbed." Ms. Tarbi felt that Dr. Rothman's report did not describe a seriously emotionally disturbed student. His diagnosis of "adjustment reaction to adolescence" is generally not considered an emotional disturbance. According to Ms. Tarbi, Peggy's problems are characterological in nature. Those problems may indeed make it difficult for her to get along well with her family. Also, her nonconforming behavior may be one way of controlling her parents.

The second witness presented by the FCPS was Miriam E. Sinken, Clinical Psychologist, Area IV. Ms. Sinken referred to her report which is contained in the record. In summarizing her evaluation, Ms. Sinken stated that she had administered a full battery of tests including assessments of the student's emotional functioning. Ms. Sinken found that Peggy was functioning in the average range of intelligence but was emotionally immature. Peggy's self-concept was inadequate and she tended to seek immediate gratification, rather than invest effort to reap benefits at a later point. Her school experiences have not been pleasurable, so Peggy opts for immediate gratification by avoiding school. She desires not to attend school, and she can obtain fulfillment of her wish because she controls her family environment. She is allowed to behave as she wishes at home, and she need not conform to the expectations of others. Her family allows her to carry on a life style which includes refusing to go to school, not accepting any household chores, sleeping very late until the afternoon, going out with friends after their school hours and not returning until the very late hours of the night, and refusing to abide by any restrictions set down by her parents. Peggy is not emotionally disturbed because, if she were, her social functioning, as well as school functioning, would be depressed. The student is clearly not withdrawing from her social life. She carries on a very active one.

Upon cross-examination, Ms. Sinken testified that Peggy is not a "normal" child. But, nor is she an emotionally disturbed child. Peggy's problem appears to be characterological in nature and supported by her home environment which she controls. Peggy's emotional development is somewhat retarded in that her impulse control is more like that of a much younger child than a child her own age. As a child grows older, he or she is more able to control his or her impulses and postpone gratification. But Peggy's behavior shows that she is not able to do this very well. Yet, she is not anxious or unhappy about her situation. She appears to be rather content. An emotionally disturbed child usually reflects considerable anxiety and unhappiness about the presenting problem.

Ms. Sinken stated that the parents might need to seek the assistance of the juvenile court in trying to establish a structured environment in the home for Peggy. She can understand Dr. Rothman's recommendation that Peggy be placed in a residential setting because Ms. Sinken believes that the parents may be incapable of providing the necessary control and structure. But such a residential setting could simply be a boarding school.

Upon questioning by the Hearing Officer, Ms. Sinken stated that Peggy does not present a case of a child who is so emotionally disturbed that she is school phobic. Such a child's emotional disturbance is so great that he or she could not function in the regular classroom setting. A child with a true school phobia would be troubled by an irrational fear and would manifest reality contact difficulties. Peggy does not exhibit such characteristics. School is simply not a gratifying experience for her, so she chooses not to attend. A child with such serious emotional disturbance that he or she could not function in school would manifest depression, in which he or she internalizes anger. The anger is self-directed and robs the child of energy to achieve on any level. This would cause the child to withdraw in other spheres of his or her life, in addition to school. Peggy seems to have the interest and energy to develop a variety of interpersonal relationships with her peers in the social sphere.

David R. Halpern, Jr., Assistant Principal, Bright High School, was also called as a witness for the FCPS. Mr. Halpern clarified Peggy's status at Bright High School. Since Peggy had missed so many days of school, she had been dropped from the attendance rolls for the purpose of financial accountability to the State Department of Education. The state government provides the local education agency with monies for education depending on the average daily attendance of students. Peggy's excessive absences caused the school officials to drop her from the rolls for the purpose of such computations. However, she was not suspended from Bright High School and she remains eligible for immediate reenrollment there.

Joseph Cooperman, Jr., Attorney, presented the case for the parents and child. He argued that Peggy has exhibited a history of learning difficulties over a long period of time. This history has been well-known to the FCPS authorities. The parents have cooperated in every respect with the recommendations of the FCPS personnel. A number of different educational programs have been tried with this student, and they have all failed. Therefore, the next step is to provide Peggy with an education in a residential facility. Such a recommendation was made in this case by Dr. Rothman, the psychiatrist to which the parents had been referred by the FCPS. The reports from the Learning Disabilities Center, which are included in the record, also support such a recommendation.

According to Mr. Cooperman, the facts in this case demonstrate that Peggy is a "seriously emotionally disturbed" child as defined in the law. Therefore, the residential educational program which she requires is a matter of legal right that the FCPS must provide her. The FCPS personnel have dealt with this child in good faith throughout. But their efforts have all been unsuccessful, and the decision of the Central Eligibility Committee was a mistake, an honest one, but a mistake nevertheless.

Mr. Cooperman stated that the FCPS personnel contended that the child's refusal to go to school was the parents' fault. It was not the parents' fault. They have another child who has gone through the FCPS successfully. They have done everything to make Peggy go to school, short of physically restraining her and transporting her to school, kicking and screaming. But regardless of the cause of Peggy's emotional disturbance, it *exists* today. The law is only concerned about whether the handicap exists in the youngster, not what it was caused by. The law defines "seriously emotionally disturbed" and details criteria therein. Peggy's behavioral manifestations meet those criteria, as shown by the professional evaluations of the FCPS personnel, and other personnel recommended to the parents by the FCPS.

According to Mr. Cooperman, the opinion of Dr. Rothman and other professionals is that this child needs residential care. The FCPS Central Eligibility Committee's decision effectively denies such services to this student. It is from that decision that the parents appeal. Mr. Cooperman requested that the Hearing Officer determine that the student is in need of such special educational services. He also requested that the Hearing Officer direct the FCPS to place this student in an appropriate residential program.

The parents of Peggy testified in their own behalf. They explained that Peggy had been adopted at four months of age. Peggy had then been identified as having a dyslexic learning disability. She was only about six or seven years old at the time.

The parents stated that they had placed Peggy in a small private school for kindergarten through grade 3. Then they placed her in the FCPS. She had been in public school through her junior high school years. It was in the 1976–77 school year, when Peggy was in eighth grade, that she had begun to have significant academic difficulties. The parents then sought professional help as recommended by the FCPS personnel. According to the parents, Peggy had begun grade 9 at Bright High School, during the 1977–78 school year. The FCPS had found that Peggy was eligible for special education services in a program for *learning disabled students*. However, she was absent for an excessive number of days during that term. Consequently, she had been terminated from the Learning Disabilities Resource program, which was located within Fairoaks High School.

The parents testified that they attempted to obtain special education services in a program for *emotionally disturbed* students in August, 1978. But the Central Eligibility Committee found Peggy ineligible for such services. The parents then withdrew her from the FCPS in September, 1978, and enrolled her in Pleasant Site Acres, a private school. However, that school terminated Peggy the next month, October, 1978, due to [her] lack of attendance.

The parents then reenrolled Peggy at Bright High School in the FCPS. She again began to have academic and attendance problems. The FCPS referred the parents to a number of psychiatrists, one of whom was Dr. Rothman.

The parents testified that Peggy began seeing Dr. Rothman in November, 1978, for regular psychiatric treatment. In January, 1979, Peggy received homebound instruction from the FCPS upon Dr. Rothman's certification that she was under his treatment and could not cope with the regular school environment at that time.

According to the parents, the FCPS had agreed to continue the homebound services only so long as Peggy was under Dr. Rothman's care. Dr. Rothman, however, terminated with Peggy because she refused to see him. Consequently, the FCPS stopped the homebound instruction in March, 1979. The parents were then at a loss as to what to do. They went back to Dr. Rothman, who agreed to see Peggy again. Dr. Rothman and the parents also agreed on a plan whereby Peggy would start to attend school for one hour a day, while still receiving the homebound instruction services. But that plan did not work. It was at that point that Dr. Rothman had recommended that Peggy required treatment in a residential program, according to the parents' testimony.

The parents further testified that the child has not attended any school since the beginning of the current school year. In November, 1979, they had again received a decision from the Central Eligibility Committee that Peggy was ineligible for special education services in a program for emotionally disturbed students. As a result of that decision, the parents filed this appeal.

The parents stated that they have done everything possible to get Peggy to go to school. They have not indulged their child. Peggy has had almost no privileges in the home. The parents would have even agreed to having the FCPS take Peggy to juvenile court, if the FCPS thought that would help.

Moreover, the parents contended that they have tried to obtain an appropriate education for her even when she refused to go to school. The parents have followed the recommendations of the FCPS personnel, and then the recommendations from the private professionals. According to the parents, Peggy is a learning disabled child and the FCPS has not addressed her needs. The parents feel as though they have been unable to convince the FCPS personnel that their child is learning disabled. Moreover, the FCPS personnel have been inconsistent among themselves in their findings about Peggy. One FCPS professional seems to have concluded that Peggy has learning disabilities, and another concluded that she does not. The FCPS personnel have genuinely attempted to help Peggy to learn, but their efforts have not worked. The evaluations and recommendations of the professionals concluded that Peggy needs a residential program. The parents asserted that such a program is Peggy's right.

EVALUATION OF THE ARGUMENTS AND EVIDENCE
Public Law 94-142 provides parents with the right to a due process hearing when the public school system takes an action, or refuses to take an action, regarding the identification, evaluation, or the provision of a free appropriate public education to a handicapped child.

In this matter, the Fairoaks County Public Schools decided that Peggy is ineligible for special education services in a program for emotionally disturbed students. This decision was made by the FCPS Central Eligibility Committee because they believed that the "data submitted does not support the fact that Peggy is seriously emotionally disturbed." In essence, the public school system was refusing to take further action with regard to placing this child in a special education program for emotionally disturbed students. It was that refusal to act which the parents challenged. This hearing was held pursuant to the parents' appeal from the FCPS decision that their child is ineligible for special education services in a program for emotionally disturbed students.

The above point of clarification is necessary because throughout the hearing, the parents and the parents' attorney seemed to have been discussing additional issues that were not before the Hearing Officer. The attorney for the parents requested that the Hearing Officer direct the FCPS to place Peggy in a residential program. The parents repeatedly emphasized that Peggy has dyslexia and other learning disabilities. They stated that they had tried on numerous occasions to convince the FCPS personnel that their child is learning disabled. But these issues were not before the Hearing Officer at this hearing. Also, the FCPS might not disagree with the parents' positions on these issues. The issue in this case is simply whether or not Peggy is eligible for a program for "seriously emotionally disturbed" students.

The threshold question under the law is whether or not the child is "handicapped." A child can only be considered "handicapped" if he or she falls into one of the categories of handicapping conditions defined in the law. The child is not entitled to special education or related services unless he or she is considered "handicapped." The particular type of special education services, such as residential placement, cannot even be addressed until it is first determined whether or not the child is even "handicapped." If it is determined that the child is not "handicapped," then the child is not entitled to any type of special education services, much less a residential placement. If the contention is that the child is "handicapped" by reason of being "seriously emotionally disturbed," then that contention must first be proven, before issues of residential placement or learning disabilities can be addressed.

In this case, the threshold question is whether or not Peggy is "handicapped" by reason of being "seriously emotionally disturbed." The FCPS contended that she is not. The parents contended that she is.

The law defines "seriously emotionally disturbed" as follows:

"The term means a condition exhibiting one or more of the following characteristics over a long period of time and to a marked degree, which adversely affects educational performance:

"(A) An inability to learn which cannot be explained by intellectual, sensory, or health factors;

"(B) An inability to build or maintain satisfactory interpersonal relationships with peers and teachers;

"(C) Inappropriate types of behavior or feelings under normal circumstances;

"(D) A general pervasive mood of unhappiness or depression; or

"(E) A tendency to develop physical symptoms or fears associated with personal or school problems."

The characteristics listed in the definition above may very well be true of all children at some times and to some degree. That is why the question of severity, reflected in the phrase "over a long period of time and to a marked degree," is of special significance. The Hearing Officer weighed Peggy's condition against each of the five definitional characteristics with the question of severity in mind.

Does Peggy exhibit an inability to learn which cannot be explained by intellectual, sensory, or health factors?

The comprehensive psychological evaluation performed by Ms. Sinken indicates that Peggy is an adolescent who possesses the intellectual abilities necessary for scholastic achievement. Dr. Rothman's report would support Ms. Sinken's conclusion in that regard. Other reports from FCPS professionals and professionals at the Learning Disability Center suggest that Peggy has specific learning disabilities. Dr. Rothman's report would also support that finding. He stated in his report that Peggy "has a normal range IQ with learning disabilities affecting reasoning, special order, arithmetic and spelling."

The Hearing Officer believes that Peggy does not have an inability to learn, or if she does, it can be explained by sensory, health, or other factors. Peggy has indeed failed to learn. But it was not proven that the reason she has failed to learn is because of an "inability to learn." Rather, it appears that Peggy has failed to learn because she did not go to school. She did not even go to school to receive specially designed instruction to meet her needs as a learning disabled student. She did not even attend when the teachers came to her home. Therefore, since the discrepancy between Peggy's intellectual abilities and her actual academic performance can be explained by other factors, the Hearing Officer cannot conclude that the discrepancy is caused by some underlying emotional disturbance.

Does Peggy exhibit an inability to build or maintain satisfactory interpersonal relationships with peers and teachers?

The evidence shows that Peggy maintains an extremely active social life. According to the FCPS social case history, the testimony of the FCPS personnel at the hearing, and the testimony of the parents, Peggy is out of the house socializing with friends until very late at night on a regular basis. From this evidence, the Hearing Officer cannot find that Peggy has an inability to build or maintain satisfactory interpersonal relationships with peers. In regard to teachers, there was no evidence provided by either party about the student's interpersonal relationships. Therefore, the Hearing Officer cannot conclude that Peggy exhibits an inability to build or maintain satisfactory interpersonal relationships with teachers. If anything, the evidence shows that the student has not had sufficient opportunity to build or maintain interpersonal relationships with teachers because she does not allow herself to come into contact with them.

Does Peggy exhibit inappropriate types of behavior or feelings under normal circumstances?

The evidence was overwhelming that Peggy has been absent from school for an excessive number of days during the prior school year, and has not even attended school this current school year. Such behavior is obviously inappropriate relative to the large majority of school-aged children. But is this behavior truly inappropriate relative to the environment in which Peggy functions?

According to Dr. Rothman's report, Peggy "has developed a strong dislike of school and external controls and for some time has found little satisfaction or sense of success at school." The testimony of Ms. Tarbi and Ms. Sinken supported the point that such *feelings* are not necessarily inappropriate among adolescents under normal circumstances. Most people even relate to this point from their own experience. Adolescents generally dislike school and external controls much of the time. It is only Peggy's *behavior* as a result of those feelings which is inappropriate, when compared to most children her age.

But the evidence shows that Peggy's behavior may not be so inappropriate or irrational in the context of her own environment. In other words, she may not be exhibiting inappropriate behavior "under normal circumstances." The circumstances in this case consist of her home environment. Ms. Sinken testified that Peggy controls her home environment. Peggy is allowed to do as she pleases. The FCPS social case history supports Ms. Sinken's assertion. That report states that, "It appears the parents have over-indulged and pampered Peggy. Discipline appears to be lacking in the home."

The parents disputed that contention at the hearing. However, the Hearing Officer finds that the weight of the evidence falls against the parents on this point. Even Dr. Rothman suggested in his report that Peggy's behavior is given room to flourish because of the circumstances of her environment. Dr. Rothman stated that, "There is no strong evidence of school phobia. Her response (to her feelings of dislike for school and external controls), to develop a pattern of avoidance of school, and to assert willfully that she can do what she wants to do, appears to be attitudinal, with the secondary gain of freedom from authority, coping with school work and the expectations of teachers."

The Hearing Officer believes that most children have normal feelings of dislike of school and desires to be free from controls by authority figures. But most children do not have the opportunity to actually live a life style based on those feelings and desires. If they could control their environment, as the evidence suggests Peggy does, then it would be likely that many more children would be living in the manner Peggy does. But the Hearing Officer does not believe that such a lack of structure and parental control is the norm in most family environments. Therefore, the Hearing Officer cannot find that Peggy exhibits inappropriate types of behavior or feelings under *normal* circumstances.

Does Peggy exhibit a general pervasive mood of unhappiness or depression?

There was no evidence submitted showing that this student exhibits unhappiness. In fact, Ms. Sinken's testimony suggested that Peggy is not unhappy with her situation. Rather, she is quite content. Ms. Sinken also testified that Peggy does not exhibit any depression to a marked degree. According to Ms. Sinken, depression is a form of anger turned inward which robs the individual of his or her energy to function in the various spheres of life. However, Peggy appears to have a great deal of interest and energy to function in the social sphere. Dr. Rothman supports Ms. Sinken's testimony by the statements in his report. He stated that "There is little overt evidence of depression. . . ." Therefore, the Hearing Officer cannot find that Peggy exhibits a general pervasive mood of unhappiness or depression.

Does Peggy exhibit a tendency to develop physical symptoms or fears associated with personal or school problems?

There was no evidence submitted to prove that this student has physical symptoms or ailments other than a normal adolescent. There was also no evidence presented to show that Peggy has a tendency to develop fears associated with personal or school problems. It is clear that this student does not want to go to school;

that she does not like school; that she does not want external controls; that she feels she is not as able as other students; and that she finds little satisfaction or sense of success at school. But there is no evidence that this student has fears related to school difficulties, or is otherwise afraid of school. Dr. Rothman clearly states in his report that in Peggy's case, "There is no strong evidence of school phobia." Therefore, the Hearing Officer cannot conclude that Peggy exhibits a tendency to develop physical symptoms or fears associated with personal or school problems.

Thus, it appears from the evidence that Peggy's problem does not fit within any one of the characteristics listed in the law's definition of "seriously emotionally disturbed." But the Hearing Officer goes beyond simply applying the definitional criteria to Peggy's case. In viewing this child as a whole, from the evidence presented, the Hearing Officer does not believe that this child manifests a true emotional disturbance. There is a danger inherent in this process of identifying as emotionally disturbed, children who choose to behave somewhat differently than their peers. Is Peggy a child whose behavioral deviation is caused by emotional problems? Or is she a child whose behavior is simply different? Behavior that is strange, unconventional, immature, unwise, or deviant cannot in and of itself be regarded as a sign of an emotional disturbance. If it were, every juvenile delinquent, Person In Need of Supervision (PINS), or other adolescent brought before the court would be labeled as being "seriously emotionally disturbed." The juvenile courts throughout the nation take jurisdiction over adolescents every day who are beyond the control of their parents, or are incorrigible for one reason or another. These children may indeed have problems in conforming to society's rules, but that does not mean that they are necessarily "seriously emotionally disturbed."

The question then becomes; "How does one know whether a child's behavior is simply deviant or seriously emotionally disturbed?"

One way of differentiating the two can be found in the testimony of Ms. Tarbi and the testimony of Ms. Sinken. These witnesses provided definitions of serious emotional disturbance which differed from the one given in the law. Ms. Tarbi stated that an emotionally disturbed child feels anxiety, guilt, and intense concern over some problem which he or she has internalized. The child may have trouble relating to other people because he or she is so uncomfortable within him or herself. Ms. Sinken stated that a child with serious emotional disturbance is unable to respond appropriately to his or her environment. Such children frequently manifest difficulty in their thought processes. They often show reality contact difficulties. They are likely to be depressed and to internalize anger. The anger is self-directed and robs the child of energy to achieve on any level. The seriously emotionally disturbed child is likely to withdraw in a number of spheres of his or her life. From the testimony of these two professionals, it can be seen that the behavior of the seriously emotionally disturbed child is not a matter of choice but of *necessity*. The disturbance controls the child.

The evidence in this case is convincing that Peggy's behavior is a matter of choice. In reaching this conclusion, the Hearing Officer attributes considerable weight to the report by Dr. Rothman. Both parties to this proceeding also stated that Dr. Rothman's report was critical. The Hearing Officer believes that the most important portion of that report is the part where Dr. Rothman discussed his findings from his mental status examination of Peggy. Dr. Rothman stated:

"Peggy is alert and oriented with intact recent and past memory functions. There is no evidence of mental confusion. She has a normal range IQ with learning disabilities affecting reasoning, spatial order, arithmetic and spelling. There is no evidence of thought process disturbance, delusions, or hallucinations. The stream of thought and content are rational and appropriate without looseness of thought associations. There is little overt evidence of depression since she actively orients to and involves herself in seeking gratification of wishes and actively and insistently avoids attending to dysphoric thoughts or confrontations from others. It is inferred that she has an underlying view of herself as handicapped, but she shows little resultant sense of loss of self-esteem. She manifests moderately high anxiety, dissipated in escape fantasies and activities. She has developed a strong dislike of school and external controls and for some time has found little satisfaction or sense of success at school. There is no strong evidence of school phobia. Her response, to develop a pattern of avoidance of school, and to assert willfully that she can do what she wants to do, appears to be attitudinal, with the secondary gain of freedom from authority, coping with schoolwork and the expectations of teachers. She does not strongly experience a sense of conflict or guilt over not attending school. She uses projection and denial as predominant defensive maneuvers obtaining gratification of dependency needs in hostile manipulating ways. Judgment is poor in most spheres of normal social expectations but consistent with her expressed goals. Insight is markedly impaired."

The consensus of the professionals, including Dr. Rothman, Ms. Tarbi, and Ms. Sinken, seems to be that Peggy's problems are primarily characterological. That is, they result from certain traits, attitudes, or notions that are part of her character or personality. Ms. Tarbi stated that Peggy's character problems may indeed make it hard for her to get along in her family, but that does not necessarily mean that the student is emotionally disturbed. Ms. Sinken stated that Peggy's character problems have been exacerbated by her family environment. While many children have character problems, their family environments provide structure and controls which socialize the children to act appropriately. The evidence in this case shows that Peggy's family environment does not provide such structure and controls. Therein lies the source of her problems, according to the FCPS testimony and Dr. Rothman's report. Peggy asserts willfully that she can do what she wants to do, and her family environment allows her to do just that.

The evidence does not show the source of Peggy's deviant behavior to be a serious emotional disturbance causing her such internal stress that it controls the way she functions. Peggy's deviant behavior appears to be a matter of choice and not of necessity. Indeed, if Peggy were only a couple of years older, her behavior could not even have been tagged as "deviant." Society does not require adolescents to attend school after they reach a certain age. Many drop out from school as soon as they may do so. Peggy may not do so at this time, and that is the fact that makes this primarily family problem a school problem as well.

The Hearing Officer believes that Peggy's behavior is more disturbing than disturbed. Since the Hearing Officer cannot conclude that Peggy is "seriously emotionally disturbed," she is ineligible for special education services in a program for such students.

The Hearing Officer will not decide any issue of residential placement for Peggy. This student may very well benefit from such a program. But she is not entitled to be placed in such a program at the expense of the FCPS. Such a placement must be at the parents' election and at their own expense. Even if the Hearing Officer were to have found that Peggy was "seriously emotionally disturbed," the FCPS would not have been obligated, necessarily, to place her in a residential program. They would have been required to place her in the least restrictive educational environment. Under the facts of this case, the FCPS might have placed her in only a day program with special transportation services to and from home to assure her attendance.

Moreover, the fact that certain professionals recommended a residential program for this student is not controlling in this proceeding. Those professionals might have recommended such a program because the student could benefit from it, even though she may not require it for reasons of emotional disturbance. Or they might have recommended such a program because the parents have not been able to control the child, even though the child is not emotionally disturbed. There are a number of reasons or considerations which influenced the professionals in recommending residential placement. But the FCPS is only responsible for the student's placement in a program for seriously emotionally disturbed students, if it is determined that Peggy is herself "seriously emotionally disturbed." It is here determined that she is not.

The Hearing Officer also will not decide the issue of Peggy's eligibility for special education services in a program for learning disabled students. There was ample evidence submitted to prove that Peggy has specific learning disabilities, or at least had them up until recently. The most recent psychological evaluation performed by Ms. Sinken suggested that Peggy does not have learning disabilities, or does not have them anymore. However, the FCPS had at one point, according to the evidence, found Peggy eligible for special education services in a program for learning disabled students. But this decision cannot concern itself with the status of Peggy's eligibility as a learning disabled student. The hearing was confined to the issue of whether or not Peggy is eligible for special education services in a program for "seriously emotionally disturbed" students. It is here decided that she is not.

FINDINGS OF FACT
After careful evaluation of the evidence, the Hearing Officer makes the following findings of fact:

1. The student had an excessive number of absences during the school year 1978–79. She has also been absent from school every day during the current school year of 1979–80.
2. The parents have been unable to provide the structure and controls over the student that are necessary to assure her attendance at school. The parents have made numerous and costly good faith attempts to help the student so that she would attend school. However, their efforts have been unsuccessful.
3. The student does not exhibit an inability to learn which cannot be explained by intellectual, sensory, or health factors.
4. The student does not exhibit an inability to build or maintain satisfactory interpersonal relationships with peers and teachers.
5. The student does not exhibit inappropriate types of behavior or feelings under normal circumstances.
6. The student does not exhibit a general pervasive mood of unhappiness or depression.
7. The student does not exhibit a tendency to develop physical symptoms or fears associated with personal or school problems.
8. The evidence strongly suggests, although it is inadequate to conclude, that the student has a disorder in one or more of the basic psychological processes involved in understanding or in using language, spoken or written, which may manifest itself in such learning disabilities as an imperfect ability to listen, think, speak, read, write, spell, or to do mathematical calculations. Further evaluation of these characteristics appears to be indicated in light of the conflicting evidence.

CONCLUSIONS OF LAW

After consideration of the pertinent law as applied to the Findings of Fact above, the Hearing Officer reaches the following legal conclusions:

1. The student is not handicapped by reason of being "seriously emotionally disturbed," as that categorical term is defined in Public Law 94-142.
2. The student is ineligible for special education services in a program for seriously emotionally disturbed students, in accordance with the guidelines for eligibility for such a program

as set forth in Fairoaks County Public Schools Regulation 29.88.

DECISION AND APPEAL INFORMATION

Therefore, in consideration of the Findings of Fact and Conclusions of Law, it is hereby decided this 12th day of May, 1980 that:

1. The student and her parents are to report to Bright High School on the first school day following receipt of this decision, for the purpose of enrolling the student in an appropriate academic program.
2. The FCPS shall consider all of the assessment data currently available regarding this student, and perform such additional assessments as they deem appropriate with parental permission. The FCPS shall then offer the student a program in accordance with the assessment information.
3. The student shall attend her assigned classes each and every day that they are in session, unless formally excused from doing so by her parents or FCPS personnel.
4. The FCPS shall assign an attendance officer, counselor, social worker, or other appropriate employee to closely monitor the student's attendance, and assist her and her parents in any way possible to assure the student's attendance at school.
5. If the parents are unable to assure the student's attendance in school, it is recommended that they seek assistance from the juvenile court, community mental health center, or other social service agencies.
6. If the parents are unable to assure the student's attendance in school, and they fail to seek assistance from community resources, the FCPS shall proceed to bring this matter to the attention of a court of competent jurisdiction.

This decision is final unless it is appealed by one of the parties. If one of the parties does wish to appeal this decision, they should contact Dr. Edith Winograd, Acting Appeals Specialist, FCPS, Department of Special Services, 185 Castlebar Road, Rochester, Ohio 65432, for information as to the procedures to be followed.

However, during the pendency of any further administrative appeal or judicial proceeding regarding this matter, the student may not remain in her status quo placement, i.e., her home without any educational program. The FCPS and the parents of the student must agree to place the student in some public school program until the completion of all proceedings. The law provides that during the pendency of any such proceedings, the child involved must remain in his or her present educational placement. But, in this case the student does not really have any present educational placement. Technically, her present educational placement is Bright High School. However, her de facto educational placement has been her home where she received homebound instruction during the previous school year, and where she received no instruction during this school year. The absence of an educational program is *not* acceptable. If the parties legally pursue this matter further, they must agree on some educational program during the pendency of the proceedings, even if that program is only minimal homebound instruction.

By copy of this decision, I would like to thank all those who participated in the hearing.

Respectfully submitted,

Michael H. Berger
Impartial Hearing Officer

Part VII

Specific Concerns

In the special education decision-making process, a number of related issues arise that impact on the due process rights of the handicapped students involved. This part discusses some specific concerns related to private schools, confidentiality of information, minimum competency testing programs, and disciplinary actions as they pertain to handicapped students.

Chapter 26

Private Schools

The Public Law 94-142 regulations include a subpart devoted to private schools. This was intended to help alleviate some of the confusion between handicapped children placed in, or referred to, private schools by the state or by local educational agencies and those whose parents choose to educate them in such schools. The major difference between these two groups of children is in who bears the cost of the private school.

PLACEMENTS BY PUBLIC AGENCIES

A free appropriate public education must be made available to each handicapped child by the public agencies of the state. Subject to the requirements on least restrictive environment, this could include placement in or referral to a private school or facility. Such a placement or referral must be at no cost to the parent. Specifically, the regulations state:

> Responsibility of State educational agency.
> Each State educational agency shall insure that a handicapped child who is placed in or referred to a private school or facility by a public agency:
> (a) Is provided special education and related services:
> (1) In conformance with an individualized education program which meets the requirements of [the section on IEPs];
> (2) At no cost to the parents; and
> (3) At a school or facility which meets the standards that apply to State and local educational agencies (including the requirements in this part); and
> (b) Has all of the rights of a handicapped child who is served by a public agency. (§ 121a.401)

In implementing this responsibility, each state must:

(a) Monitor compliance through procedures such as written reports, on-site visits, and parent questionnaires;
(b) Disseminate copies of applicable standards to each private school and facility to which a public agency has referred or placed a handicapped child; and
(c) Provide an opportunity for those private schools and facilities to participate in the development and revision of State standards which apply to them. (§121a.402)

Following is a list of suggested standards a state education agency might require of private facilities if they wish to receive referrals from public agencies:

- The facility should have an instructional program for students with one or more of the handicapping conditions listed in P.L. 94-142 and its regulations.

- The facility's program objectives must agree with the educational and treatment programs required to meet the needs of students with the type(s) of handicapping condition(s) that the facility says it serves.

- The facility must agree in its contract with the public agency that it does not discriminate against any employee or applicant for employment or student or applicant for admission because of race, creed, color, sex, national origin, or handicapping condition.

- The facility must agree in its contract that it will ensure that each handicapped child it accepts will have all of the rights of those served directly by a public agency.

- The facility must contract to provide for due process procedures in the event of the suspension or expulsion of any student placed there by the public agency.

- The facility's contract must provide for representatives of the public agency to conduct onsite inspections, evaluation, or studies of the institution, its programs, and the progress of any student placed there by the agency. The onsite visits are to assure the facility's compliance with the agency's educational standards, its contract with the agency, or any applicable federal laws and regulations.

- The facility must provide an IEP, including specialized curriculum, equipment, and methodology, that is appropriate to meet the needs of the students placed there. The IEPs it provides must provide flexibility sufficient for prescriptive planning and programming to meet individual students' needs and conform with P.L. 94-142 and its regulations.

- The facility's ratio of students to teachers must be within standards established for each profession by a nationally recognized organization acceptable to the state education agency.

- All professional staff members who teach or work directly with students must be certified or licensed by the jurisdiction in which the facility is located to work with the types of handicapping conditions served there.

- The facility must be licensed or certified by the jurisdiction in which it is located in compliance with all federal, state, and local laws. This must include evidence that the facility is in compliance with all applicable health, safety, and fire regulations, codes, and ordinances.

- The facility must not impose any fee upon parents or guardians that is not specifically approved in the contract with the public agency or as a prerequisite for the acceptance of the student.

An issue that frequently arises when a public agency places a child in a private school is how to involve the school's representative in the development of the IEP. Generally, such a child already has been receiving special education and the parents and school personnel have been involved over a prolonged period in attempting to find the most appropriate placement.

At some point in this process (e.g., at a meeting where the child's current IEP is being reviewed), the possibility of residential school placement might be proposed—by either the parents or school. If both agree, then the matter would be explored with the residential school. A subsequent meeting would be conducted to finalize the IEP. At that meeting, the public agency must ensure that a representative of the residential school either (1) is present or (2) participates through individual or conference telephone calls.

PLACEMENTS BY PARENTS

Even if a free appropriate public education is available, parents may choose not to accept it. They may opt to send the child to a private school. If this occurs, the law does not require the state or local educational agency to bear the cost of the private school.

For children placed in private schools by their parents, the state and its local educational agencies have a different duty. They must design their programs so that such children can participate in special education and related services offered by the local educational agencies if their parents so desire. Specifically, the regulations state:

> Placement of children by parents.
> (a) If a handicapped child has available a free appropriate public education and the parents choose to place the child in a private school or facility, the public agency is not required by this part to pay for the child's education at the private school or facility. However, the public agency shall make services available to the child . . .
> (b) Disagreements between a parent and a public agency regarding the availability of a program appropriate for the child, and the question of financial responsibility, are subject to the due process procedures . . . (§ 121a.403)

> State educational agency responsibility.
> The State educational agency shall insure that:
> (a) To the extent consistent with their number and location in the State, provision is made for the participation of private school handicapped children in the program assisted or carried out under this part by providing them with special education and related services . . . (§ 121a.451)

> Local educational agency responsibility.
> (a) Each local educational agency shall provide special education and related services designed to meet the needs of private school handicapped children residing in the jurisdiction of the agency.
> (b) Each local educational agency shall provide private school handicapped children with genuine opportunities to participate in special education and related services consistent with the number of those children and their needs. (§ 121a.452)

These responsibilities of public agencies raise issues concerning the needs of private school handicapped children, the number who will participate, and the types of special education and related services that the local educational agency will provide. The regulations require that these issues

> must be determined after consultation with persons knowledgeable of the needs of these children, on a basis comparable to that

used in providing for the participation of handicapped children enrolled in public schools. (§ 121a.453)

There are logistical factors to be considered by public agencies in implementing these responsibilities.

Services to private school handicapped children may be provided through such arrangements as dual enrollment, educational radio and television, and the provision of mobile educational services and equipment. (§ 121a.454)

A key point that public and private agencies should keep in mind is that the methods and settings used in providing services to handicapped children under P.L. 94-142 are essentially the same as those for educationally deprived children under Title I of the Elementary and Secondary Education Act. Thus, if a state's Title I services are provided through a variety of arrangements (e.g., dual enrollment, mobile educational services, services on the private school premises, etc.), it would be legally permissible to use the same arrangements under P.L. 94-142.

Of course, the actual service method/setting used under P.L. 94-142 would depend upon local circumstances and the needs of the individual handicapped children involved. (§ 121a.455) However, a public agency may not require a parochial school student to enroll in the public schools as a condition of receiving benefits for services funded with federal dollars according to the U.S. Department of Education, Office of Special Education.

A local educational agency may provide special education and related services to private school handicapped children that are different from those it provides to public school students if:

(a) The differences are necessary to meet the special needs of the private school handicapped children, and
(b) The special education and related services are comparable in quality, scope, and opportunity for participation to those provided to public school children with needs of equal importance. (§ 121a.455)

PERSONNEL, EQUIPMENT, AND FUNDING

Personnel and equipment are additional factors that public agencies must consider when serving private school handicapped children. Public school personnel may be made available in private schools only to the extent necessary to provide services required by the handicapped children and only when those services are not normally provided by the private school. Each state or local educational agency must maintain continuing administrative control and direction over those services in private schools. (§ 121a.456(b))

Equipment acquired with funds under P.L 94-142 may be placed on private school premises for a limited period but the public agency must retain title to it and exercise administrative control over it. (§ 121a.457(a)). It must keep records of and account for the equipment and make sure that it is used only for the specific program or project and remove it from the private school if necessary to avoid its being used for other purposes or if it is no longer needed for the program. (§ 121a.457(b))

Funds provided under P.L. 94-142 and property purchased with those monies may not inure to the benefit of any private school. (§ 121a.459) The services provided with such funds may not include:

(1) The payment of salaries of teachers or other employees of private schools except for services performed outside their regular hours of duty and under public supervision and control; or
(2) The construction of private school facilities. (§ 121a.456(c))

* * *

Provisions for serving private school handicapped children may not include the financing of the existing level of instruction in the private schools. (§ 121a.460)

Issues of segregation arise in some instances of public schools' providing services to children in private schools. For example, some programs may be carried out in public facilities that involve joint participation by eligible handicapped children enrolled in private schools and those in public schools. Such programs may not include classes that are separated on the basis of school enrollment or the pupils' religious affiliations. (§ 121a.458) It also would be a violation of Title VI of the Civil Rights Act of 1964 if services using P.L. 94-142 dollars were extended to children enrolled in schools organized principally for purposes of racial segregation.

THE EDGAR REGULATIONS

The information in this chapter is based on the P.L. 94-142 regulations, Part B, Subpart D—Private Schools. However, these provisions were largely superseded by the Education Division General Administrative Regulations (EDGAR). The EDGAR regulations apply to all U.S. Department of Education grants and applicants, including state and local education agencies. The EDGAR regulations provide general rules on how to apply for grants and subgrants, how they are made, the general conditions that apply, the administrative responsibilities of grantees and subgrantees, and the compliance procedures used by the Education Division. Rules that apply only to a particular program under P.L. 94-142 are still included in the regulations.

The EDGAR regulations became effective shortly after they were published in final form on April 3, 1980. They change some of the P.L. 94-142 regulations pertaining to handicapped children in private schools:

> *Participation of Private School Children. Regs.* 121a.450–121a.460 are revoked. Regs. 121a.450 and 121a.451 have been revised in EDGAR. Regs. 100b.650–100b.662 of EDGAR are substituted for Regs. 121a.452–121a.460 in P.L. 94-142.

However, these are largely only technical changes in language and do not significantly impact on a handicapped student's due process rights. The following is a list of the major EDGAR provisions applicable to special education:

- Section 100b.652 of EDGAR requires representatives of local education agencies (LEAs) and intermediate educational units (IEUs) to consult with appropriate representatives of private schools during all phases of program development.

- Section 100b.653 of EDGAR requires LEAs and IEUs to determine the needs of private school children and the program benefits which will be provided for those children in a manner comparable to the one used in determining the needs and program benefits of public school children.

- Section 100b.654 of EDGAR requires program benefits for private school children to be comparable to program benefits for public school children.

- Section 100b.655 of EDGAR requires equal expenditure levels for children enrolled in public and private schools.

- Section 100b.656 of EDGAR requires LEAs and IEUs to submit detailed descriptions of the participation of private school children in their application for funding.

- Section 100b.657 of EDGAR prohibits classes to be separated on the basis of religion or school enrollment when classes are held at the same site.

- Section 100b.658 of EDGAR states that program funds must not be used to finance the existing level of instruction in a private school or otherwise benefit a private school.

- Section 100b.659 of EDGAR specifies conditions under which program funds may be used to pay public school personnel who work in other than public facilities.

- Section 100b.660 of EDGAR specifies the conditions under which program funds may be used to pay private school personnel.

- Section 100b.662 of EDGAR states that program funds shall not be used for construction of private school facilities.

DIFFICULTIES IN IMPLEMENTATION OF THE PRIVATE SCHOOL PROVISIONS OF P.L. 94-142/EDGAR

Some states have had difficulty implementing the requirements dealing with the participation of private school children because of conflicts with state laws prohibiting aid to sectarian private schools and confusion about the meaning of the requirements.

Difficulties in implementation occur even when there is understanding of the requirements, since P.L. 94-142 limits the services to be provided to the extent of Part B funds available, but the appropriations (on a per pupil basis) are not sufficient to cover the costs of serving even the most mildly handicapped pupils, thus causing difficulties in determining how states can comply with the "comparable benefits" and "level expenditures" requirements of EDGAR.

Moreover, it is not clear from the regulations whether public agencies are required to extend services to children in private schools serving only handicapped children.

Generally, many state and local education agencies feel that if parents place their handicapped child in a private school, the SEA/LEA should not be responsible for the provision of services, since a free appropriate public education is available in the LEA. Organizations representing private schools feel that parents who have exercised their right to send their children to private schools should not have their children denied the benefits of federal financial support intended for handicapped children. There are clearly many issues in this area which need to be resolved in the years to come.

CASE EXAMPLE

The following is a case example to illustrate how a special education due process problem might arise in the context of a handicapped child's placement in a private school. It is developed through the decision of the hearing officer.

HEARING OFFICER'S DECISION

JURISDICTION AND PROCEDURAL POSTURE

A special education due process hearing was held in the matter of Cory Lynn on January 24, 1980. The hearing was held before Hearing Officer Roy H. Testa, pursuant to and in accordance with the *Rules of the Board of Education,* Public Law 94-142, and the regulations promulgated pursuant to that Act.

At the outset of the hearing, the Hearing Officer inquired as to whether or not the parents had been afforded their procedural rights in accordance with the above cited legal authority. The parents indicated that they had been, and were presently ready to proceed with the hearing.

THE ISSUE

After hearing opening presentations by both parties, the Hearing Officer determined that the issue to be resolved at this hearing was:

> Is the student entitled to receive special education and related services from the Public Schools of Monroe County (MCPS), while continuing to be enrolled in a private school at the expense of her parents?

APPLICABLE LAWS, RULES, AND REGULATIONS

The laws, rules, and regulations applicable to the issue in this matter can be found in the *Rules of the Board of Education,* Public Law 94-142, and the regulations promulgated pursuant to that Act.

Specifically, the following provisions of the Public Law 94-142 regulations pertain to this case:

§ 121a.403 Placement of children by parents.
(a) If a handicapped child has available a free appropriate public education and the parents choose to place the child in a private school or facility, the public agency is not required by this part to pay for the child's education at the private school or facility. However, the public agency shall make services available to the child as provided under § 121a.450–121a.460.

§ 121a.452 Local educational agency responsibility.
(a) Each local educational agency shall provide special education and related services designed to meet the needs of private school handicapped children residing in the jurisdiction of the agency.
(b) Each local educational agency shall provide private school handicapped children with genuine opportunities to participate in special education and related services consistent with the number of those children and their needs.

§ 121a.454 Service arrangements.
Services to private school handicapped children may be provided through such arrangements as dual enrollment, educational radio and television, and the provision of mobile educational services and equipment.

SUMMARY OF THE EVIDENCE

Ms. Aroesty presented the case for the MCPS. She stated that the MCPS has made available a free appropriate public education for this student. Ms. Aroesty explained that the student's needs were fully assessed with a multifaceted evaluation. The various reports and recommendations resulting from that evaluation were made a part of the record in this proceeding. (The contents of those reports are incorporated in the body of this decision by reference.)

According to Ms. Aroesty, the MCPS proceeded to develop an individualized education program (IEP) for this student after considering the information from the evaluation. Generally, the IEP calls for the student to be mainstreamed in a regular junior high school for most of the school day. However, because this student has specific learning disabilities in the area of mathematics, she would receive special education services in the Learning Resource Center at the school for a part of her day. Ms. Aroesty introduced Dr. Jane Cayne, who described the program in the Learning Resource Center, at which she is the Director.

The parents did not contest the fact that their daughter is a handicapped student by reason of her having specific learning disabilities. They also did not challenge the evaluation conducted by the MCPS. Moreover, they did not dispute the fact that the IEP proposed for their daughter by the MCPS represented a free appropriate public education. However, the parents stated that they simply *preferred* to place their daughter in a private school at their own expense. They felt that, while the MCPS program was appropriate, they could offer their daughter a program that was better for her.

However, they would like the MCPS to provide their daughter with special education services in the area of mathematics while she is enrolled in the private school. Rather than accept the whole program proposed by the MCPS, the parents requested only that portion of the program which is designed to meet their daughter's specific learning disabilities in mathematics.

The parents contended that their proposal was actually better for the school system from a cost perspective, since the parents would be paying for the major portion of the student's education. The parents expressed the hope that the MCPS could have the flexibility to adopt such an arrangement. Ms. Aroesty stated that the MCPS would abide by the Hearing Officer's determination.

EVALUATION OF THE EVIDENCE

The essential facts in this matter are not in dispute. The student is a handicapped student by reason of having specific learning disabilities. The learning disabilities adversely affect her ability to learn in the area of mathematics. She was appropriately evaluated. The MCPS has developed an IEP which is adequate and appropriate. But the parents choose to continue their daughter in the private school, where she has recently been enrolled. They are also willing to bear the expense of that schooling. However, they wish to have the MCPS supplement their daughter's program by providing special education services to assist the private school in meeting her special needs as a learning disabled student.

The issue presented in this matter is one of law, not of fact. Does the law provide for such arrangements as the parents are requesting on behalf of their daughter? The Hearing Officer believes that the answer to that question is "yes."

The law provides that a free appropriate public education must be made available to each handicapped child by the public agencies of the State. Subject to the requirements on least restrictive environment, this could include placement in, or referral to, a private school or facility. Such a placement or referral must be at no cost to the parent.

On the other hand, even if a free appropriate public education is available, the parent may choose not to accept it. The parent may choose to send the child to a private school rather than take advantage of the free public education. If this happens, the law does not require the State or local educational agency to bear the cost of the private school. For children placed in private schools by their parents, the State and its local educational agencies have a different duty. They must design their program so that handicapped children in those private schools can participate in special education and related services offered by the local educational agencies if the parents of those children so desire.

In this case, the parents so desire. They are requesting that the MCPS provide some special education services to their daughter in the academic area of mathematics, where the student has specific learning disabilities. The Hearing Officer believes that they are entitled to receive such services.

FINDINGS OF FACT

After evaluating the evidence, the Hearing Officer makes the following findings of fact:

1. The student suffers from a disorder in one or more of the basic psychological processes involved in understanding or in using language, spoken or written, which manifests itself in an imperfect ability to do mathematical calculations.
2. The MCPS has conducted an appropriate multifaceted evaluation of the student, and has developed an appropriate individualized education program to meet the student's needs in accordance with the findings of the evaluation.
3. The parents choose not to accept the program proposed by the MCPS. Rather, they intend to enroll their daughter in

a private school at their own expense. However, they want the MCPS to supplement the private school program with special education services to meet their daughter's needs in the area of mathematics.

CONCLUSIONS OF LAW
After applying the law to the findings of fact above, the Hearing Officer reaches the following conclusions:

1. The student has specific learning disabilities.
2. The MCPS has met their legal obligation to develop an individualized education program to meet the learning needs of this handicapped student.
3. Since the parents choose not to accept the program proposed by the MCPS the parents must provide the student with an education in a private school at their own expense.
4. The MCPS must provide this student with the opportunity as is appropriate with the opportunity to participate in special education and related services offered by the MCPS.

DETERMINATION
In consideration of the findings of fact and conclusions of law above, it is hereby determined that:

The MCPS shall provide Cory Lynn with the opportunity as is appropriate to participate in special education and related services offered by the MCPS.
This determination is the final state decision in this matter. Appeals on legal grounds may be made to a court of competent jurisdiction.

Chapter 27

Confidentiality of Information

Schools maintain many records on children generally but even more so on the handicapped. The files are cumulative and they follow each child from school to school. They contain information on almost every aspect of the pupils' lives. They cover such areas as family background, medical history, school disciplinary actions, grades, attendance, psychological evaluations, social development, standardized test scores of intelligence and achievement, police contacts, the type of track (e.g., advanced, slow learner, etc.), running comments by teachers and counselors, extracurricular activities, and many other types of information.

Public Law 94-142 regulations provide a number of requirements and rights with regard to such information. These closely follow what is commonly referred to as the Buckley Amendment. That is a short name for a federal law, the Family Educational Rights and Privacy Act (FERPA), 20 U.S.C. 12326 that took effect on November 19, 1974. It gives all parents and guardians of children under 18 years of age and all students over 18 or attending postsecondary schools the right to see, correct, and control access to student records. P.L. 94-142 is consistent with the FERPA (or Buckley Amendment) but does go beyond those requirements in a number of areas. The two major areas are:

1. The Buckley Amendment refers to students or pupils. The P.L. 94-142 regulations refer to children, which includes those who have not yet become students, such as preschool or unserved.
2. The Buckley Amendment is applicable to state and local education agencies. The P.L. 94-142 regulations apply to all agencies involved in the state's child identification, location, and evaluation efforts.

The first part of the confidentiality regulations defines certain critical terms:

"Destruction" means physical destruction or removal of personal identifiers from information so that the information is no longer personally identifiable.

"Education records" means the type of records covered under the definition of "education records" in Part 99 of this title (the regulations implementing the Family Educational Rights and Privacy Act of 1974). [NOTE: The Buckley Amendment covers all "records, files, documents and other materials which contain information directly relating to a student" and are maintained by an educational agency. The type or location of the record does not matter—discipline folders, health files, grade reports, and other records found in a cumulative folder—all are covered.]

"Participating agency" means any agency or institution which collects, maintains, or uses personally identifiable information, or from which information is obtained, under this part. (§ 121a.560)

The second part of the confidentiality regulations deals with notice to parents regarding the records being maintained on their child. The state education agency is responsible for the content and dissemination of the notice, which must be in the native languages of various population groups. A state plan must indicate to what extent this effort is carried out.

The regulations require the notice to contain these elements:

1. a description of the children to be identified
2. the type of data sought
3. the method(s) to be used to collect the data
4. the sources from which data will be gathered (parents, files, records, etc.)
5. the way the data are to be used
6. a description of the rights of parents and children regarding the data
7. the procedures of the agencies involved concerning
   a. agencies' storage of data
   b. disclosure procedures of the SEA and other agencies
   c. information to be retained
   d. length of time material will be held before destruction

Specifically, the regulations state the following with regard to notice to parents:

(a) The State educational agency shall give notice which is adequate to fully inform parents about the requirements under

§ 121a.128 of Subpart B [identification, location, and evaluation of handicapped children], including:

(1) A description of the extent to which the notice is given in the native languages of the various population groups in the State;

(2) A description of the children on whom personally identifiable information is maintained, the types of information sought, the methods the State intends to use in gathering the information (including the sources from whom information is gathered), and the uses to be made of the information;

(3) A summary of the policies and procedures which participating agencies must follow regarding storage, disclosure to third parties, retention, and destruction of personally identifiable information; and

(4) A description of all of the rights of parents and children regarding this information, including the rights under section 438 of the General Education Provisions Act and Part 99 of this title (the Family Educational Rights and Privacy Act of 1974, and implementing regulations).

(b) Before any major identification, location, or evaluation activity, the notice must be published or announced in newspapers or other media, or both, with circulation adequate to notify parents throughout the State of the activity. (§ 121a.561)

Each participating agency must permit parents to inspect and review any identifiable data and must comply with a request for such a look as soon as possible but no later than 45 days. As for parents' access to school files, the law provides access rights:

(a) Each participating agency shall permit parents to inspect and review any education records relating to their children which are collected, maintained, or used by the agency under this part. The agency shall comply with a request without unnecessary delay and before any meeting regarding an individualized education program or hearing relating to the identification, evaluation, or placement of the child, and in no case more than 45 days after the request has been made.

(b) The right to inspect and review education records under this section includes:

(1) The right to a response from the participating agency to reasonable requests for explanations and interpretations of the records;

(2) The right to request that the agency provide copies of the records containing the information if failure to provide those copies would effectively prevent the parent from exercising the right to inspect and review the records; and

(3) The right to have a representative of the parent inspect and review the records.

(c) An agency may presume that the parent has authority to inspect and review records relating to his or her child unless the agency has been advised that the parent does not have the authority under applicable State law governing such matters as guardianship, separation, and divorce. (§ 121a.562)

Record of access.
Each participating agency shall keep a record of parties obtaining access to education records collected, maintained, or used under this part (except access by parents and authorized employees of the participating agency), including the name of the party, the date access was given, and the purpose for which the party is authorized to use the records. (§ 121a.563)

Records on more than one child.
If any education record includes information on more than one child, the parents of those children shall have the right to inspect and review only the information relating to their child or to be informed of that specific information. (§ 121a.564)

Lists of types and locations of information.
Each participating agency shall provide parents on request a list of the types and locations of education records collected, maintained, or used by the agency. (§ 121a.565)

Fees.
(a) A participating education agency may charge a fee for copies of records which are made for parents under this part if the fee does not effectively prevent the parents from exercising their right to inspect and review those records.

(b) A participating agency may not charge a fee to search for or to retrieve information under this part. (§ 121a.566)

Parents have the right to request amendments in the files if they believe the data are inaccurate, misleading, or violate the privacy or other rights of their child. The agency must decide on the request to amend within a reasonable period and if it denies the plea, it must inform the parents of this and of their right to a hearing. The agency then must provide an opportunity for a hearing to allow the parents to challenge the data:

Amendments of records at parent's request.
(a) A parent who believes that information in education records collected, maintained, or used under this part is inaccurate or misleading or violates the privacy or other rights of the child, may request the participating agency which maintains the information to amend the information.
(b) The agency shall decide whether to amend the information in accordance with the request within a reasonable period of time of receipt of the request.
(c) If the agency decides to refuse to amend the information in accordance with the request it shall inform the parent of the refusal, and advise the parent of the right to a hearing. (§ 121a.567)

Opportunity for a hearing.
The agency shall, on request, provide an opportunity for a hearing to challenge information in education records to insure that it is not inaccurate, misleading, or otherwise in violation of the privacy or other rights of the child. (§ 121a.568)

Result of hearing.
(a) If, as a result of the hearing, the agency decides that the information is inaccurate, misleading or otherwise in violation of the privacy or other rights of the child, it shall amend the information accordingly and so inform the parent in writing.
(b) If, as a result of the hearing, the agency decides that the information is not inaccurate, misleading, or otherwise in violation of the privacy or other rights of the child, it shall inform the parent of the right to place in the records it maintains on the child a statement commenting on the information or setting forth any reasons for disagreeing with the decision of the agency.
(c) Any explanation placed in the records of the child under this section must:
(1) Be maintained by the agency as part of the records of the child as long as the record or contested portion is maintained by the agency; and
(2) If the records of the child or the contested portion is disclosed by the agency to any party, the explanation must also be disclosed to the party. (§ 121a.569)

The regulations also provide for parental consent before confidential information is released and certain safeguards to protect against improper disclosure:

Consent.
(a) Parental consent must be obtained before personally identifiable information is:
(1) Disclosed to anyone other than officials of participating agencies collecting or using the information under this part, subject to paragraph (b) of this section; or
(2) Used for any purpose other than meeting a requirement under this part.
(b) An educational agency or institution subject to Part 99 of this title may not release information from education records to participating agencies without parental consent unless authorized to do so under Part 99 of this title.
(c) The State educational agency shall include policies and procedures in its annual program plan which are used in the event that a parent refuses to provide consent under this section. (§ 121a.571)

Safeguards.
(a) Each participating agency shall protect the confidentiality of personally identifiable information at collection, storage, disclosure, and destruction stages.
(b) One official at each participating agency shall assume responsibility for insuring the confidentiality of any personally identifiable information.
(c) All persons collecting or using personally identifiable information must receive training or instruction regarding the State's policies and procedures . . . .
(d) Each participating agency shall maintain, for public inspection, a current listing of the names and positions of those employees within the agency who may have access to personally identifiable information (§ 121a.572)

The regulations also provide for the destruction of information:

Destruction of information.
(a) The public agency shall inform parents when personally identifiable information collected, maintained, or used under this part is no longer needed to provide educational services to the child.

(b) The information must be destroyed at the request of the parents. However, a permanent record of a student's name, address, and phone number, his or her grades, attendance record, classes attended, grade level completed, and year completed may be maintained without time limitation. (§ 121a.573)

The destruction notice normally would be given at the time a child graduates or otherwise leaves the agency's purview. An agency might consider establishing some specific time for informing parents about items in their child's folder that no longer are needed (e.g., at the annual IEP meeting, the opening school registration, or the completion of the program or service, such as when a speech impaired child no longer needs therapy). This is not inconsistent with the requirement to also inform parents of the right to have the child's total educational record destroyed upon request at the time the student graduates or otherwise leaves school.

The purpose of the destruction option is to ensure that nonessential records about a child's behavior, performance, and abilities, that may be stigmatizing and are highly personal, are not kept after they no longer are needed for educational purposes. Under the law, the personally identifiable information may be retained permanently unless the parents request that it be destroyed.

Destruction is the best protection against improper and unauthorized disclosure. However, the records may be needed for other purposes. In informing parents about their rights under this section, the agency should remind them that they or the child may need the information for Social Security benefits or other purposes. If the parents request destruction, the agency may retain the information in paragraph (b) of § 121a.573, cited above.

Children's rights correlate to those of their parents depending on certain factors. The regulations declare:

Children's rights.
The State educational agency shall include policies and procedures in its annual program plan regarding the extent to which children are afforded rights of privacy similar to those afforded to parents, taking into consideration the age of the child and type or severity of disability. (§ 121.574)

Under the Buckley Amendment, the rights of parents on education records are transferred to the student at age 18.

Finally, the regulations require the individual states to develop policies and procedures to ensure that the confidentiality regulation is enforced:

Enforcement.

The State educational agency shall describe in its annual program plan the policies and procedures, including sanctions, which the State uses to insure that its policies and procedures are followed and that the requirements of the Act and the regulations in this part are met. (§ 121a.575)

Chapter 28

Minimum Competency Testing

In recent years most states have developed a standardized testing program as a requirement for promotion from one grade to another and/or graduation from high school. These programs are generally referred to as "minimum competency." They appear to be the result of public opinion that students graduate from high school without mastering basic skills necessary to function productively in our society.

There is considerable variation in the way minimum competency programs are structured and administered from state to state. However, minimum competency programs generally include the determination of a set of skills that students should master at specific grade levels. Accordingly, graduation standards also require that students achieve minimum proficiency of designated skills.

There is considerable controversy surrounding minimum competency testing programs and diplomas as they pertain to handicapped students. An in-depth discussion of the merits of the positions in this controversy is beyond the scope of this book. However, it is important to note briefly the basic legal requirements involved and how they relate to the education of handicapped students.

MINIMUM COMPETENCY TESTING PROGRAMS

P.L. 94-142 and Section 504 regulations require that handicapped individuals be given equal opportunities to participate in and benefit from the policies and procedures customarily granted to all individuals. A handicapping condition, by virtue of its presence and effect upon a student, does not of itself preclude the possibility that a pupil can achieve the competencies required for graduation. Many students who are handicapped are capable of achieving the skills considered minimal in the competency program.

To exclude all of the handicapped from the minimum competency requirements would discriminate against the disabled students who would be entitled to a regular diploma at graduation. Therefore, the handicapped must be given the option of participating in the minimum competency testing program. In the event that a handicapped student does not take the competency tests, the school division should document that the ramifications of not taking it have been explained to the parents and the student, and that the parents, and the pupil when appropriate, have signed a waiver requesting that the child not participate in the examination.

Because every handicapped student is to be given the option of participating in this program, it is important that those responsible for special education programs examine their school division's curriculums, methodology, and classroom practices. Their objectives must be appropriate to the potential of the individual handicapped students, yet give them the best possible chance of passing these tests. A handicapped student's growth and development, present capabilities, talents, and potential all must be considered, along with the standards mandated by the minimum competency program.

Instruction should be planned to ensure that information and skills related to minimum competencies are included as an integral part of the special education instructional program. If the objectives are not included in the current program to which handicapped students have access, the curriculum should be revised to improve their opportunities.

Teachers should be requested to identify content and teaching strategies that relate to the competency program. They also should develop classroom management and recordkeeping systems to document progress toward the attainment of the required competencies.

Data obtained from the minimum competency tests by special education teachers should be used in their planning of individual or small-group work with their students, and similarly with regular education students who need extra help in learning certain skills.

However, it is far better not to wait for students to fail the minimum competency tests before initiating remedial help. Schools should test their younger pupils with a pair of assessment instruments, in reading and in computation, that will measure accomplishment on the same objectives that are measured by statewide examinations. Students who need extra help but who have not been identified earlier would then have more time to gain the skills they need in order to pass the minimum competency tests.

THE IEP AS A MANAGEMENT TOOL

Because the individualized education program mandated for all identified handicapped students is the management tool to ensure that they receive an appropriate education, it is important that the IEP specify when a student is eligible to take the minimum competency tests. Further, it is important to note that the P.L. 94-142 regulations require the state and local educational agencies to ensure that tests used to evaluate a handicapped child should be validated for the specific purposes for which they are being used.

Tests to evaluate children with impaired sensory, manual, or speaking skills should reflect the aptitude or whatever other factors they purport to measure, rather than the dysfunctions. When a handicapped student has failed one or more of the minimum competency tests, every effort must be made to determine whether this was a result of the handicap rather than a lack of knowledge in the areas being tested (i.e., reading and/or math).

Frequently, the student will know better than anyone else the reason for the poor test performance. Adverse testing conditions may have been responsible (e.g., testing done in a large group, or administered by someone not familiar with the coloring effect of a pupil's particular handicapping condition, or inability of the student to move from the test booklet to the answer sheet with accuracy, or an inflexible time allotment for the examination, or tests given consecutively without adequate time intervals).

If so, such adverse conditions need to be remedied and different accommodations made available before the student is retested; however, any changes must be within the parameters of the accommodations permitted for the handicapped. Permission to retest a student and conditions under which this is to be done should be stipulated in the IEP.

The minimum competency tests should not merely identify students whose skills indicate that they cannot qualify for a high school diploma; they also should provide guidance for persons responsible for trying to improve those abilities.

The tests should be constructed in such a way that they generate a performance skill profile of each individual student. Upon receiving these skill profiles, LEAs should make them available to teachers promptly. These will provide a basis for planning remediation for students who have not passed. Instruction to improve the deficient areas should become a part of the short-term objectives on the IEP.

DIPLOMAS

The establishment of proficiency standards for a high school diploma is a state function that is not addressed in either P.L. 94-142 or the implementing regulations. While there is no guaranteed right for every handicapped child to receive a high school diploma, those who meet the standards cannot be denied one on the basis of handicap. To do so would violate Section 504.

Essentially, local education agencies have two options for granting diplomas to handicapped students:

1. award a regular diploma to handicapped students who meet all requirements for graduation, including passing the minimum competency tests, or
2. grant an IEP diploma for those who meet all state requirements except passing the minimum competency tests

Of course, local education agencies may choose to adopt other forms of recognition for handicapped students who are not eligible for either an IEP diploma or a regular diploma.

Chapter 29

Disciplinary Action

Handicapped children, like others, are subject to disciplinary action pursuant to rules of local and state education agencies relating to suspension and expulsion. However, because no child may be punished solely because of being handicapped, serious constitutional questions arise when it appears that the behavior for which a student is being punished is the product of an impairment. A child cannot legally be suspended or expelled for behavior that results from a handicapping condition, because to do so would be discriminatory and would therefore violate Secton 504.

The Supreme Court has recognized children's property interests in a free public education and their liberty interests in being free from arbitrary or unjustified disciplinary action. On this basis, the Court in *Goss v. Lopez*, 419 U.S. 565 (1975), required that students be given the benefit of due process protection whenever suspension or expulsion was used against them. Specifically, for a suspension of up to 10 days, the child and parents must be given notice of the reasons and some opportunity to be heard, such as in an informal conference, to present the pupil's view of the problem. More rigorous due process protections are required for expulsions and longer suspensions.

Most jurisdictions allow a school principal, for cause, to suspend a student for up to five days. The pupil or the parents then have an opportunity for a conference with the principal and other appropriate personnel.

Generally, for suspensions for more than five days and for expulsions, procedures are set up whereby a principal must recommend the action to the superintendent, who then conducts an investigation and determines whether or not to approve the punishment.

If credible evidence is presented indicating that the child may be handicapped and eligible for special education services, an evaluation should be initiated as soon as possible and considered by the local eligibility committee. Independent evaluations obtained by the child's parents also must be considered. If it is determined that the child is handicapped and that the disabling condition was a significant cause of the behavior that prompted the disciplinary action, then the suspension or expulsion should be reconsidered and placement of the pupil should be provided in accordance with the special education regulations.

The P.L. 94-142 regulations do not directly address the question of suspension and/or expulsion. The "Comment" following § 121a.513 (Child's status during proceedings) indicates that, while the child's placement may not be changed during the pendency of proceedings brought pursuant to a complaint, an educational agency is not precluded from using its normal procedures for dealing with children who are endangering themselves or others. Also, the "Comment" following § 121a.552 (Placement) cites the analysis of the Section 504 regulations (45 CFR, Part 84—Appendix, Paragraph 24) which states: ". . . it should be stressed that where a handicapped child is so disruptive in a regular classroom that the education of other students is significantly impaired, the needs of the handicapped child cannot be met in that environment. Therefore regular placement would not be appropriate to his or her needs . . ."

These "Comments" are the major references in the regulations related to disciplining handicapped students. Both the P.L. 94-142 and Section 504 regulations fail to provide clear guidance on the extent to which school authorities are permitted to discipline handicapped children by suspending or expelling them from school. Therefore, it would appear that school officials have the same authority to suspend or expel handicapped children for disciplinary reasons as they do the nonimpaired, except for the limitation that a handicapped child may not legally be punished for behavior that results from the handicapping condition. To do so would be discrimination and a violation of Section 504.

However, this limiting point is not easily defined in practice. In fact, it really is an open question in the law as to exactly what degree a handicapped child may be subject to the disciplinary actions used for nonimpaired peers. The following are some examples of questions left unresolved by the federal regulations governing the education of handicapped children:

- What circumstances, if any, make long-term exclusions permissible where a determination has been made that a handicapped student's behavior is not related to the impairment or to any inappropriate placement?
- What circumstances, if any, make short-term exclusions permissible?
- What prior determination, if any, must an educational agency make of the relationship between a handicapped student's behavior and the disability before ordering a short-term exclusion?

- What procedures are required for what specific periods of permissible exclusion?

In one case, a handicapped child won a preliminary injunction in federal court barring a local school district from conducting an expulsion hearing. *Stuart v. Nappi,* F. Supp. 1235 (D.Conn. 1978). The student claimed that expulsion would leave her without an appropriate educational program and that the only way her education placement could be changed legally was through the procedures set out in the P.L. 94-142 special education regulations.

Although this student obtained the relief sought, effectively blocking the application of traditional disciplinary actions, not all courts have been willing to adopt this same position. Even in *Stuart,* the court made clear that its decision did not affect the school's authority to remove a student from a particular class or classes for disciplinary reasons. The court's decision focused on more substantial action, stating:

> It is important that the parameters of this decision are clear. The court is cognizant of the need for school officials to be vested with ample authority and discretion. It is, therefore, with great reluctance that the court has intervened in the disciplinary process of Danbury High School. However, this intervention is of a limited nature. Handicapped children are neither immune from a school's disciplinary process nor are they entitled to participate in programs when their behavior impairs the education of other children in the program. First, school authorities can take swift disciplinary measures, such as suspension, against disruptive handicapped children. Secondly, a [professional team] can request a change in the placement of handicapped children who have demonstrated that their present placement is inappropriate by disrupting the education of other children. The Handicapped Act thereby affords schools with both short-term and long-term methods of dealing with handicapped children who are behavioral problems.

In conclusion, the determination of whether there is a relation between behavior and handicap for some children may mean the difference between receiving a free appropriate public education and receiving no schooling at all. Suspension or expulsion therefore often can be a denial of the child's rights:

1. to "an appropriate public education"
2. to remain in the present placement until resolution of a special education complaint
3. to an education in the "least restrictive environment"
4. to have all changes of placement effectuated in accordance with prescribed procedures

Therefore, any school system's determinations in these suspension proceedings also may be challenged through the local and state level special education hearing procedures.

Glossary

The following definitions pertain to special education decision making and are based upon the P.L. 94-142 regulations and official policy statements issued by the U.S. Department of Education, Office of Special Education.

Administrator: a staff member who has been given the responsibility to manage or direct the activities of an LEA or portion of these activities.

Appropriate: see Free Appropriate Public Education

At No Cost: all specially designed instruction is provided without charge but does not preclude incidental fees that normally are charged to nonhandicapped students or their parents as a part of the regular education program.

Audiologist: a staff member who is a specialist in communicative disorders, including the scientific study and management of speech, hearing, and language disabilities. Primary responsibilities are of a clinical nature and involve diagnostic, evaluative, and therapeutic activities in the area of hearing disabilities.

Audiology: includes
1. identification of children with hearing loss
2. determination of the range, nature, and degree of hearing loss, including referral for medical or other professional attention for the habilitation of hearing
3. provision of habilitative activities, such as language habilitation auditory training, speech reading (lip reading), hearing evaluation, and speech conservation
4. creation and administration of programs for prevention of hearing loss
5. counseling and guidance of pupils, parents, and teachers regarding hearing loss
6. determination of the child's need for group and individual amplification, selecting and fitting an appropriate aid, and evaluating the effectiveness of amplification

Consent: involves the fact that
1. the parents have been fully informed of all information relevant to the activity for which consent is sought, in their native language or other mode of communication

479

2. the parents understand and agree in writing to the carrying out of the activity for which their consent is sought, and the approval describes that activity and lists the records (if any) that will be released and to whom
3. the parents understand that the granting of consent is voluntary on their part and they may revoke it at any time

Counseling Services: those provided by qualified social workers, psychologists, guidance counselors, or other qualified personnel.

Deaf: a hearing impairment so severe that the child is impaired in processing linguistic information through hearing, with or without amplification, thus adversely affecting educational performance.

Destruction: physical destruction or removal of personal identifiers from information so that the material no longer can be linked to the individual.

Direct Services and Instruction in the Regular Class: activities concerned with the teaching-learning process provided to handicapped students by special education personnel in the regular class.

Early Identification: the implementation of a formal plan for identifying a disability as early as possible in a child's life.

Evaluation: procedures used in accordance with §§ 121a.530–121a.534 to determine whether a child is handicapped and the nature and extent of the special education and related services that will be needed. The term includes those used selectively with an individual child but not basic tests administered to or procedures used with all children in a school, grade, or class.

Free Appropriate Public Education: special education and related services that
1. are provided at public expense, under public supervision and direction, and without charge
2. meet the standards of the state educational agency, including the requirements of P.L. 94-142 regulations
3. include preschool, elementary school, or secondary school education in the state involved
4. are provided in conformity with an individualized education program that meets the requirements under §§ 121a.340–121a.349 of Subpart C (IEP provisions).

Full-Time Equivalent: the amount of time for a less than full-time activity divided by the amount of time normally required in a corresponding full-time activity; full-time equivalency usually is expressed as a decimal fraction to the nearest 10th.

Hard of Hearing: a hearing impairment, whether permanent or fluctuating, that adversely affects a child's educational performance but is not included under the definition of "deaf" in this section.

Hearing Officer: a person responsible for conducting an impartial due process hearing with respect to the identification, evaluation, or educational placement of a handicapped child. The person must be impartial and may not be an employee of the education agency involved, nor have a personal or professional interest that would conflict with objectivity in the hearing. A person who otherwise qualifies to conduct a hearing based on these qualifications is not an employee of the agency solely because of being paid by the agency to serve as a hearing officer.

Homebound Instruction: individual instruction by a teacher, usually at the home of a student who is unable to attend classes.

Home-Hospital Teacher: a staff member who provides individual or small-group instruction to children unable to attend classes who receive instruction at home or in a hospital.

Hospital Program: formal instructional activities provided in a hospital.

Include: the items named are not all of the possible ones that are covered, whether like or unlike the ones identified.

Independent Educational Evaluation: an evaluation conducted by a qualified examiner who is not employed by the public agency responsible for the education of the child in question.

Indirect Services Within Regular Class: support services to the regular class teacher to enable the handicapped child to perform in the regular class.

Individualized Education Program: a written statement for a handicapped child that is developed and implemented in accordance with §§ 121a.341–121a.349.

Intermediate Educational Unit: any public authority, other than a local educational agency, that
1. is under the general supervision of a state educational agency
2. is established by state law for the purpose of providing free public education on a regional basis
3. provides special education and related services to handicapped children within that state

Itinerant/Consulting Teachers: teachers who move from school to school to provide part-day special education instruction to handicapped children, or personnel who have been delegated the responsibility of assisting teachers in the development and/or improvement of the learning situation and instructional methods for disabled pupils.

Least Restrictive Environment: the educational placement in which the handicapped child's IEP is to be carried out because it is in conformity with the following requirements:
1. handicapped children, including those in public or private institutions or other care facilities, must be educated with nonimpaired pupils to the maximum extent appropriate
2. special classes, separate schooling, or other removal of handicapped children from the regular educational environment must be used only when the nature or severity

of the dysfunction is such that study in regular classes with the use of supplementary aids and services cannot be achieved satisfactorily.

Local Educational Agency: a public board of education or other public authority legally constituted for either administrative control or direction of, or to perform a service function for, public elementary or secondary schools in any political subdivision of a state, or a combination of school districts or counties recognized as an administrative agency for its public schools. The term also includes any other public institution or agency having administrative control and direction of a public school; it also includes intermediate educational units.

Medical Services: those provided by a licensed physician to determine a child's medically related handicapping condition that results in the pupil's need for special education and related services.

Mentally Retarded: significantly subaverage general intellectual functioning existing concurrently with deficits in adaptive behavior and manifested during the developmental period that adversely affects a child's educational performance. This was taken largely from the official definition of the American Association on Mental Deficiency (AAMD). According to the AAMD, "Mental retardation refers to significantly subaverage general intellectual functioning existing concurrently with deficits in adaptive behavior, and manifested during the developmental period." Intellectual functioning may be assessed by one or more of the standardized tests used for that purpose. Significantly subaverage refers to performance that is more than two standard deviations from the mean. Two of the most widely used instruments—Stanford-Binet and Wechsler—reflect IQs of 67 and 69, respectively, in diagnosing mental retardation (Table 1). Adaptive behavior is defined by the AAMD as "the effectiveness or degree with which the individual meets the standards of personal independence and social responsibility expected of his age and cultural group."

Table 1 Levels of Mental Retardation

Levels	IQ Scores		Educational Expectations
	Stanford-Binet	Wechsler	
Borderline	68–83	70–84	Resource Help
Mild	67–52	69–55	Educable
Moderate	51–36	54–40	Trainable
Severe	35–20	39–25	Custodial
Profound	19 and below	24 and below	Custodial

Native Language: when used in relation to a person of limited English-speaking ability, this refers to the language normally used by that person, or in the case of a child, the language normally used by the parents of the child.

Noninstructional Staff: personnel who are not involved in the instruction program.

Occupational Therapist: a person licensed to provide occupational therapy services.

Occupational Therapy: includes
1. improving, developing, or restoring functions impaired or lost through illness, injury, or deprivation

2. improving ability to perform tasks for independent functioning when physical abilities are impaired or lost
3. preventing, through early intervention, initial or further impairment of loss of function

Orthopedically Impaired: a severe orthopedic impairment that adversely affects a child's educational performance. The term includes impairments caused by congenital anomaly (e.g., clubfoot, absence of some member, etc.), impairments caused by disease (e.g., poliomyelitis, bone tuberculosis, etc.), and impairments from other causes (e.g., fractures or burns that cause contractures, amputation, cerebral palsy, etc.).

Other Health Impaired: limited strength, vitality, or alertness because of chronic or acute health problems such as a heart condition, tuberculosis, rheumatic fever, nephritis, asthma, sickle cell anemia, hemophilia, epilepsy, lead poisoning, leukemia, or diabetes that adversely affects a child's educational performance.

Parent: a parent, a guardian, a person acting as a parent of a child, or a surrogate parent who has been appointed in accordance with § 121a.514, but does not include the state if the child is a ward of the state. Parent includes persons acting in the place of a parent, such as a grandmother or stepparent with whom a child lives, as well as persons who are legally responsible for a pupil's welfare.

Parent Counseling and Training: assisting parents in understanding the special needs of their child and providing them with information about child development.

Participating Agency: any entity or institution that collects, maintains, or uses personally identifiable information, or from which information is obtained.

Personally Identifiable: includes
1. the name of the child, the parents, or other family member
2. the address of the child
3. a personal identifier, such as the child's Social Security number or student number
4. a list of personal characteristics or other information that would make it possible to identify the pupil with reasonable certainty

Physical Education: special physical education, adapted physical education, movement education, and motor development; the development of
1. physical and motor fitness
2. fundamental motor skills and patterns
3. skills in aquatics, dance, and individual and group games and sports (including intramural and lifetime sports)

Physical Educators: staff members who provide instruction in the development of physical and motor fitness, fundamental motor skills and patterns, body mechanics, individual and group games and sports, skills in intramural and lifetime sports, and dance and movement education.

Physical Therapy: services provided by a qualified physical therapist.

Psychological Services: include
1. administering psychological and educational tests and other assessment procedures
2. interpreting assessment results
3. obtaining, integrating, and interpreting information about child behavior and conditions relating to learning
4. consulting with other staff members in planning school programs to meet the special needs of children as indicated by psychological tests, interviews, and behavioral evaluations
5. planning and managing a program of psychological services, including psychological counseling for children and parents

Psychometrist/Educational Diagnostician: a staff member assigned to perform professional activities in measuring the intellectual, social, and emotional development of pupils through the administration and interpretation of psychological tests.

Public Agency: includes the state educational agency, local educational agencies, intermediate educational units, and any other political subdivisions that are responsible for providing education to handicapped children.

Public Expense (Independent Evaluation): the full cost of the evaluation is paid by the public agency or it ensures that the analysis is provided at no cost to the parent, consistent with § 121a.301.

Public Residential School Facility: an educational institution in which students are boarded and lodged as well as taught and that is supported by public funds and operated by publicly elected or appointed school officials who control the school programs and activities.

Private Day School: a school controlled by an individual or agency other than a local, state, or federal government, usually supported by other than public funds, the operation of whose program rests with other than publicly elected or appointed officials, and that students attend during a part of the day, as distinguished from a residential school where students are boarded and lodged as well as taught.

Private Residential School Facility: an educational institution in which students are boarded and lodged as well as taught, and controlled by an individual or agency other than a local, state, or federal government, usually supported by other than public funds, and the operation of whose program rests with other than publicly elected or appointed officials.

Qualified: a person who has met state educational agency approved or recognized certification, licensing, registration, or other comparable requirements that apply to the area in which the expert is providing special education or related services.

Recipient: any state or its political subdivision, any instrumentality of a state or its political subdivision, any public or private agency, institution, organization, or other entity, or any person to which federal financial assistance is extended directly or through another recipient, including any successor, assignee, or transferee of a recipient, but excluding the ultimate beneficiary of the assistance.

Recreation: includes
1. leisure function assessment
2. therapeutic recreation services
3. recreation programs in schools and community agencies
4. leisure education

Recreational Therapists: personnel employed by the school system to perform recreational methods of treatment and rehabilitation other than through the use of drugs or surgery.

Regular Class: a general type of class in which most students receive instruction, including most classes other than those composed of handicapped children.

Regular Class Teacher: a person who teaches students in a general type of class in which most pupils receive instruction, including most classes other than those composed of handicapped children.

Related Services: transportation and such developmental, corrective, and other supportive services as are required to help a handicapped child benefit from special education, includes speech pathology and audiology, psychological services, physical and occupational therapy, recreation, early identification and assessment of disabilities in children, counseling services, and medical services for diagnostic or evaluation purposes; also includes school health services, social work services in schools, and parent counseling and training.

Resource Room Services: activities provided in an instructional setting designed or adapted as a place where handicapped children receive a part of their schooling.

Resource Room Teacher: a person who instructs handicapped children in an instructional setting designed or adapted as a place where they receive a part of their schooling.

School Health Services: services provided by a qualified school nurse or other qualified person.

School Psychologist: a staff member who performs assigned professional services of psychological evaluation and analysis of pupils through measuring and interpreting their intellectual, emotional, and social development and diagnosing their educational personal disabilities; also serves the school system through such activities as collaborating in planning appropriate educational programs, conducting research on pupil adjustments and behavior, and assisting other staff members with specific problems of a psychological nature and broadening their understanding of the psychological forces with which they deal.

School Social Worker: a staff member who provides professional services to help in the prevention and solution of pupils' personal, social, and emotional problems that involve family, school, and community relationships when such issues have a bearing on the quality of the students' schoolwork.

Self-Contained Special Class: a class having the same special education teacher for all or most of the daily session and composed of handicapped children, for whom a program of special education is provided.

Seriously Emotionally Disturbed: a condition exhibiting one or more of the following characteristics over a long period of time and to a marked degree, adversely affecting educational performance: an inability to learn that cannot be explained by intellectual, sensory, or health factors; an inability to build or maintain satisfactory interpersonal relationships with peers and teachers; inappropriate types of behavior or feelings under normal circumstances; a general pervasive mood of unhappiness or depression; or a tendency to develop physical symptoms or fears associated with personal or school problems. The term does not include children who are socially maladjusted unless it is determined that they are seriously emotionally disturbed.

Social Work Services in Schools: include:
1. preparing a social or developmental history on a handicapped child
2. counseling, both group and individual, with the child and family
3. working with problems in a child's living situation (home, school, and community) that affect adjustment in school
4. mobilizing school and community resources to enable the child to receive maximum benefit from the educational program

Special Class Teacher: a person who instructs students full time in a class composed of handicapped children for whom a program of special education is provided.

Special Education: specially designed instruction (including vocational), at no cost to the parent, to meet the unique needs of a handicapped child, including in the classroom, at home, in hospitals and institutions, and in physical education; includes speech pathology or any other related service if it is considered special education rather than a related service under state standards.

Special Public Day School: a nonresidential school attended by handicapped children that provides a program of special education and is operated by publicly elected or appointed school officials who have control over its programs and activities and is supported primarily by public funds.

Specific Learning Disability: a disorder in one or more of the basic psychological processes involved in understanding or using spoken or written language that may manifest itself in an imperfect ability to listen, think, speak, read, write, spell, or do mathematical calculations. The term includes such conditions as perceptual handicaps, brain injury, minimal brain dysfunction, dyslexia, and developmental aphasia; it does not include children who have learning problems that primarily result from visual, hearing, or motor handicaps, mental retardation, emotional disturbance, or environmental, cultural, or economic disadvantage.

Speech Impaired: those with communication disorders such as stuttering, impaired articulation, language impairment, or voice impairment that adversely affect educational performance.

Speech Pathologist: a specialist in communicative disorders, including the scientific study and management of speech, hearing, and language disabilities; primary responsibilities are of a clinical nature and involve diagnostic, evaluative, and therapeutic activities in the area of speech disabilities.

Speech Pathology: includes
1. identification of children with speech or language disorders
2. diagnosis and appraisal of specific speech or language disorders
3. referral for medical or other professional attention necessary for the habilitation of speech or language disorders
4. provisions of speech and language services for the habilitation or prevention of communicative disorders
5. counseling and guidance of parents, children, and teachers on speech and language disorders

State: each of the 50 states, the District of Columbia, the Commonwealth of Puerto Rico, Guam, American Samoa, the Virgin Islands, and the Trust Territory of the Pacific Islands.

State Education Agency: the state board of education or other agency or officer primarily responsible for the state supervision of public elementary and secondary schools, or, if there is no such officer or agency, an officer or agency designated by the governor or by state law.

Surrogate: a person assigned to represent a handicapped child and protect the pupil's rights whenever the parents or guardian are not known, unavailable, or the child is a ward of the state; the person is not to be an employee of the SEA, LEA, or IEU involved in the education or care of the child.

Transportation: includes travel to and from school and between schools, travel in and around school buildings, and specialized equipment (such as special or adapted buses, lifts, and ramps), if required to provide special transportation for a handicapped child.

Teacher Aide: a person who assists a teacher with routine activities associated with instruction that requires minor decisions regarding students, such as monitoring, conducting rote exercises, operating equipment, and clerking.

Visual Handicap: a visual impairment that, even after correction, adversely affects a child's educational performance; includes both partially sighted and blind children.

Vocational Education: organized educational programs that are directly related to the preparation of individuals for paid or unpaid employment or for additional preparation for a career requiring other than a baccalaureate or advanced degree.

Vocational Educator: a staff member who provides instruction directly related to the preparation of individuals for paid or unpaid employment or for additional preparation for a career requiring other than a baccalaureate or advanced degree.

Index

A

Absences from school, identification and, 71
Accessibility
  to education (mentally retarded and), 5
  to programs and buildings, 18
  Section 504 regulations and, 37
Accountability
  for child's care, 270-71
  for IEP, 113-14
  P.L. 94-142 and, 56
  school personnel and, 230
  SEAs and, 144-45
Act Concerning Surrogate Parents (P.A. 76-429), 272. *See also* Surrogate parents
Adaptive behavior, mentally retarded and, 154, 158
Administrative Procedures Act, 353
Adult education, 36
Agencies. *See* Local education agencies (LEAs); Public agencies; State education agencies (SEAs)
American Association on Mental Deficiency (AAMD), 154, 482
Annual program plans (states), 41-44, 53, 229-30
  identification and, 65-66
Appeal procedure (due process

hearing decisions)
  additional evidence and, 343, 344-45
  as administrative or judicial hearing, 340
  appeal official's decision and, 346
  appellate official and, 348-51
  closing of due process hearing and, 338
  decisions and
    affirming, modifying, or reversing, 349-51
    enforcement and, 351-54
    writing of decision and, 423
  defined, 340
  error defined and, 341
  filing, 342-43
  initiating, 342
  oral and written argument and, 345-46
  procedure for, 343-46
  right to, 339-40
  state and federal courts and, 347-48
  timelines and, 354-57
Application (local program), 44-46, 53, 229-30
Architectural barriers, 224
Articulation disorder, 174, 176
Athletics, 35, 129
  student rights and, 206
Audiological screening, 150. *See also*

Screening
Audiology, 22
    defined, 479
Audiometric assessment, hearing
    impaired and, 151-52
Autistic children, 163

B

Behavioral analysis
    emotionally disturbed and, 162-63,
        164, 165
    of hearing impaired, 150
    mentally retarded and, 154
    parent observation and, 225
    specific learning disability
        and, 171
Behavioral problems, 477
Bill of Rights for the education of
    handicapped children. See P.L.
    94-142 (Education for All
    Handicapped Children Act of 1975)
Birth defects, 160
Blindness, defined, 177. See also The
    Deaf-blind
Block grants, 25, 26-27. See also
    Grants
Braille, 179, 193
Brief (appeal procedure), 345-46
Brown v. Board of Education (1954),
    4, 123
Buckley Amendment, 463-64, 469
Budget reduction, 26-27
Burden of proof, 365-69. See also
    Evidence
Bureau for Education of the
    Handicapped, 10
Butz v. Economon (438 U.S. 478,
    1978), 254

C

Cafeteria services, 35
Census (identification), 68

Certified mail, surrogate parent
    process and, 262
Checklists
    appropriate education guidelines,
        196-201
    due process prehearing, 315-16
    evaluation, 87-88
    witness and document assessment,
        366
Child-find programs. See Identification
    (of those in need of special
    education)
Class plans
    IEP, 108
    placement and, 127-28, 193, 226-27
    regular, 485
Classrooms
    competency programs and, 472
    direct services and instruction in,
        480
    health impaired and, 162
    for hearing impaired, 153
    indirect services and instruction in,
        481
    placement and, 127-28
    school personnel and, 239
    self-contained special (defined), 486
Clubs (school), 35, 36, 129
College placement services, 140
Communication (impaired or
    professional). See Language
Community survey (identification),
    68-69
    school personnel and, 235
    state plans and, 42
Competency testing, 471-74. See also
    Tests
Compliance
    appeal decision and, 351-54
    difficulties in, 147
    private school placement and, 450
Compulsory school attendance laws, 4
Confidentiality
    Buckley Amendment and, 463-64,
        469
    consent and, 228, 243, 468

destruction of information and, 468-69
    defined, 480
enforcement of regulations covering, 469-70
hearing officer and, 256
identification and, 67
parent responsibilities and, 228
parent rights and, 216-18, 464-67
P.L. 94-142 and, 228, 463-70
record review and, 465, 466
records and, 17-18, 241, 464-70
school personnel and, 241-44
SEAs and, 464-65
student rights and, 207
surrogate parents and, 268
Congenital anomaly, 160
Congress
    accountability in education of handicapped and, 56, 144
    educational authority and, 40, 47
    educational needs of handicapped and, 12-13
    IEP and, 91
Consent (parental)
    confidentiality and, 228, 243, 468
    defined, 479-80
    due process notice requirement and, 287-94
    to evaluation, 75-76, 185, 220, 235
    identification procedures and, 67
    IEP document and, 105
    informed, 78
    initial placement and, 79
    parental competency and, 292-93
    parental knowledgeability and, 290-91
    placement and, 214, 225, 239
    P.L. 94-142 and, 16
    preplacement evaluation and, 306
    record information and parents and, 243
    voluntary, 291-92
Constitution of the U.S.
    disciplinary action and, 475
    educational authority and, 39

FAPE and, 136
    14th Amendment and, 3-4, 5-6
    notice requirements and, 279
Contract
    private school, 450
    surrogate parent, 273
Costs
    FAPE and, 31
    placement (at no cost to parent) and, 132-34, 143, 144, 147
    of private school services, 18
    of special education (P.L. 94-142), 56
Council for Exceptional Children's Delegate Assembly, 124-25
Counseling services, 129
    defined, 480
    for parents, 22, 140, 483
Courts
    decision compliance (appeal), 353
    emotionally disturbed children and, 165
    parent rights and, 270
    P.L. 94-142 and, 40, 46-48
    related services and, 147
    right to sue in state or federal (appeal), 347-48
Cover page, written decisions, 416-18, 424
Cross-examination. *See* Evidence, cross-examination; Witnesses, cross-examination *entries*
Curriculums, 18, 195
    competency programs and, 472

D

Damages, hearing officer and, 254-55
Day school (special), 128
    private (defined), 484
    public (defined), 486
    the speech impaired and, 170
Deadlines (due process hearing), 354-57
The Deaf-blind, 10, 19. *See also*

Blindness, defined; Hearing
impaired
defined (multihandicapped), 158-59
identification and evaluation of, 159
program and placement of, 159-60
Deafness, defined, 149-50, 480
Decision-making process, 203
evaluation and, 73-74, 186
parents (state plans) and, 11
placement and, 118, 119, 121, 122
safeguards for parents and, 15-16
surrogate parents and, 259, 260, 268
Decisions (of due process hearing
officer). See also Appeal procedure
(due process hearing decisions);
Hearing officer
EDGAR restrictive requirements
and, 411
case example of, 457-61
finality of (appealing), 339-40
hearing officer and, 246, 252, 258,
283, 326, 405
aptness of program and
placement and, 410
assumptions and perspectives of,
406-407
evidence and, 408, 411
handicapped definition and,
408-409
options and, 410-13
personal beliefs and, 407-408
prehearing situations and, 301-302
writing of
appeal information and, 423, 444
applicable law and regulations
and, 419, 426
case study example of, 423-45
conclusions of law and, 422-23,
443, 461
cover page and, 416-18, 424
evidence and, 420-21, 426, 434,
458, 459
final order and, 423
finding of fact and, 421-22, 442,
460-61
the issues and, 418-19

jurisdiction and procedural
history and, 418, 425
legal authority and, 418
overview of, 415-16
self-explanatory nature of, 415
testimony summary and, 427
Department of Education
appeal noncompliance and, 354
evaluation and, 77
funding and school personnel
and, 233-34
handicapped definition and, 163
hearing officer position and, 248
IEP and, 91
tape recordings and, 104
insurance proceeds and, 143
P.L. 94-142 and, 49-50
private school funding and, 453
special education laws and, 41-44
speech impairment definition and,
174, 175
state plan and, 229
Developmental characteristics (mentally
retarded, 157
Developmental period (mentally
retarded), 154
Diplomas, 472, 473-74
Direct examination. See Evidence
(due process hearing), direct
examination; Witnesses (due process
hearing), direct examination
Disciplinary action, 475-78
Discrimination, 46
evaluation and cultural or racial, 82,
155
nonacademic services and, 35-36
nondiscriminatory evaluation
and, 151, 186
hearing officer and, 256
protection against (Section 504), 29,
31
Disease impairments, 160
Disputes over education program
administrative review and, 298-99
due process and, 7, 8
due process hearing and, 227

IEP meeting and, 103-104
surrogate parents and, 268
Documents
checklist for, 366
due.process hearing
introduction of, 330, 333-34, 377
holding record open for, 337-38
writing a decision and, 420
Dress (witnesses), 391
Due process hearing. *See also* Appeal
procedure (due process hearing
decisions); Decisions (of due process
officer); Evidence (due process
hearing); Hearing officer (due
process hearing); Notice requirements
(due process hearing); Witnesses
(due process hearing)
beginning (basic components),
320-24
child's presence at, 311-12
closing, 337-38, 389
closing statements and, 328
document introduction and, 330,
333-34
holding record open for, 337-38
dress (witnesses) and, 391
due process of law and, 7-8
evaluation funding and, 139
funding services and, 142
hearing officer and, 251-52, 255,
258-59
invoking, 295-99
legal authority (statement) for, 320
notebook for, 372
oath administration and, 324
objections during, 333-37
witness and, 334-401
open or closed, 322-23
opening statements and, 325, 376-77
order of presentation (guidelines),
324-28
parent responsibilities and, 227-28
parent rights and, 215-16
planning of, 371
postponement or continuance of,
330-33

prehearing activities for, 301-315
checklist for, 315-16
procedure during, 323-24
purpose of, 203, 317, 320-21, 359
recording equipment and, 319
school personnel and, 230-31, 235,
240-41
seating arrangement and, 317-19
SLD and, 173
surrogate parents and, 268
timelines and, 354-57
Due process hearing decisions. *See*
Decisions (of due process hearing
officer)
Due process of law
analysis of, 5-8
concept of, 3, 277
evaluation and, 222
expulsion and suspension and, 475
local and state FAPE plans and, 229
overview of (training workshop),
249-50
parent decision-making safeguards
and, 15-16
private schools and, 36
procedures and, 277-78
surrogate parents and, 259, 262

E

EDGAR regulation (private schools),
454-56
difficulties in implementation of,
456-57
example of, 457-61
Education for All Handicapped
Children Act of 1975. *See* P.L.
94-142 (Education for All
Handicapped Children Act of 1975)
Educational Amendments of 1974. *See*
P.L. 93-380 (Educational
Amendments of 1974)
Educational assessment, 84-85, 152
Educational performance
emotionally disturbed and, 163

health impairments and, 160
hearing impaired and, 151
mentally retarded and, 154-55
multihandicapped and, 159
program development and, 189
specific learning disability and, 166, 168
speech impairment and, 176
visually impaired and, 178
Education Division General
    Administration Regulations
    (EDGAR, private schools), 454-56
    difficulties in implementation of, 456-57
    example of, 457-61
Education of the Handicapped Act of
    1969. See P.L. 91-230 (Education of
    the Handicapped Act of 1969)
Education of the Handicapped Act of
    1967. See P.L. 90-247 (Education of
    the Handicapped Act of 1967)
Education of Handicapped Children.
    See P.L. 89-750 (Education of
    Handicapped Children)
Elementary and Secondary Education
    Act of 1965. See P.L. 89-10
    (Elementary and Secondary
    Education Act of 1965)
Emotionally disturbed (seriously)
    defined, 162-63, 486
    identification and evaluation and, 164-65
    placement examples for, 192
    programming and placement and, 165
Employment
    P.L. 94-142 and, 53
    student, 35, 129
Environment (educational). See
    Least restrictive environment (LRE);
    Least restrictive nonacademic
    environment
Equal education opportunity, 4, 471
Equipment, 58, 140
    mentally retarded and, 158
    private school, 453-54

recording (hearing room), 319
school personnel responsibilities
    and, 234
speech impairment and, 177
visual impairment and, 179
Errors (due process hearing), 340, 349, 350
    defined, 341
Evaluation, 50. See also Reevaluation
    appropriateness of IEP and, 184-86
    child's specific needs and, 186-89
    checklist for, 87-88
    competency programs and, 473
    as continuous process, 75
    deaf-blind and, 159
    defined, 73, 480
    due process hearing notice and, 283-84
    educational assessment and, 84-85
    emotionally disturbed and, 164-65
    of evidence (hearing officer), 421-22
    family assessment and, 83-84
    handicapped student rights and, 206-207
    health assessment and, 84
    health impaired and, 161-62
    hearing impaired and, 151-52
    hearing officer and, 254-55
    identification and, 66, 67-68
    IEP and, 106, 107, 111
    ignoring data of, 146
    importance of, 74
    independent, 17, 85-86, 211, 222, 236, 281, 282, 304-305, 341, 412, 475, 481, 484
    legal requirements and, 74-75
    mental retardation and, 155-56
    notice requirement and, 280, 281-82, 283-84, 287, 288, 294
    parent responsibilities and, 220-22
    parent rights and, 210-12
    placement and, 139
    P.L. 94-142 and, 13, 16-17
    preevaluation procedures and, 77-78
    private schools and, 36
    protection of child and, 80-83

psychological assessment and, 85
reevaluation and, 80
referrals as written request for, 71
reporting results of, 86-87
school personnel and, 233, 235-36
Section 504 and, 32, 34
social assessment and, 83-84
special education decision-making
    process and, 73-74
specific learning disability and,
    168-72, 173
speech impairment and, 176
surrogate parents and, 259, 267
team approach to, 80
timelines and, 355
visually handicapped and, 178-79
Evidence (due process hearing)
admissible and nonadmissible,
    362-64, 384-85
appeal and, 343, 344-45, 349-50
    decision enforcement and, 352
burden of proof and, 325-26, 365-69
closing statement and, 389
credibility and weight of, 364-65
cross-examination and, 327, 373,
    375-76, 380-84
    expert witnesses and, 388
defined, 361
direct examination and, 373-74,
    378-79
    expert witnesses and, 388
document introduction and, 330,
    333-34
forms of (real, documentary,
    testimonial, judicial), 362
hearing officer's decision and,
    406-407, 408, 412, 458, 459
    writing of, 420-21, 426, 434
notice requirement and, 282
objections (presentation and use)
    and, 385-87
opening statement and, 376-77
parents', 327
planning for hearing and, 371-72
prehearing and, 301-302, 315
presenting, 377-78

public schools', 325-27
purpose and use of, 361-62
reexamination of, 328
secondhand, 386
sharing of, 313, 336
witnesses and
    expert, 387-88
    preparation of, 372-76
    written (obtaining), 312-14
Expert witnesses. *See* Witnesses, expert
Expulsion from school. *See also*
    Suspension from school
    disciplinary, 36, 475-76, 477
    private schools and, 36
Extracurricular services, 129
    handicapped student rights and, 206
    Section 504 and, 33-34, 35-36

F

Families, identification and, 161
Family assessment, 83-84
Federal government. *See also* Legal
    requirements
    burden of proof and, 369
    special education laws and, 39-41,
        42, 43, 44, 45
    state laws in conflict with laws of,
        54, 58
Fees
    copies of records and, 466
    private school (at no cost to parent),
        18, 449, 451
    Section 504 and, 31-32
    Texas Education Code and, 56
Fiduciary relationship (surrogate
    parents), 273-74
Financial concerns
    budget reduction and, 26-27
    placement at no cost to parents and,
        132-42
Findings of fact, 421-22, 442
Fluency disorder, 174, 176
Foster parents, 259, 261, 267
14th Amendment. *See also* Constitution

of the U.S.
  special education and, 5-6
  states and, 3-4
Free appropriate public education
  (FAPE). *See also* Individualized
  education program (IEP),
  appropriateness of
  defined, 90, 181-82, 480
  disciplinary action and, 477-78
  due process and, 7
  funding and, 142-43
  handicapped students and, 205-206
  hearing officer training and, 250
  IEP and, 91
  LEAs and, 229-30
  parents and, 209
  placement and, 121, 136, 137
  P.L. 94-142 and, 14, 50, 51, 54, 136,
    137, 181
  private school placement and, 449
  school personnel and, 229, 232
  SEAs and, 93-94, 229-30
  Section 504 and, 31-34, 50, 51, 136,
    137, 181
  the states and, 42
  surrogate parents and, 259, 268
Full-time equivalent (defined), 480
Funding
  appeal noncompliance and, 354
  cuts in, 24-28
  FAPE and P.L. 94-142 and, 14
  of handicapped education programs,
    142-44
  Medicaid and, 51-52
  penalties (noncompliance) and, 19
  placement and, 132-42
  plan acceptance and, 229
  private schools and, 453-54
  public laws concerning, 9, 10-11, 12
  school personnel and distribution of,
    233-34
  Section 504 regulations and, 29-30
  special education laws and
    local, 44, 45-46
    state, 43-44
  state, 53, 55

G

General Accounting Office (GAO), 81,
  173, 174, 175
  IEP and, 113
  report on the underserved by, 15
Goals. *See* Objectives
Grants. *See also* Block grants
  categorical, 25
  incentive, 49
  P.L. 90-247 and, 10-11
Gross v. Lopez (419 U.S. 656, 1975),
  475
Guardians, 16, 208, 259
  definition of parent and, 260
  guaranteeing, 270-71
  identification programs and, 234
  rights of, 209-218
  states and state agencies and, 261

H

Handicapped children. *See also names
  of specific disabilities*
  constitutional rights of, 3-5
  defined
    P.L. 94-142, 19, 50
    Section 504, 30-31, 50
  due process of law and, 3, 5-8
  evaluation and protection of, 80-83
  gifted, 114-16
  hearing office and definition of,
    408-409
  IEP meeting and, 101, 212
  multihandicapped, 158-59
  rights of
    confidentiality and, 469
    disciplinary action and, 477-78
    P.L. 94-142 and, 13-14
  specific needs of (evaluating), 186-89
  writing a decision and, 417
Handicapped student. *See* Student
Hard of hearing, defined, 150, 480
Health assessment, 84
Health impaired

defined, 160-61, 483
evaluation of, 161-62
identification of, 161
Health services (school), 23, 129, 140
defined, 485
school's concern over furnishing, 146
Hearing aids, 151-52
Hearing impaired. *See also* The Deaf-blind
defined, 149-50
evaluation of, 151-52
identification of, 150-51
IEP and, 153
placement and, 153
programming and, 152-53
Hearing officer (due process hearing). *See also* Appeal procedure (due process hearing decisions); Decisions (of due process hearing officer); Due process hearing
admission of evidence and, 337
appeal and, 338, 343
beginning the hearing (components of) and, 320-24
burden of proof and, 367-68
closing the hearing and, 337-38
consent refusal and, 292
continuance or postponement and, 331, 332-33
control over hearing and, 317, 329
decision timelines and, 355
defined, 480-81
documents and, 330
due process hearing and, 251-52, 255, 258-59
evidence presentation and, 327, 371-72, 376, 385
new evidence and, 314
hearing room organization and, 319
impartiality (IHO) and, 247, 253, 282
introducing, 320
keeping lists and, 240
leading questions and, 379
liability of, 254-55

monitoring, 253-54
opening statement and, 376, 377
prehearing coordination and, 301-302
preparation and, 256
procedural matter objections and, 334-37
recording equipment and, 319
responsibilities of, 256-58, 321
rights of, 255-56
role of, 245-46, 250-51, 321
protecting integrity of, 258
school personnel and, 231
selection and qualifications of, 246, 253-54
training and, 248-49
training workshop outline for, 249-52
who may serve as, 247-48
witnesses and, 392, 393, 394, 395-96, 402, 420, 421
Hearings. *See also* Appeal procedure (due process hearing decisions); Due process hearing
IEP dispute, 103, 104
information challenge, 467-68
parent's right to records and, 242
P.L. 94-142 and, 16, 18
Section 504 and, 34-35
show cause (appeal decision compliance), 352
High school diplomas, 472, 473-74
Homebound programs, 128-29
defined, 481
Hospital programs, 128-29
defined, 481

I

Identification (of those in need of special education)
appropriateness of IEP and, 183-84
census and, 68
community survey and, 68-69
confidentiality and, 67

deaf-blind and, 159
defined
  early, 22, 480
  personally identifiable, 483
emotionally disturbed and, 164-65
health impaired and, 161
hearing impaired and, 150-51
importance of, 66
legal requirements and, 65-66
mental retardation and, 155
notice to parents and, 67-68
notice requirements and, 282
parent responsibilities and, 220
parent rights and, 210
P.L. 94-142 and, 15
public awareness and, 69-70
purpose of, 66-67
referrals and, 71-72
school personnel and, 233, 234-35
screening and, 70
Section 504 and, 32
specific learning disability and,
  167-68
speech impairment and, 175-76
surrogate parents and, 259
timelines and, 355
visually handicapped and, 178
IEP. See Individualized education
program (IEP)
IHO. See Hearing officer, impartiality
  (IHO)
Immunity from damages (hearing
  officer), 255
Include (defined), 481
Individualized education program
  (IEP). See also Individualized
  education program (IEP) meeting
accountability for, 113-14
appeal procedure and, 340, 341
appropriateness and
  defining, 181-82
  evaluation and, 184-89, 194
  guidelines for, 195-201
  identification and, 183-84, 194
  legal requirements and, 194-95
  placement and, 184, 192-94, 195

program development and, 189-9.,
  194
school personnel and, 230
competency programs and, 472-74
consent and, 289
content and format of, 106-111
defined, 91-92, 481
disability definition and, 149
due process and, 7
effective implementation date of,
  95-96, 98
emotionally disturbed and, 165
evaluation and, 74, 80-81, 86, 106,
  107-111
goals and objectives and, 89-90,
  106, 108-110
handicapped gifted children and,
  114-15
handicapped student rights and, 206
health impaired and, 162
hearing impaired and, 153
hearing officer and, 256
importance of, 90-91
LEAs and, 94, 96, 99, 100, 113
  initiated placement and, 95
legal requirements and, 91
mentally retarded and, 156
parental involvement and, 280-81
parent responsibility and, 224-26
parent rights and, 212-13, 214
physical education and, 110, 112
placement and, 95, 99, 103, 104,
  129, 132
  appropriateness and, 184, 192-94,
    195
  based on IEP, 120-21
  differences in, 117-19
  funding and, 139-40, 142
  gifted handicapped children and,
    115
  LEAs and, 95
  legal requirements and, 120
  objectives and, 109
  out-of-state, 95
  parent responsibilities and, 226
  private schools and, 449, 450,

451, 455
  review of, 130
  temporary, 119-120
P.L. 94-142 and, 12, 14
present level of educational
  performance and, 107-108
programming and, 89-91
  parent responsibilities and, 224-25
purpose and function of, 92-95
related services and, 106, 110-11,
  114
school personnel and
  accountability and, 230
  development of, 236-38
SEAs and, 93-94, 99
services (duration of) and, 111
services needed (inclusion of all)
  and, 113
specific learning disability and, 172
speech impairment and, 176, 177
state responsibility for, 93
surrogate parents and, 259, 260, 262,
  267, 271
visually impaired and, 179
vocational education and, 112-13
written for each child, 17, 61-62, 91,
  92, 213, 238
Individualized education program
  (IEP) meeting. *See also*
  Individualized education program
  (IEP)
disputes in, 103-104
handicapped child's attendance at,
  101, 212
the law and, 96-98
parent rights and, 212-13
participants in, 98-102, 212, 223, 237
programming and parent
  responsibilities and, 223-24
purpose and function of, 92-93
school personnel and, 232, 237-38
size of, 100
tape recorder use at, 104-105
In Re Downey (340 N.Y.S. 2d 687,
  1973), 136
Insurance proceeds, funding

prohibition and, 143-44
Integration with nonhandicapped
  students, 17, 33-34, 193, 206. *See
  also* Mainstreaming
the deaf-blind and, 159-60
IEP and, 111
placement and, 122, 226
specific learning disability and, 172
the speech impaired and, 176
Intelligence Quotient (IQ)
evaluation and parent
  responsibilities and, 221
mentally retarded and, 154, 482
Intelligence tests, 134. *See also* Tests
evaluation and, 78, 185
mentally retarded and, 155
Intermediate care facilities, 52, 53
Intermediate educational unit
  (defined), 481
Interpreters (due process hearing), 304

L

Labeling of children, 70, 86, 149
due process and, 6
evaluation and parent
  responsibilities and, 222
not used in IEP, 107
programming and parent
  responsibilities and, 224
school personnel and, 232
special learning disabilities and, 167
Language
avoiding exaggeration and, 346, 377
avoiding flamboyant, 345
cross-examination and, 382
hearing impaired identification and,
  151, 152
interpreter (native language or sign)
  at due process hearing and, 304
native (defined), 482
parent rights and native, 211, 216,
  233
specific learning disabilities and, 168
speech impairment and, 174, 175,

176
testimony and, 394
understood by pupil (sign etc.), 207
used in closing statement, 389
used in notice requirement, 285-86
used in opening statement, 377
use of native (on tests), 82, 131
168-69, 184, 221
Language disorder, 174, 176
Lawyers
checking with before testimony, 400
child's educational interest and, 269
cross-examination and, 373, 375,
395
due process hearing and, 248-49,
322
prehearing conversations with, 373
Learning disability. See Specific
learning disability
LEAs. See Local education agencies
(LEAs)
Least restrictive environment (LRE),
17, 193, 195
defined, 481-82
disciplinary action and, 478
health impaired and, 162
placement and, 120, 122-24, 126,
129, 148
vs. mainstreaming, 124-25
misuse of, 131-32
parent responsibilities and, 226
school personnel and, 239
Least restrictive nonacademic
environment, 129. See also
Nonacademic services
placement and, 129
Legal costs, parents and due process
hearing and, 240
Legal liability
hearing officers and, 254-55
surrogate parents and, 273-75
Legal requirements. See also P.L.
94-142 (Education for All
Handicapped Children Act of 1975);
Section 504 of Public Law 93-112
appeal and, 339, 342-43, 347

decision compliance and, 352, 354
appropriate (defined), 194, 95
burden of proof and, 369
confidentiality and, 228, 241, 463-70
conflicts in, 54, 58
decisions and, 418
emotionally disturbed and, 162-63
employment and, 53
evaluation and, 74-75, 186
evidence in due process hearing and,
312
handicapped definition (hearing
officer) and, 409
health impaired and, 160
hearing impaired and, 149-50
hearing officer and, 247, 256
identification and, 65-66
IEP, 91, 181
IEP meeting, 96-98
invoking of due process hearing and,
295-99
Medicaid funding and, 51-52
mental retardation and, 153-54
minimum competency testing and,
471-74
multihandicapped and, 158
notice requirement (due process
hearing), 279-280, 285, 287, 290
parent rights and, 217
personally identifiable information
and, 416
P.L. 89-313 (exclusion from P.L.
94-142) and, 53
P.L. 94-142 and, 14-19, 49-50
private school placement and,
449-50, 452-53, 454
EDGAR and, 454-56
Section 504 and, 29-30, 50-51
specific learning disability and, 166,
169, 170
cap on counting children and, 167
problem with, 172-73
speech impairment and, 173-74, 176
states and, 53-59
surrogate parents and, 259, 260,
262, 264, 267, 272

visually handicapped and, 177, 179
vocational training and, 53
Legal rights
  constitutional, 3-5
  due process, 5-8
  handicapped student, 13-14, 205-208
  hearing officer and, 255-56
  parents, 13-14, 17-18, 209-218,
    241-43, 245
  school personnel and, 230-32
  surrogate parents, 267-68
Liability. *See* Legal liability
Life support services, problem
  concerning, 148
Local education agencies (LEAs). *See*
  also Public agencies; State education
  agencies (SEAs)
  alternative placement and, 17
  appeal and, 339, 342, 347
  competency programs and, 473, 474
  deaf-blind and, 159
  defined, 481
  disciplinary action and, 475, 478
  due process hearing and, 215
    placement and, 310
  FAPE and, 229-30
  fiscal constraints and, 146
  funding cuts and, 26, 27
  funding programs and, 138, 233
  hearing officer damages and, 254-55
  IEP and, 94, 96, 99, 100, 113
    initiated placements and, 95
  invoking due process hearing and,
    295-96, 297
  notice requirement and, 280-83, 284,
    285-87, 288-93
  placement and, 119-20, 138, 146
  P.L. 94-142 and, 13-14, 53-54
  private school placement and, 452-53
    EDGAR and, 455, 456
  SLD and, 173
  speech disorder and, 174
  surrogate parents and, 263-64, 266,
    271-72, 273
    legal liability and, 273-74
  visually impaired and, 178

Local governments
  identification and, 66
  P.L. 94-142 and, 49
  special education laws and, 39-41
    program application and, 44-46
LRE. *See* Least restrictive environment
  (LRE)

M

Mainstreaming, 124-25, 369. *See also*
  Integration with nonhandicapped
  students
  hearing impaired and, 153
  parents and, 224
Maryland State Department of
  Education, gifted handicapped
  children and, 114-16
Materials and equipment, 58, 140.
  See also Equipment
  evaluation and parent responsibilities
    and, 221
  school personnel and, 235
  speech impairment and, 177
  student rights and, 207
  visual impairment and, 179
Media, identification programs and,
  69, 234
Medicaid, funding of education and,
  51-52
Medical services, 22, 140, 141
  defined, 481
  identification and, 161
  school officials' view (problem) of,
    148
Meeting (IEP). *See* Individualized
  education program (IEP) meeting
Mental impairments, 19
  defined in Section 504, 30-31
Mentally retarded, 19
  access to education and, 5
  classification of, 6
  defined, 153-55, 482
  developmental characteristics of, 157
  evaluation of, 155-56

identification of, 155
intermediate care facilities (funding)
    and, 52
placement and, 156-58
programming and, 156
special education example and, 20-21
*Mills v. Board of Education of the
    District of Columbia* (1972), 5, 123,
    137
Minimum competency testing, 471-74.
    See also Tests
Minorities, evaluation and, 81-82
Multihandicapped, 158-59

N

National Advisory Council on
    Handicapped Children, 10
Native language. *See* Language, *entries
    concerning native language*
Nonacademic services. *See also*
    Services
    least restrictive environment and, 129
    problems concerning, 147
    Section 504 and, 33-34, 35-36
Notice of appeal, 342
Notice to parents' requirement
    amending records and, 242
    changes in programs and, 16
    destruction of information and, 469
    disciplinary action and, 475
    evaluation and, 220
    evaluation tests and, 75-80
    identification and, 67-68
    as a parent right, 209-210, 216
    placement and, 225
    programming and, 222
    referrals and, 235
    school personnel and, 232-33, 237,
        241
    Section 504 and, 34
    state plans and, 11
Notice requirement (due process
    hearing), 7
    beginning the hearing and, 322

consent and, 287-89
    elements of valid, 289-93
    parent refusal of, 284, 293-94
content of, 280-81
    description of action and, 283
    evaluation procedure description
        and, 283-84
    LEAs and, 284
    procedural safeguards and, 281-83
final notice and, 315
form of, 285-87
LEAs and, 280-83, 284, 285-87,
    288-93
meaning of, 287
purpose of, 279, 285
SEAs and, 285

O

Objections. *See* Evidence, objections
    (presentation and use of)
Objectives
    evaluation, 186
    IEP, 89-90, 106, 108-110, 213
        for mentally retarded, 156
    program development, 189-90, 191
    special education definitions
        and, 20
Occupational therapy, 22, 140
    defined, 482-83
    problems with payment for, 146
Orthopedically impaired
    defined, 160-61, 483
    evaluation and, 161-62
    identification and, 161
Otological examination, 152

P

Paper work, 26, 61
Parental consent. *See* Consent
    (parental)
Parents. *See also* Foster parents;
    Notice to parents' requirement;

Notice requirements (due process
hearing); Surrogate parents
appeal and, 341, 349-50
  decision enforcement and, 351-52
assistance for (due process hearing),
  298-99
burden of proof and, 367-68
competency programs and, 472
confidentiality and, 216-18, 464-67
counseling service for, 22, 140, 483
decision-making safeguards and,
  15-16
defined, 208, 260, 483
disciplinary action and, 475
due process hearing and, 215-16,
  298, 322
  child's presence at, 311-12
  evidence and, 327, 384
  parent rights to, 245, 321-22
  providing information and, 311
due process of law clauses and, 7, 8
evaluation and, 210-12, 220-22
  independent, 17, 85-86, 211, 222,
    236, 281, 282, 304-305, 475, 484
evaluation data and, 146
family assessment and, 83-84
fee assessment (Texas) and, 56, 58
identification programs and, 68, 69,
  210, 220, 234
IEP and, 91, 96, 109, 212-13, 214,
  226
  gifted children and, 114-15
  monitoring child's performance
    and, 105-106
  programming and, 224-25
  right to complain and, 114
  signature on document of, 105
IEP meeting and, 92, 97, 98,
  101-102, 212-213
  disputes and, 103, 104
  programming and, 223-24
  tape recording use and, 104
insurance and, 143-44
involvement of, 182
knowledgeability (consent) and,
  290-91

objections and, 386
placement and, 213-14, 225-27, 240
  at no cost to, 132-34, 143, 144,
    147
  prehearing, 306-309
  private school, 451-53
  private school service (at no cost
    to) 18, 449, 451, 479
  programming and, 212-13, 222-25
  responsibilities of
    due process hearing and, 227-28
    evaluation and, 220-22
    in general, 218-20
    identification and, 220
    placement and, 225-27
    programming and, 222-25
  rights of, 114, 209-217, 245, 280-83
  P.L. 94-142 and, 13-14
  record inspection and, 15-16,
    17-18, 217-18, 241-43
  role of, 208-209
  school personnel and, 244
  Section 504 and, 34-35
  special education definition and, 20
  speech impairment and, 175
  state plans and, 11
  transportation and, 141-42
  visually impaired and, 178
  as witness (guidelines for), 373-74,
    375-76, 402
Peers. *See* Integration with
  nonhandicapped students
Penalties for noncompliance, 19
  decision enforcement (appeal) and,
    353
*Pennsylvania Association for Retarded
  Children (PARC) v. Commonwealth
  of Pennsylvania* (1972), 4-5, 123
Personally identifiable information,
  416-17, 420
Physical characteristics
  hearing impaired and, 151
  specific learning disability and, 168
  speech impairment and, 175
Physical education
  defined, 483

IEP and, 110, 112
Physical impairments, 19
  defined in Section 504, 30-31
  defining, 160
Physical therapy, 22-23, 140
  defined, 483
  problems with payment for, 146
Placement
  alternative, 17, 32, 62
    continuum of, 125-29, 207, 214,
      239
  classroom plans and, 127-28
  consent and, 289
    initial, 79
  deaf-blind (group) and, 159-60
  defined (P.L. 94-142), 122
  disciplinary action and, 477
  due process and, 7
  due process hearing and, 305-311
  emotionally disturbed and, 165
  evaluation funding and, 139
  guidelines for, 132, 133-36
  handicapped student rights and, 206,
    207
  health impaired and, 162
  hearing impaired and, 153
  homebound and hospital programs
    for, 128-29
  IEP and, 95, 99, 103, 104, 129
    appropriateness and, 184, 192-94,
      195
    based on IEP and, 120-21
    differences in, 117-19
    funding and, 139-40, 142
    gifted handicapped children and,
      115
    LEAs and, 95
    legal requirements and, 120
    objectives and, 109
    out-of-state, 95
    parent responsibilities and, 226
    private schools and, 449, 450, 451,
      455
    review of, 130
    temporary, 119-20
  importance of, 118-19

integration with nonhandicapped
  students and, 122
LEAs and, 95, 119-20, 138, 146
least restrictive environment (LRE)
  and, 120, 122-24, 126, 129, 148
  vs. mainstreaming, 124-25
  misuse of, 131-32
least restrictive nonacademic
  environment and, 129
legal requiremens and, 119, 120, 122
  alternative placement and, 125
  LRE and, 123-24
  nonacademic requirements and,
    129
  placement costs and, 132-42
  public supervision and, 144
  review and reevaluation and,
    130-31
mentally retarded and, 156-58
no cost to parent requirement and,
  132-42, 143, 144, 147
old classification system for, 117
parent rights and, 212-14
participants in decision-making
  process and, 118, 119, 121, 122
P.L. 94-142 and, 117, 123, 124
  accountability and, 145
  defined, 122
  funding and, 142-43
  related services and, 145-48
psychiatric service funding and, 141
public school and, 449-51
public supervision of, 144-48
related services and, 120, 121, 125
  problems with, 145-46
residential, 33, 138, 146
review and reevaluation and, 130-31,
  139
school personnel and, 233, 235,
  238-40
SEAs and, 138, 144-45, 146
Section 504 and, 32, 124, 131-32,
  136, 137
services and, 126-29, 139-44
special schools and, 128
specific learning disabilities and, 172

speech impairment and, 176-77
surrogate parents and, 259, 268
temporary or interim, 119-20
timelines and, 355
transportation funding and, 141-42
visually handicapped and, 179-80
P.L. 89-750 (Education of Handicapped Children), 9-10
P.L. 89-10 (Elementary and Secondary Education Act of 1965), 9-12
P.L. 89-313 (Supplemental education services for the handicapped in state facilities), exclusion from P.L. 94-142 and, 51
P.L. 94-482 (Vocational Education Act of 1973, amendment of 1976), P.L. 94-142 and, 53
P.L. 94-142 (Education for All Handicapped Children Act of 1975). *See also* Legal requirements
  administrative reviews (not required) and, 299
  appeal and, 339, 354
  confidentiality and, 228, 463-70
  Congress and, 12-13
  definition of terms and, 19-24
  disciplinary action and, 476, 477
  disruptive students and, 309
  due process hearing and, 305, 320, 359
  due process notice requirement and, 279-80, 289, 290
  employment and, 53
  evaluation definition and, 73
  FAPE and, 14-15, 136, 137, 143, 181, 480
  financial concerns (budget reduction) and, 24-28
  handicapped students and, 205-206
  IEP and, 90, 91, 104, 105, 113, 114
  key provisions of, 14-19
  Medicaid funding and, 51-52
  minimum competency testing and, 471-74
  nondiscriminatory evaluation and, 151

  origins of, 9-12
  passage of, 5
  placement and, 117, 123, 124
    accountability and, 145
    defined, 122
    funding and, 142-43
    related services and, 145-48
  private schools and, 57-58, 449, 451, 453
    EDGAR and, 454-56
  purpose of, 13-14
  regulations and, 49-50
  Section 504 and, 50-51
  special education laws and, 39, 46, 47, 48
  specific learning disability and, 166, 167, 168
  speech disorder and, 174, 175
  state law and, 53-59
  surrogate parents and, 269, 271, 272, 273, 274, 275
  unique characteristics of, 12
  vocational education and, 53
P.L. 91-230 (Education of the Handicapped Act of 1969), 10-11
P.L. 93-380 (Educational Amendments of 1974), 11
  burden of proof and, 369
P.L. 90-247 (Education of the Handicapped Act of 1967), 10
Posture (witnesses), 392-93
Pregnancy, 161
Preschool education, 36
Primacy (state) factor in education, 40-41
Private schools
  defined, 484
  due process hearing (placement) and, 307
  EDGAR regulation and, 454-56
    difficulties in implementation and, 456-61
  funding and, 453-54
  IEP and, 93
  personnel and equipment and, 453-54

placement and, 449-53
P.L. 94-142 and, 57-58, 449, 451, 453
EDGAR and, 454-61
school personnel and, 232, 234, 237, 239
Section 504 and, 36
services in (at no cost to parent), 18
Procedural safeguards, 46, 50
appeal and, 344
notice requirements (due process hearing), 281-83
parent rights and, 210
Section 504 and, 34-37
state plans and, 11
Process disorder, 166
Professionals, as witnesses (guidelines for), 373-74, 375
Program application. *See* Application (local program)
Programming
appropriateness of IEP and, 189-91
deaf-blind and, 159
defined, 89
emotionally disturbed and, 165
health impaired and, 162
hearing impaired and, 152-53
hearing officer's decision and, 410
IEP and, 90-91
mentally retarded and, 156
parent rights and, 212-13
role of, 89-90
Section 504 and, 32
specific learning disabilities and, 172
speech impairment and, 176-77
surrogate parents and, 268
visually handicapped and, 179-80
Program plans. *See* Annual program plans (states)
Property interest (public education) 5-6, 475
Psychological assessment, 85
Psychological services, 140, 148, 165
defined, 484
funding for, 141
Psychologist (defined), 485
Public agencies. *See also* Local

education agencies (LEAs); State education agencies (SEAs)
adherence to requirements and, 62
appeal and, 342
consent and, 76, 79
defined, 54, 483, 484
due process hearing and, 296, 298
funding and (insurance proceeds), 143-44
IEP and, 93, 95
accountability and, 113-14
disputes and, 103-104
parent participation and, 101-102
progress reviews and, 106
services and, 110
signing of document and, 105
teacher participation and, 99-101
notice requirements and, 280
private school placement and, 449-51
surrogate parents and, 260, 261, 262-63
duty of, 263-64
selection of, 265-67
transportation and, 141
Public awareness, identification and, 67, 69-70
Public Laws. *See* P.L. *entries*
Public schools
due process hearing and
evidence and, 325-27
placement and, 305, 306, 307, 308, 309
educational needs of handicapped and, 12-13
mentally retarded and, 156
residential, 484
school personnel and, 234, 239
special education definition and, 20

Q

Qualified person (defined), 484
Questionnaire (identification), 68-69, 235

R

Reading, visually impaired and, 179
Recipient (defined), 484
Records
  confidentiality and, 17-18, 241,
    464-70
  due process hearing, 231
  due process hearing (verbatim),
    303-304, 319
    appeal and, 343, 344, 346
    requests for, 337
  evaluation and school, 84
  hearing officer responsibility and,
    257
  hearing officer's review of, 408
  IEP meeting, 232, 238
  notice requirement and, 280, 281
  parent responsibilities and, 218, 228
  parent rights and, 17-18, 217-18,
    241-43
  school personnel and, 233, 234
  Section 504 and, 34
  special education laws and, 44, 46
  student rights and, 207
  surrogate parents and, 267
  tape recordings as, 105, 319
  witness preparation and, 373
Recreation, 23, 129
  defined, 485
Reevaluation, 80. *See also* Evaluation
  mentally retarded and, 158
  parent responsibilities and, 222
  parent rights and, 212
  placement and, 130-31, 139
  surrogate parents and, 268
Referrals
  health impairment identification
    and, 161
  identification and, 67, 71-72
  mentally retarded and, 155
  of multihandicapped, 159
  school personnel and, 235
  specific learning disabilities and, 167
  speech impairment and, 175
  visually impaired and, 178

Regulations. *See* Legal requirements
Rehabilitation Act of 1973, 29
Related services. *See also* Services
  defined, 21-24, 58, 485
  IEP and, 106, 110-11, 114
  Medicaid funding and, 52
  placement and, 120, 121, 125
    problems with, 145-48
  school personnel and, 232, 236-37,
    238
Residential placement, 138. *See also*
  Placement
  private school, 484
  speech impaired and, 176
Residential school, 128
Retarded children. *See* Mentally
  retarded
Review
  disputes and administrative, 298-99
  due process hearing and, 231, 240
  hearing officer and, 408
  IEP and, 106, 213
  parent responsibilities and, 223
  parent rights and, 217, 465, 466
    records and, 241-43
  placement and, 130-31
  surrogate parents and, 267
  testimony, 392
  timelines and, 355

S

Scheduling, IEP and, 106, 111
Scheuer v. Rhodes (416 U.S. 232,
  1974), 255
Schizophrenic children, 163
School achievement. *See* Educational
  performance
School clubs, 35, 36, 129
School day, funding beyond regular,
  142
School health services, 23, 129, 140
  school's concern over furnishing,
    146
School personnel

chief state school officer (appeal
   compliance), 353-54
disciplinary action and, 475
due process hearing and, 297
   placement and, 309
   as witnesses at, 314
noninstructional, 482
private school, 449, 450-51
responsibilities of
   confidentiality and, 241-44
   in dealing with parents, 244
   due process hearing and, 240-41
   evaluation and, 235-36
   in general, 232-34
   identification and, 234-35
   IEP development and, 236-38
   placement and, 238-40
rights of, 230-32
role of, 229-30
timelines and, 355
Screening, 230
   identification and, 70
   identification of hearing impaired
      and, 150
   parent responsibilities and, 220
   parent rights and, 210
   school personnel and, 235
   speech impairment and, 175
   visually handicapped and, 178
SEAs. See State education agencies
   (SEAS)
Section 504 of Public Law 93-112. See
   also Legal requirements
   administrative reviews (not required)
      and, 299
   burden of proof and, 369
   criteria for protection under, 30-31
   disciplinary action and, 476
   disruptive students and, 309
   FAPE and, 31-34, 136, 137, 143, 181
   handicapped students and, 205-206
   least restrictive environment and,
      124, 131-32
   minimum competency testing and,
      471-74
   nondiscriminatory evaluation and,

151
   passage of, 5
   placement and, 124, 131-32, 136,
      137
   P.L. 94-142 and, 50-51
   procedural safeguards and, 34-37
   regulations in, 29-30
   special education laws and, 46
Senate Committee on Labor and
   Public Welfare, 137
Seriously emotionally disturbed. See
   Emotionally disturbed (seriously)
Services. See also Related services
   "continuum" of, 126-29
   defined, 480, 481
   dual enrollment and, 453, 454
   handicapped student rights and, 206,
      207
   IEP and, 111, 113
   individualized plans for, 107
   parent rights and, 214
   placement and, 139-42, 143-44
   P.L. 94-142 and SEAs and, 54
   priority for, 15
   private schools and, 18
   program development and, 190-91
   resource room (defined) and, 485
   school personnel and, 232
   Section 504 and, 32
   social work, 486
   surrogate parents and, 268
Sex (gender), evaluation and, 81
Shelton v. Tucker, 123
Sign language. See Language, entries
   concerning sign
SLD. See Specific learning disability
   (SLD)
Social assessment, 83-84
Socially maladjusted children, 165
Social worker (defined), 485
   services of (defined), 486
Social work services, 23
   school's concern over furnishing,
      146
Special day school, 128
   private (defined), 484

public (defined), 486
speech impaired and, 176
Special education. *See also*
   Individualized education program
   (IEP)
   congressional perception of, 12-13
   constitutional rights and, 3-5
   the courts and, 40, 46-48
   definition of, 19-21, 147, 486
   due process of law and, 5-8, 277
   hearing officer and, 248-49, 409-410
   local government and, 39-41, 44-46
   placement and, 117-19
   P.L. 94-142 and
      budget reduction and, 24-28
      Congress and, 12-13
      definition of terms and, 19-24
      origins of, 9-12
      provisions and purpose of, 13-19
   school personnel and, 232, 236-37
   states and, 39-44
Special education decision-making
   process. *See* Decision-making
   process
Special education due process hearing.
   See Due process hearing
Specific learning disability (SLD)
   defining, 166-67, 172, 486
   evaluation and, 168-72, 173
   identification and, 167-68
   program development example for,
      190-91
   program and placement and, 172
   regulation problems with, 172-73
Speech analysis
   hearing impaired and, 151
   specific learning disability
      and, 168
Speech impairment
   defined, 173-75, 486
   evaluation and, 176
   identification and, 175-76
   program and placement and, 176-77
Speech pathology, 23
   defined, 487
Speech therapy, 140, 174

Staff development programs, 234
State advisory board, 18
State education agencies (SEAs). *See*
   also Local education agencies
   (LEAs); Public agencies
   accountability and, 144-45
   alternative placement and, 17
   appeal and, 342-43, 347-48
      decision enforcement and, 352
   confidentiality and, 464-65, 466, 467
   deaf-blind and, 159
   defined, 487
   disciplinary action and, 475, 478
   due process hearing and, 215-16,
      227, 296
   FAPE and, 229-30
   fiscal constraints and, 146
   funding cuts and, 26, 27
   funding programs and, 138
   hearing officer liability and, 254-55
   hearing officer service and, 248
   IEP and, 93-94, 99
   notice requirement and, 285
   placement and, 138, 146
      accountability and, 144-45
   P.L. 94-142 and, 13-14, 54-56, 57
   private school placement and,
      449-51, 452-53
      EDGAR and, 456
   SLD and, 173
   surrogate parents and, 263-64, 266,
      271-72, 273
      legal liability and, 273-75
   timelines and, 354
   visually impaired and, 178
The States
   burden of proof and, 369
   consent refusal (parental) and, 294
   constitutional rights of handicapped
      and, 3-5
   deafness definition and, 150
   defined, 487
   due process of law and, 5-8
   federal laws in conflict with laws of,
      54, 58
   funding FAPE and, 142-43

health impaired definition and, 160
IEP and, 93
mentally retarded definition and,
    154
P.L. 94-142 and, 53-59
P.L. 93-380 and, 11
special education laws and, 39-41
    annual program plans and, 41-44
    primacy factor in education and,
        40-41
    surrogate parents and, 261, 262-63,
        269, 273
    selection of, 265-67
Stenographer (due process hearing),
    303, 304, 319
Structural changes, 37
Stuart v. Nappi (F. Supp. 1235,
    D.Conn., 1978), 477
Student
    competency programs and, 472, 473
    responsibilities of, 208
    rights of (through parent's rights),
        205-108
    role of, 205
Stuttering, 175
Supplemental educational services for
    the handicapped in state facilities.
    See P.L. 89-313 (Supplemental
    educational services for the
    handicapped in state facilities)
Surrogate parents, 16, 207. *See also*
    Foster parents; Parents
    child's natural parents and, 261-63,
        266
    definition of, 259-60, 261, 487
    effort to locate natural parent and,
        261-62
    implementing provisions for, 272-73,
        274
    legal problems in providing, 269-75
    monitoring of, 264
    need for, 260-63
    parental rights and, 269-70
    potential legal liabilities of, 273-75
    public agencies' duties and, 263-64
    responsibilities of, 268-69

role of, 259-60
selection of (criteria for), 265-67
student's age of majority and, 264
Suspension from school, 241. *See also*
    Expulsion from school
    disciplinary action and, 475-76, 477,
        478
    due process and, 310

T

Tape recorders, 104-105
    due process hearing record and, 303,
        304
    in hearing room, 319
Teacher aide (defined), 487
Teachers
    competency programs and, 472
    evaluation for SLD and, 169
    home-hospital (defined), 481
    IEP accountability and, 113
    IEP meetings and, 99-101, 212, 223
    itinerant, 127
    itinerant and consultant defined,
        481
    placement funding and, 140
    preparation programs for, 234
    regular class and resource classroom
        defined and, 485
    special class definition and, 486
    speech impairment and, 175, 177
    visually impaired and, 178
Teacher training, 12, 13, 18. *See also*
    Training
Team approach
    disciplinary action and, 477
    to evaluation, 80, 185
        school personnel and, 236, 238
    to IEP, 91
    parent rights and, 211, 221
    placement and, 119
    specific learning disability and,
        169-71
Testimony. *See* Witnesses (due process
    hearing)

Tests. *See also* Intelligence tests;
  Wide range achievement test
  (WRAT)
  "adverse effect," 175
  emotionally disturbed and, 164
  evaluation
    appropriateness of IEP and,
      185-86
    native language use and, 82, 131,
      168-69, 184, 221, 226
    notice to parents and, 75-80
    protection of child and, 81-82
  health impairment and, 161
  hearing impairment and, 150, 152
  hearing officer, 256
  mental retardation and, 155-56
  minimum competency, 471-74
  nondiscriminatory, 62
  notice requirement and, 280
  parent responsibility and, 219, 221,
    222
  parent rights and, 211
  placement and, 213
  P.L. 94-412 and, 13, 17
  reevaluation and, 131
  school personnel and, 233, 235-36
  screening and, 70
  specific learning disability and,
    168-69
  speech impairment and, 175, 176
Texas Education Code Section, 56, 58
Therapy. *See* Occupational therapy;
  Physical therapy; Speech therapy
Timelines (due process hearing),
  354-57
Training. *See also* Teacher training
  constitutional rights of handicapped
    and, 5
  hearing officer, 248-49, 256
    workshop outline for, 249-52
  parent and, 483
  surrogate parent and, 274
Transportation, 21, 23, 129, 140
  defined, 487
  funding for, 141-42

U

U.S. Department of Education. *See*
  Department of Education

V

Visually handicapped
  defined, 177, 487
  evaluation and, 178-79
  identification and, 178
  program and placement and, 179-80
Vocational education, 18, 140
  defined, 53, 487
  IEP and, 112-13
  mentally retarded and, 158
Vocational Education Act of 1963,
  amendment of 1976. *See* P.L.
  94-482 (Vocational Education Act of
  1963, amendment of 1976)
Voice disorder, 174, 176

W

Ward of the state, 260, 263
Wide range achievement test (WRAT),
  187. *See also* Tests
Witnesses (due process hearing)
  answering questions and, 393-96
  avoiding arguments with, 383
  checklist for, 366
  compelling attendance of, 314-15,
    320
  cross-examination and, 375-76,
    380-83
    guidelines for handling, 396-400
    of parent, 327
    redirect examination and, 384
    of school personnel, 327
  direct examination and, 373-74,
    378-79
  document introduction and, 330
  dress and, 391
  effective information presentation

and, 400-402
expert, 387-88, 399, 400, 401
hearing officer and, 392, 393, 394,
    395-96, 402, 420, 421
leading questions and, 379, 381, 382
nervousness and, 392-93
objections and, 334, 401
posture of, 392-93
preliminary matters and, 324-25
preparation of, 372-76
presentation of, 328-30
    order of, 372

professionals as (guidelines for),
    373-74, 375
providing list of, 312, 315
reexamination of, 328
testimony preparation and, 391-92
testimony and testimony
    modification and, 328-30, 334
Wood v. Strickland (420 U.S. 308,
    1975), 255
Writing a decision. *See* Decisions (of
    due process hearing officer), writing
    a decision
Writing, visually impaired and, 179

About the Author

James A. Shrybman is a lawyer who specializes in problems of children. He currently serves as an Impartial Hearing Officer for special education due process hearings in Maryland, Virginia, and the District of Columbia. He also practices as a private attorney in matters of child abuse and neglect, adoption, foster care, mental illness, and retardation commitment.

He has worked as a teacher for self-contained programs for seriously emotionally disturbed children, director of a resident summer camp, program director of a settlement house, staff member of the Boston Children's Museum, and a legal intern to the U.S. Senate Subcommittee on Children and Youth.

Mr. Shrybman received a Bachelors degree in Political Science from Boston University, Boston, Massachusetts. He received a law degree from Antioch School of Law, Washington, D.C.

Mr. Shrybman also provides consultation and training for school systems, parent groups, and individuals in the area of special education due process.

Date Due